D0772354

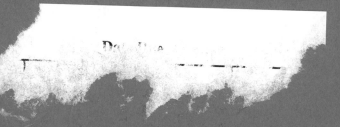

ICELANDIC ENTERPRISE

ICELANDIC ENTERPRISE

 Commerce and Economy in
the Middle Ages

by Bruce E. Gelsinger

University of South Carolina Press

TO

R.

"... in the chronicle of wasted time
... we ... lack tongues to praise."

Library of Congress Cataloging in Publication Data

Gelsinger, Bruce E.   1938–
   Icelandic enterprise.

   Bibliography: p.
   1. Iceland—Commerce—History. I. Title.
HF3655.G44   382'.094912   80–26116
ISBN 0–87249–405–5

⚓ Contents

TABLES

CHARTS

⚓ Preface

From the time it was first colonized about 870 until nearly the end of its independent Commonwealth in 1264, Iceland had a commerce that was usually able to satisfy the island's considerable foreign needs. This trade took place despite hundreds of miles of often tempestuous waters that separated Iceland from the rest of Europe and despite a general poverty of natural resources. It began at a time when a largely self-sustaining manorial economy was dominant in much of western Christian Europe and when long-distance trade, intermittent as it was, usually concerned articles of luxury, not necessity. It is remarkable even when compared with the earlier, more distant, and, in its way, perhaps equally danger-ous Scandinavian eastern trade, or even compared with the more consequential trade of western Europe after its commercial revival beginning in the eleventh century. These commercial achieve-ments were made possible largely because of the many geographical advantages and natural resources Iceland was denied.

As remarkable as Iceland's foreign trade during the Com-monwealth may seem to us, it was not especially noteworthy to men of the time. Like the sources for most other aspects of medieval economic history, those directly touching upon Iceland's commerce during this period are scanty. But there are numerous sources that can yield, however reluctantly or unintentionally, a significant amount of indirect evidence.

Properly collected and dated, archaeological material can help to tell us, among other things, how Icelanders lived, what they imported, what resources of their own they used, and how goods were transported at sea. But the sign language of artifacts is usually unable to express more specific information about domestic economy and foreign trade. For instance, an English sword dating from the eleventh century found at Kaldárhöfthi in southwestern Iceland[1] obviously shows that swords on occasion were obtained from abroad and that iron production and sword manufacture might not have been highly developed in Iceland, for otherwise such a weapon would not have been brought to the island. But, of course, the sword alone cannot answer more specific questions of direct concern to trade: Did an Icelander or someone else bring it? How was it acquired? If purchased, what was exchanged for it? Was it brought directly from England or not? The written record is better able to deal with such questions, but its answers are often vague and subject to various interpretations, and these answers cannot always be trusted, even though they might have been intended to be truthful. Separately, both the archaeological and written record have drawbacks, though some of these can be overcome if both kinds of evidence are combined, the one to check and to amplify the other. This ideal, however, cannot always be attained in a study of commerce, and so archaeological evidence mainly has to be cast in a subservient but still important role of balancing and adding to the written evidence whenever appropriate.

The most important collection of factual written sources bearing on trade is composed of Icelandic and foreign documents such as commercial agreements, deeds, church inventories, separate laws and proclamations, most of which are printed in *Diplomatarium Islandicum*.[2] This collection also includes part of the corpus of Icelandic Commonwealth law known as *Grágás*. Of another type are works intended to be historically accurate written well after most of the events described. These may be based on the accounts of at least some participants or witnesses to the events or on earlier, now lost source material such as chronological, genealogical, or biographical data. Two important examples are *Íslendingabók (Book of the Icelanders)*, written by Ári Thorgilsson about 1130, and *Landnámabók (Book of Settlements)*, originating undoubtedly from the early twelfth century, though the earliest redaction comes from only about 1275. In a final group are non-documentary works that describe, at least partially, contemporary life. These include such Icelandic material as the "Leitharvísir" ("Pilgrimage Guide") of Abbot Nikolás Bergthórsson of Mún-kathverá written about 1155 and various versions of annals covering mainly the thirteenth and fourteenth centuries. Foreign works of this nature include Adam of Bremen's *Gesta Hammaburgensis ecclesiae pontificum* from about 1075 and *Konungs skuggsjá (King's Mirror)*, written about 1250 by a Norwegian.

Far surpassing in quantity such sources as these are the appealing historical sagas with their usually inherently credible plots, their psychologically believable characers, their convincing physical environments.[3] Like the best of modern historical novelists, authors of these sagas entertained contemporary audiences by so skillfully reconstructing the past that they often must have seemed to be narrating only what actually happened. As a literary attribute this quality is admirable, but it is dangerous for historians because they, who should be more critical than medieval audiences, might still be tempted to accept the truthfulness of almost everything these authors say. While the actual historical content of each saga writer's work is dependent upon his methods of gaining information, all of these men provide useful evidence, nonetheless. Since they can be counted upon not to include any element in their historical backdrop that would strike nonscholarly contemporaries as untrue, they can be trusted to reflect reality as known to their own times. For instance, if an author who was writing his saga about 1230 states that an Icelander went on a trading trip to England in the early eleventh century, purchased a red kirtle there and returned with it to Iceland, we can be reasonably certain that sometime before about 1230 such trading trips did take place and that red kirtles were brought from England.

Whether the event itself actually occurred during the early eleventh century, however, remains questionable.

Though they included dialogue and possibly exaggerated some situations for artistic effect, some authors may have been able to approach historical accuracy even for the time of their narratives. The most reliable in this respect are the writers of so-called Contemporary Sagas, which can be divided into the following categories: the collection known as *Sturlunga saga*, dealing mainly with secular Icelandic events during the twelfth, and especially the thirteenth centuries; the "Bishops' Sagas," describing mainly the activities of Icelandic bishops from the eleventh to the fourteenth centuries; and a few "Kings' Sagas," most notably *Sverris saga* and *Hákonar saga gamla Hákonarsonar*, concerning these late twelfth- and thirteenth-century Norwegian monarchs. Many authors of these sagas wrote soon after the described events took place, and they consequently often had direct, personal knowledge of their material by acquaintance with participants in the events or with those who knew those authorities; and sometimes they may have gained their knowledge by having participated themselves in some of the events they describe, as did Sturla Thórtharson, author of *Íslendinga saga*, part of the *Sturlunga* collection.

In general, the narrative of *Heimskringla*, the largest collection of "Kings' Sagas," is only somewhat less historically trustworthy for the time of its events. Written by Snorri Sturluson during the 1220s, it deals with the reigns of Norwegian kings from the ninth century until 1177. Only for the very latest period of his narrative could Snorri have had direct knowledge of his subject from eyewitnesses, yet like the modern historian Snorri made up for this disadvantage by carefully using reliable earlier sources. In the Prologue to this work he discusses the credibility of his sources, thereby making clear his wish to write factually. He says that expeditions and battles described in skaldic poems must be truthful because the poems concern activities of the very kings before whom they were recited; consequently if those poems had contained misstatements about these achievements, the kings would have been ridiculed rather than praised. Snorri states that his other main source is a collection of the lives of Norwegian kings written by Ári Thorgilsson in a now lost, longer version of *Íslendingabók*. Snorri says Ári drew upon the lives by Odd Kolsson; Odd in turn depended upon the knowledge of a certain Thorgeir who lived in the tenth century. Ári also was well acquainted with the events of the reign of St. Óláf (1015–1030), writes Snorri, because he grew up with Hall Thórarinsson, who had been a retainer to that king. And Snorri says that other sources used by Ári were points of information gained from his teacher, Teit, son of the first bishop of Iceland, Ísleif Gizurarson (1056–1080), and from Thuríth, daughter of the important chieftain, Snorri gothi (d. 1031).[4] Both Teit and Thurith were in a position to know about eleventh-century events in Norway, especially when Iceland was concerned. Snorri thus makes a good case for the reliability of his own work and that of Ári upon whom he so much depended.[5]

Unlike "Contemporary Sagas," "Sagas of Icelanders," which concern affairs of islanders who lived between about 930 and 1030, were written by men who generally lived at least two or three hundred years after the events they describe. And unlike Snorri, these authors usually specify few if any previous sources. How much faith can the historian place on the events described by these men? The question involves the problem of saga origins, at one time a vigorously debated subject. One viewpoint, espoused by the so-called freeprose school, insisted that soon after the events took place they were committed to memory by men who founded an oral tradition. Repeated unchanged by succeeding generations, these oral renditions were ultimately committed to writing. This school upheld the general historical validity of these sagas. The opposite viewpoint, and the one now more generally accepted, contends that the influence of oral tradition is impossible to measure accurately even though it undoubtedly did play a part in forming the written saga. The accuracy of oral tradition, this bookprose school claims, is questionable because a story, even if memorized, was likely to change over a period of two or three centuries. In addition, the writer of the saga undoubtedly asserted his own creativity when dealing with earlier tradition. Previous written sources too may have played a part in shaping many sagas, yet information gained from them could be altered to suit an author's own purposes. This school stresses that the origins of every saga must therefore be studied independently and that generalizations about origins are impossible. Consequently, in general, the historical accuracy of the "Sagas of Icelanders" cannot be upheld.[6]

But even according to the rigorous standards of the bookprose school a considerable measure of historical reliability must be granted to some sagas of this group. For instance, *Eiríks saga rautha* and *Grœnlendinga saga*, both of which concern expeditions to Vínland and other places west of Greenland, must contain at least a basic core of truth. The completely independent testimony of Adam of Bremen and that of other, later sources, mainly Icelandic, all support the exploration of North America and the general location of Vínland as given by these two sagas. Recently, archaeological evidence has appeared to buttress the general accuracy of these two works. Beginning in 1961 excavations were made at L'Anse aux Meadows in northern Newfoundland. Remains unearthed there seem to be of Scandinavian origin, and carbon dating has placed their deposit within the period when Leif Eiríksson and his immediate successors are said to have gone on their famous voyages.[7] *Eiríks saga* and *Grœnlendinga saga* are particularly fortunate in having their basic narratives supported by this independent evidence. If many other "Sagas of Icelanders" were equally favored, our opinion of the historical worth of the group as a whole could be much less skeptical.[8]

In general, then, while no historian of medieval Iceland can ignore the large body of saga evidence, he must be judicious in using it. In this study emphasis is placed upon those sagas more likely to be truthful for the events they relate, "Sagas of Icelanders," except in broadest outline, usually being accepted as sources of historical evidence only for the time of their composition.[9]

Despite existence of the large amount of mainly indirect evidence found not only in sagas but also in more strictly historical works, the Icelandic Commonwealth's foreign trade has not received the comprehensive attention it deserves. An interest in the subject among comparatively modern scholars began, however, as early as 1755. In that year Johannes Erichsen (Jón Eiríksson) had his *Disqvisitiones de vetervm septentrionalivm inprimis islandorvm peregrinationibvs* published in Copenhagen, in which he included a brief discussion of the Commonwealth's trade. He later wrote a short essay more directly pertaining to commerce based in part on his previous study. Entitled "Udkast til en islandsk Handels Historie," it was published in the third edition of Ludvig Holberg's *Dannemarks og Norges Geistlige og Verdslige Staat* (Sorø, 1762). In both studies the Commonwealth's trade is treated only incidentally, and the discussions are based on the presumption that the sagas faithfully recorded historical fact. Consequently, Erichsen's two short works lack a critical assessment of the evidence upon which they are based. He cannot be blamed for this because in his day it was the commonly held opinion that all sagas did state absolute truth; he can be commended for making the initial effort to stimulate further interest in his subject. Not long afterward, the next work on Icelandic trade appeared, Olav Stephensen's *Kortfattet Underretning om den islandske Handels Førelse fra Aar 874 til 1788* (Copenhagen, 1798). As the title suggests, Stephensen's work was ambitious in scope, yet this very quality makes it, at least for the period of the Commonwealth, inferior to his predecessor's. While Stephensen adopted the same viewpoint of the sagas as Erichsen did, he was forced by the chronological terms of his endeavor to give an even briefer presentation of the early trade. His seventy-one-page work, in fact, includes only four short pages devoted to the Commonwealth.

Finnur Magnússon published in 1833 the first truly perceptive study of any aspect of medieval Icelandic trade, "Om de Engelskes Handel og Færd paa Island i det 15de Aarh," in the second volume of the Copenhagen journal, *Nordisk Tidsskrift for Oldkyndighed.* Unlike the period of the Commonwealth, no sagas pertained to this later time of Icelandic history, so Magnússon was forced to rely upon annals, governmental records, laws, and other evidence that were more dependable than uncritically accepted saga material. Perhaps influenced by Magnússon's approach, when Konrad Maurer in 1861 published an article, "Kaflar úr verzlunarsögu Íslands," in the twenty-first volume of the Icelandic periodical *Ný félagsrit*—a study that for the first time since the eighteenth century dealt with the Commonwealth's trade—he drew upon sources more strictly historical than most sagas, especially legal materials. When he used the sagas, he looked at them more critically than had Erichsen and Stephensen, perhaps because as a non-Scandinavian he did not feel a nationalistic need to uphold saga historical accuracy. In 1870 he published another article, "Islands und Norwegens Verkehr mit dem Süden vom IX bis XIII Jahrhunderte," in the second volume of *Zeitschrift für deutsche Philologie,* an article exhibiting the same critical attitude as his earlier one.

Despite Maurer's earlier examples, Bogi Th. Melsteth, the next scholar to be attracted to the study of the Icelandic Commonwealth's foreign trade, reverted to an uncritical acceptance of the sagas as his main evidence. He published about 1896 an article of twenty-eight pages in the ninth volume of *Búnatharrit* entitled "Hverjir ráku verzlun milli Íslands og annara landa á dögum hins íslenzka thjóthveldis?" in which he attempted to show the extent of Icelandic active trade during the Commonwealth by examining mainly evidence in the sagas, with only cursory reference to other sources such as *Landnámabók* and *Grágás*. Not only did he accept the sagas at face value, but also he made little attempt to interpret the other evidence he cites. In spite of his faults—seen from the viewpoint of present scholarly standards—Melsteth still made more extended use of the sagas and more thoroughly examined them than had his predecessors.

The editor of *Búnatharrit* appended a note to Melsteth's article saying that the periodical planned to publish a series of studies dealing with Icelandic trade from the beginning of the island's history to the present. That plan was not implemented, but Melsteth himself did further work on the trade of the Commonwealth. Apparently using as a basis his *Búnatharrit* essay, as well as his "Utanstefnur og erindisrekar útlendra thjóthhöfthingja á fyrri hluta Sturlungaaldar: 1200 til 1239," published in 1899 in the twenty-first volume of *Tímarit bókmentafélagsins,* he wrote the first extensive treatment of Commonwealth trade, "Ferthir, siglingar og samgöngur milli Íslands og annara landa á dögum thjóthveldisins," a work of 325 pages appearing in the fourth volume of *Safn til sögu Íslands* between 1911 and 1914. Like his previous studies, this treatment is based primarily on the saga evidence, but it makes more references to other sources, for Melsteth exhaustively cites virtually every direct indication of Icelanders leaving their country and foreigners entering it. But treating all his evidence equally, he made no attempt to establish its relative veracity, and he drew from it only rather superficial conclusions, his main purpose being to estimate the number of voyages made by Icelanders and Norwegians during various periods of the Commonwealth.

Melsteth's is the only lengthy study of Commonwealth foreign trade to have been made.[10] A number of excellent articles, however, have appeared recently. Particular mention should be made of the summaries by G. J. Marcus, in his "Norse Traffic with Iceland," and by Björn Thorsteinsson, in his "Thættir úr verzlunarsögu: Nokkur atrithi úr norskir verzlunarsögu fyrir 1350," as well as the succinct, dependable, and readily obtainable entries of relevance in the volumes of *Kulturhistorisk leksikon for nordisk middelalder.* In addition to these articles, there are sections treating Commonwealth trade included in works of a more general nature; especially valuable among them is Jón Jóhannesson's *Íslendinga saga,* vol. 1: *Thjóthveldisöld,* translated into English by Haraldur Bessason as *A History of the Old Icelandic Commonwealth.*

Because of the unusual and remarkable qualities of the Icelandic Commonwealth's foreign trade, the not inconsiderable sources for gathering at least inferential knowledge about it, and the lack of a comprehensive treatment of the subject based upon a critical use of the evidence, it is clear that a full study of the subject should be undertaken. This work is an attempt to fulfill that need.

A few words should be added concerning this study's organization, as well as some technical matters relating to it. Part One briefly discusses environmental, economic, governmental, social, legal, and other matters pertaining to Iceland. Together with methods of overseas transport, these might be considered as prerequisites to the island's commerce and certainly as significant influences upon it. Part Two is a discussion of Iceland's foreign trade itself, arranged according to geographical area. On the whole, descriptions of foreign economies have been limited to their bearing on the Iceland trade; in the sections on other North Atlantic Scandinavian islands and Norway, however, those discussions have had to be far-ranging in order to properly assess Iceland's commercial role. Part Three summarizes various conclusions made earlier; its primary purpose is to give a rounded picture of the trade by considering interrelationships between aspects that previously had to be given separate treatment. This approach has the further advantage of allowing a more strictly chronological arrangement than was possible earlier. The epilogue is a brief survey of Iceland's commerce during the later Middle Ages, a subject already examined by Björn Thorsteinsson in his two works, *Íslenzka skattlandith* and *Enska öldin í sögu íslendinga*. A short account nevertheless is needed here to put the Commonwealth's trade into clearer perspective, for the later period witnessed both a change and a continuance of some important earlier commercial traits.

The chronological limits of this work present some minor technical difficulties with dates. The medieval Icelandic Commonwealth (or Republic, as some prefer to call it) usually is not considered to have been officially founded until the island's National Assembly (Althing) was established about 930. The earlier period, the so-called Age of Settlement, beginning about 870, thus perhaps should be regarded as a time of only quasi-independence. Nevertheless, for convenience, the term Commonwealth is sometimes used here to include the Age of Settlement. The end of the Icelandic Commonwealth also presents problems in dating. At the Althing in 1262 Icelanders representing two of the quarters into which their island was divided agreed to become subjects of the Norwegian king. It is debatable whether their action was legally binding on all of Iceland,[11] but in any case their decision was confirmed by the remaining leaders in 1263 and 1264. Rather than to refer pedantically always to 1262–1264 as the end of the Commonwealth, 1264 alone has been used.

Old Icelandic spellings of Icelandic localities and of Scandinavian personal names, except of course translated nicknames, are used as consistently as possible. An exception is that the final "-r" is normally omitted when preceded by a consonant. Also, because of high printing costs and in consideration for readers who would be distracted by the Icelandic character, " ," representing in English the unvoiced "th" as in "thorn," and by the " " indicating the voiced "th" as in "the," both of these Icelandic letters have been changed to "th" throughout this book, in names of places and persons as well as in other Icelandic words, including those in titles of works. These two transliterations may be disagreeable to some scholars in the field—to whom I extend my apologies—but I am consoled by at least the partial precedent set by Lee M. Hollander in his recent monumental translation of *Heimskringla*. All Old Icelandic accents are retained, and the OI "ǫ" and "ø" have been rendered, as in modern Icelandic, as "ö"; all orthographical distinctions are ignored in alphabetizing. A few Icelandic words are presented in their original forms but not italicized. Frequently used Icelandic words are to be found in the Glossary. All dates given in parentheses following the names of monarchs and ecclesiastics refer to terms of office, unless otherwise stated.

My obligation to scholars past and present can be repaid only partially by acknowledgements in the notes. For their kind and generous advice after reading an early version of the manuscript, I wish to thank Professors Lynn White, Jr., and Erik Wahlgren of the University of California, Los Angeles, and, in Iceland, Dr. Björn Thorsteinsson. My greatest debt of gratitude is to Professor Rudolph E. Habenicht for his unstinting counsel and untiring encouragement.

PART ONE

Icelandic Prerequisities for Foreign Trade

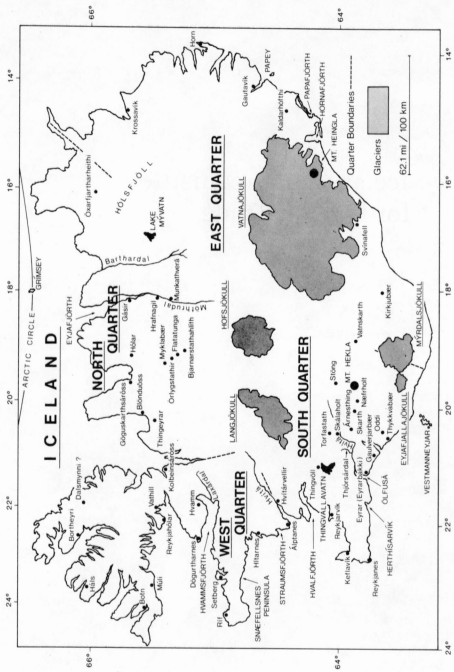

CHAPTER ONE

Environment, Resources, and Material Needs of Medieval Icelanders

SETTLEMENT

Before the first Scandinavian discovery of Iceland about 860, and before the beginning of the first serious Scandinavian settlement of the island about ten years later,[1] Iceland may have been inhabited by a few Irish monks. Dicuil, an Irish monk writing about 825, mentioned that thirty years before some of his countrymen went to an island, which he called Thule, where no darkness occurred at the time of the summer solstice.[2] If Iceland was the island Dicuil mentioned, his authority seems to be supported by an independent Norse tradition. When Scandinavians arrived on Iceland they were supposed to have identified the men already there as Irish monks because they found bells, crooks, and Irish books, which presumably fleeing monks would have left behind.[3] The places where these objects were found were afterward called Papey and Papýli— logically enough, for "papar" means "monks." This specific story seems perhaps too plausible; indeed, it could have been invented later to explain the already existing place names, as so often was clearly done in other cases. But a similar reason may have been

3

responsible for these names, just as for those of other places such as Papafjörth ("Monk-Fjord"), which have no story, plausible or otherwise, connected with them.[4]

While the settlement of Iceland may have started with a few who came to the isolated island for solitary contemplation, permanent colonization began when Scandinavians arrived, more intent on this world than the next. *Landnámabók (Book of Settlements)* mentions about four hundred of the more important who came during the sixty-odd years before about 930 when the Age of Settlement came to a close. Taking into consideration that many unnamed family members and some slaves also must have come, that there would have been a certain natural increase among the earlier pioneers, and that a population figure of perhaps eighty thousand was attained by the end of the eleventh century, there must have been a total population of close to thirty or even thirty-five thousand on Iceland by about 930.[5]

That large numbers sought a new home across the wide sea implies compelling reason. Icelandic saga writers insist on two interrelated political reasons more than any others: welding together the first Norwegian monarch by King Harald the Fairhaired (c. 860–c. 933) and the tyranny that he imposed upon the vanquished. Seeking to expand his domain beyond that of his ancestors in eastern Norway, Harald waged war with other petty chieftains, especially those of the fjord districts in the west who were particularly resistant to conquest. Rather than obey a despotic king, many of the chieftains migrated to Iceland with their families and retinues. Yet despite what the saga writers say, political motivation was probably not the only reason to move to Iceland; the great majority of settlers could not have been so directly affected by King Harald's tyranny. Overpopulation during Viking times existed to some extent in all Scandinavia, but nowhere more than in mountainous Norway where good farmland was scarcer than in either Sweden or Denmark. Since Iceland offered land free for the taking, economic reasons must have been among the most important for sacrificing an old home in Norway in order to make a new one in Iceland.

Both literary tradition and economic circumstance, among

other indications, suggest that most immigrants were from Norway, with apparently only a few from Sweden and Denmark.[6] But not all of them came to Iceland directly. Like Auth the Deep-Minded, several other colonists mentioned in *Landnámabók* had previously lived in other North Atlantic Norse settlements—the Faeroes, Shetlands, Orkneys, Hebrides, Man, or Ireland.[7] Those who had resided on these islands sometimes brought spouses and slaves from there, adding a Celtic element to the dominant Scandinavian descent of the Icelandic colonists.

NATURAL ENVIRONMENT

When the pioneers arrived, they found a harsh land. Glaciers and lava fields prevented most of the interior of Iceland from being used,[8] and even where conditions were suitable for human habitation life was far from easy. Long after the settlement period, about 1355, Abbot Arngrím of Thingeyrar monastery wrote a biography of a thirteenth-century bishop of Hólar, Guthmund Arason, in which he gives a graphic picture of the island's natural environment, conditions that probably were much the same as those experienced by the original settlers:

> Readily at God's service was the bishop in this land which books call Thule but Scandinavians call Iceland. It must be said that the name of this island is appropriate because ice is there in abundance, both on land and on sea. In its immense extent, it fills the northern harbors; and on the high mountains of the country there are unmeltable glaciers with such surpassing height and width that their size might be thought unbelievable. Sometimes calamitous torrents flow from these glaciers with overwhelming currents and with a stench so foul that birds in the air and men or beasts on land die from it. There are other mountains in this land which emit terrible fire with the fiercest casting-up of stones. The horror can bring so great a darkness that with the wind at midday at midsummer one cannot see his own hand [before him]. . . . On Iceland . . . boiling pits and sulphur are plentiful. No forests are there but birch, and yet [they are] stunted.[9]

The Icelandic annals readily confirm Abbot Arngrím's description. They frequently mention ice surrounding Iceland, as in 1261 when apparently it remained unmelted throughout the year. Devastating floods too are prominently cited. In 1336, for example, severe rains came in spring, killing much livestock, and when another rain spell came the same year at St. Barbara's Mass (4 December), it was impossible for one to venture out even to a nearby stock-house.[10] Eruptions of Mt. Hekla in the south, the island's largest active volcano, also did not go unnoticed by the annalists. During the first recorded eruption of 1104, "blood was seen flowing from [its] mouth," and its fifth known eruption in 1300 was the worst experienced until then: the noise was loud enough to be heard even in the northern part of the island, hot pumice burned the roofs of the houses of the farm at Næfrholt nearby, and wind-driven sand was so thick between Vatnskarth and Öxarfjartharheithi that "men could not tell night from day." That same year, soon after Christmas, there was a severe earthquake in the south. Other noteworthy earthquakes occurred there before and after that time, but the one of 1339 was particularly bad—three men died because of it, and hot springs ten fathoms in every direction developed on Mt. Heingla.[11]

Had Iceland been nothing more than these dramatic descriptions suggest, an island of ice and fire, of earthquakes and boiling springs, of floods and stunted birches, it would not have been settled in the first place, shunned as a wasteland suitable only as a setting for Hell itself, an entrance to which, as some believed, was the mouth of Mt. Hekla. In fact, Iceland offered much more, making life not only possible but even more than tolerable. Belying its name, Iceland had wide grasslands often stretching considerable distances from the coast. Its climate was fairly mild during most of the period before 1250, being similar then to that prevailing during the years 1901–1930. About 1200, however, the average yearly temperature began to decline, and during the century following 1250 it was usually as low as what was typical during the cool eighteenth and nineteenth centuries.[12] Thus, some of what the fourteenth-century Abbot Arngrím and the annalists after 1250 say about natural phenomena, while generally reflecting conditions known during the settlement and the following period of the Commonwealth, might have been somewhat more evident in their times than before.

HUMAN ENVIRONMENT: POPULATION

After the period of settlement, the numbers of Icelanders can be estimated at three different times: about 965, about 1095, and in 1311. But the evidence on which these calculations is based is so imprecise that only the most general tendencies can be observed. Unfortunately, the first accurate census was not taken until 1703 when there were 50,444 people on the island.[13]

Snorri Sturluson tells of a poet, Eyvind Finsson, who composed a poem about 965 in which he honored "all" Icelanders. As a reward, they contributed three silver pennies each. At the island-wide assembly, the Althing, where the money was collected, these pennies were reduced to pure silver and made into a buckle weighing fifty merkur.[14] Björn M. Ólsen thinks that 3,000 to 4,000 persons contributed to the reward, depending upon how much pure silver was in the buckle. He estimates that the ratio between those contributing and those who did not was about one to seventeen, yielding a population of between 51,000 and 68,000. Consequently Ólsen estimates that there were about 60,000 inhabitants in Iceland by about 965.[15]

The basis for calculating population about 1095 is furnished by Ári Thorgilsson. In his *Íslendingabók*, written about 1130, he says that Bishop Gizur Ísleifsson of Skálaholt counted the number of farmers in all four quarters of the country: there were 700 in the East Quarter of the island, 1,000 in the South Quarter, 900 in the West Quarter, and 1,200 in the North Quarter.[16] Since Ári gives the figures in hundreds only, these numbers must be accepted as only approximate. Perhaps Ári meant by the "C" that he uses to designate "hundred" the Old Icelandic "hundrath," which equalled 120. If so, the number counted by Bishop Gizur would have totalled 4,560. This figure is patently too low for the total population of farmers. If it is supposed that the bishop counted only those who paid a tax for going to the Althing or other assemblies and that the ratio between those paying it and those who did not was about one to three, as it was in 1753, the total number of farmers would have been 13,680. If, moreover, there were seven persons per household on the average, the population of all of Iceland would have totalled almost 100,000.[17] But because Ári indicates the number one hundred by the Roman numeral, it seems more likely that 100 persons were intended rather than 120, considerably reducing the final total. In this case, using the same multiplication factors as before, the total population would have been almost 80,000 in 1095.[18]

The estimate of Iceland's population in 1311 is based on a report made then of the number of farmers who paid the tax for going to the Althing. According to that information, accepting the Roman numeral "C" as equalling 100 rather than 120, there were 970 men in the North Quarter, 484 in the East Quarter, 838 in the South Quarter, and 920 in the West Quarter:[19] the total is 3,212. Once again using the proportion of those heads of households paying the tax in 1753, about one-third, and assuming seven people per household, the total population of Iceland in 1311 would be 67,462.[20]

It seems clear that during the period of the island's first settlement until about 965 there was a very great expansion of population. Initially the growth was due, of course, to the large influx of colonists that lasted until about 930 when, as we have seen, perhaps thirty to thirty-five thousand were living on the island. At that time the land was all supposed to have been claimed, but as yet it hardly could have been densely occupied; therefore during the thirty-odd years afterward, with plenty of land still available, the population was able to practically double; later it had to slow down to a more normal growth rate, attaining its known medieval maximum about 1095. That high level was probably maintained for almost another century, for there is no reason to believe that during this time there was any long-lasting change in conditions affecting human survival. But the generally favorable circumstances did not last. Though there had been plagues and famines earlier, both appeared with extraordinary force in 1192 when annal entries state, "2,400 men died in the North Quarter from disease and hunger between winter and spring."[21] Plague and famine are always close associates, and it is often difficult to know which brought the other in its train. But if not in 1192, at least somewhat later, famine must have taken precedence. Trade abroad, which hitherto had regularly given valuable supplementary support to the islanders, was beginning to be interrupted, and the worsening climate beginning about 1200 seriously affected the domestic economy. These conditions must have caused an increase in the mortality rate, which is reflected in the population figure for 1311. Because the adverse conditions remained during all or most of the remainder of the fourteenth century, population must have continued to be relatively low. Abbot Arngrím, writing in the mid-fourteenth century about Bishop Guthmund of the early thirteenth, would not have been exaggerating the conditions of at least his own time when he said that it is "a characteristic of Iceland that during both winter and summer destitution goes from house to house among the common people, and [they] have scant nourishment except [for] the charity of good men."[22] The increasingly harsh natural environment, aided by plague and commercial difficulties, finally seemed to have claimed its due.

MEANS OF SUSTENANCE

Fortunately for Icelanders, the period of bleakness was long in coming. Before then they succeeded quite well in wresting from their natural environment both direct support and surpluses to trade abroad for necessities and luxuries that they could not adequately obtain at home.

Admittedly, agriculture was never very rewarding. At first Icelanders tried putting land to the plow in widely separated parts of their island. Most important to them was the grain crop of barley, though hardy vegetables such as turnips, cress, and carrots probably were not neglected.[23] But even with the long summer days heat was insufficient in the northern part of the island for much agricultural success, and so by 1100 all attempts to grow barley there had ended.[24] Though crop yields were probably reduced in the warmer south and west as summer average temperatures declined during the thirteenth century and later,[25] agricultural efforts were never totally given up in these areas. About 1250 the presence of plow oxen and as late as 1362 of kilns for drying grain show that some barley was being raised even during the period of cooler weather.[26]

A far more successful alternative to using land for agriculture was to put livestock on it. For instance, at the southern farm of Svínafell, though agriculture could still be practiced there in the mid-thirteenth century, stock raising apparently was given the greater emphasis. *Svínfellinga saga* says that in 1250 Sæmund Ormsson and Ögmund Helgason had to divide property they held in partnership; once the church's and that of Ögmund's wife were taken away, Sæmund took as his share thirty cows, young steers worth twelve cows, four plow oxen, fifty geldings, seventy sheep a year old, twenty horses, twenty-five pigs, and fifty geese in addition to weapons, armor, and personal belongings.[27] In places less suitable for agriculture, even during the warmer earlier period, stock raising must have been given still more attention.

The two most important kinds of livestock, not only at Svínafell, but all over Iceland, were cattle and sheep. From cattle the important foods of meat, milk, butter, and cheese were produced, as well as hides for clothing and vellum.[28] Even the membrane enclosing a newborn calf, stretched on a frame, was used as a window. Until the introduction of the glass pane near the end of the twelfth century this was the best type of translucent window covering available, and at least until the nineteenth century it was still being used.[29] Sheep similarly were a source of various food products, but they were especially valuable for their wool. Wool was braided into cloaks and spun and woven into a coarse cloth called vathmál; the fabric was used not only for clothing, but for tents and sails. In addition, sheep produced tallow and parchment. There is no direct documentary evidence concerning the extent of sheep raising before the fourteenth century, and so it is difficult to know for sure whether sheep or cattle were given the greater attention during most of the Commonwealth[30]—that both were of considerable importance to the economy is attested by the fact that both vathmál and cows were used as the two practical monetary standards. It is probable, however, that even in the earliest days of settlement sheep received greater attention. Sheep could make better use of available grass because they could graze in many places the year around, even on highlands such as Hólsfjöll and Möthrudal, where grass might be too scant for cattle and where snow seldom fell in winter.[31] During winter, the hungry, more vulnerable cattle had to be provided with hay[32] and protected from the cold with stalls.[33] Certainly after the twelfth century when the worsening climate caused less grass and hay to be available, cattle raising must have been limited.[34]

Icelanders did not have to rely exclusively on agriculture and stock raising to support themselves. Sandwort, a weed growing in sand dunes, if threshed, dried, and ground, could be made into meal suitable for porridge or bread, but the result hardly warranted the effort: forty pony loads of the original sandwort were needed to yield one barrel of meal.[35] Moss could be eaten in porridge or with readily obtainable, vitamin-rich seaweed.[36] More appetizing perhaps were wild bird eggs, or even the bony birds themselves. Abbot Arngrím, describing a practice that undoubtedly took place well before his own time, states that innumberable seafowl laid eggs in high mountains and many Icelanders made their living by collecting both eggs and birds, even though the occupation was very dangerous.[37]

Other significant food products of Iceland were obtained from the waters—from the numerous rivers, fresh water fish, especially salmon, and from the sea, not only cod and other saltwater fish but whales, important for their meat and blubber.[38] The value Icelanders placed on whales in particular is reflected by elaborate provisions for the division of those that were cast ashore. A document of about 1270, for instance, states that any whale larger than 1,080 pounds that drifted ashore between Ásuberg and nearby Keflavík was to be divided into nine parts; the allocation of each part, or portion of that part, is described in detail.[39] Fish formed a staple of the Icelandic diet, along with the milk of cattle and sheep.[40] Having at their disposal not only the well-stocked waters of the North Atlantic but innumerable fjords, glacial rivers, and lakes, Icelanders had many opportunities for catching them. Abbot Arngrím describes what must have been a typical way of doing so, not very different from that of the present. A fisherman rows far out to sea to places where fish are habitually known to be; then after casting anchor by letting down a line with a stone at the end until it hits bottom, the fisherman casts his hooked lines, using a lure shaped like a fish. When he feels a bite, he hauls the fish into the boat.[41]

Iceland also possessed other natural resources that were useful to its inhabitants. Bog iron, smelted from hematite ore, was forged in Iceland.[42] Until the beginning of the fifteenth century, its production played an important role in everyday life in areas where hematite deposits were found, provided that enough charcoal from shrublike birches could be obtained for processing the ore, as for instance in the highlands forming the continuation of the valley called Bárthardal.[43] Salt played a small but vital part in the economy. It was produced by evaporating sea water.[44] And the very soil itself, combined with grass roots as sod, might be classified as a resource for Icelanders who had no trees large enough on their island for building purposes.[45] Sod-built houses were so common that they must have been the "underground caves" that Adam of Bremen mentioned in his late eleventh-century description of the island.[46] Indeed, similar houses are still being used in Iceland, quite satisfactorily keeping out cold and preserving warmth.

Icelanders, with utilization of their resources in this manner, might have been able to satisfy their basic requirements for food, clothing, and shelter with little if any help from overseas. But if they wanted to enjoy a more civilized life than their island alone could provide, they would have to rely on imports paid for with exports.

GENERAL EXPORTS

The most important exports were the sheep products of undyed tweedlike vathmál and cloaks called röggvarfeldir and vararfeldir, made by braiding shaggy tufts of wool to imitate as much as possible the pelts of squirrels or other wild animals.[47] The fact that vathmál was used as a standard of payment in Iceland testifies not only to its importance there, but also its acceptance abroad in exchange for other goods. Vathmál and tufted cloaks were apparently so widely exchanged in Norway, the most important foreign country with which Iceland had commerical contact, that they must have been found on virtually every ship arriving there from

Iceland. They could be used to pay the requisite toll at least from the time of King Óláf the Saint (1015–1030) and probably from the time of King Harald the Fairhaired (c. 860–c. 933). Besides plain vathmál, two other grades of the cloth were commonly known. Mórent (brown-striped vathmál) and hafnarvathmál (vathmál for clothing) were both somewhat more expensive and probably of better quality than regular vathmál. Undoubtedly, both of these fabrics were sold abroad. In addition, hides, butter, and cheese from cattle were produced in sufficient quantity to serve as export goods.[48] And, while fish was not an export commodity during the Commonwealth, there is a slight possibility that some whalemeat was sent abroad.[49]

Apart from these essential goods, products of a luxurious or semiluxurious nature could be used as export wares. They included arctic fox and seal skins,[50] but most important were falcons. Iceland was well known during the Middle Ages as a source for these birds of prey, in demand abroad for hunting: Giraldus Cambrensis about 1185 stated that "this land [Iceland] produces and sends large and noble gerfalcons," and in the next century Emperor Frederick II mentioned in the book, *De arte venandi cum avibus* (1248), that Iceland is the place where one finds gerfalcons, which "are the best birds for hunting."[51] Some especially valuable white falcons were also captured in Iceland and sent abroad.[52]

The only polar bears known to have been taken overseas by Icelanders were intended as gifts. Most of these came from Greenland, where bear traps could be laid far from populated areas; such traps were not practical in Iceland because coastal areas, where the bears were likely to come on drift ice, were usually too densely inhabited for them to come ashore.[53] But there were exceptions. In 1274, twenty-two polar bears were killed on Iceland; and in 1321 a large white bear came ashore at Strandir on the western coast of the island, killing eight persons at Keflavík and ravaging the general area before it was finally killed.[54] And, in spite of the danger, some polar bears were tamed and kept as pets by their owners.[55] Given these circumstances, possibly a few polar bears from Iceland reached foreign shores as commercial products.[56]

The only mineral that had any use for the Icelandic export

trade was sulphur.[57] In all of northern Europe only volcanic Iceland had it, and, as a product useful in alchemy and eventually warfare,[58] the foreign demand, though limited, might have been rather advantageous to Icelanders.

GENERAL IMPORTS

With important regular exports limited mainly to woolens, Icelanders had to rely essentially on them to trade for the foreign goods they needed or desired. Since they were never able to grow adequate amounts of grain for themselves, large amounts had to be imported. With a lack of sizable local timber and its by-products, such as tar for preserving ships, they had to import these as well. They also were unable to provide themselves with certain luxuries such as fine cloth and, after the legalization of Christianity in 1000, articles needed for religious services and for church decoration. Thus the oldest collection of Icelandic law, *Grágás*, written starting in 1117–1118 but including material from earlier times, stipulated that grain, linen, timber, wax, and tar were the products most essential for Icelanders to import.[59] The period that this statement refers to is uncertain, but surely not much wax had been imported before the introduction of Christianity.

Barley was brought to Iceland in various forms: sometimes as the whole kernel separated from the chaff, most often as ground meal, and occasionally as malt for brewing beer.[60] Other less essential but still important foodstuffs were hops, giving home-brewed beer a good taste, sometimes beer itself, and honey, useful by itself as a sweetener and as an ingredient of mead. Besides these staples, sometimes exotic foods and spices may have been imported by the wealthiest Icelanders. At least in the time of Bishop Lárentíus Kálfsson (1324–1331) among the distinctive possessions of his cathedral at Hólar were the spices and drinks that he had on hand.[61]

Though Iceland lacked timber, driftwood could be carved for decorative purposes and it might even have been found in sufficient quantity and size to build a small building.[62] Because it was in such demand, rights to driftwood were as well defined and complicated as those for beached whales.[63] The wealthier secular and spiritual leaders, however, were not content with driftwood and abundant sod, they demanded good imported timber for their more imposing buildings.

As *Grágás* suggests, imported linen was especially popular, but other foreign fabrics apparently were in common use by the upper classes during the thirteenth century. Fustian hoods and copes and other vestments of fine cloth are frequently mentioned in church inventories for clerical use, but this fabric was not used by the clergy exclusively. Most fine cloth came from England, and cloth from other parts of Europe, though known, must have been rare in Iceland.[64] Whether English or not, especially fine fabrics are sometimes said to have been presented by kings to worthy Icelanders. As early as the mid-eleventh century, Frisian cloth, for example, may have been given by King Harald the Harsh-Ruler of Norway (1046–1066) to his skalds, among whom was the Icelander Thorbjörn the Raven.[65] While this presentation could have taken place, others are probably anachronistic. For instance Gunnlaug the Serpent-Tongued was supposed to have been given a fur-lined "skarlat" cloak by King Ethelred II of England (979–1016); but if so, he could not have brought it home because skarlat was not known in Iceland until the mid-thirteenth century.[66] Dependable documentary reference is made to "fland" and "arest," designating cloth from Flanders generally and in particular from Arras; a German cloth, "thýthest," probably coming from Saxony, was known in Iceland as well.[67]

The introduction of Christianity to Iceland seems to have provided a stimulus for importing foreign articles. The church in particular needed wax for candles, incense for rites, and wheat flour and wine for the sacrament, though these articles could have been used for nonreligious purposes as well.[68] The higher clergy and secular supporters of local churches also felt a desire to adorn places of worship with many other luxuries in order to make religious services more effective, partly by appealing to the aesthetic sense. Numerous inventories of various churches provide a startling array of imports, these inventories citing perhaps a greater variety of foreign articles than any other type of medieval Icelandic document. The list of goods at the church at Skarth made in 1259 is typical:

> 2 large chalices. 2 vestments with "pell" [some costly material, perhaps velvet] copes. And another two with green and blue copes. And one least expensive with a linen cope. One priest's gown of pell and another of fustian. 2 priests' gowns. 4 altar cloths of pell and two of fustian. 2 of silk. Bearskin. Old hangings all around the church. Dyed clothes. 2 glass windows in the roof. 3 candlesticks. 2 small wash basins and the third somewhat larger. Inexpensive watercan shaped like a man. Fire pot. 10 bells with small bells [clappers?]. A statue of Mary. One enamelled cross and some of wood. Latch and chest. 2 standards. And a large supply of books and some goblets.[69]

Since Skarth was only a relatively modest church, mention is not made of gold or silver chalices and other valuable accoutrements that were in the cathedrals at Skálaholt and Hólar.[70] But liturgical books like those at Skarth are mentioned in virtually all inventories, and occasionally English graduals and psalters are included as well.[71] The church at Múli was particularly well supplied with manuscripts, probably many of them imported. Among others, it had the *Expositiones* of St. Gregory, the sermons of St. Jerome, the *Acts of the Apostles* and the *Legends of the Saints* in two volumes bound in sealskin, *Lives of the Fathers*, sermons of St. Augustine, old Christian laws, and Alcuin's *Martyrologium*.[72]

In sum, despite unfavorable living conditions, many Icelanders during most of the four hundred years following their settlement were able to support themselves surprisingly well. A few natural resources were capable of providing not only sustenance but an exportable surplus. Icelanders thereby had some means for obtaining not only supplementary necessities from abroad, but also many of the luxury wares to be found in the rest of Europe.

CHAPTER TWO

Icelandic Institutions
and Commercial Practices

GOVERNMENT, RELIGION, SOCIETY, AND PARTICIPATION IN TRADE

During the Commonwealth, Icelandic government was dominated by chieftains who used paganism and Christianity to support their authority and augment their wealth. These men, together with those closely associated with them, were able to participate most actively in trade and to exercise the most decisive influence on commercial practices.

The development of legislative and judicial authority in Iceland before the establishment of the National Assembly, the Althing, about 930 can be discussed only in light of later developments about which more is known. It may well be supposed that the colonists, when settling their lonely island, tended to group around a leader who could offer them protection and a means of support; the leader in return enhanced his authority and self-esteem. Even before the actual settlement, leadership had been asserted by men who were wealthy enough to own the ships that brought settlers to the island. And because *Landnámabók* mentions many men of aristocratic lineage who came to settle in Iceland, perhaps respect for family ties also helped a man to gain a

17

following. An individual already of prominence before he made an especially large land claim when reaching Iceland would continue to be held in respect by his neighboring landowners because of his more extensive lands. He would also be given special honor by those to whom he eventually made land grants from his own large domain.

However leadership was first acquired, the relationship between a chieftain and his men came to be strictly defined by custom and law. Though effective protection of his followers as well as arbitration among them were the main duties of any chieftain, he was also obliged to provide a place for pagan worship and to officiate at services there.[1] The chieftain's followers—apart from eventually paying him certain taxes—in turn had to support him at times of physical and, later, of judicial conflict with others.

After about 965, when Iceland was divided into four parts for governmental purposes, followers had to reside in the same quarter as their chieftain. Otherwise, a chiefdom was not necessarily a geographical entity, though it tended to be; strictly defined, it was only personal authority.[2] In fact, if a man thought that his chieftain was not fulfilling his obligations properly, he could give his support to another, provided the latter was willing to accept this new responsibility. Any chiefdom could be sold, given away, lent, inherited, given as a dowry, and divided: in other words, it was treated as personal property.

Even before the Settlement Age ended about 930, it would have grown clear to the chieftains that they could not exist with absolute autonomy, much as they may have wished to do so. Some degree of cooperation among them when their common interests were at stake became all the more necessary as the number of settlements increased and as disputes between their followers became more likely. Thus the need for assemblies (sing. and pl., "thing") to deal with legislative and judicial problems that lay beyond a single chiefdom became apparent. Although there is no way of knowing how many of these local assemblies existed before the Althing was founded, by 930 there were probably twelve and by about 965 there were certainly thirteen, each including three chiefdoms. By about 965 each of them met twice a year. The much more important May meeting was composed of thirty-six men, each of the three chieftains in the district having chosen twelve men from among his followers, called thingmen. Each spring assembly's judicial and legislative functions were combined until about 965 when those duties were more clearly differentiated. The custom for each district assembly to meet again in July or August surely started only when the Althing was founded, for that later district meeting's main duty was to make known to those who had not attended the Althing what had happened there; this session of the local assembly also may have possessed some legislative function, but it certainly was not a judicial body.

The establishment of the Althing, which met for two weeks every June at Thingvöll ("Thing Field") in southwestern Iceland, fulfilled a basic governmental need that had emerged by then. By about 930, because all parts of the island had been claimed more or less completely, contact between widely separated areas had become more frequent: there thus had to be an assembly that could enact legislation for the island as a whole and that could settle disputes between men from widely separated local thing districts.

The legislative body of this National Assembly was the Lögrétta. Originally it consisted of one chieftain from each of the thirty-six chiefdoms, each with two "advisers" whom he chose from among the thingmen who had come along with him.[3] After about 965 when three "new" chiefdoms were added in the North Quarter, the chieftains from the other three quarters, not wishing to suffer any loss of realtive strength, chose one additional man for every three of their chiefdoms. This meant that then there were forty-eight men, each having two advisers. In addition, there was a "lawspeaker" serving a three-year term of office, whose main duty, before the laws were first committed to writing in 1117–1118, was to recite the corpus of law from memory;[4] he also clarified interpretations of law when asked and proclaimed when the judicial courts should make their verdicts public. After Christianity was introduced, the two bishops who were eventually created also had the right to sit on the Lögrétta, bringing the total membership to 147. These men had five main duties: to "right the laws" (probably to decide what *was* the law, in the early medieval sense of "finding" the law); to decide on new laws (and probably to amend old ones); to grant exemption from a law; to choose a lawspeaker; and to act as the representative body of Iceland in foreign affairs.

The Althing had a separate judicial court. It originally consisted of thirty-six men, one man chosen by every "full" chieftain (one who owned all of his chiefdom himself). Little is known about this early court except its existence, but there seems little doubt that it was concerned with cases involving parties from different local assembly districts. Before long the number of cases the court handled must have grown too large to be dealt with efficiently because in addition to hearing cases from widely separated parts of the island, the judges seem to have acted together as a court of appeal for decisions handed down at the spring assemblies. Another difficulty was the formidable power of individual chieftains to sway decisions in cases involving them or one of their men. To cope with these problems, about 965 Lawspeaker Thórarinn Óleifsson successfully urged a new judicial organization.[5] Iceland was now to be divided into quarters, each with its own insignificant assembly. Simultaneously four new Quarter Courts were created to sit at the Althing, replacing the old court. Every chieftain who completely owned one of the thirty-six "old" chiefdoms (the owners of the three "new" ones in the North Quarter were excluded) named one of his thingmen to sit on each Quarter Court, yielding for each therefore a total of thirty-six judges. Because men from all parts of Iceland sat on every Quarter Court, the impartiality of their decisions thus could be more certain than before. The Quarter Courts had original jurisdiction in all but minor matters, with appellate jurisdiction even over those when juries at local assemblies were deadlocked. But it was possible that a Quarter Court might be unable to reach a decision. Therefore, to serve mainly as a court of appeal in these cases, another court—the Fifth Court—was instituted between 1004 and 1030 to sit at the Althing. Its membership was determined in an especially convoluted way, but the number of men hearing a specific case would always be thirty-six. The Fifth Court was the last major change in the Icelandic Commonwealth's judicial system.

Complicated as the Commonwealth's legislative and especially its judicial procedure became—of which only some indication has been given here[6]—legislation and justice were far from
being exercised with impartiality. The chieftains as a group, or at
least the most powerful among them, always remained the con-
trolling element in Commonwealth government because directly
or indirectly they controlled all legislative and judicial proceedings
at all levels.[7] Spurning the concept of a single executive—a
monarch—and protected by geographical isolation from having it
forced upon them, the chieftains had to cooperate among themselves if a stable society was to be achieved in Iceland. The assemblies of the Commonwealth were designed to bring that cooperation about, yet the difficulty of the task is revealed by the
growing complexity of the legislative and judicial system during
its early stages. The independence of the chieftains was too strong
a force to be overcome by recourse to mere constitutional gymnas-
tics. In spite of law-making bodies and courts of continually increasing jurisdiction, no chieftain was always willing to place his
individual authority at the disposal of the collective authority of
his peers. Any chieftain, or indeed anyone else with sufficient
support, might willfully ignore any judicial or legal decision of an
assembly. After the last major constitutional revision at the beginning of the eleventh century, it must have become obvious that
such governmental changes were only palliatives in limiting the
abuse of power by chieftains. Restraint, however, still could come
from other directions. Christianity, with its ideals of self-
effacement and otherworldliness may have dulled for a time the
personal ambition of some newly converted leaders. But spiri-
tuality alone cannot always satisfy the appetites of men hungry for
power in this world. Then, too, Icelandic chieftains, like all those
in authority, were ultimately responsible to those they governed.
Chieftains well knew that the allegiance they commanded from
their followers might be transferred to another if they lost the
respect of those men. But available choices for alternate chieftains
were always limited; the same geographical isolation that favored
chieftain independence could also mean a prison for the island's
discontented inhabitants.

Restrained but not altogether subdued by any force, certain Icelandic chieftains gradually but inexorably were able to increase their power at the expense of others among them and society as a whole. By the 1220s all chiefdoms came to be held by only five families,[8] and Iceland sank into a state of almost continuous civil war. Consequently the very independence of chieftain spirit that had worked against the institution of monarchy now played a major role in permitting it. Profiting, as shall be seen, by religious and economic circumstances as well, the Norwegian king was able to gain the allegiance of all Icelanders by 1264. He finally provided the strong executive power that had been the most serious deficiency of Icelandic government.

When Christianity was introduced to the island, the chieftains tried to control the church almost as carefully as they controlled the government. With pressure from Norway and with the urging of two powerful chieftains, Gizur the White Teitsson and Hjalti Skeggjason, both of whom previously had been converted by Thangbrand, a German missionary, the Althing agreed to adopt Christianity in 1000.[9] Buttressed by the earlier tradition of providing places for pagan worship and of performing pagan rites, the chieftains were easily able to continue to hold much religious power when Christianity was introduced, albeit usually less directly. Instead of providing for pagan services, they or their relatives now built churches, which were treated as personal property. If they wanted them to have their own priests, chieftain families might undertake the education of young boys with that aim in mind. Economically dependent as they were, all parish priests, whether resident at particular churches or not, were controlled far more by their secular patrons than they ever would be either by the bishop of Skálaholt, whose diocese was established in the south in 1056, or by the bishop of Hólar, whose see in the north was established in 1106. Priests who provided religious services at a single church were given food and lodging with a small annual salary by the church owner; others who had no fixed residence, but who sang masses at churches that had no priests of their own, were paid by the church owner according to the actual amount of service performed.[10] Though supposedly independent, parish priests with fixed residence were hardly more than the church owner's personal property, for they, like thralls, were to be apprehended in case of an attempt to flee their duties, unless they had provided replacements for their jobs. The greater dependence on an occasional benefactor by a roving priest who lacked even the security of a slave can be imagined.[11]

In an attempt to improve the financial independence of the Icelandic church, as well as to bring the island into accord with a well-established religious practice in most other parts of Christian Europe (though no yet in the rest of Scandinavia) the tithe was introduced, mainly through the efforts of the second bishop of Skálaholt, Gizur Ísleifsson (1082–1118).[12] Ári Thorgilsson, who lived at the time, said that at the bishop's urging, "it was made law that all men count and appraise all their property, and swear that it was correctly valued, whether it was in land or in chattels, and give tithes thereof."[13] The practice was accepted by the Althing, according to the Icelandic annals, in 1097.[14] Unlike the tithe elsewhere, in Iceland it was not 10 percent of income, but, with some exceptions, 1 percent of total net wealth. Still, some correspondence with the usual custom existed, for in Iceland the legal interest rate was 10 percent of the value of property, and the 10-percent tithe of this income would equal 1 percent of the value of the property itself.[15]

One of the reasons the tithe law was easily accepted at the Althing was that the collection of religious revenue was not new to Iceland. During the pagan period a "temple-tax" had been paid to the chieftains for maintaining pagan temples or sanctuaries. Little is known about this tax, but it may have been substantial. The temple-tax probably was introduced by the founders of the Althing who hoped thereby to strengthen the economic basis of paganism; even after Christianity was introduced in 1000, it still may have been collected until the tithe was brought into law to strengthen Christianity rather than paganism.[16] Familiarity with the practice helped, but there was probably a far more important reason that chieftains supported the tithe. Though it succeeded in giving badly needed financial support to the bishop of Skálaholt, and, after his see was established, to the bishop of Hólar, it did not strengthen the independence of parish priests and the church as a whole, but instead it substantially contributed to the income of secular leaders, probably yielding more revenue for them than the temple-tax ever had. Within each diocese, tithe revenue, as elsewhere in Europe, was to be distributed in equal parts for the maintenance of the bishop, poor, priests, and churches. Because the chieftains and their relations continued to own churches and to pay their priests themselves, the chieftains received the half of the total tithe that was intended for church upkeep and priests.[17] The sums they paid for their own share of the tithe, for actual church maintenance, and for salary to a resident priest or small sums on occasion for actual religious services performed usually must have been greatly outweighed by the total amount collected. Revenue the chieftains gained from the tithe was all the more important to them because, compared to it, income gained as a result of their political power in the forms of levies or fines must have been quite small.[18]

Considering the economic significance of the tithe to the chieftains and other church owners, they were reluctant to see any reforms introduced that limited their access to this revenue. Until the last quarter of the twelfth century their control of priests and churches was left unchallenged by the two bishops, partly no doubt because they both were always members of chieftain families themselves or under their influence. A change in this situation occurred after 1178 when Thorlák Thorhallsson became bishop of Skálaholt. Urged to do so by his superior, Archbishop Eysteinn Erlendsson of Nidaros, Bishop Thorlák attempted reforms that struck at some of the main problems that had limited the autonomy of the Icelandic church. He tried to take churches away from the control of those families that had built them and make them instead subject to his own authority; in doing so, he would make those churches' priests also more greatly obedient to his authority, for they presumably would be paid by him from proceeds of the tithe, rather than as formally by the church owners; and he was intent upon dissolving consanguineous marriages and discouraging the habit of taking concubines, practices that were traditional among chieftains.[19] But the bishop's program gained only very limited success in the face of chieftain opposition,[20] and after his death in 1193 the reforms that he had been able to make were dropped. Success for the church was just as elusive at Hólar when Bishop Guthmund Arason (1203–1237), more forcefully than Thorlák, attempted to introduce much the same program, with, like Thorlák, the full support of the archbishop. Open battle was waged with the bishop by his former supporter Kolbeinn Tumason in 1208, and although Guthmund emerged victorious then, his success was only temporary. The next year he was driven from his see, and he did not return to it until 1218. He had to relinquish possession of his diocese again in 1221, not regaining it that time until 1232. The stubborn twenty-four-year struggle with the chieftains ended only in the failure of Guthmund's reforming attempts.[21]

During the years when the two bishops tried to bring Gregorian reforms to Iceland, chieftains resisted their efforts so strongly not just to keep much of their financial power, but thereby also to help safeguard their own political strength—in the latter sense it was an Icelandic echo of the main reason that Emperor Henry IV had resisted the reforms of Pope Gregory VII himself in the 1070s and early '80s. With the island subject to the Norwegian archdiocese since its founding in 1152 or 1153, rather than as previously to the more distant archiepiscopal see at Lund, and before that to the even more distant see of Hamburg-Bremen, the religious ties between Iceland and Norway were bound to become stronger. If strict conformity to a religious policy of the archbishop by way of either Icelandic bishop led to any significant weakening of the chieftains' financial power, aspirations of the Norwegian monarch to exercise a greater degree of political influence on Iceland would be furthered. One wonders to what extent there was cooperation between the Norwegian archbishop and monarch with the goal of eventual annexation in mind, particularly during Bishop Guthmund's dispute, when Iceland was also having especially difficult political and economic problems with Norway. Certainly it might have been interpreted as an ominous sign, in view of the fact that previous bishops had all been Icelandic, when two Norwegians were appointed by the archbishop to fill the sees of Hólar and

Skálaholt in 1238, both Guthmund and his Skálaholt colleague, Magnús Gizurarson, having died the previous year.

As important a source of revenue to the chieftains as was the tithe, it could only have been considered supplementary to ordinary income. For these men, as for all other Icelanders, their most significant revenue was always earned by raising livestock and, in some cases, by tilling the soil. Of course, those holding the largest amounts of acreage also would usually earn the largest farming incomes, provided that they had an adequate labor supply.

When Iceland was first settled, some of the first arrivals claimed huge tracts of land. Ingólf Árnarson, traditionally considered the first Icelandic colonist, claimed all the land between Ölfusá and Hvalfjörth, an area of several hundred square miles. Auth the Deep-Minded took all the land around Hvammsfjörth, an inlet that itself is more than twenty-five miles long, together with all the valleys adjacent to it. And Geirmund Hell-Skin claimed land north of Auth, as well as the whole of the north by northwestern peninsula of the island.[22] These holdings were so large that they very quickly had to be divided. Land itself was still relatively cheap, and some gave away part of their original claims to relatives, friends, and even freed thralls.[23] The problem of the time was not scarcity of land, but of labor. There were exceptions of course,[24] but most settlers contented themselves with only the amount of land that could be worked by their own family unless they could afford thralls. The Icelandic chieftains, who were wealthy even before they came to Iceland, who had often gained or increased their wealth by Viking expeditions in earlier years, were also the very ones most likely to bring with them significant numbers of slaves, procured either directly during Viking raids or indirectly by purchase. With this labor force, they were able not merely to claim larger amounts of land than others, but to make effective use of it as well.

As useful as thralls were when free men were usually not willing to work for others, slave labor presented problems to owners. A thrall as valuable human property had to be adequately provided with food, clothing, and shelter; yet his labor might not be commensurate with these expenses because he was reasonably certain of a minimal support that was not likely to be greatly improved no matter how hard he worked. Therefore, as long as free labor remained unavailable—labor that could be hired at a fixed rate for particular tasks and that would either perform satisfactorily or be fired—there would be little desire on the part of the large landowner to invest in still more land, provided he was able to maintain his accustomed living standard, and, if he was a chieftain, his political power. For his increasing descendants old lands might not remain adequate for these purposes, and new ones might have to be purchased or otherwise acquired; nevertheless, these new lands would be kept to a minimum, being viewed more as a necessity than as an investment. When the number of thralls that were owned expanded beyond what was needed for farm labor, steps were taken to control their increase. Child exposure was apparently the preferred means; castration does not seem to have been widely practiced.[25] Alternately, surplus thralls might be sold if a buyer could be found or, if not, given their freedom. When Christianity was introduced in 1000, child exposure was expressly forbidden; thereafter, manumissions increased accordingly.

An increase of thralls was part of the general population growth in Iceland. With only a limited amount of habitable land, the time would come when the hired labor of free men would be more available. From what is known of Icelandic population expansion that point appears to have been reached no later than the end of the eleventh century, probably even a hundred years earlier. An estimated population of thirty to thirty-five thousand about 930 must have been rather small compared to the available amount of useful land because of the greatly increased population by about 965. Usable land seems to have become more scarce during the next century because population increased only about another third; thereafter, when population probably remained fairly static and eventually began to decline rather than increase, undoubtedly one of the main reasons was that land had become very scarce indeed. Until about 965, pastureland held even by a family not of the chieftain class might have been adequate to raise the additional livestock required for support of increasing numbers of family members. But later, by about 1000, there might not be enough land to support whole families. Some members would have to find part-time or full-time work on the still extensive lands of chieftains. During the next two-and-a-half centuries such labor provided by free men would become increasingly available for employment by chieftains and their families. Another recourse for families with inadequate land was to establish a new home in Greenland, following the first Icelandic settlers who went there about 986 with Eirík the Red. For expenses of establishing the new settlement the family might sell its old farm at a good price, thereby taking advantage of the growing scarcity in Iceland of such land. This solution, though, might have seemed rather drastic to many, and as the eleventh century proceeded it also would have become less practicable because of an expanding population and growing shortage of good land on Greenland. Instead of moving elsewhere, as a short-range solution to economic problems part of the family land could be sold for a good price to a rich landowner. Using the proceeds, the family could lease back from the buyer the same parcel and more land as well. If this process continued, eventually the family would be left with high rent to pay in return for land that soon would be, or already was, inadequate for a decent living. This stage for many families was reached during the earlier thirteenth century.[26]

Discouraging as were future prospects for relatively small landowners, their plight was beneficial to both thralls and larger landowners. With free hired labor becoming increasingly available after about 1000, manumissions took place not merely to avoid excess numbers of thralls, but to replace their labor partially or entirely with that of free men. As the eleventh century progressed, thralldom had generally disappeared as a result.[27] With the thriftier labor of free men becoming more abundant, already rich men had a strong incentive to acquire more land. Whereas before they had increased their acreage to maintain social or political rank, now they would do so to gain profit for its own sake. If the landowner did not wish to supervise his new lands directly, he could still draw income from them by leasing them to tenants on the profitable legal basis of 10 percent of their value per annum. Furthermore, the leases usually were available on only a yearly basis, which meant that a reassessment of the land's value and hence its rent could always be made often enough to keep pace with rising values. Moreover, equipment and livestock could also be rented to tenants and others, again for a yearly rate of 10 percent.[28]

By the early thirteenth century there were several men of relatively great wealth. Snorri Sturluson is a good example. He received the equivalent of 16,000 aurar from Bersi the Wealthy and 800 aurar as his share of his patrimony; he also had custody of the property of Klaeng and Orm, sons of Hallveig and Orm, worth another 16,000 aurar. From these sources alone Snorri was worth 32,800 legal aurar, easily making him a millionaire by present standards. *Íslendinga saga*, written by Snorri's nephew, says, "Snorri had far greater wealth than any other man in Iceland."[29]

When investment in additional land became increasingly desirable for members of chieftain families during the eleventh century, it began to replace expenditures for ships and cargoes for foreign trade.[30] Land investment was much safer, and trade was becoming less necessary for Icelanders because more Norwegian merchants began coming to their island. As Icelanders relinquished direct participation in overseas trade, higher prices would have to be paid for imports and lower ones received for exports; these were relatively small sacrifices for chieftain families who were favored by increasing wealth gained from additional land. Nevertheless, as the wealthiest and hence a most important group of Icelandic customers for imports, and as the main distributors of those products at least indirectly to other islanders, chieftain families would have to try to prevent foreign merchants from demanding excessive profits. This they hoped to achieve with their customary rights and their control of legislative and judicial procedure.

During the heyday of Icelandic participation in foreign trade, the period before the mid-eleventh century, one of the most important prerequisites was access to a ship and a cargo for it. Because members of chieftain families had a considerable amount of surplus woolens and other goods to sell, they might wish to purchase a ship of their own for voyages abroad. But though they could afford to buy an expensive ship, they might hesitate using significant capital for its purchase and a great deal of their yearly exportable surplus for its cargo space because of the inherent risks of seafaring. A ship with its cargo might be lost or destroyed at sea. And, even if the crossing was made safely, once the vessel arrived at a strange port it or its cargo might be confiscated or stolen. Either would be a considerable economic loss for a single individual. As a form of insurance against such extensive loss, partnership in one or more vessels seems to have been used as a way of sharing the risk. This practice apparently was popular among the wealthy chieftains and their families, to judge from the elaborate procedure enacted into law that was to be followed in case of arguments between partners. If two partners disagreed on whether to make a journey or not, the owner who objected summoned the other to appear at the ship with witnesses in fourteen days; seven days before then the five landowners nearest the ship were to have estimated the value of the vessel and its equipment. The owner who did not want to make the voyage had the choice of being bought out or of buying the ship from the other owner, the amount fixed by the assessed valuation. If he chose to be bought out, the money was due fourteen days later; if he chose to buy out his partner, the money was due in seven days.[31]

In addition to chieftains and their close relatives, there were others who had means of their own to trade abroad. The two Icelandic bishops, though usually related personally to chieftains, had independent episcopal incomes that were quite large after the end of the eleventh century. Episcopal estates would have produced a considerable amount of exportable surplus, and, in addition, the bishops gained substantial revenue from tenants on their lands, from their share of the tithe, and from a less substantial tax levied on parish priests for the wine and wheat flour necessary for the sacrament.[32] Because the episcopacies, however, had been founded only after land investment had started to become more appealing than foreign trade, the bishops, like secular members of chieftain families at that time, would usually have preferred to buy additional land with their income. And by the middle of the twelfth century, these bishops, like other churchmen, were under strict orders not to engage in trade for personal profit. The eleventh article of the Canons of Nidaros (1152), all of which were valid for Iceland, stated that no member of the clergy was to "go to village or market in order to buy cheaply and sell expensively, for the canons of the Church say that clerics who carry on trade shall be removed from office. But if they are poor they can carry on the necessity of handiwork without detriment to their office."[33] This prohibition does not seem to have included trading that was necessary to acquire goods needed by the church, as long as no personal gain was involved. Therefore, on their trips to Norway for other clerical business Icelandic bishops undoubtedly exchanged some of their merchandise for churchly needs—certainly this was done after the Commonwealth when both dioceses had their own ships. Except for some abbots whose monasteries had significant incomes from their lands, only rarely would other members of the clergy have traded abroad if they were dependent upon their clerical incomes alone. Some would have been able to do so as members of secular wealthy families, their agents, or intermediaries for a bishop.[34]

Some farmers who were not part of a chieftain's family, like those wealthier members of society, also might have had the means and desire to trade their surplus animal products abroad themselves. Without more than medium-sized parcels of land, though, they would be unlikely to accumulate enough of a surplus to make a voyage worthwhile as often as larger landowners. When these medium landowners did sail abroad, they almost never had a ship of their own, or even a partnership in one; instead, they usually would have served as crewmen, being alloted a share of a ship's cargo space sufficient for their limited needs.[35] Those farmers holding small parcels of land very rarely if ever would have traded abroad, for such surplus that they could accumulate would have been too small to warrant it being taken abroad personally; these goods would have been reserved to exchange for necessary imports brought to them by others.

Medieval Iceland never had a merchant class, those who made their living exclusively from trade. Even members of large land-owning families, who would have had more means for trading abroad than others, and who before about 1050 would have seen foreign trade as both a necessity and a good investment, would have regarded it as only a supplement to their normal farming activities. They could not have become professional merchants without neglecting supervision of the very land that made their trade possible. Also, the prolonged and continuous absences from Iceland necessary for a merchant would have helped undermine the political power of these chieftain families.

The lack of professional Icelandic merchants during the Commonwealth is reflected in an absence of towns. Domestic trade was carried on at fairs or other temporary marketplaces instead. Fairs were held at the various assemblies at the same time they met, as well as at the two cathedrals at Skálaholt and Hólar and at important monasteries at certain times of the year— locations that in themselves testify to the domestic commercial importance of large landowners. In addition to these occasional fairs, markets were more frequently held wherever and whenever at least one merchant ship cast anchor. Certain harbors were particularly favored, creating especially popular marketplaces where more than one ship might come at once. Three of the most important were at Gásir in the north, Hvítá in the southwest, and Eyrar (Eyrarbakki) in the south.[36] Just as at the assembly fairs, these markets were dominated by chieftains because, until late in the Commonwealth, they had the right to set prices on incoming ships' cargoes.[37]

The lack of professional merchants is also mirrored by the short life of Icelandic guilds, if in fact they ever developed into something close to true mercantile associations. Three guilds are said to have existed during the twelfth century. "If grain was available to buy," the "Óláfs-Guild" met at Reykjahólar every summer at St. Óláf's Mass (29 July) "and many guildbrothers were there." Another met at Hvamm on St. Matthew's Mass (21 September). A third is mentioned at the monastery at Thingeyrar.[38] It is most probable that these guilds were mainly religious brotherhoods, meeting socially for drinking bouts,[39] and that they never developed into actual merchant guilds. The chieftain families who did most of the domestic trading on Iceland had no need of a merchant guild in the ordinary sense of the term because of their already dominant role in trade. If smaller farmers had attempted to form these guilds as a cooperative means of assuring profits, the guilds were destined to fail.[40] Such members of merchant guilds in essence would have had to make a concentrated effort to buy local products in quantity and to sell imports at prices that the members regulated themselves, independent of outside control. Such organizations, however, would have been inimical to Icelandic society. Guild members would not have been able to procure enough Icelandic products, and certainly not at prices advantageous to them, because those who controlled directly or indirectly the largest sources of surplus production, the chieftains and the upper clergy, were too powerful to submit to pressures from guild members composed of small farmers. Efforts to sell imports at their own prices would have been just as fruitless because prices of goods even brought by foreigners were carefully controlled by individual chieftains, who as domestic tradesmen themselves would have been powerful enough to prevent any inroads on their privileged trading position. Whether these guilds were just social gatherings or nascent mercantile associations, they are not mentioned again.

MERCANTILE STANDARDS AND PRICING POLICIES

For Icelandic trade to function with reasonable efficiency, some standards of weight, currency, and measurement had to be observed.

The basic units of weight were the "eyrir" ("ounce," pl. aurar) and "mörk" ("mark," pl. merkur). If the eyrir weighed 27.125 grams, *avoirdupois*, in Iceland,[41] or almost an ounce (28.3495 grams *avdp.*), then the mörk, which was eight times as heavy, would weigh 217 grams—nearly half a pound (.479 lb.). The "vaett" and "fjórthung" were other units of weight: "It is legal weight when eight fjórthungar [quarters] are in a vaett [weight]; and twenty merkur shall be in a fjórthung."[42] Since there are thus 160 merkur in a vaett, a vaett weighed about 80 pounds (actually 76.64 lbs.; 34.72 kg) and a fjórthung about 10 pounds (actually 9.58 lbs.; 4.34 kg). Merkur are divided into aurar, "örtugar" (3 to an eyrir), and "penningar" (10 to an örtug), and thus in a vaett there were 1,280 aurar, 3,840 örtugar, and 38,400 penningar.[43]

"Pundar" ("pounds") were still another way to measure weight. The smallest type of "pund" probably used in Iceland was the "skálapund" ("scale-pound") weighing two merkur[44] or about one pound (.958 lb.; 434.55 g); the "lífspund" ("Livland-pound") was 24 merkur or 11.496 lbs. (5.22 kg); a "skippund" ("ship-pound") was 24 lífspundar or 275.904 lbs. (125.15 kg). One "lest" ("last") was 12 skippundar or 3,310.848 lbs. (1.5 metric tons); and there were 12 lestir in an "áhöfn" ("cargo of a ship") or 39,730.176 lbs. (18 metric tons).[45]

Iceland, like most parts of Europe at the time, based its monetary values upon silver.[46] To a large extent this basis was only theoretical, as is testified to by the absence of Icelandic mints during the Middle Ages. A great deal of Icelandic trade, both domestic and foreign, consisted of exchange by barter. One frequently exchanged item might be equated with another during ordinary times; less common articles might be exchanged for as much else as they would bring. But whether any silver was actually involved in an exchange or not, the value of any item had to bear some relationship to this monetary standard. At the time of settlement Icelandic production of livestock and woolens was not as thoroughly developed as it later became, and during that period a considerable amount of silver was brought to the island as a result of Viking expeditions abroad. For these reasons, silver probably had a greater actual use then than later. Even afterward, silver could be used to pay fines, to settle an imperfectly balanced exchange of goods both at home and abroad, to pay foreign mercantile taxes, or to settle large accounts. During the period after about 930, when Iceland's population greatly increased, exchanges increased in proportion, and Viking raids declined and eventually stopped, the available supply of silver was not always adequate to meet even limited needs. Iceland had no silver mines, so this means of increasing holdings of the metal was not available. Thus silver nuggets and foreign coins mixed with alloy ("bleikt silfr") came to be accepted at half the value of pure silver ("brannt silfr," "burned silver").

Vathmál served as another monetary standard, probably even during the period of settlement. Always valued in terms of silver, vathmál served this purpose well. Its production was the most important industry during the Commonwealth and probably during the period of settlement as well. It was readily available and, as the mainstay of the island's foreign trade, could be easily exchanged abroad.

As an important item of trade and as a monetary base, it was necessary for measurements of vathmál to be standardized. The basic unit of measurement was the "öln" (pl. "alnir"), originally meaning the length of the under part of the arm from behind the elbow to the fingertips. A shorter öln, extending only to the end of the thumb, later became more common. These measurements were obviously too approximate, so attempts were made to standardize these lengths throughout the island. About 1100, the long öln was set at about 22" (about 56 cm), the short (or legal) öln ("lögöln") at about 18" (about 46 cm).[47] The longer the measurement, the more exact each smaller unit within it is, and so the "stika" ("stick," pl. "stikur") of two short alnir was used as well, starting shortly after 1100.[48] About 1200 the Althing legally enacted this measurement, stating that the width of "vathmál, linen, and all cloth shall be measured with stikur which are so long that ten of them correspond to twenty [legal] alnir, [a length] which is marked on the wall of the church at Thingvöll."[49]

Although used as weights, the eyrir and mörk were used as monetary designations as well. A piece of vathmál six alnir long by two alnir wide corresponded to a legal eyrir ("lögeyrir," "legal ounce," pl. "lögaurar," or simply aurar).[50] Although there is no sure proof, it is likely that during the period of settlement, and perhaps even later, one legal eyrir was worth one eyrir of impure silver, and two legal aurar were equal to one eyrir of pure silver.[51] Probably by about 930, certainly before another century had passed,[52] this ratio was changed, so that four legal aurar were worth one eyrir of impure silver, and eight legal aurar equalled one eyrir of pure silver.[53] The reason for this change could be either that vathmál declined in value after its manufacture became more common[54] or that silver rose in value due to an increasing need for the metal in trade and an inadequate supply. Probably it was a combination of both.

The 8:1[55] correspondence between the number of legal aurar to one eyrir of pure silver lasted until shortly before 1200. At that time the ratio was temporarily changed, at least in one district, to 10.83:1, a 35 percent increase in the old price of silver compared to vathmál. Then about 1200 the ratio throughout the island was set at 7.5:1, a 6 percent change compared to the old 8:1 ratio; by about 1300 the ratio was set at 6:1, or an additional 20 percent change.[56] In the latter cases, either silver fell in price or the value of vathmál, upon which the legal eyrir was based, was increased. The latter alternative seems the more likely.[57]

Since the mörk was worth eight times as much as the eyrir, using the common ratio between legal aurar and an eyrir of pure silver of 8:1, 48 alnir of vathmál equalled one legal mörk, and 384 alnir of vathmál equalled one mörk of pure silver. Table 1 gives equivalent values for aurar and merkur of pure and impure silver according to the various ratios between legal aurar and an eyrir of pure silver.

Because vathmál was both an article of trade and a monetary unit, its two functions are sometimes confused in Icelandic documents. Thus even though the amount of vathmál per se is the point of interest it is often expressed in monetary terms, merkur or aurar, instead of in terms of measurement, alnir; in these cases the legal valuation of the given monetary unit was intended. This must be converted into the equivalent number of alnir: for instance, ½ a mörk of vathmál is 24 alnir (according to the usual 8:1 ratio).

Cows were also used as a monetary standard during the Commonwealth, but only for local areas because of the inconvenience of sending cows any considerable distance. The "standard" cow was "three years old or older, ten years or younger," which can "bear calves and give milk." It must be "horned and faultless, no worse than the average, capable of being driven from the local vicinity ["herath"] in one day and of giving enough milk for one calf."[58] Even though this "standard" cow's characteristics were so carefully delineated, there is no set value for a "standard" cow ("kúgildi") for the whole island, no doubt because of its purely local use as a monetary base. Since the price was set by the local spring assembly, not by the Althing, its value could vary in differ-

TABLE 1   EQUIVALENT VALUES FOR SILVER, LEGAL AURAR, ALNIR OF VATHMÁL

Ratio	Silver	Legal eyrir (aurar)	Alnir
	1 eyrir impure	1	6
2:1	1 eyrir pure	2	12
	1 mörk impure	8	48
	1 mörk pure	16	96
	1 eyrir impure	3	18
6:1	1 eyrir pure	6	36
	1 mörk impure	24	144
	1 mörk pure	48	288
	1 eyrir impure	3.75	22.5
7.5:1	1 eyrir pure	7.5	45
	1 mörk impure	30	180
	1 mörk pure	60	360
	1 eyrir impure	4	24
8:1	1 eyrir pure	8	48
	1 mörk impure	32	192
	1 mörk pure	64	384
	1 eyrir impure	5.415	32.49 [32.5[a]]
10.83:1	1 eyrir pure	10.83	64.94 [65[a]]
	1 mörk impure	43.32	259.92 [260[a]]
	1 mörk pure	86.64	519.84 [520[a]]

[a] In practice.

ent parts of the island depending upon local conditions.[59] The Gula Thing for part of western Norway set the value of a cow at 2.5 aurar of pure silver; in contrast to the Icelandic "standard" cow, it usually could not be more than eight years old.[60] The typical price for a kúgildi probably must have been the same—20 legal aurar—in Iceland from the period of settlement until well afterward, although a price equivalent of 20 legal aurar is first mentioned in a document only from about 1186 or somewhat later.[61] In both the twelfth and thirteenth centuries, however, the value of a kúgildi was sometimes set at 2 aurar of pure silver. Thus during the twelfth century the kúgildi must have been sometimes 16 legal aurar (when the ratio of legal aurar to an eyrir of pure silver was 8:1); in the early thirteenth, sometimes 15 legal aurar (when the ratio changed to 7.5:1); and about the beginning of the fourteenth century, sometimes 12 legal aurar (when the ratio became 6:1).[62]

Whether values were expressed in terms of silver, legal aurar, vathmál, or cows, exchanges of domestic and foreign merchandise could be effected only when the value of the articles in question was agreed upon by the parties concerned. If a certain article of a certain quality was commonly traded, and if both demand and supply was fairly regular, its value would be set within narrow limits by the force of custom, but obviously a transaction would still be subject to bargaining by both parties.

An important exception to this free negotiation was the power of chieftains to set, after they bought all they wished, what they considered to be a fair value on goods brought into harbors subject to their authority. Though this practice seems to have existed in Norway and in Scandinavia generally long before Iceland was settled,[63] local chieftains there must have had to surrender this right to royal representatives when monarchies grew strong enough to impose their jurisdictions on the matter. But in Iceland, this practice of chieftains seems to have existed until quite late in the Commonwealth. In fact, during the time of settlement and the earlier Commonwealth this power may not have been invoked as often as it would be later. While Icelanders still went abroad frequently to trade, and while foreign merchants still did not come to the island as frequently as later, native shipowning merchants—almost always chieftains or their relatives—no doubt would usually bring their ships back to harbors they controlled. There they could ask whatever price they wished for goods they did not need themselves. Still, some curb to those prices would have existed because if they were too high, customers might buy hardly any at all, or, seeking a better buy, they might be able to find similar goods at another convenient harbor where a less demanding chieftain also might have just returned from abroad with imports. Occasionally, at the same time that a chieftain put in to his own harbor, another merchant might do so. In this case, the chieftain would need to exercise his right of pricing to make sure that his rival did not undercut him. Later in the Commonwealth, during the eleventh century and afterward when Icelanders traded abroad less often and relied instead upon foreign merchants to bring imports, the pricing power of the chieftains would be particularly valuable. Instead of sometimes being concerned, as he had in earlier years, that a merchant's prices might be too low without his intervention, now a chieftain would want to make sure that they were not too high; the possibility, though, that the merchant might go elsewhere if those prices were set excessively low probably would encourage the chieftain to exercise his powers fairly.[64]

Toward the end of the twelfth century and the early thirteenth this system showed signs of breaking down, partly due to severe and general economic disruption in Iceland. Yet now chieftain intervention in pricing imports would be particularly necessary, for without it, in view of the scarcity of imported goods that existed, a foreign merchant who did make a voyage to Iceland might charge extortionate prices for his goods unless restrained, prices that would be magnified even more when the goods were later retraded. But toward the end of the twelfth century a considerable reduction in the number of chieftains had already taken place, and their ranks would be depleted even more during the early thirteenth century; consequently even though ships from abroad were coming to fewer harbors than before, there always would not be a chieftain available to exercise his traditional pricing rights. To combat this difficulty and to stabilize prices for domestic goods traded within the island, chieftains who remained, first those in at least one district and then those on the whole island, agreed to surrender for a certain time their traditional pricing rights for some incoming goods in order that fixed maximum prices for commonly traded goods, both those newly arrived from abroad and those traded domestically, could be enacted into law.

The maximum price list of one of the spring assemblies, the Árnes Thing in southern Iceland, was issued probably a few years before 1200, or about 1186. This list states that 300 (i.e., 360) alnir of vathmál is worth 100 (i.e., 120) "legal aurar." The value of these

"legal aurar," of course, was valid only for the district of this
assembly, and they were equal to only half the value of usual legal
aurar (720 alnir were usually required for 120 legal aurar).[65] A few
examples of comparable exchanges of goods are made, for instance
one öln of English linen was equal to three alnir of vathmál.
Inasmuch as only half as much vathmál as usual was in a "legal
eyrir" for this assembly district, these exchanges do not seem
unusual, for they correspond to exchanges stated in other, later
price lists, and the same equivalents must have been typical for
many years both before and after this time. But one highly unusual
equivalent is given: one eyrir of gold is said to be equal to 43⅓
"aurar" (or 86.67 usual legal aurar). Gold undoubtedly is mentioned in this instance only to avoid confusion between pure and
impure silver. According to this stated equivalent, one eyrir of pure
silver consequently would be worth ⅛ as much or 5.416 "aurar"
(or 10.83 usual legal aurar). This new ratio of usual legal aurar to
pure silver, 10.83:1, represents slightly more than a 35 percent
change in the old price ratio of 8:1. Since the legal eyrir was based
on vathmál, this new ratio represented a 35 percent decline in the
value of that product and a corresponding 35 percent increase in
the relative cost of other goods. The price list of this local assembly
clearly was intended to hold prices on nonwoolen goods down, but
still the maximum prices were so much higher than before that the
shortage of necessary foreign products and the declining value of
woolens must have been severe. This price list is the only one that
exists issued by a local spring assembly, but it is not improbable
that similar attempts to stabilize rapidly increasing prices for
nonwoolen goods were made in other areas at the time, although
Icelanders elsewhere may not have suffered from such high prices
as those living in the Árnes Thing district.

To combat the extraordinarily ascending prices for non-
woolens all over the island, reflected by the list of the Árnes Thing,
the Althing issued a price list for the whole island somewhat later,
about 1200.[66] It is the most complete record of values for the
Icelandic Commonwealth, and in most cases it shows what must
have been a typical relationship between goods:[67]

6 alnir of vathmál = 1 eyrir
1 tufted wool cloak 4 "thumb alnir" long and 2 alnir wide with 13 strips
    across = 2 aurar
6 arctic-fox skins = 1 eyrir
6 sheep fleeces = 1 eyrir
6 shorn wethers = 1 eyrir
2 skins of old tom cats = 1 eyrir
3 furs of summer-old tom cats = 1 eyrir
5 alnir of mórent = 1 eyrir
1 eyrir of gold which withstands fire [i.e., pure gold] = 60 aurar
1 mörk of burnt [i.e., pure] silver = 60 aurar
1 iron kettle, new and unused, weighing ½ vætt and as large as 8 buckets
    = 15 aurar
3 tempered scythes, with steel handles, edges fired, and weighing 18
    aurar = 2 aurar
1 vætt of bog iron = 5 aurar
1 vætt of forged iron = 6 aurar

      . . .

3 cattle a year old = 1 cow
2 cattle two years old = 1 cow
1 cow not giving milk and a two-year-old cow capable of bearing calves
    = 1 cow less 2 aurar
1 four-year-old ox, gelded or not = 1 cow
1 steer and an ox three years old = 1 kúgildi

      . . .

6 ewes, 2 being two years old and 4 older, thick-haired without bald
    spots, with their lambs = 1 cow

      . . .

6 goats with kids [and above qualifications] = 1 cow

      . . .

1 four-year-old horse or older and less than ten years, healthy and
    faultless = 1 cow
1 four-year-old mare or older and less than ten years, healthy and
    faultless, giving no milk = ¾ cow

      . . .

1 two-year-old sow or older with 9 piglets = 1 cow
3 alnir of broad linen = 2 aurar
2 alnir of English linen two alnir wide = 1 eyrir[68]
2 merkur of wax = 1 eyrir

. . .

3 vættir of old sheep's wool = 1 cow
3 vættir of food, valued at the standard of meal = 1 cow
1 vætt of year old lamb's wool or an old bull's hide = ⅓ kúgildi (either
    also exchangeable for aurar)
2 cows' hides = 1 old bull's hide[69]

This list also included another group of items described as "prized wares" ("met fé") for which prices could not be set by law:

Rigging cloth, newly cut or uncut
Hafnarvathmál
New tufted wool cloaks sold abroad
New things made flat with a hammer [wrought iron?] and wooden or
    metal work
Iron bars
New brass kettles[70]

Of the latter group, the first three items were important exports, the latter probably important imports. Though these "prized wares" could not have been imported or exported with the frequency of items with set prices, they must have been sufficiently common to be included in this list. The law stated that these "prized wares" had to be appraised by a surveyor ("lögmetandi") and a law-seer ("lögsjándi") and that the goods had to be purchased at the prices they agreed upon. If they could not agree on a price, then each had to swear that his price was fair for a specific item.[71]

The most important aspect of this list, insofar as prices are concerned, is that one mörk of pure silver is worth only 60 aurar (i.e., one eyrir of pure silver is worth 7.5 legal aurar) compared to the traditional value of 64 aurar (or one eyrir of pure silver being worth 8 legal aurar). The result of this change would be to lower prices on nonwoolen goods and to raise those for woolens almost 31 percent compared to what was stated by the Árnes Thing (or, conversely, prices set by the Árnes Thing had been 44 percent higher than these). But the price levels established by the Althing were not just a conservative return to the traditional levels that had existed for at least the previous century and a half when the ratio between legal aurar and one of pure silver was 8:1. The further reduction to 7.5:1 was slightly more than 6 percent compared to that earlier ratio. One reason for this departure from tradition, making goods paid for with woolens cheaper than ever despite the growing scarcity of nonwoolen goods, could well have been to allow them to become available to especially poor islanders who otherwise could not afford them even at ordinary prices. Throughout the twelve-month period that the stated prices were to be in effect they were not to fluctuate, which is to say the goods could not be sold for more during the hard winter months, when no shipping from abroad was possible and when it was difficult to move goods any great distance within Iceland itself, than during the summer months, when shipping and domestic transport were possible. Trading these products for more than the stipulated prices carried a punishment of three years' exile.

It must have been difficult to enforce such a stringent punishment during the year the prices were in force, especially considering the power of chieftains to ignore regulations at will. The Althing list was not renewed, and even if it had done some good while in force, after its expiration prices must have increased again. During the early thirteenth century many of the poor were seen roaming the countryside, often in the company of their heroic bishop, Guthmund Arason, begging for food.[72]

After the expiration of the Althing list, the traditional chieftain practice of setting prices on incoming goods was resumed, at least occasionally, but not without opposition from foreign merchants. About 1203 Snorri Sturluson insisted upon setting the price of meal on a ship from the Orkneys, but the captain, Thorkell the Walrus, was equally adamant about pricing it himself. The result was a violent argument.[73] In 1215 an even more serious disagreement arose when two powerful chieftains, Saemund Jónsson and Thorvald Gizurarson, attempted to set prices for the cargo brought on a Norwegian ship that landed at Eyrarbakki, which was within their chiefdom. The Norwegians, upon returning home, spread news of the incident, causing continuing discontent among their fellow merchants in Bergen.[74] Clearly the foreign merchants in these cases were unhappy, having their dreams of high profits unrealized because of intervening chieftains, especially since these merchants had become accustomed to charge what they wished when a chieftain was not present at a harbor. To avoid such serious misunderstandings in the future, new pricing regulations had to be made in order to prevent excessive charges for foreign goods and to make sure that those regulations could be effectively enforced even though the numbers of chieftains had become depleted.

Therefore, about 1219, when the country was on the verge of war with Norway partly as a result of what Norwegians regarded as its unfair pricing practices, Iceland was divided into districts that apparently corresponded to the boundaries of the spring assemblies.[75] Three men were elected for each whose duty was to decide prices on goods coming from the east (i.e., mainly from Norway) before any purchase could be made. If anyone paid more than the agreed prices, he had to pay a very large fine—576 alnir of vathmál. The prices were to be established at least two weeks after the ship's arrival, or if there were more than one ship at a harbor (or in the district), the prices had to be decided upon one week after arrival. If anyone bought before the prices were agreed upon, he was to have the punishment that was decided as just for him.[76] Chieftains, when they were available, might well have been among the three elected men; yet because the law does not specifically state that any or all of them had to be chieftains, it seems likely that this law attempted to fill a void in their number by allowing nonchieftains to take on this duty. It also appears that the chieftains' privilege of "first-buying" before prices were set, as was once their right, was now definitely abrogated by law. There is no way of knowing how effectively the stipulations of this law were enforced.[77]

The Icelandic trader of the medieval Commonwealth was, in sum, most often a chieftain or a member of his family because of the wealth of his class; he was more likely to participate in trade before about 1050 than afterward; and he gave only part of his attention to trade. Unrivalled by merchant guilds, he sold his wares in Iceland either at fairs or marketplaces because towns did not exist. And, although he was not bound by any law if he was sufficiently powerful, the Icelandic trader found it commercially advantageous to himself and to other islanders to agree upon common standards of weight, currency, measurement, and, within limits, prices.

CHAPTER THREE

Old Norse Merchant Ships and Navigation

That seafaring was highly developed in medieval Scandinavia is most dramatically seen by the massive seaborne marauding carried on by Vikings against the coasts of England, Scotland, Ireland, and France.[1] More mundane, but offering equal and longer lasting evidence of a strong seafaring tradition, was the Scandinavian use of ships for trade. For mountainous Norway, indented by fjords penetrating far inland, the sea afforded the most convenient paths for commerce, while for islands like Iceland, there was obviously no other means of contact with the outside world. Seafaring employed for Icelandic Commonwealth trade reflected the tradition of Scandinavia generally, particularly that of Norway. Ships and navigational techniques used for Icelandic commerce therefore cannot be discussed alone but must be considered within the whole tradition.

SHIPS

Until fairly recently archaeological evidence was slight for gaining knowledge of medieval Scandinavian merchant vessels. The best known examples of Norse ships, found on the western side of Oslo Fjord in 1904 and 1880, are still the ships from Oseberg (dating from c. 800) and from Gokstad (c. 850). The Oseberg ship, with its elegantly carved prow and stern and its fine lines, must have been mainly intended for coastal traffic. The Gokstad ship, larger, more solidly built, and not as elaborately decorated, was a more worthy ocean-going craft, as proved when its replica, *The Viking*, sailed from Norway to the Columbian Exposition in Chicago in 1893.[2] Yet the Oseberg ship was a type of longship and incapable of sailing uprotected waters, and the Gokstad ship, while capable of managing the high seas, was not completely typical of the merchant ship that was used in open seas during the Viking and post-Viking period.[3]

Several other ship finds of various periods, especially in Norway and the southern Baltic, make possible some calculation of the development of Scandinavian ship types—knowledge that can be supplemented by pictoral representations on rune stones from Sweden, on rock carvings from Norway, and on wood carvings from "Bryggen," the medieval wharf at Bergen. This visual evidence, together with literary descriptions, yields a considerable body of information; yet the question still remains: what exactly were the main characteristics of a typical merchant ship ("knörr," pl. "knerrir")?

This question can now be answered thanks to the excavation of five separate ships between 1957 and 1962 in Roskilde Fjord, mainly eleventh-century ships, near Peberenden, not far from Skuldelev, Denmark. Of the five, two were merchant vessels, the only sure examples of their kind.[4] The main characteristics of all of these ships, together with the Oseberg and Gokstad ships, are compared in Table 2. From their dimensions as well as from other features of construction, it is evident that besides Wrecks I and III having been types of merchant ships, II and V were transport vessels capable of carrying a maximum of about fifty to sixty men and about twenty-six to thirty men respectively, and Wreck VI was possibly a ferry or fishing boat.

Wreck I is of particular interest because not only was it the kind of ship that regularly engaged in the Iceland trade, but it is the best preserved as well. Considering its sizable cargo space alone, Wreck I could carry approximately three tons of vathmál, or thirty tons of finely milled grain, or five tons of whole barley. Most ships of this kind, however, would carry a variety of products, and, because the bulk of the product would sometimes have to include containers, the actual cargo would be somewhat less than these maximums. Because the full cargo of a ship was probably set in Iceland at about twenty tons, the cargo capacity of this ship can be taken as typical of most knerrir. So much of the available space was used for cargo that the crew would be limited to between fifteen and twenty men,[5] or even somewhat fewer; with less cargo, more space might be available for passengers.[6]

The "búza" (pl. "búzur") was another type of cargo ship, not represented in the Skuldelev finds and introduced later than the knörr. It is known as early as 1026, referred to then as a warship; yet certainly by the twelfth century it was used mostly as a merchant vessel, eventually supplanting the knörr by the first half of the fourteenth century.[7] The height of its gunwales seems to have been its distinctive feature. About the middle of the thirteenth century King Hákon Hákonarson of Norway had a warship named *Króssuthinn,* which seems to have been an especially large búza, whose "bulwarks were as high as the awning poles [to support coverings over the deck] on [other ships at harbor]. The gunwale was nine alnir [c. 13.5'; 4.12 m] above the water."[8] The length of most búzur, at least those intended as open-sea vessels (sing. and pl. "hafskip"), was probably not significantly more than most knerrir, for the length of hafskip was limited, apart from other considerations, by the size of obtainable strong timber for a keel.[9] Yet because of a búza's greater height, its cargo space was larger than that of a knörr; this advantage would be somewhat offset, however, because compared to a knörr its heavier construction and greater cargo would mean that it would have a deeper draft, and therefore it not only would be less speedy, but also unable to use the more shallow harbors frequented by knerrir.

In contrast to the knörr and búza, both of which could be, and usually were, open-sea vessels, the "byrthing" and the "ferja" were small merchant vessels used mostly for coastal traffic. The byrthing was occasionally used to ship cod and herring from Norway overseas;[10] and the ferja or "ferry," which might attain a size large

TABLE 2 COMPARATIVE MEASUREMENTS OF SHIPS

Ships	Skuldelev I (c. 1040 at earliest)	Skuldelev II (c. 1020)	Skuldelev III (c. 1060)	Skuldelev V (c. 990 at earliest)	Skuldelev VI (before c. 1060)	Gokstad (c. 850)	Oseberg (c. 800)
Length	52.8–54.1' 16.1–16.5 m	c. 91.9' c. 28 m	c. 44.3' c. 13.5 m	59.1' 18 m	c. 39.4' c. 12 m	76.25' 23.24 m	70.8' 21.58 m
Beam	14.4–15.7' 4.4–4.8 m	c. 14.8' c. 4.5 m	c. 10.5' c. 3.2 m	8.5' 2.6 m	c. 8.2'[a] c. 2.5 m[b]	17.06' 5.2 m	16.73' 5.1 m
Height from bottom of gunwale amidships	5.9–6.2' 1.8–1.9 m	—	c. 4.6' c. 1.4 m	c. 3.6' c. 1.1 m	c. 3.9'[c] c. 1.2 m[d]	6.63' 2.02 m	5.18' 1.58 m
Draft loaded (unloaded)	4.9' (2') 1.5 m (0.6 m)	—	c. 3.3' (c. 2') c. 1 m (c. 0.6 m)	1.6–2' 0.5–0.6 m	c. 2.3' (c.1')[e] c. 0.7 m (c. 0.3 m)[f]	c. 3' c. 0.9144 m	?
Ratio of length to breadth	3.5:1	6:1	4.2:1	7:1	4.8:1[g]	4.5:1	4.2:1
Volume of hold to edge of gunwales	c. 1039 ft.³– c. 1236 ft.³ c. 30–35 m³	—	c. 353 ft.³ c. 10 m³	—	—	—	—
Number of strakes per side	12	—	8	7	—	16	12
Number of oarholes	4 (+?) pair	—	5 fore 2 aft	24	—	16	15

TABLE 2 COMPARATIVE MEASUREMENTS OF SHIPS CONT.

Dimensions for the Skuldelev ships from Olaf Olsen and Ole Crumlin-Pedersen, "The Skuldelev Ships. (II)," *Acta Archaeologica* 38(1967):108–9, 118, 130–32, 144–45, 152–53, 170; for dating I–V, p. 163, and especially p. 164 n 1.Dimensions for the Gokstad and Oseberg ships from Thorleif Sjøvold, *The Oseberg Find*, pp. 19–20, 57–58; draft for the Gokstad ship from P. H. Sawyer, *The Age of the Vikings*, p. 69. All measurements for the Skuldelev ships are provisional; Wreck IV was found to be part of Wreck II.

[a]Skuldelev VI was found to have been altered before it was sunk in Roskilde Fjord. Before enlargement, this figure would have been c. 7.4'.
[b]Before enlargement, c. 2.3 m.
[c]Before enlargement, c. 3'.
[d]Before enlargement, c. 0.9 m.
[e]Lightly loaded.
[f]Lightly loaded.
[g]Before enlargement, 5.2:1.

enough to be classed a cargo ship, also might have traveled abroad at times, if the evidence derived from the name of a ship can be believed.[11] With a crew of about twelve men,[12] the byrthing was smaller than either the knörr or búza, as was the ferja,[13] as Skuldelev VI exemplifies.

The knörr, búza, byrthing, and the Icelandic version of the ferja[14] were driven by both oars and sail. On the knörr, such as Skuldelev I or III, and on the búza intended for cargo, oars were fewer than found on a longship, and they were used only in special instances, as when maneuvering a ship back on course after drifting during a calm or when entering or leaving harbor. On cargo ships oarsmen could only use space fore and aft, not amidships as on the longship, because the area was needed for cargo. The rudder on all medieval Scandinavian ships was shaped as an especially strong and large oar, mounted aft to starboard.

The sail of all Norse ships consisted of one square-rigged sail fastened by ropes to the yard which in turn was attached to the mast situated in the middle of the ship.[15] The sail could be raised or lowered along the mast by the halyard, fastened to the middle of the yard. Unlike that of a warship, the mast of a hafskip could not be lowered; it could be removed only when the ship was not in use.[16] Consequently in violent storms the mast of a hafskip was quite liable to be broken, accounting no doubt for the loss of many ships plying the North Atlantic. On merchant ships the sail was usually made of vathmál, and in rough weather or in strong winds this material was liable to be torn if unfurled. Consequently the son in *Konungs skuggsjá* (c. 1250) is wisely advised to "keep aboard with you two or three hundred alnir of vathmál which is suitable for mending sails . . ., many needles, and iron thread or cord."[17] This especially tough cord, made from long twisted strips of walrus hide or sealskin, was also used for the mast tackle as well as for the anchor rope.[18]

Like medieval northern ships in general, Scandinavian merchant vessels were clinker built, one strake partially overlapping the one below it, either lashed together inside with pliable spruce roots[19] or nailed with wooden or iron spikes from the outside;[20] and of course the hull was well caulked and tarred. It would be a mistake to think that the pliability of the hull indicates a weakness of the ship, for if Skuldelev I is as typical as it seems, not only the oaken keel but the soundly reinforced frame system gave these ships a great deal of inner strength. The resulting combination of flexibility and solidity made the ships superb open-sea vessels.

The merchant ship, built for carrying cargo rather than warriors, was not as speedy as the longship. Primarily propelled by sail rather than oars, it might be forced to drift for long periods during a calm, and its generally greater height and draft and its lesser length-breadth ratio meant that it would encounter greater water and air resistance. Even when these limitations are taken into consideration, as well as the heavy cargo, the average speed made under the most favorable conditions was excellent, about six knots.[21]

Most of the larger ocean-going vessels owned by Icelanders must have originated in Norway, for, in contrast to barren Iceland, it was far better supplied with the necessary timber. Among certain privileges that King Óláf the Saint of Norway gave to Icelanders about 1022 was the right to cut as much timber as they wished on royal lands, much of which was undoubtedly used for building ships on the spot. Not only did Icelanders go to Norway to build a ship for themselves, but also certain worthy individuals were given one as a gift.[22] Consequently, even when ships were obtained in Iceland they usually must have been built elsewhere.[23]

Nevertheless, the building of smaller ships in Iceland itself cannot be precluded. If the timber was imported, such ships or boats would be expensive to build, except when large amounts of salvageable wood could be obtained from other ships, either wrecked or otherwise no longer usable. And some ships might have been built in Iceland from driftwood.[24] Surprising as they seem, references to such a practice cited by the sources cannot be dismissed out of hand because fishing and cargo boats were built of such material in the eighteenth and nineteenth centuries. Nor were these later boats especially small. The *Ófeigur*, built in 1875 completely of driftwood, measured 38.8′ (11.83 m) in overall length, 10.8′ (3.3 m) in beam, and 3.6′ (1.1 m) in height amidships, dimensions that are similar to Skuldelev VI. Lúthvík Kristjánsson argues convincingly that ships of this type were being built at the time of Greenland's settlement at the end of the tenth century and that these ships made up the greater part of the original colonization fleet.[25] If so, ships built of driftwood also would have been useful to local merchants plying protected waters.

Once acquired, a ship had to be carefully looked after. The Norwegian father in *Konungs skuggsjá*, always ready with advice for his son, but equally applicable for Icelanders as well, tells him to "keep your ship attractive; then good men will join you and it will be well manned."[26] Tarring and caulking was done usually between October and April when seafaring was not feasible:

> If you should prepare to trade overseas and you have your own ship, then have your ship well tarred in the fall and keep it tarred in the winter if possible. But if the ship is put on timbers too late to be coated in the autumn, then tar it at the beginning of spring and let it dry well afterward.[27]

If a merchant protected his investment in a well-built ship by conscientiously caring for its upkeep, it probably would remain seaworthy for a considerable time. For example, Archbishop Eysteinn Erlendsson of Nidaros had a ship built that was unusually well constructed; frequently used at sea, it was still being sailed in 1239, fifty-six years after it was built.[28] This example, however, might well be exceptional, for judging from the Icelandic annals a more typical lifespan for a ship appears to have been between twenty and thirty years.[29]

NAVIGATION

Crossing the North Atlantic was always a dangerous affair for the Norse mariner, but especially so between October and April when weather conditions were so bad that rarely if ever could a voyage to or from Iceland be made. The father in *Konungs skuggsjá* tells his son that if a

> sea is wide and full of dangerous currents, . . . one needs to exercise great caution; and one must not travel over such open waters when the season is late. . . . One should hardly travel overseas later in the year than the beginning of October. For after then the sea starts to become

very restless, and storms always grow more violent as fall passes and winter approaches. . . . Men may venture out on almost any sea except the largest toward the beginning of April. For toward the seventeenth of April [March?], the days lengthen, the sun rises higher, and the nights grow shorter . . ., the rains let up, the waves sink to rest, the breakers diminish, the swell of the noisy ocean dies away, all the storms weaken, and quiet comes after restless turmoil.[30]

Even during the favored season between April and October the moods of nature were not always benevolent. The wind could suddenly shift, the heavens might be hidden by blanketing clouds, and ice might block harbors. Mainly for these reasons, though sometimes because of a merchant ship's immovable mast, ship-wrecks are recorded frequently in Icelandic annals, sometimes many in one year.[31] That more casualties did not occur and that an ocean crossing could usually be made without mishap owes a great deal to the navigational art of the Norse mariner.

On early sailings to Iceland one method of finding the island was to use birds to lead the way. When Flóki Vilgertharson sailed to Iceland about 868 he is supposed to have departed with three consecrated ravens. "When he let the first loose, it flew back behind the bow; the second flew up into the air and back to the ship; but the third flew ahead of the prow in that direction where they found land."[32] The presence of migratory birds helped in navigating because they eventually would lead one to land, and when coming rather close to unsighted land, birds and whales furnished valuable clues of location. Hauk Erlendsson, in his version of *Landnámabók* (c. 1307), says that when a sailor sails from Norway to Greenland he will pass "north of the Shetlands, which can be seen on a clear day, and south of the Faeroes, so that the sea is [will appear to be] halfway up its slopes, and then [that point] south of Iceland where there are birds and whales."[33] As this passage suggests, sightings of island promontories also were most useful to the seafarer. In this respect Iceland was particularly noticeable. As the thirteenth-century *Breve chronicon Norwegiae* says, Iceland has many glaciers which can be seen from far out at sea, thus guiding seamen to harbor;[34] and the regular route between Iceland and Greenland, until the fourteenth century, was a course within sight of a glacier at either end.[35] Icefloes, the temperature of the water when close to Greenland, and areas known to be usually engulfed by fog, as well as the sense of smell—land yields a scent in stark contrast to salty sea air—must have been other natural indications useful to the skilled navigator.

Fundamental as were such aids, more reliable and accurate navigational methods also were used to try to prevent a ship from straying off course. The nature of winds and tides had to be studied, and careful observation of the heavens had to be practiced by a competent sailor.

The father in *Konungs skuggsjá* gives a lengthy, although very general explanation to his son concerning the nature of the eight main winds[36] and rather poetic descriptions of their natures at various times of the year. For instance, about 7 November the east wind "breathes heavily and violently, as if mourning a recent loss," the southeast wind "knits his brows under the hiding clouds and blows the froth violently about him," the south wind "blows vigorously," the southwester "sobs forth the grief of his soul in heavy showers, . . . leads forth very heavy winds, wide-breasted waves, and breakers that yearn for ships. . . ."[37]

To avoid sandbars, reefs, and other obstacles when coming into harbor, the Norse mariner had to have some knowledge of tides. The cause of tides is well understood by *Konungs skuggsjá's* father. He says that it varies in accordance with the phases of the moon. When the moon is full or new the tide is greatest; when at its quarter phases it is weakest. Every seven days the tide changes, "for the tide rises [approximately] one seventh part [daily] from the time when the rise begins [i.e., when the moon waxes from first quarter to full]; and after it turns and begins to diminish [i.e., when the moon wanes from full to third quarter], it ebbs in the same way during the next seven days."[38] Whether this exact information was known by all may well be doubted, for the father himself says that "merchants are . . . scarcely able to notice these changes because the course [of the moon] is so swift; for the moon takes such long steps both in waxing and waning that for that reason few men can determine the divisions of its course."[39]

Astronomical observation was the most accurate way to get a

directional bearing on the open sea. Sighting the North Star as the simplest way to get a bearing was long known to European navigators. Using the sun as an indication of direction was more complicated, yet it was particularly useful during the long summer days of the northern sailing season. Because the sun traverses the meridian, time must also be known for the sun to be useful for giving direction. At dawn and at sunset the position of the sun indicates east and west;[40] midway through its transit, at noon, it indicates due south; when visible at midnight during the summer, it indicates due north. The experienced navigator, taking a well-known route, would soon learn the maximum height of the sun: the sun would then be south and the time noon. Halfway between sunrise and the sun's zenith, the sun's direction would be southeast and the time about 9 A.M.; halfway between the zenith and sunset, the sun's direction would be southwest and the time about 3 P.M. Except for the sun being due south at noon (and, on the occasions when it could be observed, due north at midnight), the other directions were only approximate, hence they would be used less often and only when sighting the sun at noon was not feasible.

The most usual way of using the sun as a navigational aid for reaching, from Norway, the North Atlantic islands of the Orkneys, the Shetlands, the Faeroes, Iceland, and Greenland must have been what is called "latitude sailing." Running in a generally north-south line, the coast of Norway faces all of these places, and by sailing due west from various points along the Norwegian coast, one can reach any of these destinations. For instance, Sturla Thórtharson in his version of *Landnámabók* (c. 1275) states that one would reach Hvarf in Greenland (just north of Cape Farvel, which is 59° 41′ N) by sailing due west from Bergen (60° 4′ N).[41] How could such a direct westerly course be maintained during so long a voyage? It almost goes without saying that the experienced Norse seaman realized that the farther north he sailed, the lower the sun would be at its greatest altitude, noon, and the farther south, the higher the sun. In other words, he was well acquainted with comparative latitude. On a direct voyage to Greenland from Bergen, the distance at noon between the bottom of the sun's disc and the horizon would be measured, before leaving, with a simple device such as a straight stick of the same length or with a longer one notched at the proper place. Every subsequent day at noon the distance between the sun and the horizon would be measured again. If the distance was greater than the stick or notch on it, the ship had sailed too far south; if lesser, too far north. The ship's route could then be corrected until the following noon, when position would be checked again.[42]

For north-south trips, the method was less reliable. For instance, when sailing from Iceland to Ireland, a pilot would know he was proceeding in a southerly direction because of the ever widening interval between the horizon and the sun every noon. But he would be much less sure, from the position of the sun alone, whether he had been traveling due south, east by southeast, west by southwest, or some direction between these, though in the latter cases he would know that the sun seemed to climb more slowly day after day compared with what it would do were he traveling due south. Still, if he knew the height of the sun at noon in northern Ireland at various times during the sailing season, he could continue to sail until this height was observed. When it was, he could strike a due easterly course until he hit Ireland. Actually, because Ireland lies southeast of Iceland and westerly winds prevail over the intervening waters, in this case a mariner probably would usually reach his destination without recourse to deliberate alteration of his southerly course.[43] Although the Norse seafarer was able to determine comparative latitude, he had no way to decide with any accuracy what his longitude was,[44] and so he had to rely upon significant lapses of time to establish his westerly or easterly progress across the sea, periods that were expressed as "days' sailings," each of which was an interval of either twelve or twenty-four hours.[45]

Besides depending upon his own experience and skill to interpret natural conditions and phenomena, the Norse mariner also used some navigational instruments. One of the simplest and oldest was the lead and line for taking soundings. Unlike the Mediterranean, which is mostly deeper than 100 fathoms, the Baltic and North seas are sufficiently shallow to make soundings feasible. The varying depth of the Continental Shelf, or even the qualities of material picked up from the sea floor by wax attached to the lead, were important indications of location to an experienced seaman.[46] Of course, the Atlantic, like the Mediterranean, was generally too deep for the practice of navigation by soundings, yet a seaman would be able to tell that he was approaching an island like Iceland when it was obscured by fog by, among other ways, noting the increasing shallowness of the ocean floor.

Though latitude sailing was probably the most important open-sea navigational technique practiced by Scandinavians during the Middle Ages, two instruments for ascertaining direction, the lodestone and the sunstone, eventually came to be used also. Both were possibly known to Icelanders during the later Commonwealth. The lodestone device, a primitive type of magnetic compass, consisted of a needle rubbed on a piece of naturally magnetized iron (lodestone); it was placed through a straw and allowed to float on a bowl of water. This device was known to Icelanders sometime before 1307;[47] the evidence possibly indicates that it was known as early as between about 1213 and 1230.[48] This instrument provided an important aid for checking direction, particularly for north-south routes when latitude sailing could not be directly employed. The more sophisticated mariner's compass had two important advantages compared to the simple lodestone device. The needle was placed on a stationary pivot over a compass card on which was inscribed at least the eight main "winds." Nonnorthern courses could be set more accurately compared to the guesswork involved with the lodestone device. And the whole instrument was encased, making it easier to use at sea, for it avoided the floating suspension of the earlier version of the instrument. The mariner's compass appears to have been known in Iceland by 1394, perhaps even as early as 1362.[49]

The sunstone, sometimes apparently confused in the documents with a lodestone, was a separate instrument. According to a recent plausible interpretation, it was a type of polarizing crystal, such as Iceland spar or andulacit,[50] known by at least the earlier half of the fourteenth century as a directional indicator.[51] During overcast weather, a pilot would still be able to locate the position of the sun, thanks to the instrument's polarizing qualities. It therefore would be quite useful for latitude sailing.[52]

Helpful as these instruments for ascertaining direction were, one must be careful not to underestimate the cumulative empirical experience of Norse mariners. Skillful dead reckoning, emphasizing latitude sailing, made it possible for a merchant seaman to sail his well-built ship in open waters with ease well before either the lodestone or the sunstone were known as aids.

PART TWO

Iceland's Commercial World

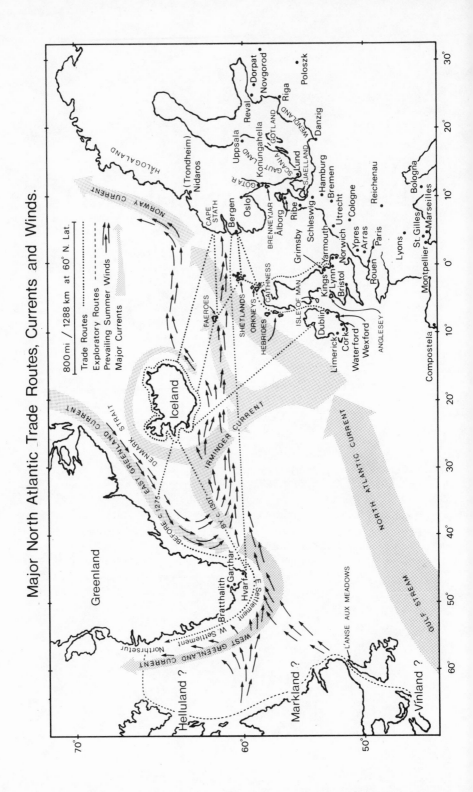

Major North Atlantic Trade Routes, Currents and Winds.

CHAPTER FOUR

Icelandic Trade with Norway, Denmark, and Sweden

NORWAY

Throughout the time of the Commonwealth, Iceland depended upon Norway as its main supplier of imports and main customer for exports. To some extent this choice can be explained in noneconomic terms, for cultural affinities between the countries were always strong, and, at least during the early period of Iceland's history, so were those of kinship. Norway also attracted Icelanders who occasionally served at the royal court and who more often traveled there for religious purposes after the establishment of the Norwegian archiepiscopacy in the mid-twelfth century. A strong Norwegian monarch and archbishop would also be attentive to Iceland for their own political and religious reasons. But these ties provide only indirect reasons for the Iceland-Norway commerce. The more direct economic causes can be appreciated only against the general background of Norway's own early commercial development.

Toward the end of the ninth century when Iceland was being settled, a Norwegian named Óttar met Alfred the Great of England and gave him straightforward information about his financial and

61

commercial activities.[1] He lived far to the north in Hålogaland, and apparently he was quite wealthy. As a chieftain he said he had the right of exacting a tribute from Lapps, consisting of pelts, eiderdown, whalebones, and rope made from sealskin or the hide of the walrus; to augment this income, he himself hunted whale and walrus. He must have invested at least some of this revenue in purchasing tame reindeer—he said he owned six hundred—and at least sometimes he must have taken a considerable part of the goods he collected to trade abroad, for he told his royal host that once he had traveled from his home to the vicinity of the Kola Peninsula and had made another voyage to Hedeby in southern Denmark. Enroute to Hedeby Óttar mentioned stopping at Skiringssal, a market probably located on the western bank of Oslo Fjord.[2] The site was well favored as a trading center. Grain—mainly barley but also rye and possibly oats—was produced on both sides of the wide-mouthed fjord, especially in present-day Swedish Bohuslän. It was grown to the north of the fjord as well, on lands surrounding Lake Mjøsa and in fertile eastern valleys such as Gudbrandsdalen, which themselves communicated with another grain producing area, Trøndelag, adjacent to Trondheim Fjord on the west coast midway between the northern and southern extremities of the country.[3] Another resource was found to the west of Skiringssal, in Telemark, then as now especially rich in timber.[4] Óttar might have been tempted to exchange all of his northern goods at Skiringssal fairs had he not been planning to continue farther south, perhaps before reaching the great Viking emporium of Hedeby stopping at the fairs often held at Brenneyjar, islands at the mouth of the Göta River near present-day Göteborg. Because he may have gone on to England directly after Hedeby, Óttar does not refer to one area of major commercial importance in his country, the western districts—Vestlandet—which had little tillable land compared to pasturage and which thus had to import supplementary grain from either Trøndelag or the eastern part of the country (Østlandet).[5] But even with this omission, Óttar's report of economic and commercial conditions in the Norway of his time is exceptionally valuable.[6]

Until about 1000 Norway, like Iceland throughout the Middle

Ages, could be characterized generally as a country without true towns, for even Skiringssal undoubtedly was not inhabited by a permanent populace of merchants devoting themselves exclusively or mainly to trade. The first obvious sign that this situation was changing came when King Óláf Tryggvason (995–1000), according to saga tradition, founded Nidaros (Trondheim) about 997.[7] What distinguished Óláf's marketplace from others, either possible ones established there in Trøndelag earlier or those known to have existed elsewhere in the country, was its greater permanence. The king made it his residence, maintained a large garrison there, and urged others to build houses there, presumably hoping by such acts to reduce the area's resistance to his insistent efforts to introduce Christianity. A sizable group of administrators and soldiers, together with others such as servants and artisans, would cause a number of merchants to make the place their permanent headquarters also, having to provide continually not just foodstuffs grown in the vicinity, but foreign needs and luxuries as well. In other words, Óláf's marketplace would have had some of the characteristics of a small town. Later, a number of circumstances furthered its growth. King Óláf Haraldsson (1015–1030), who also made it his residence, built a church dedicated to St. Clement there,[8] thus causing several clergymen to become permanent residents. After his death at Stiklestad, his memory stimulated the town's growth even more, for, almost immediately venerated as a saint, he brought worshipers from all over the Scandinavian world and eventually beyond to his burial place in Nidaros. Besides the indirect benefit to trade that this growing administrative, military, and ecclesiastical population entailed, Nidaros's commercial prosperity was more directly enhanced during the eleventh century by a royal trade monopoly in Hålogaland. Instead of being shipped abroad directly, as often had been the practice in Óttar's time,[9] now the far northern products—probably increasingly dried fish—would have been brought first to Nidaros where the royal accounting would be convenient and where some of the products would be used locally before being sent elsewhere in Norway or abroad.[10] When Nidaros received the honor of being selected by Norway's first archbishop as his residence, his choice must have been due almost as much to the reputation the town had gained as a commercial and governmental center as to its fame among pilgrims. Though by the mid-twelfth century or soon afterward Nidaros would have been deprived of its role as the main emporium for more northerly products, the archbishop's own large bureaucracy and commercial interests would have continued to assure the place of permanent importance. The town had become a city.[11]

Nidaros provided a model for other towns. During the eleventh and early twelfth centuries several monarchs, imitating Óláf Tryggvason, are said to have directly encouraged the growth of commercial centers. Besides his support of Nidaros, St. Óláf founded Sarpsborg about 1016; his half-brother, Harald the Harsh-Ruler Sigurtharson, established Oslo about 1050; Harald's son, Óláf III the Quiet, founded Bergen about 1075; and Óláf III's grandson, Sigurth the Jerusalem-Farer Magnússon (1103–1130), promoted the prosperity of the most southerly Norwegian town, Konungahella (mod. Kungälv, in Bohuslän), by making his chief residence there.[12] These cities had more in common with Nidaros than royal establishment: except for Bergen, they were all situated in particularly rich agricultural regions of the country, and all, including Bergen, had good harbors; Sarpsborg and Konungahella may have been founded originally as defenses against Swedish or Danish military threats; and Bergen and Oslo became important ecclesiastical centers as episcopal sees. With permanent occupants consisting of soldiers, administrators, and clergy, these centers, like Nidaros, would become most attractive to merchants.[13]

Icelandic sagas give most of the credit to monarchs for promoting Norwegian urban development. But the role of these men, together with that of prominent clergy, should not be exaggerated. General economic circumstances must have been even more important.

Beginning about 800, large-scale Norwegian emigration, which resulted in the settlement of Iceland among other places, had provided a great measure of relief for overpopulated areas of the country. After about 950, however, it grew more difficult for Norwegians to find new homes abroad, and certainly with the close of the Viking Age about 1030 extensive emigration came to an end. The first part of the country to feel the effects of a confined but growing population would have been the mountainous fjord districts of Vestlandet. Consequently this area, as well as the far north of the country, would have to be provided with additional grain from more fertile districts. Certain centers, well suited geographically to collect foodstuffs and other goods and to distribute them, would have had an especially important commercial function even before they started to have permanent governmental administrators, soldiers, or clergy residing there. Once such men began living in these places, however, those towns that were in fertile areas would have required much more of the local grain production for their own use, leaving less for the poorer districts. After about 1050, as Norwegian towns proliferated, and as population expanded in them and in Norway generally, a sharply increased effort, compared to a century before, undoubtedly had to be made to try to provide enough grain to keep pace with this rising demand. New clearings and a more intense use of old farmland, especially in fertile areas, must have been vigorously attended to. But even so, the resulting increase of grain production may have been inadequate at times. Thus foreign sources of grain might have already begun to supplement that grown domestically.[14] In heavily forested areas that were potentially suitable for growing grain, new clearings not only made it possible for more grain to be grown, but the timber could be exchanged abroad for more grain. A cargo of bulky timber, however, undoubtedly could not be exchanged for as much foreign grain as dried fish. Increased exploitation of the rich fisheries of Hålogaland might well have taken place during the second half of the eleventh century, providing Norway with an abundant, easily transportable, and profitable export. It does not seem accidental that this century was the very time that the royal trade monopoly was established in Hålogaland.

The monarch benefited not just from his control over the export of Hålogaland fish but also from the new clearings taking place energetically in Østlandet and Trøndelag: when they occurred on commons the man who had done the work became a royal tenant.[15] Already in possession of a large amount of land from conquest, inheritance, and purchase, the king as a landlord collected a portion of his tenants' harvests or part of their livestock products.[16] The church too was able to profit substantially from the agricultural and commercial energy of the time, particularly when the tithe began to be collected during the second decade of the twelfth century. Tithe revenues—also often payable in kind[17]—in addition to other incomes, bequests, and financial and commercial privileges received from the monarch, gave churchmen, especially the archbishop of Nidaros, considerable means to profit from domestic and foreign trade as well as to invest in more land than they already owned, yielding further products to sell.[18]

With a sizable amount of domestic agricultural products and fish with which to carry on interior and exterior commerce concentrated in relatively few hands—the monarch, his aides, and the higher clergy—it was obviously impractical for them to undertake all that trade themselves, even had their governmental, military, or religious activities not consumed much of their time and even had not social convention discouraged it at least for clerics.[19] By the end of the eleventh century foreign merchants, who then began to make trips to Norway, would conveniently be able to make some of the necessary exchanges themselves, but they were not yet numerous enough to handle most of the business of rich landowners. Thus from before 1100 until well afterward the great men of the kingdom would have to rely upon other Norwegians as their mercantile agents to make most domestic and foreign commercial transactions. A new Norwegian merchant class on either a part-time or full-time basis was thereby created which, usually based in towns, was itself an important cause of Norway's growing urbanization.[20]

Of all Norwegian cities, Bergen prospered most from the economic circumstances after 1050. Even before it was officially founded, an earlier center might well have had commercial importance there, for it would have been situated on the coast and yet within convenient access to the agriculturally poor interior via Hardanger Fjord to the south and Sogne Fjord to the north: it would have been at a natural point of distribution for grain grown elsewhere in Norway and at a natural collection point for its own area's livestock products to offer in exchange. The new town inherited not only its district's earlier function in domestic trade, but it also became Norway's most important center for a foreign commerce that was mainly directed toward the North Atlantic islands and increasingly toward grain-rich England. These advantages could not be matched by any other Norwegian port. Except for Stavanger, founded after Bergen's role in the commerce had been established, it was closer than other Norwegian towns to England, and it was only slightly less convenient than Nidaros to the rich northern fisheries that were used for buying English goods; its location was more favorable than either Nidaros or Stavanger as a gateway to the most populous part of the interior that increasingly was having to depend upon foreign grain as the fertile lands of Trøndelag and eastern Norway were becoming more densely settled; and it was at a convenient point as well for carrying on trade with grain-needy North Atlantic islands. To be sure, amateur merchants from markets on Oslo Fjord, since at least Óttar's time in the late ninth century and probably before, had been in the habit of trading not just in the Baltic and eastern Europe,[21] but in England and western Europe also. And that activity continued in St. Óláf's day when Oslo Fjord merchants were said to have been in the habit of going to Denmark, Saxony, England, and Flanders.[22] But as Norwegians started to become more active in wholesale foreign trade in necessities during the second half of the eleventh century, none of the towns on Oslo Fjord could offer much competition to Bergen as an international port. Access to English grain and Hålogaland fish was much less convenient for eastern merchants; and the Baltic countries, though easier for them to reach, were not yet in as much need for fish as England with its more substantial urban population. There was, in any case, only a relatively small amount of herring in Oslo Fjord compared to the abundance of cod in Hålogaland waters; and eastern Norway, with more of its own grain, had less need for importing it than Vestlandet and the North Atlantic islands—thus most eastern grain imports ultimately would have had to be sent to such a port as Bergen anyway.

With all of Bergen's unrivaled commercial advantages, even just after its founding "many rich men lived there and foreign merchants came there."[23] And when Kali (or Rögnvald) Kolsson from the Orkneys visited the town about 1120 after a stay in England, he was supposed to have found "a large number of men, both from the north and south [of Norway] and many from other lands who had brought many products there."[24] Though Kali is not said to have noticed dried fish specifically, during the twelfth century more and more often it must have been sent, not to Nidaros, but to the newer center from where it could be more conveniently shipped abroad by Norwegian and foreign merchants. By at least the last decades of the century Bergen must have superseded the older center as the main depository for Hålogaland catches, a role which caused its merchant population to grow well beyond what it had been in Kali's day. When the Norwegian monarch, Sverrir Sigurtharson, made a speech there about 1186, he had occasion to praise directly merchants from England, the Orkneys, Shetlands, Faeroes, and Iceland for bringing useful products to the port. Though a substantial number of merchants, domestic and foreign, in Bergen was beneficial to Norway as a whole, their mercantile success could also be a disadvantage for the country. King Sverrir recognized this when he criticized merchants from Germany, presumably from the Rhineland, because they brought mostly wine and sold it for butter and dried fish, a practice, said Sverrir that was impoverishing the Norwegian people.[25] Bergen's trade was based on necessities, but success would tempt Bergen merchants to seek luxuries like wine abroad and foreign merchants to bring them. Though that practice if stressed unduly might create problems for Norway as a whole, apparently most merchants in Bergen continued to stick to trading goods of basic need for Norway. Just a few years after the royal speech some Danes who came there about 1191 reported what appears to have been a healthy amount of necessities in the city, though they found luxuries there as well:

> Such a great quantity of dried fish which is called "skreith" is there that it exceeds all measure and number. A large number of ships and people come there from everywhere: Icelanders, Greenlanders, Englishmen, Germans, Danes, Swedes, Gotlanders, and so many other nationalities

besides that there are too many to enumerate. If you wish to be diligent, you can find many things in this place. There is an abundance of wine, honey, wheat, fine clothes, silver, and other goods for sale, and anyone can buy what he wants.[26]

On the threshold of the thirteenth century Norway, and particularly Bergen, had achieved at least many of the material advantages of civilization.[27]

Norway's first regular trading partner of importance was Iceland, an association that considerably antedated Norway's eleventh-century commercial expansion. The trade was born of an obvious Icelandic desire to gain such Norwegian products as grain and timber and a somewhat less obvious Norwegian willingness to accept mainly Icelandic woolens in exchange. Demand for this Icelandic export was real enough, for raising cattle was much more important than breeding sheep throughout Norway:[28] it was probably for this reason that until the end of the Middle Ages plentiful cows continued to be used as a monetary standard, whereas scarcer Norwegian wool cloth (vathmál) ceased to be used for that purpose at an early date.[29] And Norway's significant population expansion after about 950 meant that its desire for supplementary Icelandic woolens would have increased correspondingly. But for the Iceland trade there was a less happy aspect to Norway's population growth: it also meant that Norway's ability to provide Iceland with native grain eventually decreased. Even aside from that, there was another threat to the trade: Norway had only a limited capacity, after all, to absorb the ever increasing amounts of woolens Icelanders would be using in exchange for products they needed for their own expanding numbers. Thus when Norwegian commerce with the Continent and especially with England enabled it to import supplementary grain and to open additional markets for Icelandic woolens, this dual danger to trade with Iceland was avoided.[30]

Norway's general commercial expansion was more than an adventitious benefit for the Iceland trade, the two were intimately connected. About 1022 Norway and Iceland made what amounted to a reciprocal commercial agreement, one of the earliest between two countries not only in Scandinavia but also in all of northern

Europe. To take full advantage of this profitable agreement Norwegians would have been anxious to promote their trade connections with other countries, even if they had had no other reasons to do so, in order to obtain extra grain for Iceland in exchange for extra woolens from there. And the agreement would enhance Norway's position as commercial intermediary: trade by Icelanders at non-Norwegian ports was discouraged because they, as it turned out, were not able to gain similar rights at those places, and, because of the agreement, outsiders would not be able to trade with Iceland as profitably as Norwegians.

The immediate cause of this commercial agreement, however, was probably due more to political than to economic considerations. Ever since Iceland was settled, Norwegian kings had tried to exercise at least a nominal suzerainty over the island, which could easily lead to outright annexation.[31] One of the most insistent of these would-be rulers of Iceland was St. Óláf. In 1024 the king sent a spokesman there to ask at the Althing that Icelanders grant him certain taxes and possession of Grímsey, an island off the northern coast, in return for which "he would give whatever good things from his own land Icelanders would ask him for." At first these proposals seemed to be supported, but then Einar Eyjólfsson spoke up:

> If Icelanders want to keep their freedom, which they have had since they settled here, then they should not let the king get any advantage here, whether a piece of land or our promises to pay him taxes which could be considered dues from his subjects. . . . Concerning Grímsey, I say that . . . many could find food there. And if a foreign army sailed from there with warships, I think many Icelanders would be in difficulty.[32]

This speech was enough to defeat the propositions.[33] Because St. Óláf made these political requests only about two years after he gave Icelanders their extensive privileges in Norway, those concessions must have been largely caused by the king's desire to weaken Icelandic resistance to the less generous proposals he was planning.[34] But wily Icelanders were able to avoid the hook and keep the bait, for the agreement of about 1022 was to remain in force for almost another two and a half centuries, while annexation would be delayed equally long.

According to the agreement's terms,[35] an Icelander when in Norway had the same legal standing as a free Norwegian ("höldsrétt"), though if he stayed there for three years his social rank and attendant rights were then to correspond to his actual social station. Icelanders could claim inheritances in Norway up to three years after a benefactor's death; those who had gained movable property from some other kingdom than Norway were not to have their goods confiscated while they were in Norway, presumably on their way back home. Icelanders had the right to water and wood in the forests of the Norwegian king. Unless Norway was at war, they were free to leave the country. They were specifically allowed to travel from Iceland to any country they wished, and any Icelander could come to Norway provided he was healthy and able to pay the landing fees ("landaurar"). Almost all of these privileges were of direct benefit to Icelandic merchants:

Possession of the status and attendant rights of a höld were a distinct advantage to Icelanders because other foreign merchants in Norway were considered as belonging to only the ordinary farmer class, which is to say to the next lower rank.[36]

The provision concerning property gained outside of Norway is worded in such a way—if an Icelander "comes into" ("tømiz") property—that it seems to apply only to inheritances. It is far from inconceivable, though, that this stipulation also would apply to goods purchased by a merchant. If so, the privilege was very important. Unless a merchant could be sure his non-Norwegian goods would not be confiscated in Norway, he would either have to avoid that country on his return home, or he would have to limit his trade to Norway alone. Since the latter possibility is specifically negated by another clause of the agreement, this provision might well have been intended to allow a reselling of foreign goods by Icelanders in Norway.

The right to "wood" in the forests of the king must have been one of the most valuable aspects of this agreement to merchants. Possibly the word refers only to firewood,[37] but it is unlikely, judging from the specific permission for Icelanders to "cut all the

wood they want in the king's forests" and from the frequent references to Icelanders acquiring timber in Norway for building ships
on the spot or for exporting to Iceland for other construction
purposes. Furthermore, as soon shall be seen, what timber was sold
in Iceland was so low in price compared to grain that this low cost
may have been partly due to free access to trees in royal Norwegian
forests. In any case, this stipulation must have been intended as an
encouragement for Icelandic merchants to trade in Norway.

Freedom to leave Norway except during war was not an insignificant promise to Icelanders. Not long before, in 999, King
Óláf Tryggvason had forbidden Icelanders from leaving the country
in an effort to force them to accept Christianity.[38] Though in later
times prohibitions against leaving Norway were made as well,[39]
when this agreement was executed the stipulation seemed to provide security for Icelandic merchants.

Specific permission for Icelanders to travel to any country
they wished from Iceland is somewhat surprising. Even before the
agreement was made, Icelanders certainly had gone where they
pleased; so this permission was superfluous. It can well be taken as
an indication of nascent Norwegian claims to suzerainty over
Iceland, though at the time Icelanders may have understood it only
as an assurance that Norway did not intend to monopolize their
foreign trade.

In return for these privileges, Icelanders had the two fairly
heavy responsibilities of helping to defend Norway in wartime if
they were there and of paying the landaurar.

The responsibility to serve in Norway's defense may have had
roots in earlier custom.[40] At least by the time of the agreement, all
Icelanders in Norway were conscripted for wartime service, and,
because of this duty, they were forbidden to leave during the period
of emergency.[41] The necessity of defending the country was a task
that merchants, though they might be capable of bearing arms,
might dislike, but the possibility that they would not be able to
leave should a war break out must have been even more burden-
some.

The landaurar was certainly not a new idea. Ári Thorgilsson

states that it originated under King Harald the Fairhaired (c. 860–
c.933) and that it was only standardized by King Óláf the Saint:

> At that time such very large numbers of men came out here [to Iceland]
> from Norway that King Harald forbade it, because it seemed to him that
> the land was becoming deserted. Then they agreed that every man who
> traveled here [Iceland] from there [Norway], unless he was exempt,
> should pay the king five aurar. . . . This was the origin of that tax which
> is now called the landaurar; and sometimes more and sometimes less
> was paid until Óláf the Fat [the Saint] commanded that every man
> should pay the king half a mörk [four aurar] who traveled between
> Norway and Iceland except women and those men whom he exempted
> from it.[42]

Ári does not give all details of the landaurar provision in the
agreement of about 1022. According to it, the landaurar was payable when Icelanders arrived in Norway unless they had already
paid the tax on the Shetlands or on other islands near them. If
anyone lost so much of his cargo at sea that he could not pay the
fee, or if he had been driven to Norway when intending to go to
Greenland or on an exploratory voyage, he was exempt from it.
Apart from having to pay fees for Norwegians officiating at the sale
of his goods, the Icelander was not to be subject to any further
taxes. Though the landaurar could be paid with half a mörk of
silver, it could be paid instead with six tufted wool cloaks and six
alnir of vathmál.[43]

Besides omitting these details, Ári differs from the text of the
agreement more subtly. By saying that every man had to pay the
tax who traveled between Norway and Iceland, he suggests that
the old tax payable by Norwegians when leaving Norway was
continued, though reduced, while Icelanders now also had to pay
the same tax, presumably (as the agreement says) when entering
Norway. The agreement, on the other hand, makes no mention of
Norwegians paying the tax either when leaving their country for
Iceland or returning home from the island. Since the agreement
concerns rights of Icelanders and Norwegians in each other's country but not in their own, it might seem that this omission can be
explained thereby and that consequently no real discrepancy exists

between the two sources. Nevertheless, Ári is at least misleading in light of a law made after St. Óláf's time. After St. Óláf's defeat and death at the Battle of Stiklestad, the young Sveinn, son of Canute (Knút) the Great and Álfífa, became king of Norway (1030–1035); he or his mother instituted several new laws, the so-called Álfífulög ("laws of Álfífa"). One stipulated, according to Snorri Sturluson, that everybody, Icelanders as well as Norwegians, had to pay the landaurar when traveling to Iceland.[44] It is inconceivable that Icelanders now had to pay the tax twice, when entering and when leaving Norway: they undoubtedly paid it as the earlier agreement had stated, only when coming to Norway. But collection of the landaurar from Norwegians upon leaving their country for Iceland met with much opposition, as did the other laws.[45] Later, many of the Álfífulög were abrogated, sometime during the time of Sigurth the Jerusalem-Farer, who ruled first with his brothers and then alone (1102–1130),[46] but the one concerning a landaurar to be paid by Norwegians was kept in force.[47] Therefore, because Sveinn's collection of a landaurar was greatly resisted and its collection from Norwegians is said to have been a new practice—though it actually was a return to the law of King Harald the Fairhaired—it seems almost certain that St. Óláf had exempted Norwegians from paying the landaurar either when leaving Norway for Iceland or when returning from there.

Assuming this interpretation to be correct, the changes in royal policy regarding the collection of the landaurar must have been due as much to considerations of commerce as to revenue. When Ári says that King Harald originally forbade migration to Iceland because he thought his country was becoming deserted, the statement must not be understood literally but that the exodus was so great that it was depriving him of a significant portion of his taxpayers. Therefore, to regain some of those losses, as well as to slow the migration, he imposed the landaurar upon those leaving the country. After Iceland's settlement period ended about 930, migration there from Norway practically ceased, and thus income from the landaurar dried up as well; traffic by then was flowing in the opposite direction, however, for increasingly Icelanders were coming to Norway to trade. When St. Óláf reversed earlier policy regarding the landaurar—exempting Norwegians and collecting it from Icelanders arriving in Norway—he gained an immediate and sizable increase of revenue for himself, and he benefited his own merchants greatly because their exemption from the tax provided them with a competitive advantage over Icelanders, an advantage that must have greatly enouraged trade to Iceland. During the eight years or so that the exemption for Norwegians remained in effect, their trade with Iceland must have become so well established that King Sveinn was able to further increase the royal revenue by imposing a landaurar on them (as well as continuing it for Icelanders) without causing them to lose interest in the trade. Even almost a century afterward it must have been a lucrative royal income, for King Sigurth or his brothers apparently could not afford to dispose of this law of the unpopular Sveinn, though many others were repealed.

To balance the privileges and responsibilities for Icelanders who came to Norway, the c. 1022 agreement stipulated that the king and his subjects should benefit from and honor certain rules in Iceland. If the king had a legal case raised there, it was to be judged without any special privilege. If a Norwegian died there without heirs, his property was to be safeguarded until an heir arrived from Norway—there was no time limit for the heir to make his claim, unlike the three-year limit for Icelanders claiming inheritances in Norway.[48] Finally, Norwegian subjects were allowed the same rights in Iceland as Icelanders themselves. This provision was that which most directly concerned Norwegian merchants. The clause should be construed as meaning only that they would have the same rights as ordinary Icelanders, not chieftains. This meant that at least now, if not possibly before, they would be exempt from Icelandic tolls that were payable by other foreigners and that they would still have to submit to the pricing policies of chieftains.

Because the agreement stipulates that one way of paying the landaurar was in vathmál and woolen cloaks, Icelandic woolens undoubtedly were being brought to Norway in large amounts at least by about 1022. Consequently Icelandic ships going to Norway almost always must have carried these goods, and when

Norwegians again were made responsible for paying the landaurar, they, like Icelanders, probably were allowed to pay it with these products. Norwegian demand for these goods also can be seen by the higher value given to them in Norway than in Iceland. Because the landaurar clause of the agreement stated that either six tufted cloaks together with six alnir of vathmál or half a mörk of silver could be used to pay the toll, obviously the goods and the silver must have been regarded as of equal value in Norway. But they were not in Iceland. Since this stipulation of the agreement, like most others, remained in effect until the end of the Commonwealth, it is not inappropriate to compare the Icelandic values for these goods in the c. 1200 price list issued by the Althing. The worth of one cloak was set at two legal aurar, equal to twelve alnir of vathmál, a relationship of value that must have existed since the tenth century. Thus in Iceland six cloaks plus six alnir of vathmál equaled seventy-eight alnir. In Iceland the number of alnir equaling half a mörk of impure silver (the kind the agreement must have intended) was ninety-six from probably about the mid-tenth century until nearly the end of the twelfth, when the ratio of legal aurar to one of pure silver was 8:1; at the time of the Althing list, when the ratio was set at 7.5:1, there would have been ninety alnir for each half mörk of impure silver. According to the 8:1 ratio, then, the goods were worth 23 percent less in Iceland than the value of half a mörk of impure silver; according to the 7.5:1 ratio, they were worth 15 percent less. Consequently, in Norway where the landaurar was paid according to Norwegian, not Icelandic values, the value of impure silver could have been 15 or 23 percent less than in Iceland, or the cloaks and vathmál could have been worth that much more, or the difference could have been due to a combination of both. The first possibility might have been true during the height of the Viking period, but then only in certain hoard-rich parts of Norway; it is inconceivable, however, that silver remained so much cheaper during all the years between about 1022 and 1264 when this agreement was in force; in fact the value of silver must have been almost the same in the two countries since at least 1022. Therefore, most of the difference in the value of cloaks and vathmál in Norway must have been due to a correspondingly greater value of woolens there. This represented a good profit margin for Icelandic merchants selling these goods in Norway, or Norwegians buying them in Iceland.

According to tradition, Icelandic tufted wool cloaks first became popular in Norway when an Icelandic ship came to Hardanger Fjord between 961 and 970. Snorri Sturluson, who included the story in his *Haralds saga gráfeldar*, says the ship was laden with these garments. Thus, if not completely comprised of these woolens, which were made to look like animal pelts, at least the cargo must have consisted of a great many of them. The merchant had difficulty selling them until he met King Harald Eiríksson, who was there with several of his men. The trader told the king his trouble, and Harald asked to have one for himself to use as a cloak. As a result he gained his nickname, "Gray-Cloak" or "Gray-Pelt." The king's example provoked all his men into buying these sheep "pelts" also, to be used in the same way. A few days later, hearing of the new practice, many others in the vicinity came to the ship to buy this latest fashion, but the lucky trader could provide only half the crowd with them before his stock ran out.[49] Usually legends embellish the truth to some extent at least. It is not likely that a merchant would have taken a large cargo of woolen "pelts" to Norway without being reasonably sure that at least some could be sold there without the intervention of the king. Therefore, if we believe that the "cloak-pelts" were indeed taken to Norway during the reign of Harald Gray-Cloak, they also must have been taken there previously.[50]

Unlike Icelandic woolen cloaks, whose supposed introduction to Norway had the makings of a good story, not even a legendary time is given for that of vathmál, yet surely it had been sent to Norway since Iceland's early settlement period. Though the cloth must have been too common to warrant specific notice of the first shipment abroad, this very circumstance suggests that it was sent to Norway in even greater amounts than woolen cloaks. Indeed, that this cloth, not cloaks, formed a main unit of practical account in Iceland for ascertaining the value of almost all other goods also suggests vathmál's comparatively greater importance for foreign trade in general. Because it was a unit of account, though, it is often difficult to decide whether vathmál itself was the export involved in specific instances or merely its equivalent in other goods. But there can be little question that, in one most important example, an Icelandic cloth of some kind, but most probably ordinary vathmál, was regularly sent to Norway in large amounts. When King Magnús Erlingsson was crowned by Archbishop Eysteinn Erlendsson in 1163 or 1164, at the same time or soon afterward the king granted the archbishop several perpetual rights in a document known as the Letter of Privilege. One of these allowed the archbishop to send thirty lestir of grain meal to Iceland every year.[51] In a letter to the archbishop of Nidaros in 1194 confirming the earlier privilege from the king, Pope Celestine III made clear that the grain was to be sent "to buy cloth for the use of St. Óláf's servants [the archiepiscopacy]."[52] The amount of cloth required in exchange for the thirty lestir of grain meal would have been 51,840 alnir of vathmál.[53]

As the archbishop's trade in large quantities of vathmál in return for grain helps to illustrate, cereals were the most important of Norwegian exports to the island. But though the archbishop's grain shipments to Iceland were large, they were not the largest known. The equivalent of about eighty tons is recorded in a detailed and suggestive manner by Snorri Sturluson:

> He [King Harald the Harsh-Ruler Sigurtharson (1046–1066)] was the best friend here [in Iceland] to all inhabitants of the land. When there was a very bad season [or "famine": hallæri] in Iceland, King Harald permitted four ships laden with [grain] meal to sail to Iceland and stated that a skippund should be no more expensive than 120 alnir of vathmál. He allowed all the poor to come to Norway if they could get transportation across the sea. And thus our land recovered with better seasons and better conditions.[54]

In this passage the term *bad season* has been taken to mean a period of inadequate harvests because of bad weather.[55] During unusually severe weather conditions in Iceland, not only would the even normally small harvests of grain be greatly reduced or even eliminated, but so would other forms of nourishment, for livestock would die of cold or starvation from lack of fodder, and fishing would be more difficult in ice-covered bays and fjords. The shipments of Norwegian grain meal certainly would have helped to alleviate such a general food shortage. Snorri does not give the time that these shipments were made during Harald's reign, but the years between 1056 and 1058 are known to have been very bad seasons for Iceland.[56] There were also bad harvests at the same time elsewhere in Scandinavia, at least in Sweden, although perhaps not as bad as in Iceland;[57] if Norway at the time was itself undergoing a period of deprivation, as seems likely, it is odd that Snorri does not refer to it when praising Harald, for the king's act would have appeared all the more munificent.

Thus, it is possible that the grain meal was sent at another time during Harald's reign, and that Snorri, rather than using the word *hallæri* to mean a time of bad harvests, intended instead for it to refer to a famine that resulted from an interruption in shipping from Norway because of a war with Denmark. During much of his reign, Harald was engaged in disputes over possession of the Danish realm. Just after he first came to power, he and his comonarch, his nephew Magnús Óláfsson, fought in Denmark in 1047 against the Danish claimant to the throne, Sveinn Estridsson. After the death of Magnús that year, Harald continued the war in Denmark during all the summer of 1048, but that campaign ended when Sveinn was able to chase Harald back home. Though Harald had political problems in Norway, he continued to make minor attacks against Denmark in following years, culminating in 1062 when he again raised a great fleet and prepared for a major offensive against his rival. The Danes were defeated in a naval battle, but Harald, suffering great losses himself, did not stay to hold Denmark. Definitive peace was finally concluded in 1064.[58] Snorri does not make any direct connection between this war and trade with Iceland, but we may be sure that during hostilities most or all of the trade would have ceased: virtually all Norwegian ships would be needed for attacks, and Icelandic merchants who were in Norway then would have had to help defend the country according to the c. 1022 agreement. What we can only presume from Snorri, we are told was true by the author of another work. *Halldórs tháttr Snorrason hinn síthari*, written at about the same time or somewhat before Snorri was composing his work, says quite clearly that trade with Iceland was severely disrupted because of Harald's Danish war. And this statement is immediately preceded by another, "the next spring men prepared to make trading voyages [from Norway]."[59] Because of what he says about the war, the author obviously means that the voyages were made during a peaceful time, which could have been either after the conclusion of the first phase of the war late in 1048 or after the peace of 1064. Though Snorri does not make the same overt connection between the war and trade, he strongly suggests it because he also places his account of Harald's grain shipments in close conjunction with the war—immediately after his description of the first phase of it. All in all, it thus seems most probable that the shipments were made at a time of peace, of "better seasons and better conditions," during late 1048 or the spring of 1049, most likely the latter.

Because the grain appears to have been sent to Iceland when Norwegian or Icelandic merchants were not prevented from leaving Norway for military reasons and when Norway's climate was not, so far as is known, anything less than typical, producing normal grain harvests, why did Harald have to give his permission for the grain shipments to be made? Could it not well have been because of the Norwegian scarcity of grain even at times of normal harvests that was now becoming evident? In such a circumstance Iceland might receive more than its fair share because of still higher prices compared with Norway that it would fetch there, where it was grown in far smaller amounts relative to population. If Norwegians who had grain surpluses beyond their personal needs sold a disproportionate amount to Iceland for the sake of extra profit, other Norwegians might suffer as a result. To insure a fair amount of grain for Norway before any was sent to Iceland, there would have to be regulation of the trade by the monarch. Thus, Harald's permission for the shiploads of grain to be sent to Iceland probably would have been a normal procedure by his time for any grain shipment there. It is true that these four shiploads represented an unusually large amount to be sent at once, an amount that certainly would require royal permission to export. But in granting leave in this case, Harald undoubtedly would not have been irresponsible in the exercise of his regulatory authority: if shipping had been interrupted because of war with Denmark the previous two years, grain that normally had been sent to Iceland would have accumulated from surpluses of Norwegian harvests; the eighty tons thus could have been spared for Iceland without involving undue hardship for Harald's country. In his role as regulator the king also insisted that Norwegian merchants not overcharge for the grain. It was to be sold to Icelanders at most at only the normal price in spite of the severe shortage the islanders were experiencing.[60]

During the century following King Harald Sigurtharson's reign, Norwegian-grown grain must have become even more inadequate, and correspondingly a greater reliance must have been placed upon supplementary imports. During this time royal control over grain exports to Iceland would have become all the more necessary. The Letter of Privilege granted by King Magnús Erlingsson to the archbishop of Nidaros about 1164 seems to lend support to these assumptions. The thirty lestir of grain meal the archbishop was allowed to ship yearly to Iceland amounted to either 82,771 lbs. (37.55 metric tons), or, less likely, 99,325 lbs. (45.05 metric tons). This privilege, as well as later confirmations of it by Pope Celestine III in 1194 and King Magnús Hákonarson in 1277, was not absolute, for the stipulation always was included, "if supplies in the country allow it." If anyone in Norway would have had the right to export grain at will, he would have been the archbishop. Yet young Magnús Erlingsson, though he was not well in charge of his throne and though he owed what security he had largely to Archbishop Eysteinn for supporting his claim to the crown with a coronation, insisted on exercising what appears to have been an unquestioned royal prerogative by his time: export of grain was possible only by the grace of the king. Since in this case the right was given in perpetuity, it was necessary for the archbishop to exercise restraint on the same basis as apparently the king did with regard to prospective exports over which he still retained direct control: Norway as a whole, not just the archbishop, had to be able to spare it without hardship. Even though he controlled much land in Trøndelag, one of the richest grain-growing areas of Norway, as well as other grainlands elsewhere in the country, the archbishop might have had difficulty in making sure that this condition was met without having to import some supplementary grain. It seems likely, therefore, that this was the reason that Archbishop Eysteinn sought and was granted by King Henry II, probably in the early 1180s, the right to export from England a shipload of grain and other provisions every year, regardless of whether or not English harvests were poor, and, furthermore, without payment of any export toll and without any other hindrance.[61] Some of the archbishop's English grain must have been paid for with the Icelandic woolens—far more ample than his archiepiscopal clergy could personally use—which he received in return for his yearly grain shipments to Iceland; some of the English grain, in turn, might have been used by the archbishop for reexport to Iceland.[62]

For Icelanders, timber, with its by-products of tar and pitch, was second in importance to grain as an import from Norway. Not only was timber useful, but it was cheap, even when brought over the wide sea.[63] In a saga written about 1200 two Norwegian ships are said to have arrived in northern Iceland at Eyjafjörth during the period of settlement carrying mostly timber, both ordinary and choice. In accordance with the custom, the chieftain of the district set the worth of it all at 360 alnir of regular vathmál and paid six aurar (or 36 alnir of vathmál) for the better timber.[64] The timber cargoes on these ships had an average worth of only thirty legal aurar each, representing in about 1200 only the cost of two cows. There were, however, somewhat more valuable cargoes of timber said to have been sold in Iceland: in another saga written about the same time as the last, two Norwegian brothers in the late tenth century supposedly sold some or all of their ship's timber to an Icelander for eighty legal aurar,[65] but this price still must have been quite low. Useful it was, but timber's very cheapness paradoxically caused it to run only a distant second to grain as an import. A cargo of timber could never attain the value of a cargo of grain, which, according to King Harald's pricing rule in the mid-eleventh century, sold for about the equivalent of 2,880 or 3,456 aurar per shipload. The reasons for a lower price for a timber cargo are numerous and obvious. A ship could not carry as much bulky timber as grain; as useful as it was for house and church construction, for bridge building or fishing boats, imported timber was not necessary: buildings could be made of sod, fishing boats of driftwood, and temporary bridges of stones; because Norway was plentifully supplied with timber, a scarcity did not exist there which would have driven up the price; and finally, timber of course was not necessary to support life. Thus, it is likely that Norwegians would have usually preferred bringing more lucrative cargoes than timber to Iceland, and when Icelanders fetched it themselves, they usually must have combined it with a more profitable cargo to take home.

Thus the core of the Norway-Iceland trade remained grain in exchange for woolens. Many other Icelandic imports from Norway—common, such as hardware, or uncommon, such as "Russian hats," tapered axes, "stained saddles," and religious articles—probably had to be brought first to Norway from elsewhere. Like woolens, other Icelandic products sent to Norway—usually luxuries or semiluxuries such as falcons, sulphur, and possibly polar bears—frequently were destined for reshipment abroad from Norway, often as gifts.[66] These lesser items in the trade thus serve to underscore Norway's role, not only as Iceland's most important trading partner, but also as its chief commercial link with the greater European world.

Before leaving this discussion of the Norway-Iceland trade, one additional point should be mentioned. For the trade to exist, as indeed for any foreign trade that Iceland had, the value of the products exchanged on each side usually had to be in fairly exact balance, for it was essentially a trade of barter. Quite apart from an Icelandic inadequacy of silver, and even more so of gold—at least by the end of the tenth century—with which to make good an excess of imports over exports, there was the far more important consideration of Iceland's geographical isolation. When an Icelandic or Norwegian merchant made an infrequent, long, and dangerous trip to the other's country, both legs of the journey had to count. A merchant had to acquire goods of the other land by exchanging a like value of his own wares; he would not make the voyage abroad merely to sell his goods for silver or gold, even if the metals were always available, and return home with his ship empty of cargo.

During most of the Commonwealth Icelandic woolens were usually sufficient to balance Iceland's need for Norwegian grain and other goods. Since grain, however, was far more of an absolute necessity than woolens, there was the lurking danger for Icelanders that if a trade balance with Norway could not be maintained, and consequently if the trade declined, they would suffer far more than Norwegians. The realization of this danger came in the thirteenth century, and it was a significant cause of the loss of Icelandic independence. Before the end of the Commonwealth, though, Icelanders made at least tentative commercial contacts with other lands than Norway. Had that non-Norwegian trade been more successful, Icelanders might have been spared many of their thirteenth-century economic problems.

DENMARK

Examples of Icelanders traveling to Denmark for the express or implied purpose of trade can be found during each century of the Icelandic Commonwealth. But references to this trade are relatively rare, and they can be briefly summarized.

About 970 an Icelandic merchant ship was wrecked in Danish waters; an official of King Harald Gormsson confiscated all of its cargo, for it was subject to seizure as jetsam. This incident understandably provoked the anger of Icelanders; unable to force the return of the cargo, they resorted to composing verses lampooning the Danish king.[67] The tenth century was not, however, a period of continuous discord, for some Icelanders are said to have profited from the Danish trade. One was able to purchase a large knörr in Denmark with all of its cargo, while another spent a long time on trading journeys in both Denmark and England.[68]

Early in the eleventh century an Icelander, Bolli Bollason, is said to have arrived in Denmark. Previously he had come to Norway with a large amount of Icelandic wares on a ship that he owned with his brother. Though King Óláf the Saint urged him to stay in Norway, Bolli insisted on leaving. He let his brother have his own share of their ship, and he himself went to Denmark on another merchant ship, apparently Norwegian. He almost certainly intended to trade there because he took many goods along.[69] Another possible indication of Icelandic trade with Denmark during the late eleventh century and before is a note to Adam of Bremen's *Gesta Hammaburgensis ecclesiae pontificum* (c. 1075), a gloss which itself may not have been written long afterward. It says that it is a journey of thirty days' sailing from Ålborg to Iceland. This statement implies that at least some sailing took place directly between the two places, probably for commercial reasons since Ålborg was an important trading center.[70]

An indication of trade with Denmark in the twelfth century is an entry in *Annales regii* for the year 1188: "Magnús Gizurarson made a round trip to Ribe from Iceland."[71] Ribe was one of the most important commercial centers in Denmark from the early ninth century until the mid-fourteenth.[72] It specialized in exporting horses, but it also dealt in goods that were common to all Denmark such as grain, cattle, butter, and tallow. And Ribe had strong trade connections with England, Flanders, and the Baltic lands from which it gained such products as fine cloth and wine.[73] Therefore, Magnús Gizurarson must have been at least partly attracted to Ribe by the products to be found there.

In the thirteenth century, since Icelanders are mentioned in the laws of the commercial town of Schleswig (c. 1201),[74] the successor to the older Hedeby, they presumably went there to trade. Schleswig was not as important a commercial center as Ribe, but like Ribe it did have foreign contacts, particularly with Flanders, from which it imported cloth, and with the Baltic countries, from which it imported furs. The city also had native horses, cattle, and oxen.[75] During the thirteenth century Schleswig suffered a setback in its trade, much of it being transferred to Hamburg. Possibly it is a measure of that decline, even with the opening year of the century, that Icelanders, perhaps before excluded, were now allowed to come to the city. If Icelanders were allowed to trade there by about 1201, it is possible that they continued to do so at least for a few years afterward.

Hardly any definite conclusions concerning Icelandic trade with Denmark can be drawn based on such sparse evidence. That very scarcity, though, does suggest that the trade was infrequent and that it took place only under exceptional circumstances.[76]

The 1188 entry in *Annales regii* in particular suggests that Denmark was visited only during unusual times. It is the only reference in any series of Icelandic annals that mentions an Icelandic voyage directly to Denmark; it is also exceptional because it states that a round trip was made in one year, whereas typically a round trip would be spread over two. Both the unusual destination and the unusual round trip suggest exceptionally compelling motivation. What that purpose was can be answered by an entry found in two other annals, *Skálholts annáll* and *Gottskálks annáll*, as well as in *Annales regii* itself, for they all say that the previous year "no ships arrived [in Iceland] from Norway."[77] Apparently then only because of an interruption in the usual Norwegian trade was the trip undertaken to Ribe, which, having access to the crops of the exceptionally fertile Danish islands and Scania, was therefore capable of replacing foodstuffs from Norway in an emergency.[78]

Icelanders must have normally preferred dealing with Norway because until the beginning of the thirteenth century — and then with just one city — they lacked any commercial understanding with Denmark similar to what must have existed for them in Norway even before about 1022; the specific story concerning the seizure of the Icelandic ship's cargo by the Danish king in the tenth century must reflect a tradition of the generally poor trading conditions Icelanders encountered in Denmark. Certainly trade would be discouraged even had not similar untoward incidents occurred, for if Icelandic merchants went as usual to Norway first, paid their landing fees, and then continued to Denmark, they would have had to pay additional tolls there[79]—perhaps this partly explains why Bolli Bollason's brother did not wish to continue to Denmark after arriving in Norway.

If Icelandic traders came only infrequently to Denmark, Danish merchants all the less often must have traveled to Iceland. Danish traders as such are not mentioned being in Iceland by any source. The only indication that some Danes might have been there — at least occasionally for some purpose, whether for trade or otherwise — is that they are mentioned in the sections on prosecution of manslaughter cases and on inheritances in *Grágás*.[80] The reasons for the probable typical absence of Danish traders basically must have been similar to those that discouraged Icelanders from trading in Denmark. Danes had easier access to most products Iceland could offer; indeed, unlike Norwegians, they probably produced all the woolens they needed themselves. If Danes had wished to engage in the trade for profit, they would be discouraged by having to pay the Icelandic toll, which was applicable to them but not to Norwegians. This Norwegian competitive advantage would make trade with Iceland lose even any small attraction it might have held for Danes. Ordinarily Norway must have acted as the intermediary in providing any desirable Icelandic products to Denmark, or Danish products to Iceland.

SWEDEN

According to the sources, Icelanders apparently made the journey to Sweden more to enhance their reputations than to gain necessities or trading profits. For instance, Snorri Sturluson says that an Icelandic skald, Hjalti Skeggjason, who accompanied a Norwegian envoy of St. Óláf's, was sent in the early eleventh century on a mission to the king of Sweden to help solve boundary disputes between the two kingdoms. Another Icelandic skald, Sighvát Thórtharson, went with them. Hjalti believed that he would be viewed by the Swedish king as a neutral in the dispute, and he also hoped to gain confidential information concerning the feelings of the court from his two friends there, Gizur the Black and Óttar the Black, who were also Icelandic skalds. Ultimately he succeeded in his mission and thus fulfilled his earlier dictum, " 'Kings are to be so served that their men have great honor and are valued more than others. . . .' "[81] Some honor too came alone from being a skald in the service of a monarch. Icelanders, who were particularly renowned practitioners of skaldic poetic forms, often displayed their art for kings. That king with whom Hjalti carried on negotiations must have been particularly fond of skaldic poetry since he already had two skalds at his court before Hjalti and Sighvát arrived; and another famous Icelandic skald, Gunnlaug the Serpent-Tongued, visited him on a separate occasion.[82] The success Hjalti gained in his capacity as diplomat may have been partly due to his capability as a poet.

Although such illustrious Icelanders as Hjalti, Sighvát, and Gunnlaug may have carried on a certain amount of incidental trade when they were in Sweden,[83] there is only one recorded instance of an Icelander who is said, rather unreliably, to have gone there specifically for commercial purposes. According to a late thirteenth-century saga, about 966 Thorgils Thórtharson went to Norway on a buying trip. After a foray as a Viking in the Hebrides and Scotland, he returned to Norway to continue with his more peaceful occupation as a trader. He made a buying expedition not only to Norwegian Uppland, but he also went to Sweden to trade; after these adventures he returned to Iceland.[84]

Some Swedes are known to have gone to Iceland. The island itself, according to *Hauksbók*, the early fourteenth-century version of *Landnámabók*, was discovered by Garthar, a native of Sweden.[85] And well after the period of settlement, at the beginning of the twelfth century, a Swede was in Iceland giving sermons at the Cathedral School of Hólar.[86] Because Swedes were in Iceland, some of whom may have been merchants, stipulation is made for prosecution of cases on the island involving their killing and presumably for their inheritance rights in *Grágás*.[87] Swedes in Iceland, whether merchants or not, may have promoted trade relations between the two lands, just as Icelandic skalds who were at the court of the Swedish king may have stimulated interest in Sweden when they returned home to Iceland.

According to two generally unreliable authorities, one Swede who was said to be a merchant and another who can be inferred to be came to Iceland. The first, Thorsteinn Ragnhildarson, is supposed to have come to Eyjafjörth in northern Iceland about the beginning of the eleventh century and spent the winter with Thórárni [Thórarinn] Nefjólfsson; after the passing of winter, they both went to Norway. The second, Tófi Valgautsson, supposedly came to Hornafjörth in eastern Iceland in 1024. He was of an aristocratic Swedish family and had been trading for a long time; he therefore would probably have come to Iceland with commercial intent.[88]

That trade between Sweden and Iceland was not more

significant than this evidence indicates must have been due
partly to disagreements between Norway and Sweden such as
occurred during the reign of St. Óláf. During such periods trade
would be difficult for Norwegians as well as for Icelanders, and
St. Óláf wished a reconciliation with the king of Sweden in
hopes of reestablishing commercial intercourse between their
two countries.[89] During a period of commercial disruption
Icelanders may have been especially discouraged from trading
with Sweden because if they went to Norway on their trip as
well, as they surely would have done, they would probably have
had to pay the landaurar twice, for at such times the king of
Sweden would be sure to exercise to the full what he considered his
rights. The Swedish king claimed ultimate jurisdiction over the
realm of St. Óláf because Sweden was traditionally the place of
origin of the Ynglings, the family of eastern Norway that began,
under Hálfdan the Black, to unify eastern Norway and later the
whole country.[90] As the Swedish king said, in the words of Snorri,
" 'I am the tenth king at Uppsala, our relatives . . . having been
monarchs over . . . other kings in Scandinavia.' " When Hjalti
Skeggjason met him hoping to bring about a diplomatic reconciliation, he took pains not to offend him. Hjalti therefore said, " 'It is
the law between Iceland and Norway that Icelanders, when they
come to Norway, pay the landaurar there. And when I crossed the
sea, I took the landaurar of all my fellow shipmates, and because I
know that rightfully you have power over that kingdom which is
Norway, I traveled to your court to bring you the landaurar monies'
— then he showed the king the silver and poured into the lap of
Gizur the Black ten merkur of silver."[91] Even during peaceful
periods between Norway and Sweden, the Swedish king may have
demanded the payment of a landaurar, although perhaps not an
amount equal to that which already would usually have been paid
in Norway. As in the case of Dano-Icelandic trade, the lack of
commercial privileges in each other's country discouraged direct
trade between Icelanders and Swedes. Norway thus would usually
have to act as intermediary for any Swedish products in demand by
Icelanders.[92]

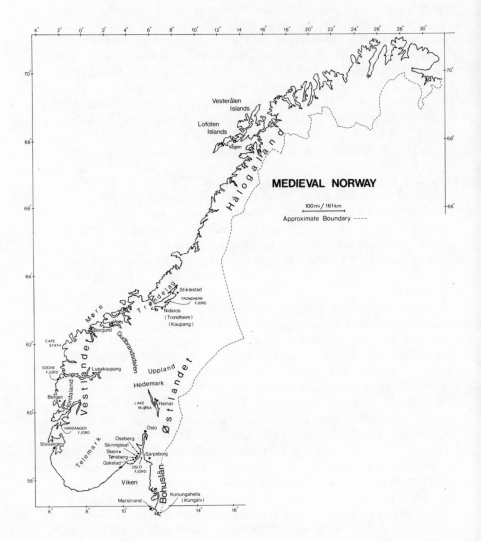

MEDIEVAL NORWAY

100 mi / 161 km

Approximate Boundary ----

Vesterålen
Islands

Lofoten
Islands

Vågen

Hålogaland

Stiklestad

TRONDHEIM
FJORD

Trøndelag

Nidaros
(Trondheim)
(Kaupang)

Møre

Veøy

Borgund

Gudbrandsdalen

CAPE
STATH

Vestlandet

SOGNE
FJORD

Lusakaupang

Uppland

Østlandet

Hedemark

Hordaland

LAKE
MJØSA

Hamar

Bergen

HARDANGER
FJORD

Oslo

Oseberg

Skiringssal

Telemark

Stavanger

Skein

Tønsberg

Sarpsborg

Gokstad

OSLO
FJORD

Viken

Bohuslän

Marstrand

Konungahella
(Kungälv)

CHAPTER FIVE

Icelandic Trade with Other North Atlantic Settlements

From the beginning of the ninth century until the end of the tenth, Scandinavians settled the Shetlands, Orkneys, Hebrides, and Faeroes, then Iceland, and finally Greenland. Sharing a common culture and similar environments, reenforced in some cases by personal and family bonds, these pioneers at first must have had a strong sense of community. One of the early benefits of their communal sense was that it encouraged trade. Yet paradoxically the very similarity of their living styles and natural surroundings meant that long-lasting trade among them could hardly be maintained because they produced and required so many of the same goods, even though Icelanders, the most numerous group of these settlers, overcame some of the major commercial obstacles for short periods. Eventually either the groups of more isolated islanders surrendered to their natural loneliness, keeping only a weakened sense of community with each other by mutual trade with Norway, or those living on islands close to Britain and Ireland broke away from most of their earlier Norse connections and adopted an identity and trade with their nearer neighbors.

GREENLAND

A sense of community with Iceland was perhaps most marked

in the case of Greenland. Just as Iceland's population had been formed largely by those originally from Norway, Greenland's original Norse colonizers can be looked upon as a group of Icelandic separatists. These more westerly pioneers were far less numerous, for they never exceeded four or five thousand.[1] On both islands the population was confined to the coasts. Greenland's huge interior ice field limited areas of settlement not only directly but indirectly because of the adverse effect it had on climate. Not even the warming benefits of the Gulf Stream, or more properly a continuation of it, the North Atlantic Current, compensated Greenland for this interior ice, for the island's coasts were struck only by the cold Greenland Current, originating in the Arctic. When the first Norse colonists, led by Eirík the Red, came from Iceland about 986, they found that they had to restrict their settlement to two favored, protected, and thus relatively warm places on the western side of the island — Eystribygth ("Eastern Settlement") toward the southern tip in the area of modern Julienhåb, and Vestribygth ("Western Settlement"), a colony about half as large to the northwest of the other in the district of modern Godthåb.

It is axiomatic that any settlers in a new land are forced to accommodate their living style to their new environment; at the same time they wish to preserve their traditional way of life as much as possible. The Norse Greenlanders inherited the raising of livestock from traditional Scandinavian practice, and, until the last of them disappeared at the end of the fifteenth century, it remained the basis of their domestic economy.[2] Due to the rigorous climate, cultivation of the soil was far less rewarding. As the learned author of *Konungs skuggsjá* says,

> as to whether any kind of seed or grain can grow there, I believe that country has little success from that. And yet there are men who are regarded as the wealthiest and most prominent who have tried to sow grain experimentally; but still the great majority in that country do not know what bread is because they have never seen it.[3]

Of course hunting and fishing were carried on by all Scandinavians, but the Norse Greenlanders may have emphasized them more, though not so much as later Eskimo inhabitants of their settlements. Indeed, the author of *Konungs skuggsjá* suggests that Greenlanders habitually ate more game than Norwegians, for he felt a need to say that they "also eat the meat of all kinds of game, such as reindeer, whales, seals, and bears."[4]

Hunting was vitally important to Greenlanders not just for food, but also because the products so derived formed their most consequential exports. The author of *Konungs skuggsjá* shows this when he says "men bring back from there these goods: buckskin or cattle hides, sealskins, and that rope . . . which is called 'svar-threipi' which is cut from the [hide of that] fish called the walrus, and also the teeth of the walrus."[5] Though he seems to include them only as an afterthought, walrus tusks were probably the most important export of all.[6] Though he does not mention them here, falcons, polar bears, and bearskins, also seem to have been exported in limited quantities.[7] To judge from the foods that the Greenlanders themselves ate, some reindeer skins, blubber, whalebone, and whale and seal oil may have been exported, too. What was imported in return for these goods is neatly summarized in *Konungs skuggsjá:* "everything that is needed to improve the land must be purchased from other countries, both iron and all the timber they need to build houses."[8]

With only a few luxuries to sell, Greenland could not enjoy a prosperous foreign trade in the best of circumstances, much as the island depended upon necessities from abroad. This perilous situation was made all the worse because Iceland was something of a competitor in the sale of luxury wares: seals and polar bears were found off Icelandic coasts and falcons on land, though in fewer numbers. Walrus tusks (and other walrus products) were apparently the only important export Greenland had that Iceland lacked. Since more populous Iceland also demanded the same imports, it definitely had a competitive advantage, especially because it was not so far from Europe.

Though conditions certainly were not propitious for trade between the two islands, during the first half of the eleventh century a few Icelandic merchants came to Greenland. They may have been attracted by a desire to participate in North American explorations, news of which may have reached Iceland before they left. But such a motive is difficult to prove. Disregarding the chance of pure coincidence, the merchants may well have come because of hopes for profit. Without much competition from Greenlandic merchants and probably none from Norwegians at this time, Icelanders might have realized that they had a good chance of trading on particularly advantageous terms. To understand how such a circumstance occurred, a digression is necessary to examine the ability of Greenlanders to act as merchants themselves and the beginning and extent of Norwegian trade with Greenland.

During the Greenland colony's existence, the voyages that the islanders made abroad seem to be remarkably few. When the most famous of all — the ones to North America — are excluded,[9] those reported number only a handful, and some are probably spurious. *Grœnlendinga saga* tells of an Icelandic merchant named Bjarni Herjólfsson who owned his own ship and came to settle in Greenland. About fifteen years later he sailed to Norway to visit Jarl Eirík Hákonarson (ruler of Norway, 1000–1015) who "received him well."[10] No other motive for the voyage is given by the saga, but it is hard to believe that a man as responsible as Bjarni is said to be would have made his trip for only a good welcome. Either this trip was a literary invention on the part of the composer of the saga to suit his own purposes,[11] or, if the voyage actually took place, further motivation must have existed. In the latter case, it seems unlikely that Bjarni would have so forgotten his earlier instincts as not to make his trip a commercial venture.

Eiríks saga rautha, treating much the same subject matter as *Grœnlendinga saga*, does not mention Bjarni Herjólfsson's voyage to Norway, nor even his name. It substitutes a similar voyage on the part of Leif, son of Eirík the Red. According to this work, Leif went on this trip before he made his famous Vínland voyage, at a time somewhat before Bjarni would have been in Norway. The saga does not specifically say so, but it is assumed that Leif went on his own ship. He seems to have engaged in some mercantile activity: on the way to Norway, his ship was driven off course to the Hebrides, where he gave gifts consisting of a gold ring, a Greenland cloak of vathmál, and a belt of walrus ivory.[12] Except for the ring, these gifts of specifically Greenlandic origin suggest that Leif had loaded his ship with similar goods to trade in Norway. On his way back to Greenland, he is said to have been driven off course, during which time he discovered Vínland. Even more than in the case of Bjarni's trip, however, there is room for doubt that Leif's voyage to and from Norway ever took place, although there is little doubt that he went to North America on another occasion under different circumstances.[13]

More certain reference to Greenlandic voyages abroad, also involving trade, is offered by *Fóstbrœthra saga*. It mentions two separate Greenlandic merchants who traded during the first half of the eleventh century, presumably in the 1020s. One was Thorgrím Einarsson, who on his way back from Norway stopped over in Iceland, where it was noted that he had a large ship with forty men aboard and a valuable cargo. The other was Skúf, who owned a ship in partnership with another Greenlander: he made at least two trips to Norway.[14]

Hereafter, apart from certain Norwegian bishops of Greenland, there are three more references to men of Greenland going to foreign lands, but in contrast to earlier instances they do not seem to have gone on their own ships nor in most cases even for trade. Adam of Bremen, the late eleventh-century historian of the archbishopric of Hamburg-Bremen, says that some Greenlanders, among other Scandinavians, visited Archbishop Adalbert about 1050, asking him to send them clergymen.[15] Though this brief notice carries no implication of trade, a trip made soon after 1123 by the Greenlander Einar Sokkason does suggest that some trade might have been involved. On his voyage to Norway to urge creation of a Greenlandic bishopric,[16] he took along a large quantity of walrus tusks and walrus rope, as well as a polar bear, to use as well-timed gifts for King Sigurth the Jerusalem-Farer:[17] Einar conceivably might have sold some of the walrus ivory and rope or taken other goods of Greenland to trade while he was abroad, but this was not his main purpose. No mention is made in the account that Einar traveled on his own ship—indeed, if he had, the saga undoubtedly would have mentioned the point, for its author was very conscious of the scarcity of ocean-going ships in Greenland.[18]

After a gap in the evidence for most of the rest of the twelfth century, about 1191 *Historia profectione Danorum* mentions Greenlanders being in Bergen.[19] Because they are referred to in a commercial context, they probably were merchants, but, like other known Greenlandic travelers after the 1020s, there is no reason to believe that they had come on their own ships.

After this reference, the records cease to mention or even to imply that Greenlanders traded abroad. Indeed, the well-informed mid-thirteenth-century author of *Konungs skuggsjá* clearly suggests that in his time they were only the passive recipients of goods brought by Norwegian merchants.[20] As previously implied, one of the reasons that the active trade of Greenlanders would have disappeared altogether by then and would have been extremely sparse even before was a scarcity and then a virtually complete lack of ocean-going ships.

Initially, some ships belonging to the first Norse settlers of Greenland provided them with the vessels they needed for overseas trade. Part of the original fleet of Eirík the Red and his followers must have consisted of true cargo ships (knerrir).[21] Of these, some conceivably might have been used during the later stages of the settlement of Iceland itself, ending about fifty-six years before: thus, they would have already been quite old by the time of the Greenland settlement about 986. The useful life of the fourteen ships that made Greenland—including virtually all of the knerrir unless some were particularly delapidated—might have been prolonged for a time afterward by being kept in good repair with driftwood. Other Greenlandic ocean-going ships were those brought by later immigrants. Although there must have been more of these immigrants than the sources directly mention,[22] the very lack of evidence suggests that they were not numerous.

Those ships brought by settlers, whether they came with Eirík the Red or later, were virtually the only ocean-going vessels Greenlanders would have possessed. Like Icelanders, Greenlanders had no sizable timber on their island to build more of them. Large pieces of driftwood could be used for building relatively small boats, but, practical as these vessels were in protected waters for fishing and hunting seal, walrus, or whale, they probably could not have been used in crossing wide seas for trade.[23] Timber was imported from Norway, but it was used for building houses, not ships. Indeed, it is hard to believe that any imported timber could be of a size sufficient for constructing a large ship.[24] Ships acquired by Greenlanders when abroad, by building them there, purchasing them there, or being given them there are unknown, though sales in Greenland reportedly took place.[25] Like Norwegian timber, what was brought back from North America was too small for ocean-going ships. The possibility that large ships were built there on the spot cannot be ignored, but there is no proof of it.[26]

A few of the ocean-going ships brought by immigrants apparently lasted until the 1020s when the last known voyages overseas by Greenlanders definitely on their own vessels took place.[27] Afterward, as the old ships were no longer worth repairing and the number of new settlers coming on their own ships declined, Greenlanders who wished to trade abroad had to depend upon whatever foreign ships came to their shores.

But after the 1020s, fewer Greenlanders than before were in a financial position to trade abroad because of a shrinkage in the size of most individual land holdings. Though their land holdings probably still produced a salable surplus for the immediate descendants of Eirík the Red and other large landowners of his time,[28] and though these descendants probably could afford to obtain directly or indirectly the desirable exports from Northrsetur, a well-frequented haven for walrus north of the Western Settlement, sooner or later their own descendants would not be able to enjoy such easy circumstances. With each new generation, either earlier settlements had to be expanded or old lands had to be divided. Because the Western Settlement had been founded either contemporaneously with the Eastern Settlement or shortly afterward,[29] and because there was no other area suitable for habitation, the growing population first must have caused both settlements to be enlarged as much as possible and then to be more densely settled. When a maximum population of four or five thousand was reached, not all young men could be provided with a large estate. Thus, the original settlers and their children and perhaps their grandchildren might have been in a position to carry on some foreign trade, but members of later generations would have lacked sufficient surpluses of livestock products from their home lands to warrant trading abroad, and fewer still would have been able to finance teams for hunting expeditions to acquire large quantities of more desirable exports. The turning point apparently came sometime during the 1020s when we last hear of a Greenlander who was certainly a merchant going overseas.

Individual ownership of large amounts of land must have been curtailed even further after the introduction of a permanent diocese to Greenland in 1125. After his appointment, Bishop Arnald set the tone of things to come when he said, " 'If it should happen that I am consecrated bishop, then I wish that Einar [Sokkason, heir to the main chiefdom at Brattahlíth] swear an oath to me to strengthen and support the bishopric and those properties that are given to God, and to punish those who try to take them away. And he shall be the protector of the episcopacy in every respect.' "[30] Einar and his successors evidently strengthened and supported the church well, for by the first half of the fourteenth century the Greenlandic clergy owned nearly all the land surrounding the fjords where they had establishments.[31] Even though the prosperity of secular Greenlanders greatly diminished, due partly to the absorption of good land by the Greenlandic church, the bishops of Greenland were relatively rich. Considering the size of their holdings and incomes, supplemented by tithes and other clerical levies, they might have traveled abroad themselves to exchange some of their goods. But no bishop of Greenland is actually known to have traveled on his own ship nor even to have acted as a merchant abroad, though several did leave Greenland after they initially arrived from Norway. These trips were undoubedly undertaken for affairs of the church and some of that business must have involved trade, but these men, who remained essentially Norwegians, were not in any real sense Greenlandic merchants.[32]

When, by about 1030, Greenlanders no longer had access to ocean-going ships and the means to undertake a voyage abroad, they had little choice but to rely upon foreign merchants to bring necessary goods to them. The only conceivable ones were Icelanders and Norwegians. In the case of Norwegians, they apparently did not begin sailing to Greenland just when they were so badly needed. The earliest instance known of a Norwegian merchant voluntarily sailing to Greenland does not occur before about 1061 when a certain Thórir from Møre is said to have gone there,[33] and surely others did not begin sailing there regularly much before that time.

Why did Norwegian merchants not come earlier? The lack of experience in sailing to Greenland could well have been the most important deterrent. Granted that some Norwegians might go to the new settlement for the compelling reason of establishing a home; others might be driven to Greenland by unfriendly winds or currents. But until such trips had provided a dependable body of sealore, Norwegians would be reluctant to sail to the remote island only to exchange their goods for nonvital Greenlandic ones at considerable risk to their cargoes and perhaps even their lives. Routes to other lands were better known and safer as well.

Sailing to Greenland from Norway was particularly difficult because the North Atlantic Current might push a ship off course, and the prevailing westerly winds would tend to drive it in the opposite direction.[34] Tacking against the wind could be employed, but until knowledge of at least the approximate comparative latitude of the southern tip of Greenland was attained by ascertaining the height of the sun above the horizon at noon at certain intervals throughout the sailing season, this practice could be extremely hazardous. If a navigator caused his ship to tack too far north, his ship might reach the desolate and isolated eastern coast of Greenland; he would be fortunate to reach Iceland instead. If one tacked too far south, his ship might reach North America. By contrast, with the same contrary current and winds existing in the case of the passage to Iceland, a navigator would know well the comparative latitude of his destination since the crossings were much more frequent. Naturally during unusually heavy weather, a ship might be driven well off course, in which case knowledge of comparative latitude, or the lack of it, would make little difference. An element of adventure always existed. The king of Norway, St. Óláf, apparently was well aware of the dangers of sailing unknown North Atlantic waters because in the agreement that he made with the Icelanders about 1022 provision is made for being driven to Norway while on a voyage of exploration as well as on one that might be made to Greenland.[35] Snorri Sturluson, though writing in the thirteenth century, preserves what appears to be a valid memory of St. Óláf's time when he has a sailor experienced in sailing familiar seas say, " 'Now it may happen, king, as is not unlikely and can easily occur, that we cannot make Greenland but are driven to Iceland or to other lands. . . . ' "[36] Sailing to Greenland was particularly fraught with danger during the early eleventh century. Certainly accidents happened after that time,[37] but that consistent reference is made to misadventure during the earlier period suggests that navigators inexperienced with Greenlandic waters were more at fault than nature.

By about 1061 when enough experience apparently had been gained for at least one Norwegian trader to purposely travel to Greenland, more followed in his path, each adding to the store of navigational knowledge and making the route safer for later voyagers. By the first part of the twelfth century, sailing to Greenland for trade was apparently not unusual because *Grœnlendinga tháttr* records several Norwegian merchants there at that time.[38] Besides the bishops of Greenland who probably traveled abroad on Norwegian ships from about 1150 onward, several references in the Icelandic annals to vessels involved in the Greenland trade that encountered accidents or were noteworthy for other reasons also indicate Norwegian merchants' interest in Greenland, since there were undoubtedly other ships going there that did not encounter any misfortune or that were not otherwise worthy of record.[39]

By about 1275 when Sturla Thórtharson wrote in his version of *Landnámabók* that one would reach the southern tip of Greenland by sailing due west from Bergen, the route to Greenland by latitude sailing already must have been established for some time. That it could be so accurately plotted speaks well of the cumulative experience of previous seafarers, and that it could be referred to as a not uncommon occurrence indicates that Norwegian traffic to the island was far from negligible by then. The author of *Konungs skuggsjá*, writing his work only somewhat earlier, has the son in his book ask his father why men sail to Greenland since the seas are so dangerous. The father answers that it

> is to be sought in the three-fold nature of man. One motive is fame and rivalry because it is man's nature to go where great dangers are encountered and thus to win fame. A second motive is curiosity, for it is also in man's nature to see and learn about the things that he has heard of and thus to learn whether what was told to him is true or not. The third motive is to accumulate wealth, for men seek riches wherever they have heard that money is to be made, even though, on the other hand, there may be great dangers attached to it.[40]

The attractions of profit as well as curiosity could compensate for the usual hazards of the seas, especially when they were no longer exaggerated by a lack of knowledge.

Still, the extent of Norwegian trade with Greenland must not be overestimated, as the author of *Konungs skuggsjá* reminds us when he writes that "this land lies so distant from other countries that men seldom travel to it."[41] Distance alone was not the only hindrance. Greenland's main economic advantage over Iceland, its unusual or particularly abundant luxury wares, could not command so great a market that merchants would make numerous trips to obtain them. The only remaining economic advantage for Norwegians to trade in Greenland was that possibly they could gain a better return for their wares than they could in Iceland because Greenland was less frequently visited. If many considered this reason enough to travel there, even that advantage would be diminished as imports became more easily available.[42]

Before regular Norwegian commerce began, enterprising Icelandic merchants had already visited Greenland. They must have been especially welcomed by the isolated Greenlanders because as intermediaries they provided badly needed Norwegian imports which the Greenlanders could acquire for themselves only infrequently if at all. Of course, the Icelanders must have been attracted by the luxuries that were found in Greenland, and they must have received more of them—or at least more of the ordinary Greenlandic goods—in return for what they sold to the islanders than they would have received for much the same things in Iceland, otherwise there would have been little incentive for them to make the trip. Because Norwegian merchants did not yet come to their island and because their own trade overseas was infrequent, Greenlanders had little choice but either to do without the goods Icelanders brought, or to pay, in effect, inflated prices.

Icelandic merchants would come to Greenland only when they were reasonably knowledgeable about the sea passage, and, for all their problems when making their first sailings to Greenland,[43] Icelanders were the first to gain experience in these waters. Not only did the first settlers of the Norse colony come to Greenland from Iceland, most of those who came afterward probably came from there as well. It was apparently not until relatively late, about 1125, that some Norwegians attempted to make a new home on the island. With relatives on Greenland, some Icelanders who stayed behind had more reason than Norwegians to keep in touch with the Greenland colony, particularly during the early years of the settlement. *Grágás*, the Icelandic codification of traditional law dating from 1117–1118, provided for legal problems Icelanders might encounter as a result of contact with Greenland, for one eventuality considered was the inheritance of property that had been taken there:[44] for such provision to be made, Icelanders might have often made trips to that island and back during these early years. Gradually knowledge of sailing to Greenland would be accumulated from the experience at sea of each of these men, whether settlers or visitors.

In the first gropings for their route Icelanders benefited from generally favorable winds and currents. Most left from western Iceland, usually the Snæfellsnes Peninsula, and sailed directly across the Denmark Strait to the eastern coast of Greenland, then south along that coast and around the southern tip to the settlements on the west coast. This is the way that Eirík the Red went on his initial exploration of Greenland, and this was the passage still indicated by Sturla Thórtharson almost three centuries later.[45] On his first exploratory visit to the island, before he led the first settlers there, Eirík must have found that once he crossed over the intervening waters to the larger island he could avail himself of the presently named Greenland Current, which flows down the east coast of Greenland and around its southern tip to the western side; prevailing northerly winds down the eastern Greenland coast and prevailing southerly ones up the western coast would have helped to drive him in the right direction. The main obstacle that Eirík and Icelanders in general always would have was rounding the southern tip of the island, for at that point they would pick up the same westerly winds that caused Norwegians trouble as soon as they left their homeland on their way to Greenland.[46]

Although Icelanders had knowledge of a route to Greenland before Norwegians, and although the general trading climate from about the late tenth century until shortly after the mid-eleventh would never be better for them, only a few are actually known to have made the trip. If it were not for the narrative of *Eiríks saga rautha*, even that number would be considerably reduced.

Though generally *Grœnlendinga saga* should be taken as more historically reliable than *Eiríks saga* with its later date of composition and other defects, the latter has more of the ring of truth concerning Icelandic merchants.[47] Both sagas say that Thorfinn Karlsefni, a wealthy Icelander, visited Greenland and stayed with Eirík the Red at his estate in the Eastern Settlement. Apart from these scant details, the two narratives do not agree on much else concerning the circumstances of Thorfinn's visit or the extent of the Icelandic presence in Greenland at the time of the early voyages to North America. *Grœnlendinga saga* states that Thorfinn came from Norway, presumably about 1006. It says nothing about the crew that he had on his ship at that time, although when he decided to sail to Vínland, he took on board sixty men and five women:[48] presumably many or all were from Greenland, but some could have been from Iceland or Norway. Apart from Thorfinn, the only Icelanders mentioned by this work who came to Greenland—and they also are said to have come from Norway— were two brothers, Helgi and Finnbogi; they later traveled on the ship they commanded to Vínland, not with Thorfinn, but at the same time that Freythís, Eirík's illegitimate daughter, made her trip there.[49] *Eiríks saga* is more expansive concerning both Thorfinn and the participation of Icelanders in the Vínland voyages. Thorfinn, who was a merchant of "great distinction," had come to Greenland from Iceland; and his ship partner was another Icelandic merchant, Snorri Thorbrandsson. They had a crew of forty, all of whom were apparently Icelanders. Another ship, owned by two more Icelandic traders, Bjarni Grímolfsson and Thorhall Gamlason, also went to Greenland at the same time; again its crew of forty seems to have been exclusively Icelandic. When all the skippers reached Brattahlíth, Eirík the Red's estate, they gave him whatever he wanted from their cargoes. During winter Eirík confessed to Thorfinn that there would be a poor Christmas. " 'That should not be' said Karlsefni. 'We have both malt and grain aboard our ships and you may have as much as you wish and prepare as generous a feast as you would like.' " The feast was so lavish that "people thought they had hardly ever seen one so magnificent in that poor land."[50] Having talked about Vínland a great deal that winter, the Icelandic traders as well as the rest of the eighty who formed the crews of their two ships decided to make an expedition there the next summer.[51] And some Greenlanders joined them on probably two more ships. One was captained by Thorvarth, Eirík's son-in-law—this ship previously had been brought to Greenland from Iceland by Thorbjörn Vífilsson; the other, of unknown origin, was apparently skippered by a certain Thorhall the Hunter.[52] These men probably took other Greenlanders on for their crews. Since a total of 160 men went on this expedition, and since the two Icelandic ships had crews of forty each, probably it is to be understood that the Greenlandic crews were each the same number.

Comparing the information in the two saga accounts, *Eiríks saga* seems to be the more reliable for several reasons. *Grœnlendinga saga* has the Icelanders coming to Greenland from Norway. As has been seen, such voyages would have been highly exceptional for this period. And because this was so, it is doubtful that the saga writer would have missed the opportunity to emphasize the point; as it is, these voyages are mentioned only as matters of due course. Probably the direct route from Norway given by this saga reflects later traditions. As *Eiríks saga* has it, the Icelanders came to Greenland from Iceland itself, certainly a voyage more believable for the

time. As *Grœnlendinga saga* says, Thorfinn's single ship, whose
even comparative size is not given, was loaded with sixty-five people, together with ample livestock and presumably everything else
the hopeful colonists might have needed for establishing their new
home in Vínland. That this is true is inconceivable, for an ordinary
knörr, with a normal cargo, might hold between fifteen and twenty
men, or perhaps somewhat more if the cargo was especially small.
But with the size of the cargo described for Thorfinn's ship, even
fewer than usual should have been able to come aboard. *Eiríks saga*,
while similarly exaggerating the size of the crew and passengers on
each ship making the voyage, at least pares the number down to
apparently forty each. Considering that a new settlement was contemplated, it also seems more reasonable, as *Eiríks saga* says, that a
convoy of several ships would have been used to sail to the new land.
Eiríks saga is also more believable here than *Grœnlendinga saga*
because the historicity of certain Icelanders mentioned in its account is partially confirmed by *Eyrbyggja saga* and *Grettis saga*. The
former mentions Snorri Thorbrandsson going to Greenland and
Vínland,[53] and the latter gives Thorhall Gamlason the nickname of
"the Vínlander."[54] Finally, *Eiríks saga* is much more attentive to
Thorfinn Karlsefni than is *Grœnlendinga saga*. The author of *Eiríks
saga* consequently might be trusted to have done a better job collecting available information concerning him. True, the author added
some elements that were fictional as well, as when he has the
stubborn pagan Eirík the Red show a concern that his guests would
not be able to enjoy a merry Christmas without certain foods. But
this inconsistency may only have been an attempt to illustrate the
generosity of Thorfinn and the others or to show the nature of their
actual cargoes.

Apart from the evidence in *Eiríks saga* and *Grœnlendinga saga*,
two other Icelanders are known to have been in Greenland during
the earlier half of the eleventh century. There is no way of telling
how concerned they were with trading. One was Thormóth the
Coal-Browed Skald. As his nickname shows, he was a poet among
other less honorable occupations, but none of his activities included
being a merchant.[55] The other Icelander is mentioned by Ári Thorgilsson. Writing his *Íslendingabók* about 1130, he included a short

account of the settlement of Greenland. He says that Eirík the Red began colonizing the island fourteen or fifteen winters before Christianity came to Iceland, according to what a man who had accompanied Eirík told his uncle, Thorkell Gellisson, while that uncle of Ari's was in Greenland.[56] Thorkell must have been in Greenland sometime about the middle of the eleventh century to be able to get this information from the aged Greenlandic settler and to relate it many years later to his young nephew. The only other Icelanders who are definitely known to have been in Greenland after the time of the original settlement were Hermund Kothránsson and his brother Thorgils; they had a "large crew" on their ship, a crew that probably was mostly Icelandic. They went there to trade and were in the Western Settlement about 1130—at the same time that Norwegian merchants were there.[57]

When Thorfinn Karlsefni and the other Icelanders came to Greenland during the early eleventh century, they were there quite obviously to make substantial profits by exchanging vitally needed foods—which must have composed a great deal of their cargoes—during a time when such foods must have been in short supply in the colony. As we have seen, Eirík the Red, the first settler and undoubtedly the wealthiest inhabitant on the island, did not have adequate grain or malt. Having aboard those very products, Thorfinn and the other merchants must have known about this short supply when they came to Greenland. Although Eiríks saga says that they gave some of their cargoes to their host, they must have made substantial profits selling the remainder to other less illustrious Greenlanders.[58]

Even during the first half of the eleventh century when good profits were to be made by Icelandic traders in Greenland, there could not have been many more than those we know about who would have taken advantage of the opportunity. Because in Iceland such a relatively scarce but necessary import as grain was high in price, there must have been few Icelanders like Thorfinn Karlsefni and the others who would have had the chance to buy substantially more than they needed themselves, who would have had available capital to do so, and who would have had the desire to go to Greenland to sell it, when, despite the profit to be made there, a good profit still could have been obtained by selling the grain in Iceland itself.[59] But if an Icelander were selling some grain in Greenland, he would expect to be rewarded for his efforts by obtaining in return more woolen goods, for example, than he would have received had the exchange taken place in Iceland. However, because the Icelandic merchant was also a farmer who raised his own sheep products at home, he probably already had all the woolens he needed for foreign trade if he was rich enough to go to Greenland in the first place. It thus would be somewhat pointless for him to go to Greenland only to acquire more, regardless of a more favorable exchange there. The same would be true for other livestock products. Instead, the main Greenlandic products of interest to Icelanders, like Norwegian merchants after them, would be luxury wares. Because by their very nature these were not necessary, and because they had only a limited resale market, Icelanders would not go to Greenland often to obtain them.

After Norwegian merchants began coming fairly regularly to Greenland during the 1060s, the earlier deterrents would have been magnified. As far as such an essential import as grain was concerned, Icelandic traders, dependent themselves upon a Norwegian supply, were hardly in a position to compete with Norwegians for the Greenlandic market. But even when Icelanders managed to obtain such Greenlandic luxury exports as walrus tusks, if they took them to Norway to resell rather than the much more limited market of their homeland, again they would have to face stiff competiton: Norwegians, having had a surplus of grain to sell to Greenlanders more often than Icelanders, also returned from there more frequently with Greenlandic exports to resell. Icelanders thus might have great difficulty in finding customers for their expensive goods. Because of these adverse circumstances, it is probably not coincidental that there is only one recorded instance, once Norwegians began sailing there, of any Icelandic merchants being in Greenland, those who came about 1130.[60]

The remote Greenland colony, unable to provide itself sufficiently with foreign goods, was given only slight commercial assistance by Iceland. Even that limited trade evaporated in the face of Norwegian competition; until their own foreign trade grew weak in the fourteenth century, Norwegians were far better able to provide Greenland with commercial links to the outside world.

THE SHETLANDS, FAEROES, ORKNEYS, AND HEBRIDES

A section of the agreement made about 1022 between the Icelanders and St. Óláf says "if Icelanders pay the landaurar in the islands or in the Shetlands, then they do not have to pay it again in Norway, unless they travel away [i.e., do not come to Norway directly] in the meantime."[61] This statement seems to show clearly that Icelandic merchants would have conducted at least some trade with the Shetlands and certain other islands on their way to Norway during some of the 240 years the agreement was in force.

Before discussing this obvious implication of the clause and others less so, the "islands" (nom. pl.: "eyjar"; here, dat. pl.: "eyjum") mentioned here need to be determined. They must have been geographically associated with the Shetlands (Hjaltland), but did they include all or only some of the other island groups nearby, the Faeroes (Færeyjar), Orkneys (Orkneyjar), and Hebrides (Suthreyjar)? From a philological standpoint, frequently when "the islands" are mentioned in such a context as a kind of abbreviation, the Orkneys alone are intended.[62] If then only the Shetlands and Orkneys were affected by the stipulation, the saga evidence available for discussing their somewhat dissimilar economies and the nature of an Icelandic trade with them is both limited and comparatively extensive: very little concerns the Shetlands as such, but there is much more about the Orkneys. The Shetlands, however, were economically similar to the Faeroes, about which more is known from the literary standpoint, and so with some justice the economies of those two island groups may be discussed together. For the same reason, material concerning the Orkneys can help to illuminate the obscure economy of the Hebrides.

If, from a wider viewpoint than philology, certain aspects of St. Óláf's North Atlantic political policy are briefly considered, it is apparent that the Hebrides and ultimately the Faeroes also may have been included in the agreement's clause. During his reign between 1015 and 1030, St. Óláf made strenuous efforts to gain control over all North Atlantic islands that had been settled earlier by Norwegian emigrants. Perhaps because he had a strong case with the Shetlands, Orkneys, and Hebrides, he approached these islands first. At the end of the ninth century King Harald the Fairhaired had conquered them, and in St. Óláf's eyes they had rightfully been part of the royal Norwegian possessions ever since.[63] But despite occasional instances when the claim of Norwegian suzerainty had been reiterated after Harald's reign,[64] the islands had fallen away from Norwegian control by St. Óláf's time. He thus saw it as his duty to reassert Norwegian power in these places once again. In 1021, making sure that he cited the relevant precedents, he forced the two Orkney jarls, the brothers Thorfinn and Brúsi, to acknowledge him as their overlord, though he still allowed them to govern in his name.[65] There is no question that the Shetlands were part of the territory ruled by the Orkney jarls at the time of this reannexation and that those islands then became part of the royal possessions along with the Orkneys themselves.[66] The relationship of the Hebrides to the Orkney jarls, on the other hand, is more problematical. After Harald the Fairhaired had conquered the Hebrides, he may have given jurisdiction there to another jarl instead of Rögnvald, to whom he entrusted the Orkneys and Shetlands. Snorri Sturluson, in his *Haralds saga hárfagra*, states quite specifically that the king gave Rögnvald the Orkneys and Shetlands, but he does not include the Hebrides.[67] Rögnvald, however, transferred his title of jarl to his brother Sigurth, and the latter, with Thorsteinn the Red, took possession of the Hebrides as well as Caithness in northern Scotland.[68] Did this acquisition of the Hebrides establish an actual control over them which Rögnvald or Sigurth had nominally held before, or was it at the expense of a separate ruler's authority? No sure answer can be given. Later, though, Sigurth's son, Thorfinn, who with his brother had agreed to the desires of St. Óláf, is credited with ruling not only the Orkneys, Shetlands, and Caithness, but also the Hebrides.[69] There is no way of knowing whether he held actual control over the Hebrides only after the reannexation by St. Óláf was made in 1021, or whether he had held them before. From a legal standpoint, if not necessarily from a practical one, the Hebrides probably were regarded as lands of the Orkney jarls since at least the time they were claimed by Sigurth back in the days of Harald the Fairhaired. Therefore, when the agreement between the Icelanders and St. Óláf was made about one year after the surrender of the Orkney jarls to the king, the "islands" it mentions in addition to the Shetlands would have included not just the Orkneys, but probably also the Hebrides.

In 1027 St. Óláf summoned to Norway various prominent Faeroese, including the lawspeaker of the islands, to demand their oaths supporting his self-given right to have taxes collected from the islands and to have his laws accepted there—these claims would amount to annexation. The men had little choice but to accept, and thus from that point onward the Faeroes were also numbered among the royal possessions.[70] Just as the agreement with the Icelanders about five years before this time had made provision for the islands annexed in 1021, so this 1027 acquisition of the Faeroes, having much the same relationship to the kingdom, henceforth in all probability would have been included in the landaurar exemption clause of the agreement, being easily incorporated within the ambiguous term, "the islands."

What was the economic nature of the Faeroes and Shetlands, and, if the Faeroes were included in the stipulation eventually, how did this nature affect the desire of Icelanders to take advantage of their privilege to trade in both these places without having to pay an additional toll in Norway?

The circumstances that lay behind some of the earliest Scandinavian voyages to Iceland during the 860s illustrates that the islands could later serve as important way stations across the North Atlantic. The first Scandinavian visitors to Iceland had intended sailing to the Shetlands or Faeroes when their ships were driven off course by unfavorable winds.[71] These first voyages were accidental, but when the first intentional trip was made to Iceland, the ship's captain, Flóki Vilgertharson, on his way there prudently took his vessel from southwestern Norway first to the Shetlands,[72] and then, according to one account, to the Faeroes.[73] And much later, even when voyages usually were made to Iceland directly from Norway, evidently the Faeroes sometimes were used as a stopping place on the way.[74] Well placed for east-west voyages, the

Faeroes and especially the Shetlands were also located at a crossroads between Iceland and Norway and islands farther south— the Orkneys, Hebrides, Ireland, and Britain.[75] This geographical position in relationship to more important places was probably the greatest commercial advantage the Faeroes and Shetlands were to have.

Both island groups had been settled by Scandinavians about 800,[76] and by the time a century passed, there were some from these islands who, for one reason or another, went to settle in Iceland, following the way pointed by the first ships.[77] Although they would have badly needed whatever they brought with them as cargo, undoubtedly there were occasions when some of those goods were exchanged with settlers who had come earlier. During these early years, Icelanders would need replenishments of livestock that had not survived the first hard winters, not to speak of the inanimate paraphernalia necessary for living. Some Icelanders, in turn, perhaps partly encouraged by family ties, but even more so by the desire to acquire necessities, also may have traveled to the Faeroes or Shetlands during the settlement period. These smaller islands, having been occupied longer than Iceland, might have been able to spare a few sheep, cattle, horses, and other livestock.

But whatever attractions the Faeroes and Shetlands may once have had, they diminished as Iceland achieved some maturity. Family ties grew weaker with every new generation, and, even more importantly, Iceland quickly outgrew its need for any provisions the Faeroes or Shetlands might have formerly provided. A long-lasting commerce between Iceland and these other North Atlantic islands was out of the question basically because of the similarity of their environments and the poverty of the Faeroese and Shetlanders.

Even more so than in Iceland, sheep were the mainstay of the Faeroese and Shetlander economies. Products that these thick-coated and tasty animals provided were supplemented for use at home by those of other livestock and by whatever else could be garnered from the environment, such as whales, seals, and fish from the sea, as well as birds from the skies.[78] Much else the islanders needed, from tools to timber, had to be brought from

overseas to their barren homes. Again their sheep were of fundamental importance because, until the end of the thirteenth century when their fish began to be desirable abroad, the islanders
relied, to the virtual exclusion of everything else, upon woolens to
exchange for those imports. The Faeroes were aptly named
(Færeyjar: "Sheep-Isles"), but both island groups were inhabited
mainly by shepherds and sheep, at least so far as outsiders were
concerned.

Occasionally Faeroese and Shetlanders are known to have
gone abroad to obtain for themselves what they needed or could
resell at home. For instance Thránd í Gata, one of the most powerful chieftains in the Faeroes at the time of St. Óláf's annexation, is
said to have sent two lazy nephews on his ship to Norway with a
cargo of woolens. But men such as Thránd were rare in either the
Faeroes or Shetlands, for few would regularly have enough sheep
products of their own to warrant trips overseas, and still fewer
would be able to afford the expenses required for a ship and its
upkeep. Even Thránd, who must have been wealthy compared to
others in the Faeroes, does not seem to have been free from these
considerations. He taunted his nephews into taking his ship
abroad by telling them that in earlier times, when he was as young
and healthy as they, his ship would not be in its shed practically
rotting under its strakes from disuse while plenty of wool was
available everywhere as cargo.[79] Thránd apparently had a gift for
rhetorical exaggeration because that very ship was taken to Norway. But it seems as though the ship had to remain on its timbers
in storage for quite a long time until enough woolens could be
saved to make a voyage worthwhile. Despite Thránd's reference to
abundant woolens, if enough had been available before, surely
someone else besides his nephews could have been found to take
the ship overseas. Thránd may have appealed to his nephews'
self-respect, but he also must have had in mind his own need to
make a profit on those woolens to pay for the storage expenses of
his ship and, as we would say today, to justify the capital outlay for
the ship itself.[80]

If even relatively powerful and wealthy men like Thránd
lacked sufficient woolens to make regular trips abroad worth-

while, there is reason to believe that most of the other inhabitants of the Faeroes and probably the Shetlands were quite poor. Apparently poverty was brought about by overpopulation, for a lack of excess woolens to sell others suggests the local population had to use too many themselves in proportion to the number of sheep they were able to maintain. Since woolens were virtually the only product these islanders could exchange for necessary imports, a lack of sizable woolen surpluses would mean that they had to do without many foreign products, as vital as they may have been.

There is no way to estimate accurately what the populations of the Faeroes and Shetlands in the Middle Ages were, nor even what that population was relative to usable land.[81] But some tendencies can be suggested. Both of these island groups have only about 550 square miles of land, good or bad. During the ninth and tenth centuries population pressures would have been somewhat eased by men going on Viking expeditions, but as local populations increased again, and as the amount of available land for each family correspondingly diminished, some would leave their homes not for adventure and hope of quick wealth, but for the mundane purpose of finding more ample pastures for their sheep. Some went to Iceland about a century after their ancestors had colonized the islands, this at a time when the congestion of the emigrants' former homelands would not be as severe as it would be later.[82] As time passed and as family members expanded even more, the choices of reasonably near places like Iceland where land could simply be taken came to be ever more limited. Just as on their own islands, most nearby lands, including Iceland after about 930, were totally claimed by their own populations. Most Faeroese and Shetlanders would have had little choice but to stay at home, trying their best to survive with what resources they had. By the early eleventh century, at the time of the annexation by St. Óláf, the Faeroes already must have been densely settled, as the story about Thránd í Gata seems to show. In succeeding generations, the population increase must have led to more severe poverty. If other Scandinavian bishops can be taken as typical, the bishop of the Faeroes must have been a relatively large landowner during these later times.[83] Yet, even he apparently was not able to hold enough land to be called prosperous. Although his episcopacy was founded at the beginning of the twelfth century at Kirkebø, a cathedral was not begun there until the late thirteenth century. Even after that time the bishopric was so poor that the structure was never completed.[84] These examples concern the Faeroes, but the Shetlands certainly could not have been much more prosperous.

Faeroese and Shetlander overseas trade, because it could not be maintained adequately by the islanders themselves, especially from at least the eleventh century onward, had to be entrusted to foreigners. But for many of the same reasons that largely prevented their own inhabitants from trading abroad, the islands were not an attractive market for foreign merchants. Only part of the reason was that customers were limited both in relative numbers and wealth. Another disadvantage for trade was that the islanders could offer essentially only sheep products in exchange for any purchase of imports. True, these products were also the main export of other North Atlantic islands, and the market for them was good in such a place as Norway. But other places such as Iceland, besides having a larger and generally more well-to-do population, also offered some attractive exports besides woolens. For these reasons foreign merchants would probably come to the Faeroes and Shetlands, when they came at all, only as an incidental part of a longer but more lucrative voyage.

Commerce with these islands could be undertaken better by Norwegians than Icelanders. In fact, the market would be so disadvantageous to Icelanders that it is quite believable that they rarely traded there voluntarily.[85] Since these islands had only sheep products to sell, of which an Icelandic merchant usually would have had plenty himself from his own lands and from exchanges at home, there would be little reason for him to acquire more there. Norwegians, on the contrary, might want even a small quantity of woolens to help satiate their local demand and that created by their relatively strong commercial ties with other parts of Europe. Since they could get larger quantities of woolens in such a place as Iceland, however, they certainly would not be content with stopping only at the Faeroes and Shetlands; they would include Iceland on their trip as well. In exchange for woolens of the Faeroes and

Shetlands, Norwegians could sell goods which would be more desirable to the islanders than those of Icelanders. Norwegian barley, timber, and hardware could more readily be sold to them, of course, than Icelandic luxuries such as falcons. The more ordinary goods that Iceland had were the same as those of these islanders, those of Norwegians far more necessary. There would be a greater absolute demand, however, for Norwegian imports in Iceland than on these islands; so for this reason too Norwegians would want to come to the large island on the same trip.

The exemption from the double payment of the landaurar in the c. 1022 agreement, insofar as it concerned the Shetlands, and somewhat later probably the Faeroes, must, then, have been exercised rarely if ever by the Icelanders whom it was intended to benefit. Icelanders would not find that the privilege balanced the disadvantages of the trade for them.

The economy of the Orkneys and Hebrides was more prosperous and varied than that of the Faeroes and Shetlands. If the landaurar clause applied to both of these groups of more southerly islands, the privilege would be at least potentially more important for Icelandic merchants.

Superficially these islands had much in common with the Faeroes and Shetlands. Like them, they were geographically well situated for trade, in fact even more so, because they were less isolated, being not far from England and Ireland. Men from these islands too had come to help colonize Iceland during its period of settlement, and during those early years they also may have carried on a trade with the larger island, especially needy at that time.[86] And, like other North Atlantic islanders in general, they emphasized sheep raising, thereby gaining products they could use themselves and export elsewhere.

Unlike those living on islands farther north, men of the Orkneys and probably the Hebrides, in addition to depending upon sheep as their economic mainstay, also were able to raise a significant amount of barley, so much so in fact that at least occasionally they had a surplus to sell to others.[87] This surplus indicates another important difference compared to the Faeroes and Shetlands: population density must have been much lower on

these more southerly islands. Indeed, even that ordinarily enough
grain apparently could be raised by these islanders for their own
needs points in the same direction. Compared to sheep raising,
which, as far as climate was concerned, was almost certain to be
consistently productive, barley harvests were much more subject
to fickle changes in weather conditions: the inhabitants of the
Orkneys and Herbrides must have been certain of having enough
sheep for their needs before valuable pastureland was used for
cultivating barley. It thus must have been because of a relatively
low population density that so much land nevertheless could be
devoted to this grain to regularly provide for the islanders' own
needs, as well as sometimes a surplus for others.[88]

With surplus woolens to sell, and occasionally barley, Orcadians and Hebrideans were also better able than Shetlanders or
Faeroese to carry on trade themselves. Though Orkney merchants,
as has been seen, were in Bergen about 1186, Norway was not as
good a choice for these traders as Ireland, or, even better, England.
Norway was farther away, and it offered little or no economic
compensation for the extra distance traveled. Imported grain probably would rarely be needed by these merchants for use on their
home islands, and if so, England or Ireland could supply it; luxuries
could be obtained more cheaply in those closer countries; and
England—where much local wool was used to make cloth of fine
quality from at least the early eleventh century onward—would
pay as much or more than Norway for the ordinary woolens these
islanders had to sell.[89] A commercial orientation toward Ireland
and England was also quite natural because of a general familiarity
with those places since Viking times. It is therefore not surprising
that during the twelfth century relatively large numbers of merchants from both the Orkneys and Hebrides were found in England, especially in the east coast city of Grimsby—a town whose
very name is of Norse origin—situated in an area that had been
heavily settled by Scandinavians. The islanders' trade with that
city, or others, continued into the next century and later.[90] As
another example of trade with England, when about 1200 an
Icelandic pilgrim on his way farther south, Hrafn Sveinbjarnarson,
visited the Orkneys, the bishop there gave him splendid gifts of

dyed cloth and fine saddles:[91] known for its locally manufactured multi-colored cloth as well as cloth of one color,[92] and having had a leather industry since at least Anglo-Saxon times,[93] England must have been the source of these articles.

Even though merchants of the Hebrides were closer to Ireland than were those of the Orkneys, after the Viking Age they, like Orkney merchants, usually must have preferred trading their woolens in England because Ireland made much the same inexpensive cloth themselves. During the Viking Age in Ireland and somewhat afterward, however, when large amounts of Viking luxuries were available, Hebridean merchants would have gone there more often than later, being willing to accept less than the best price for their woolens because of the particularly alluring goods they might get in exchange. All that time, too, their sense of community with Irish merchants remained strong enough to go on trading voyages in partnership with them. A passage in *Eyrbyggja saga* illustrates both the types of luxuries available in Ireland during the late Viking Age and a close relationship between Hebridean and Irish merchants, a relationship that probably was being practiced for trade not just to Iceland, but to England also:

> That summer when Christianity was accepted in Iceland [1000] a ship arrived at Snaefellsnes; it was a "Dublin-farer," and Irishmen and men from the Hebrides were on it, but few from Scandinavia. They stayed quite long in the summer at Ríf and waited to start sailing into the fjord at Dögurtharnes. Many men went out from the headland to carry on trade. On the ship was a woman from the Hebrides whose name was Thórgunna. The crewmen said of her that she had brought goods along that must be rare in Iceland. [When another woman on Iceland heard about these goods, she traveled to the ship, wishing to buy some from Thórgunna, but was refused. Later Thórgunna, in making up her bed, displayed the luxuries she had.] She spread over the bed English colored cloth and a silken quilt. She took out from the chest the bed curtains and all the precious bed hangings too. They were such valuable items that people believed that they had not seen such things before.[94]

One cannot say who owned the vessel, whether someone from Ireland, the Hebrides, Scandinavia, or someplace else, but clearly it was manned by an association of merchants, mainly Irish and

Hebridean. Many of the goods on the ship, such as the silken quilt and the English colored cloth, must have been imported earlier to Ireland and, via Ireland, to the Hebrides.[95]

Both the Orkneys and Hebrides would be important to Icelandic consumers, then, as sources for barley and for luxury articles from England and, at an early time, from Ireland. Even though these advantages were shared more or less equally by the Orkneys and Hebrides, an Iceland-Orkney trade was apparently much more frequent than one between Iceland and the Hebrides.

When Hebrides or Orkney merchants came to Iceland, they must have brought with them, whenever a surplus was available, a cargo of barley in some form, for the large amount would bring greater profits than a few Irish or English luxuries. Therefore, barley probably formed the main cargo of the ship Thórgunna was on, less worthy of mention than the vain woman's luxurious bed furnishings. The noteworthy rarity on Iceland of those fine articles, however, suggests an important aspect of the joint Irish and Hebridean voyage: similar voyages were probably not frequent. Such indeed seems to be the case, for there is no record of any being made after this time by either Irish or Hebridean merchants acting together or separately.

Examples of Orkney merchants going to Iceland are more numerous. About 1200 or somewhat later, an Orkney ship, having come by way of the Faeroes, arrived in Iceland, bringing along twenty-four merkur (about 12 lbs. or 5.4 kg) of wax, which was later taken to Skálaholt.[96] Of course, the cargo of this ship must have consisted of much else besides, especially grain, but since wax attracted the attention of the saga writer, there is good reason to suppose that this ship, or another one from the Orkneys, had previously been to England, for that country was well known for its bee products. An Orkney merchant, Thorkell the Walrus, came approximately the same time, about 1203, and stayed with Snorri Sturluson. What we can only presume in other cases, we know about his cargo: it consisted of barley meal and malt, which, though only ordinary products, were worthy of attention this time because they gave rise to a bitter dispute resulting in Thorkell's death.[97] A better end came to some merchants traveling on a ship from the Orkneys to Iceland, saved by a miracle attributed to St. Jón Ögmundarson of Hólar. The story of the miracle gives a hint that the ship had previously been to England, for when a heavy fog enshrouded the ship, making it impossible for the navigator to find his way, an Icelander aboard suggested that the crew should pray for the aid of St. Jón and donate (presumably later, to Hólar) half an English penny each; the fog then lifted and the men were able to reach their destination safely.[98] Like the other voyages, this one seems to have taken place about 1200, when Jón was declared a saint.

Rather than rely on merchants from the Orkneys, or much less likely, the Hebrides, to bring cargoes to Iceland, Icelanders would find the trade more advantageous by coming to those islands themselves for grain and for other products that had been previously imported there. In contrast to Orcadians' voyages to Iceland, which seem to have been especially numerous during the early thirteenth century when all those we know about occurred, Icelanders seem to have come much more consistently to the Orkneys. At least supposed instances can be drawn from the tenth until the thirteenth centuries. Thorkell Thorgrímsson, who was probably a merchant, is said to have visited the islands sometime in the tenth century accompanied by a Norwegian trader. The Orkney jarl gave Thorkell an axe decorated with gold, as well as especially good clothes. Better than these presents though, Thorkell also was given a ship with a cargo of his own choosing:[99] barley must have been his main choice. Probably like Thorkell Thorgrímsson, Odd Ófeigsson, an enterprising Icelandic merchant of humble beginnings, came to the Orkneys in the mid-eleventh century primarly for grain; though he definitely is said to have obtained some, he had to exchange goods for it, because the jarl of that time was not so generous with him.[100] Sometime during the twelfth century an "Iceland-farer" came to the Orkneys: an Icelander was on this ship engaged in the Iceland trade, though the vessel itself was not necessarily Icelandic.[101] But in the middle of that century Jarl Rögnvald of the Orkneys was able to take a merchant ship definitely belonging to an Icelander from Norway back to his home.[102] At the end of this century or the beginning of the next, St. Jón Ögmundarson, ever ready to help distressed sea-farers, again is said to have aided merchants, probably including Icelandic ones: this time they were on their way from Iceland to the Orkneys.[103] And in the early thirteenth century, when Hrafn Sveinbjarnarson came to the Orkneys, he may have been accompanied at least that far by other Icelanders who had come mainly for trade.[104]

If Hebrides merchants seldom came to Iceland, Icelandic ones equally rarely came to the Hebrides. Only one instance is known, occurring in 1202 or 1203; but even in that case, anticipated trade was aborted. When Guthmund Arason, soon to become bishop of Hólar, and several Icelandic merchants arrived there, someone claiming to be a royal official demanded 120 alnir of vathmál from every man on the ship as the landaurar. The merchants would not pay this fee, knowing that they would have to pay a toll again when they continued to Norway as was their plan.[105] This story suggests the main reason Icelanders hardly ever came to the Hebrides. If the islands were included in the landaurar exemption clause of the c. 1022 agreement, as they probably were at least technically, the privilege must not have been honored there, certainly not at the time this voyage was undertaken by Guthmund and the other Icelanders. According to the landaurar privilege, the Icelandic merchants aboard the ship almost certainly would not have had to pay any amount for a landaurar in excess of what was demanded in Norway itself, but the one claimed here was probably either 25 or 33 percent higher than the Norwegian one. Nor could the privilege, insofar as it concerned the Hebrides, have been recognized by this time in Norway, for according to that privilege if the fee was paid, it would not have had to be paid again in Norway if the visitors continued there directly afterward, as was their intention. The reason for this state of affairs is not hard to find: even before the c. 1022 agreement was made the Hebrides had been unwilling to submit to Norse authority, and they had continued to drift from Norwegian control even after an attempt had been made to restore it at the end of the eleventh century.[106] It was probably because of these generally unfavorable circumstances that Icelandic visits to the islands were discouraged, as indeed the very account of this single known instance suggests: if earlier trips to the Hebrides had been frequent, Guthmund and the others would have been prepared for the high landing fee demanded there.

The privilege, on the other hand, always seems to have been honored in the Orkneys, helping to explain why Icelanders went there much more often. Nevertheless, an Icelandic merchant usually would have preferred going to Norway alone, though in all but one respect the Orkneys might appear at least equally attractive. The merchant would be aware that the value of his woolens—usually the main product he would be selling—probably would be lower in the Orkneys than in Norway, for on the islands local production probably completely satisfied local demand. As far as barley was concerned—one of the main things an Icelandic merchant would want in exchange for his woolens—its value might be approximately the same in the Orkneys as in Norway. Though the Orkneys grew less, this lower supply was balanced by lower demand, for not only did the islands have a far smaller total population, but also they had little or no agriculturally nonproductive administrative, military, and professionally mercantile population to support. If the Icelandic merchant wanted some English goods, their price might have been lower in the Orkneys than Norway because those islands were closer to the source, and again the demand would not be as great.[107]

But the Icelandic merchant probably would far more greatly desire barley than English luxury imports, and he might want other necessities and luxuries besides. In this case, Norway would be the more attractive alternative. With its larger trading area, it would have a larger variety and a greater amount of imported goods than the Orkneys. It also would have available certain abundant domestic products such as timber, of which the Orkneys had none. And, even with increasing domestic demand, usually Norway would have enough barley to sell the merchant what he wanted, whereas in the Orkneys there might not be enough to provide him with all he expected. If the price for barley was the same as in the Orkneys, and the value of his woolens higher, the Icelandic merchant would have all the more reason to prefer going to Norway. Finally, the merchant would have a better market in Norway, not just for his woolens, but for other goods as well, including luxuries; thus he could dispose of a varied cargo of Icelandic wares more easily than in the Orkneys.[108]

There still would be some reason for the Icelandic merchant to go to the Orkneys if he did so as an incidental part of his voyage to Norway. For example, if he wanted some English goods, which he might get for less than in Norway, he might stop first at the Orkneys to make his exchange. Or, if there was a known shortage of barley in Norway, he might stop first in the Orkneys to buy what he could. In either case, he would continue to Norway where he would dispose of the rest of his cargo in return for whatever else he needed. A limited Icelandic trade with the Orkneys such as this was made possible largely by the privilege of having to pay the landaurar only once. Without that privilege, any savings the Icelandic merchant made in acquiring English goods in the Orkneys would be reduced; and, unless there was a total lack of grain in Norway for him to buy, he might not want to stop in the Orkneys for any grain at all if he had to pay a double toll.[109]

The landaurar exemption clause of the c. 1022 agreement was therefore useful enough for Icelandic merchants in the case of the Orkneys. But since it had little or no practical value in the Shetlands, something that surely St. Óláf could have anticipated, a question remains: why did he specifically include those islands in the agreement? He might well have done so for immediate diplomatic and long-range political reasons. Because the agreement as a whole provided considerable advantages for Norwegians in Iceland and because it exacted the fairly heavy burdens of payment of a landaurar and the possibility of military service from Icelanders when they came to Norway, St. Óláf would need to balance these by granting as many concessions to Icelanders as possible, even though, as in this landaurar exemption clause, those privileges actually might amount to less than they seemed. Also it was to St. Óláf's advantage to appear as solicitous of the needs of Icelandic merchants as possible because of his plans of later annexing their island, which would be the major victory in his quest to gain a Norwegian hegemony in the North Atlantic. Granting to Icelandic merchants privileges of any kind, useful or not, St. Óláf might have thought, would help to promote the good reputation he was anxious to establish.

There was probably another reason that St. Óláf granted the privilege to Icelanders for all the islands he had recently put under his control. The Orkneys, Shetlands, and Hebrides had an important political distinction within the Norwegian realm: St. Óláf entrusted their government to lieutenants, the Orkney jarls, and he thus governed the islands only indirectly; nevertheless, in practice, he dominated at least the foreign affairs of these islands (with the possible exception of the Hebrides) just as much through the jarls as he did those of Norway directly.[110] It might have been obvious, therefore, that the landaurar was to be paid whenever an Icelander entered the lands of the king, whether they be these islands or Norway itself; as long as the Icelander did not leave those lands, he would not have to pay the toll again. Since, however, the agreement was made between the Icelanders and St. Óláf as king of Norway, strictly speaking the payment of a landaurar in these islands would not be required. To avoid this possible misunderstanding, the landaurar clause of the agreement had to state clearly that Icelanders were exempt from the toll in Norway if they had come directly from the islands and had paid it there. Though the inclusion of this clause might have been due partly to this legal technicality, that legalism concerning all the islands, not just the Orkneys, had the advantage of further pleasing Icelanders in general, not only merchants who might take advantage of its terms. By tacitly admitting that a misunderstanding over political allegiance could occur, St. Óláf recognized the still remaining semi-independent political status of all the islands despite his imposition of power over them the previous year. Because he was anxious to annex Iceland in the near future, this point could be to his credit when he began those negotiations. For the time being, this clause could be used as yet another example of his generous nature, showing that his newly acquired dominance over these islands had not involved a complete subordination to his power.

⚓ CHAPTER SIX

Icelandic Trade with England, Ireland, and the Continent

Icelandic commerce beyond Scandinavia itself and the North Atlantic Norse islands was most substantial with England, less so with Ireland. While Iceland may have had some commercial contact with certain continental countries or areas—France, Germany and Frisia, the southern Baltic area, Russia, and Byzantium—much of the evidence concerning it is highly circumstantial and indicates that trade with these places would have been tenuous at best.

ENGLAND

In 789 "three ship of Norwegians from Hörthaland" arrived on the southern coast of England; "and then the reeve rode thither and tried to compel them to go to the royal manor, for he did not know what they were; and then they slew him. These were the first ships of the Danes [i.e., Scandinavians] to come to England."[1] In this terse manner the Anglo-Saxon Chronicle notes for the first time the appearance of Viking marauders not only in England but in all of Europe. The reeve of course could not have known this—he probably believed they were only peaceful traders.[2] This mistaken opinion shows that Scandinavians in all likelihood traded with England before 789, and it helps to explain one cause of the event

124

itself: peaceful trading might well have whetted impatient appetites to use more direct means of gaining England's wealth. Despite Viking attacks on England that lasted intermittently for more than two centuries, some Scandinavians continued to trade. A number of examples testify to it. While King Alfred was building a navy to defend England from hostile Vikings, at his court he listened to the tales of the Norwegian merchant, Óttar. In 991 Óláf Tryggvason, later to become king of Norway, promised Ethelred II that merchant ships of foreigners in English ports would be unharmed by his Vikings as would those of English subjects in foreign ports: at least some of those foreign ports must have been in Scandinavia.[3] And at York, Danish and doubtless some Norwegian merchants had a colony that existed soon after 1000;[4] surely they carried on much of their trade with Denmark and Norway. Nor did English trade with Scandinavia stop after the end of the Viking period— which in England may be placed at 1042 when Harthaknút lost his throne—for English coins found in Scandinavia date not just from the reigns of Ethelred and Canute the Great but from those of Edward the Confessor and the Norman kings, after the Scandinavian military and political presence had ended. Some of these coins, especially those of Edward's time and afterward, bear witness to a continuing peaceful trade.[5]

Several circumstances were favorable for Norway, of all Scandinavian countries, to have the strongest trade relations with England after the mid-eleventh century. The urbanization and growing population of both countries[6] would lay an essential economic basis for an exchange of primarily Norwegian fish for English grain, but that Norway and England looked to each other for these supplementary foods after the conclusion of Viking contact owes much to strong religious and, later, to common political interests. The establishment and early development of the Norwegian church during the earlier eleventh century had been greatly influenced by the English example, and a continuing exchange of clergy was maintained during the twelfth and thirteenth centuries.[7] Therefore, as the Norwegian church, particularly the archiepiscopacy of Nidaros, became an important commercial force in Norway, it was only natural that it would take advantage of its religious orientation to establish a mutually beneficial trade with England. In fact the archbishop of Nidaros and the monks of the Cistercian foundation at Lyse, near Bergen, a daughter house of Fountains Abbey, became the first known Norwegian beneficiaries of formal trade concessions in England, probably between 1180 and 1183 and in 1217 respectively.[8] Contact of a peaceful political nature perhaps first began when King Sigurth the Jerusalem-Farer in 1107 stopped in England on his way to the city after which he came to be named,[9] and thereafter friendly relations between the English and Norwegian monarchs were maintained by an exchange of gifts. Those the English king apparently liked to receive most were falcons and hawks, while the favorites of his practical Norwegian counterpart seem to have been grain and malt.[10] Surely from the point of view of both monarchs, their own friendly relations would promote an ease and safety for their merchants traveling to each other's country. Those merchants gained privileges on a formal basis in 1223 when a mutual trade agreement was signed by Henry III and Hákon IV.[11] It was, then, amid these circumstances of strong Anglo-Norwegian religious, political, and economic contact that Iceland, as a kind of commercial extension of Norway, conducted its trade with England.

As in the case of Norway, the most important category of Icelandic imports from England were foods, and the most significant of them was grain. For instance, a saga says that in the mid-tenth century King Ethelstan II gave Egill Skallagrímsson a good merchant ship filled with a cargo of both wheat and honey.[12] Although this event cannot be unhesitatingly accepted for the tenth century, it does seem to reflect the later circumstances of the time of the saga's composition, about 1200, for, by way of example, when an Icelandic priest, Ingimund Thorgeirsson, came to Bergen from England in 1189, the ship on which he had made his voyage also carried grain and honey, as well as some wine.[13] This cargo was stolen, otherwise Ingimund might have taken his share on to Iceland. Only somewhat less importantly, England was also a source of cloth for Icelanders who wanted finer materials than their own vathmál.[14] Both one of the typical fabrics made in England and cloth imported there are mentioned in *Egils saga Skalla-*

grímssonar. In York—at least by 1200 an important center of the cloth industry—Egill Skallagrímsson is said to have met his friend Arinbjörn who gave him a robe of silk embroidered with gold and a complete suit made of newly cut English cloth of many colors.[15] Though the embroidered silk probably would have been imported, the multi-colored cloth was one of the specialities of York at least by 1200,[16] and, because Egill is said to have received it along with the silk, it must have been considered almost equally luxurious. Luxurious too must have been sixteen alnir of brown and red cloth which was part of the ill-fated cargo of Ingimund's ship:[17] that there was so little cloth aboard to be stolen shows its high value. But Icelanders were most familiar with more common English linen. In the Icelandic price list of about 1186 it was valued at the equivalent of two alnir for one legal eyrir, a price three times the value of ordinary vathmál; the same price was repeated in the later lists of about 1200 and about 1300. Because the value of a legal eyrir, in terms of pure silver, changed with each of these price lists, so did that of both English linen and Icelandic vathmál; but they always varied in step with each other, for the 3:1 price ratio between the two cloths was always maintained. Since the relationship evidently was traditional for the compilers of these lists, it is likely that English linen was both well known and frequently traded in Iceland for a considerable period before even the earliest list appeared.[18] The three price lists also mention several kinds of hardware. Since Britain had tin in Cornwall, copper in North Wales and Anglesey, and iron in Kent,[19] it is not unlikely that at least some of this hardware originated there, as did probably many of the bells so often mentioned in church inventories. Occasionally sagas directly mention Icelanders obtaining bells in England: during the early eleventh century, for instance, the Icelandic merchant Odd Ófeigsson supposedly went to England where he purchased some, and, at the end of the twelfth century, Markús Gíslason did the same.[20]

Icelandic products that were exchanged for English food, cloth, and hardware are not often mentioned, but they usually must have been one version or another of vathmál, Iceland's typical export. This is shown by correspondences between English and

Icelandic cloth measurements which are so striking that they cannot be just coincidental. In 1101 King Henry I introduced the yard to England. It was composed of two ells, and the standard ell, according to William of Malmesbury, was equal to the king's own right forearm.[21] It was at about the same time that the "short" or legal öln, exactly corresponding to the length of this English ell (18"; c. 46 cm), was standardized in Iceland, thereby suggesting that measurement in stikur, each of which was the same length as Henry's yard, began to be used in Iceland at the same time as well. In 1196 King Richard I issued the Assize of Measures stipulating that all cloth everywhere in England had to be woven in widths of one yard;[22] again, just a few years later, about 1200, Iceland's "stika law" was made, stating that "vathmál, linen, and all [other] cloth" had to be two alnir in width, which was the same as the English yard.[23] The clear purpose of this Icelandic law and probably the use of the "short" or legal öln a hundred years before was to facilitate the sale in England of Icelandic cloth, presumably mostly ordinary vathmál. Since cloth manufactured in England was usually one yard wide after 1101—and legally had to be after 1196—Icelandic cloth of the same measurement could be sold more easily there if for no other reason than that English customers had become used to that size. Because the measurement was adopted in Iceland in response to English custom and law, vathmál must have been sent in one form or another in considerable quantities to England.

It may seem surprising that any Icelandic cloth could find a market in England. Medieval English wool production is practically proverbial, and even though a considerable portion of it was sent across the Channel for Low Country weavers, until the thirteenth century there seems to have been no shortage of it remaining for the use of English craftsmen.[24] As far as the cloth itself is concerned, in the countryside, where every farm had at least some sheep, there usually would be no shortage of an ordinary fabric because as much as a family needed could be made at home. In urban areas, however, where such convenience was not possible, cloth available for purchase might be beyond the means of many. Town weavers, having to face high everyday city costs themselves, would naturally specialize, if they could, in the types of cloth that brought the highest return for their labor—fine cloth that would be exported. Merchants might bring back from their buying trips in the countryside some ordinary cloth from an available rural surplus, but usually their main intent was to procure raw wool destined for the domestic and foreign looms of craftsmen. With an urban cloth industry geared for production of high-priced, luxury fabrics, the needs of the majority of townsmen would be neglected. Demand would thus exist for Icelandic vathmál, an ordinary cloth that remained inexpensive even though imported.[25] Until technological innovations helped increase production, helping, in turn, to lower prices for fine cloth and to allow craftsmen to give more attention to ordinary cloth, England would be a most important customer for Icelandic vathmál.

Occasionally luxuries from Iceland were found in England. Many of the falcons sent from Norway to England, for instance, must have been originally found in Iceland; in 1169 and 1177 they are specifically said to have come from there.[26] Icelanders like Hrafn Sveinbjarnarson, who made a pilgrimage to Canterbury about 1195, may have brought other luxuries from other parts of the Scandinavian North. In Hrafn's case, he presented the shrine of St. Thomas Becket with walrus tusks in gratitude for aid the saint had given when his name was invoked during a walrus hunt,[27] presumably in Greenland. And in 1224 some Icelandic luxuries might have been brought to Yarmouth. On 23 August of that year King Henry III ordered his bailiff in the city to allow ships bringing merchandise from Iceland, Norway, and other places to leave the port without impediment.[28] There is no way of knowing from this order whether ships from Iceland were involved or whether they were Norwegian ones engaged in the trade to Iceland. But for the Icelandic goods to have been identifiable as such, some or even many of them may have been luxuries: to Englishmen vathmál alone might not be perceived as distinctively Icelandic, but luxuries like falcons could more easily be recognized as such.

Although Icelanders came to England[29]—most of them probably to trade—their number should not be exaggerated. Both points are indirectly illustrated by two stories about the Icelandic saint, Thorlák Thórhallsson. An Icelandic biography written about 1206 says that he was able to help men when his name was invoked and that therefore much money was given to his former see at Skálaholt from all countries where his name was known. Apart from Iceland itself, most donations came from Norway, but many too from other places, including England.[30] Surely St. Thorlák's fame in England must have been abetted by Icelanders who were there. Nevertheless, the cult of the saint could not have been widespread in England, for when an Icelander named Authunn is said to have erected a statue of St. Thorlák in a church in King's Lynn ("Kynn") sometime at the beginning of the thirteenth century, he had to explain to an English cleric whom the statue represented.[31] Though of course not conclusive, the ignorance of the English priest suggests Icelanders were not frequent visitors to King's Lynn even though it was the fifth busiest port in England at the time and among the most favored by other Scandinavians, particularly Norwegians.[32]

Almost always whenever Icelanders are known to have come to England or to have returned to Iceland from there, they are said clearly to have traveled via Norway, usually on Norwegian ships. Surely, however, some who came directly to Ireland on their own ships would have gone to western England as well, but such instances are not recorded.[33] Probably the main reason Icelanders usually came with Norwegians was because of the Norwegian trading concessions that they lacked,[34] and for this reason Norwegian merchants must have acted as intermediaries in the sale of Icelandic and English goods most of the time. For instance, as we have seen in an earlier chapter, there is a strong possibility that the archbishop of Nidaros, who was the largest known regular supplier of grain to Icelanders by shortly after the mid-twelfth century, sold Icelandic vathmál in England in return for at least some of the grain he sent to Iceland. Because of the activities of the archbishop, as well as other Norwegians before and after the mid-twelfth century, Icelanders desiring English products could have obtained them in Norway, where they had trading concessions.

Of course, without traveling abroad themselves, Icelanders could also obtain English goods brought to the island. In this case Norwegians, such as agents of the archbishop, were far more likely to bring them than English merchants, for the latter had little reason to come to Iceland. Inexpensive Icelandic woolens might be sold profitably enough in England, but the English demand for them would not be great enough to warrant an Englishman going to Iceland just for them. Of primary interest was Icelandic luxury goods. For many of the same reasons, however, that Icelanders preferred dealing with Norway as an intermediary, so did the English. English demand for Icelandic luxuries was always limited, and usually the relatively few customers would be satisfactorily provided with those goods by the Norwegians and the few Icelanders who came to England. If English merchants went to Norway for them, a place they knew well and where they had trading rights, they would be able to buy other desirable goods besides. No doubt English merchants could have obtained Icelandic luxuries for a lower price and could have sold such of their own products as grain for a higher one if they came directly to Iceland. But most must have been content journeying only to Norway, for no merchant from England is stated specifically to have come to Iceland during the Commonwealth period. In the section of *Grágás* on inheritance laws affecting the property of certain foreigners who die in Iceland, Scandinavians are grouped together; in another category belong Englishmen or "those whose origin is unknown." The property of the first category could revert to their heirs even though they did not live in Iceland. The property of those of the second was sold usually by the chieftain of the district in which the death occurred unless the son, brother, or father of the dead man had been in Iceland before, and one of those relatives was known.[35] Apparently Englishmen so seldom came to Iceland (or Icelanders to England) that word of a death would scarcely reach any heirs back home. Although this provision shows that at least a few Englishmen visited or lived in Iceland, some of whom may have been merchants, the paucity of other specific reference to Englishmen in the sources for the Commonwealth confirms that they were seldom found on Iceland during that time.[36]

IRELAND

Norsemen began settling Ireland probably very soon after the first raid there in 795, just north of Dublin, and Dublin (or Dýflinn in Old Norse) became essentially a Norse city, as did Waterford, Wexford, Limerick, and Cork. There were numerous disputes for political control among Irish, Norwegians, and Danes, quarrels that finally ended in 1014 at the Battle of Clontarf with a definitive Irish victory. That battle for all intents and purposes brought to a close the Viking period in Ireland, but even during the earlier period of hostility the Scandinavians had a reputation among Irish as merchants: a tenth-century Irish source speaks ruefully of the Norse "gift of habitation and commerce," and an Irish poem mentions with evident disgust "the gluttony of the Norse and their commerce."[37]

These Irish comments were probably truthful enough, for the Norse settlements were repositories of considerable riches gained from plunder and trade. When native Irish sacked even the secondary city of Limerick in 968, they discovered gold, silver, oriental satins and silks.[38] As the Norse capital, Dublin must have been even richer. In 941 the city was able to pay its temporary conqueror, Muirchertach, a tribute consisting of "gold, colored mantles, and foodstuffs for his men," and in 989 Dublin again was forced to pay the extraordinarily large tribute of one ounce of gold per house.[39] In 1014 when King Brian Boru gained his great victory at Clontarf, the Irish discovered in nearby Dublin

> the greatest quantities of gold and silver, and bronze and precious stones, and carbuncle-gems and buffalo horns, and beautiful goblets. All these valuables were collected by them [Brian's men] to one place. Much also of various vestures of all colours was found there likewise.[40]

Luxuries such as these, not to speak of the grain that the island had in abundance,[41] would have attracted Icelanders to Ireland, particulary because, except for those who accompanied Thórgunna in 1000, merchants from Ireland are not known to have traded in Iceland. They had little reason to do so, for, like English merchants, they would not wish to sail there merely for vathmál or a few arctic luxuries, and they could dispose of their grain and other products for export more conveniently than by going to Iceland to make the sales.[42]

During the tenth century, Icelandic trade with Ireland must have been restricted because of the almost constant warfare between Irish and Scandinavians. Icelandic merchants might be mistaken easily for warriors by wary Irish if they landed in non-Norse districts, as an incident in *Laxdœla saga* suggests. Óláf the Peacock Höskuldarson was supposedly outfitted by Queen Gunnhild of Norway with a ship and a crew who appeared "more like warriors than traders." Drifting in dense fog for some time at sea because of lack of wind, the ship finally made port in Ireland, evidently in a non-Norse district where foreigners were not welcome. According to their law, the saga says, the Irish attempted to seize the illegally moored ship as flotsam but Óláf sought to prevent it by telling them in their native tongue—he was taught it by his Irish mother—of the peaceful nature of the mission; he said, furthermore, that a ship could not be seized if a translator were aboard.[43]

More peaceful conditions for trade must have prevailed after the Battle of Clontarf. Somewhat before or after 1014 Hrafn Oddsson earned his nickname, "the Limerick-Farer," because of his frequent voyages between Iceland and that Irish city. Perhaps because Hrafn traded in more distant ports, using Limerick as a base for his operations, he was said to have been there a long time.[44] Descendants of those Scandinavians who had resided in Norse-held Ireland in the tenth century not only continued to be active as traders after 1014, but, if Hrafn can be taken as an example, their numbers may have been supplemented occasionally by additional Scandinavian merchants.[45]

Though some Icelanders like Óláf the Peacock apparently took the much longer route to Ireland via Norway, others must have gone there directly: the earliest extant version of *Landnámabók*, written by Sturla Thórtharson about 1275, gives the number of days' sailing directly from southwestern Iceland to northwestern Ireland.[46] This geographically convenient direct route, not via Norway, is an exception to the general habits of Icelanders trading with non-Scandinavian lands. Sturla's comment also implies that Icelandic overseas merchants were reasonably acquainted with sailing to Ireland, for that island was chosen as a geographical reference point for Iceland's own location. But however true this may have been once, one cannot be certain that Icelandic merchants still went to Ireland in Sturla's time. In fact, since his *Landnámabók* is mainly a copy of a lost earlier version, written about 1130, itself based partly on older materials,[47] Sturla's sailing direction and even a similar one of the 1130 version of the book may be only repetitions of sailing lore that was no longer put to practical use.[48]

Although it cannot be decided solely on the basis of the c. 1275 version of *Landnámabók* whether sailings to Ireland were actually still being made, other considerations suggest that if they were, they were not frequent. Though Ireland could provide foods that Icelanders needed, there the market for Icelandic woolens would not have been as good as in nearby England, for Ireland did not export either raw wool or fine cloth in the quantities that England did, and so its demand for relatively cheap Icelandic cloth would not be as great.[49] An Icelandic merchant who made his way to Ireland and was faced with this circumstance would find that by sailing on to England he undoubtedly would get a better price for his vathmál and at least the same price for any of his Icelandic luxuries; there in England also he probably could obtain grain as easily as in Ireland. After the first disappointing attempts to sell Icelandic woolens in Ireland, few other Icelanders would have followed.

Instead of going to Ireland for grain in exchange for woolens, Icelanders like Hrafn the Limerick-Farer went there primarily for the unusually plentiful luxuries. During the Viking period in Ireland lack of peaceful trading conditions could be braved and a relatively poor market for ordinary woolens could be suffered because such luxuries were highly profitable when resold either in Iceland or Norway. But after the Irish victory at Clontarf and during the rest of the eleventh century when Norse-Irish more often spent their accumulated wealth and less often acquired more by plunder, Icelanders would find that once plentiful luxury wares in Ireland were growing increasingly scarce. Even in earlier years an Iceland-Ireland trade based mainly on a one-sided desire on the part of Icelanders for Irish luxuries could not have been strong; when that limited desire could not always be satisfied, the trade must have greatly diminished.[50] That time certainly had come well before Sturla wrote his *Landnámabók;* it probably had arrived even before the c. 1130 version of the book had been written.

FRANCE

In general, medieval Icelanders gained their knowledge of France more through the distorted medium of romantic literature than by the practical one of trade. The French chivalric tradition was formally introduced to Norway and Iceland when the story of Tristram and Isolde was translated Old Norse in 1226 at the instigation of King Hákon IV Hákonarson. Later, especially after the Commonwealth, French literary tastes began to compete with native Icelandic ones; Icelanders wrote sagas in a chivalric style based on the exploits of other Arthurian heroes and of such foreign historical figures as Charlemagne and Alexander the Great. Yet even before the literary heritage of France became so well known, some direct and concrete knowledge of the country was gained by Icelandic scholars and pilgrims. Between 1076 and 1078, for example, Sæmund Sigfússon returned to his home at Oddi after having studied at Paris,[51] and perhaps his experience abroad encouraged later on another Icelander to go overseas to study. Thorlák Thórhallsson, the future bishop of Skálaholt and saint, had been raised at Oddi by Sæmund's son Eyjólf; between about 1153 and 1159 Thorlák too went to Paris.[52] Finally, near the end of that same century, the indefatigable pilgrim Hrafn Sveinbjarnarson, who had already been to Canterbury and who would later go to Compostela, was to be found at St. Gilles in Provence,[53] not far from Montpellier, well known at the time for its medical studies. It is hard to estimate exactly what knowledge was gained by these travelers, but the influence they had upon Iceland's civilization could have been almost as profound as French chivalric literature was to have at a later time. A strong supporter for the introduction of a tithe to Iceland at the end of the eleventh century, Sæmund may have taken this position partly because of his knowledge of the practice in France.[54] His early training in Paris may have helped him later to gain a reputation as a man of learning in his own time, and it even may have inspired him to write the first histories of the kings of

Norway, thereby founding a long tradition of historical scholarship.[55] Similarly there might have been a relationship between Thorlák's stay in Paris, where Gregorian reforms were well known, and his later attempts to introduce some of those reforms to Iceland once he became bishop of Skálaholt (1178–1193). Even Hrafn, who was well known to his contemporaries as a physician, might have applied some Montpellier medical practices to his own attempts at healing. The possibility too that these men may have convinced a few of their fellow Icelanders to travel to France for trade should not be overlooked, nor indeed that they themselves may have traded some Icelandic goods while they were in France. In Hrafn's case, it seems particularly likely, because during his pilgrimage he had purchased timber and bells in Norway for a church in Iceland, and, as we already know, he had brought with him walrus tusks to donate to Canterbury. He also may have purchased goods in France to bring home, or he may have sold, rather than donated, some exotic Icelandic products while he was in St. Gilles.

Before and during the times of Sæmund, Thorlák, and Hrafn, Normandy would have been more likely than other areas of France to have had trade relations with Iceland and other parts of Scandinavia. During its early history Normandy differed from the rest of France most obviously because of its element of Scandinavian population. True, the original Viking settlers soon became at least superficially Gallicized following a grant of the area about 911 to a Norwegian, Rollo (Hrólf), by the Frankish king, Charles the Simple; yet Frankish civilization did not immediately replace older Scandinavian traditions, instead the two existed side by side for at least the next century.[56] Both the geographical position of Normandy and its dual civilization during these early years were beneficial for trade. Normandy was on a most important trade route between interior France and England. The Norman Seine valley connected the Channel ultimately with Lyons and Marseilles, and goods from the towns of the Loire reached the Channel only after passing through Normandy. Because Normans early assumed some aspects of Frankish civilization, they were able to make the best of this favorable geographical position by trading all the more easily with interior France, thereby supplementing purely Norman goods, such as dairy products, grain, and fruits, with products from more distant areas, such as wine from the Loire and spices from Marseilles, which themselves had been brought from even farther places. Gallicized Normans must have benefited commercially as well by imitating Frankish trading practices, thereby strengthening commercial ties and increasing profits. On the other hand, because the Normans still retained a partial Scandinavian identity, northern trade relations could be maintained, stimulated by the abundance of desirable products that Normandy possessed.

It thus probably would have been due to Normandy's attractive products and its Scandinavian atmosphere during this early period that the Icelandic skald, Sighvat Thórtharson, supposedly traveled there to trade about 1025.[57] Despite any possible business inspired or carried on by later scholars and pilgrims, Sighvat is the only Icelander who is said specifically to have traded anywhere in France. Even his trip is questionable, but if it actually occurred, he probably would not have traveled to Normandy directly from Iceland in any case. His father was a merchant who later became a retainer to King Óláf the Saint, and when Sighvat grew up, he left Iceland with some Norwegian merchants, joined his father in Norway, and like him, became the king's man.[58] No doubt with this background Sighvat would have come to Normandy from Norway. Though probably very few Icelanders other than Sighvat came to France to trade, long after his time some Icelandic products apparently were to be found there. In *Tristrams saga ok Ísöndar*, the Norse tribute to French literature already mentioned, the translator glossed the story by having a ship come to Tristram's castle in Brittany from the North: on the ship were merchants with "all kinds of Scandinavian wares," including squirrel skins ("grávara"), white fur, beaver, black sable, teeth goods (walrus ivory), bearskins, hawks, gray falcons and many white falcons, wax, hides, buckskin, dried fish, tar, train oil, and sulphur.[59] The translator no doubt added this episode for purpose of verisimilitude, probably basing his imaginary incident on actual Norwegian vessels that brought these very products to France. The author had his ship come to Brittany rather than to Normandy, but after all, he had to make his comment have some bearing on the story. The list of products includes one that certainly was of Icelandic origin—the sulphur—and others that might have been, such as the white fur and falcons.[60] Probably the conclusion can be drawn, therefore, that usually any trade that Iceland had with Normandy was only via Norway, as was true for so many other places.

There remains one piece of testimony, however, to be considered. Though equivocal, it may indicate that Icelandic merchants once came directly to Rouen. One of the entries in the income accounts of the Norman duke for 1198 says "Radolfus of Calais received for himself and for all the commune of Rouen 213 pounds, 6 shillings, 8 pence for 80 marks of silver from the sale of seventeen of the remaining sacks of wool on the Icelandic ship. And 56 pounds for 21 marks of silver from the sale of that ship."[61] On the face of it, it would seem self-explanatory that the "Icelandic ship" was from Iceland; but instead it could have been a Norwegian vessel that was regularly engaged in the trade to Iceland, the kind of ship that would have been known in the North as an "Íslandsfar" ("Iceland-farer").[62] The latter interpretation might seem the more likely because Norwegian merchants, even though they may not have come to Normandy often, still would have come more so than Icelanders, and because, as shall be seen in Part Three, there is the strong likelihood that Icelandic ownership of sea-going vessels had greatly declined by 1198. Nevertheless this case could have been an exception to the general tendencies. Icelandic merchants might have visited Normandy in 1198, though they seldom had before—just as they came to the Hebrides a few years later, a place equally unfrequented by them—in search of a new marketplace during a period of economic distress at home. And, though they might have had few ocean-going ships by then, they still could have used an old one that they believed was seaworthy enough to make the voyage. Although this ambivalence about the origin of the ship cannot be resolved definitively, more light might be shed on the matter by studying other aspects of the record more closely.

Each of the seventeen sacks of wool sold by Radolfus brought a price equal to more than one-fifth of that gained from the sale of the ship itself. Therefore either the wool was very high in price or that of the ship very low. A high demand for raw wool during these years might account for a good price being paid for these sacks, helping to explain in turn why this is the only known example of raw wool being exported from Commonwealth Iceland (where the wool must have originated, regardless of whether or not the ship carrying it was Icelandic or Norwegian). No matter how desirable the wool was, however, it is impossible to believe that any could be so expensive compared to the value of a good sea vessel. Rather than the wool's price being very high, the alternate explanation must be favored—that the ship's value was extraordinarily low. It is quite believable that Icelanders might have sailed a ship that was already delapidated when it left their island; when it finally got to Rouen, it would have been in even worse condition just because of the long voyage, not necessarily because of any untoward events during the trip; a very low price gained for a ship whose bottom was rotted out or was nearly or actually a wreck is understandable. On the other hand, it is not so believable that Norwegians, who had no lack of ships, would have embarked on a vessel that was in poor condition to begin with. Their ship, however, might have been nearly wrecked during heavy weather at sea and it might have barely made port at Rouen. But unless it had been, a ship in poor condition would have been more likely to be Icelandic than Norwegian.

It appears that the ship and its cargo were confiscated and sold, but there is no way of knowning exactly why. We do know that Duke Richard IV of Normandy, who was also King Richard I of England, was hard pressed for revenue during much of his reign, largely because of his numerous military campaigns. One of them, lasting from 1194 until his death in 1199, broken only by a temporary truce for much of 1198, was a costly defense of Normandy itself against Philip II of France. To pay for his unusually large expenditures, Richard had greatly increased his revenues from loans, tallages, and fines.[63] Perhaps therefore almost any excuse would have sufficed to confiscate this ship and its cargo, as a means of helping to increase ducal revenue during this difficult time.

Since the ship appears to have been a wreck, or nearly one, when it arrived at Rouen, perhaps the vessel and its cargo were confiscated as flotsam and jetsam. Or perhaps the reason for it was related to a commercial privilege granted to Rouen merchants by Richard's father, Henry II: they had the right to trade everywhere in England without the payment of any toll.[64] In return, there may have been certain prohibitions for foreign vessels, such as this "Icelandic ship," from making port at Rouen, in order to encourage those ships to come to port across the Channel instead where their arrival could benefit English merchants. But regardless of the reason for the confiscation, Norwegian merchants could be expected to be more familiar than Icelanders with regulations affecting trade in Normandy because they previously would have come there more often. Thus they would have done whatever possible to avoid confiscation, even to the extent of avoiding Rouen on this trip altogether, if at all feasible. From this point of view too, then, there is a greater likelihood that the ship was actually Icelandic.

Whether this ship in Rouen was Icelandic or Norwegian cannot alter what must have been the basic nature of Icelandic trade with Normandy or other parts of France. If the ship was Norwegian, it provides an example of Norwegian mediation; if it was Icelandic, the direct trade was only an isolated exception.[65]

GERMANY AND FRISIA

Of the total number of coins deposited about 1012 at Gaulverjabær in southern Iceland, the largest coin hoard yet found on the island, 161 were minted in the Holy Roman Empire. Of this number, 107 were from Saxony and 12 from Frisia. These coins may well have been Viking loot gathered first in Denmark, then seized by an Icelander who brought them home.[66] But in the unlikely event that at least the coins from the Empire represented trade, they must have been the outcome of only indirect contact, for the literary evidence suggests that there was hardly any direct commerce between Iceland and either Germany or Frisia during the Commonwealth.

One German merchant is known to have come to Iceland before 1264.[67] He was Thangbrand, son of Count Vilbaldus (Willibald) of Saxony, and he arrived at Gautavík in eastern Iceland about 997.[68] Although Thangbrand was a merchant by profession, his primary purpose for coming to Iceland was not commercial. In fact almost as soon as he arrived on the island, as though to divest himself of any taint of commerce, he turned over for marketing what goods he had brought along to an Icelander, Hall-Sítha. Thangbrand had been sent to Iceland by the king of Norway, Óláf Tryggvason, to convince the islanders that they should adopt Christianity and renounce their paganism. Not only was trade less than incidental to Thangbrand's main purpose for coming to Iceland, but it is quite likely that he left for his destination not from his native Saxony but from Norway.

For their part, Icelanders were not unfamiliar with Germany. Those who are known to have traveled there went, however, not for commercial profits but for religious benefits. Germany lay on an important pilgrimage route for Icelanders, a fact substantiated by Nikolás Bergthórsson when he wrote, about 1155, a guidebook for Icelandic pilgrims.[69] To be sure, even before Nikolás pointed the way, Icelanders had realized the importance of the route, to judge from a register of the monastery at Reichenau which, dating from about 1100, listed thirty-eight names under the heading "Hislant Terra."[70] In addition, because the archbishopric of Hamburg-Bremen was in charge of Icelandic ecclesiastical affairs until 1104, the first two bishops of Skálaholt, Ísleif Gizurarson and his son Gizur, went there to be consecrated during the second half of the eleventh century; and even before he became bishop, Ísleif was said to have studied at Herford.[71]

As in the case of Icelandic visitors to France, the possibility that these pilgrims and prelates may have exercised an influence on trade cannot be totally discounted. They may have brought Icelandic products with them to either sell or present as gifts while in Germany.[72] Such Icelandic goods may have created, to some extent, a desire for more. Besides, upon returning home, Icelanders, with tales of their experiences, may have encouraged Icelandic merchants to travel to Germany for specifically commercial purposes or at least may have created a desire for German products in Iceland.

As far as Frisia is concerned, there are two accounts telling of voyages from there to Iceland. Writing about 1075, Adam of Bremen says that some Frisians sailed to Iceland and beyond; they encountered difficulties at sea, landed on an island, stole valuables, were chased away by giants and dogs, and finally somehow got to Bremen.[73] The time of this voyages has been set at sometime between 1035 and 1045.[74] Adam gives no reason in his account for the voyage, nor does he make clear whether the adventurers were supposed to have landed on Iceland or some other island. No accurate information concerning Iceland is noted in this account; instead the supernatural tales included in the description of the trip raise doubts concerning the authenticity of any of the events. If a voyage to Iceland or elsewhere did occur, the tales lead one to suppose that the return trip actually was not made, or at least that the voyagers gained no sure knowledge of Iceland or another island while they were there. The unrealistic elements also suggest that there were virtually no other voyages to Iceland or someplace else when more accurate knowledge might have been obtained. Indeed, Adam does not record that the journey was repeated.

Nevertheless an Old High German poem, "Merigarto," like Adam's work written during the late eleventh century, also mentions an apparent Frisian trip to Iceland. The poet states that he met a priest in Utrecht named Reginbert who had visited Iceland. Reginbert said that the island had sufficient grain and wine, but trees were so rare that a stock of firewood costs a penny, and the ocean surrounding the island was flammable ice as hard as stone.[75] Because the date of the poem's composition is roughly of the same period as Adam's work, it is possible that Reginbert's voyage was the very one Adam was thinking of. If it was a separate trip, either Adam did not know of it or it took place after Adam wrote his account. In any case, this report is more illuminating than Adam's. Evidently trade was of interest to the voyagers, otherwise "sufficient" grain and wine, two products which Frisian merchants surely would wish to sell to Icelanders, and which they might acquire from Germany, would not have been so prominently mentioned in the poem. The correct observation that there was a lack of wood on Iceland similarly indicates an interest in goods that might be sold to the islanders. This poem, while furnishing more detail than Adam's account, and while it therefore is a more convincing piece of evidence, nevertheless contains great inaccuracies. The burning ice can be explained partially as a deposit of sulphur; but still less easy to justify is the "sufficient" grain and wine, for grain at least was one of the products most necessary to be imported to Iceland. Therefore, if the voyage in fact did occur, it must have taken place just at a time when grain and wine had been brought to Iceland by other merchants, probably Norwegians or Icelanders themselves. In addition, the voyagers could not have had any prior knowledge of conditions on Iceland, otherwise they would have known that these goods had to be imported from abroad. This voyage too probably must not have been preceded by earlier ones.

Although Adam's account and that of Reginbert are both notably weak and inaccurate, the fact that their two reports, dating from approximately the same period and describing events which occurred at about the same time, are independent of each other in itself does lend a degree of credibility to the voyage or voyages they describe. But even if some Frisians went to Iceland during the mid-eleventh century, there is no evidence that any of their countrymen had direct contact with Iceland afterward;[76] nor is there any definite proof that Icelanders went to Frisia for any commercial purpose during the entire period of the Commonwealth.[77]

Thangbrand's trip to Iceland, the only recorded one of an inhabitant of the Holy Roman Empire before about 1012 when the 161 coins minted there were deposited at Gaulverjabær, surely cannot account for the deposit of such a large number of coins commercially gained, even had his trip been primarily for trade. Indeed, even if the date of the hoard were a century later, neither Icelandic pilgrims and prelates returning from Germany nor the two admittedly suspicious reports of trips to Iceland by Frisians would adequately explain the presence of the coins. If they were not the result of a Viking raid by an Icelander but were acquired instead by trade, how then can their presence be explained?

Compared with Iceland, a very large number of coins from the Empire have been found in Norway. Of the 2,500 found there, most date from the eleventh century and come especially from Saxony and Frisia.[78] Probably most of those eleventh-century coins are evidence of commerce rather than of raids, especially in view of the extensive general trade of Norway, Germany, and especially Frisia during the period.[79] Because of imperial-Norwegian trade, direct commerce between the Empire and Iceland was not necessary, for Norway once again could act as intermediary. The coins from the Holy Roman Empire found at Gaulverjabær, if they were the result of trade, probably would have reached Iceland, then, via Norway.[80]

THE SOUTHERN BALTIC, RUSSIA, AND BYZANTIUM

Despite Iceland's geographical remoteness to the Baltic southern shore, Russia, and Byzantium, it may have had some commercial acquaintance with these areas. The evidence supporting such an association is, however, meager.

According to *Fóstbrœthra saga*, an Icelander in the early eleventh century went on a trading expedition to the "Land of the Wends" on the southern Baltic coast. Before going there he sailed to Norway. He may have made his expedition, therefore, in the company of more knowledgeable Norwegian merchants. In spite of the fact that merchants generally were not particularly welcome there at the time, the Icelander returned to Reykjahólar in Iceland a wealthy man two years later,[81] apparently because of his commercial success in "Wendland" despite the adverse circumstances.

There is no explicit documentary indication that Icelanders, as such, actually traded with Russia. There are suggestions though that some commerce may have taken place. A Norwegian trader, Björn Skútathar-Skeggjason, who later settled in Iceland, was nicknamed, *Landnámabók* says, "Fur-Björn" because of his frequent trips to Novgorod where he specialized in trading furs. *Thórthar saga hrethu* adds that these furs were grayskin (squirrel), beaver, and sable.[82] Fur-Björn was not technically an Icelandic merchant, for his activities in the east were suspended before he settled in Iceland during the late ninth or early tenth century. His example, noteworthy enough to be recorded in *Landnámabók*, however, may have been followed later by other Icelanders who might have traded in Russia after hearing of his exploits there. For this reason and because of the circumstances of their visits, certain Icelanders who are known to have gone to Russia, though they are not specifically said to have traded, might have done so.

Thorsteinn Geirnefjufóstri is said to have been in Novgorod before he started on some Viking forays one spring in the tenth century. He was visited by another Viking, Úlfhethinn, who had been to Ireland. In the middle of the summer, in preparation for an expedition, they apparently combined their resources of three ships and crews well equipped with clothing and weapons.[83] To provide his share of the equipment, Thorsteinn may have engaged in trade in Novgorod the previous winter. Another example of an Icelander who may have gone to Russia to trade was Björn Arngeirsson. At the beginning of the eleventh century he supposedly went to Norway and then proceeded to Russia in the company of Norwegian merchants.[84] Either he was not prosperous, since he did not travel on a ship of his own, or he was unfamiliar with the route to be taken; in any case his association with these traders of Norway makes one suspect that he traded also. A final example is Barthi Guthmundarson. Unlike Björn Arngeirsson, Barthi is stated to have bought a ship in Iceland about 1020, then to have gone to Russia where he joined the company of other Scandinavians, known as Varangians, who permanently lived there; he remained with them for some time.[85] It is possible that Barthi traded in Russia because he purchased a ship and associated with Russo-Scandinavians but not apparently as a partner in any Viking forays.

As in the case of Russia, there is no proof that any Icelandic trade existed with Byzantium. One Icelander, Sigurth Oddsson, however, was nicknamed "the Greek" because he had traveled to the Byzantine Empire. When he returned to Iceland about 1217, he brought back with him from Constantinople a sword named Mail-Biter.[86] Because a good sword was difficult to make and was a highly desirable article in Scandinavia, particularly rare in Iceland, it would have had a considerable value. Perhaps Sigurth was able to earn enough money from trade to purchase his sword; and because such swords were desirable at home, conceivably he brought back to Iceland other swords to sell at a profit.

How can this evidence, slender as it is, of Icelandic trade on the southern Baltic coast and possibly in Russia and Byzantium be explained? In the first place Iceland had several noncommercial points of contact with eastern Europe, contact that in turn may have prompted Icelanders to trade in these areas, encouraged by tales of wares and profits. Noncommercial links could be of various types. Religious contact is seen on the one hand by Icelandic pilgrims to the Holy Land who returned home by way of Byzantium and Russia,[87] and on the other by bishops from the Baltic area, Russia, or Byzantium who are said to have appeared in Iceland during the mid-eleventh century.[88] Military contact occurred when Icelanders joined the Varangian Guard of the Byzantine emperor, a group originally recruited from Scandinavians living in Russia.[89] And artistic contact may be seen in the panels of a church in northern Iceland upon which were carved a depiction of the Last Judgment and which possibly show the influence of Byzantine art.[90]

A second general explanation for the presence of Icelandic traders in eastern Europe is furnished by the strong commercial ties that mainland Scandinavia had with the area.[91] Icelandic commercial contact with Norway, as well as some with Denmark and Sweden, may have prompted an Icelandic interest in the places where these other countries already had trade connections. Swedes had been the pioneers in this trade, establishing themselves in Russia as early as the eighth century, and perhaps before; in 860, 907, 911, and 945, Russo-Scandinavians, probably mostly of Swedish descent, gained commercial treaties with Constantinople.[92] Swedes were the leaders in the eastern trade, but Danes and Norwegians were also fairly active.[93] When Icelanders are said to have gone to "Wendland," Russia, and Byzantium, usually they went via Norway. Thus, as in the case of almost all of the places discussed in this chapter, Norway usually must have been the intermediary for trade between Iceland and these areas.[94]

PART THREE

The Course of
Icelandic Foreign Trade:
A Summary

CHAPTER SEVEN

Icelandic Foreign Trade, c. 870–1264

Between Iceland's settlement and its annexation by Norway, the strength of its foreign trade depended mainly upon the activity of its merchants, the demand for its exports abroad, and the ability of foreigners to provide its necessary imports. Foreign trade during the settlement period established many traits that were to last for centuries, and the lessons learned then were largely responsible for the commercial prosperity attained during the first century of the Commonwealth, more specifically, from about 930 until about 1022. After 1022 Icelanders became less active as merchants abroad; but the foreign market for their exports expanded and their supply of imports remained adequate until almost the end of the twelfth century. From about 1180 until the end of the Commonwealth, foreign markets were less able to provide Iceland with necessities and to absorb the island's products. A solution to the resulting economic hardship seemed to be for Icelanders to submit to annexation by Norway.

THE EARLY PERIOD: c. 870–c. 1022

When the first pioneers left their old home for their new one on Iceland, they must have had only a general idea of what to expect. From reports of the first explorers who preceded them, they might have known something of the island's size, climate, and

terrain. But because the explorers had been on the island too
briefly, the settlers could have only guessed at the average duration
of good summer weather and the rigor of typical winters, the full
extent of good pasturage and the feasibility of raising various crops.
They would have brought as many supplies on their ships as they
thought they would need for establishing a new Scandinavian
home, but lack of knowledge about their future life as well as
limitations of cargo space meant that additional goods would have
to be brought later. Soon after arrival, for instance, though some
found bog iron, smelted it, and fashioned ironware themselves,
even they would have to import essential pieces of hardware that
they could not make themselves. Or when some of the few, pre-
cious farm animals the settlers brought with them died during the
first unexpectedly hard winters, others to take their place would
have to be brought from overseas. And perhaps these pioneers
hoped they eventually could grow grain in enough quantity to
provide for all their needs, but it would become plain before much
time had passed that the climate was usually not suitable and that
what could be raised would be most inadequate. Balancing that
disappointment, though, the amount of pasture land suitable for
sheep as well as for other livestock might have exceeded the
expectations of many. As sheep multiplied, flourishing in an ideal
environment, woolens made from their fleeces, the islanders must
have hoped, would provide an increasing means for acquiring what
was needed from abroad.

The volume of Icelandic imports during the Age of Settlement, lasting from about 870 until about 930, would have been
unusually large relative to population. Then not only did such a
staple as grain have to be imported in large quantities, just as it
always would have to be, but also there was the need to supply the
new home with items that seldom or never would have to be
imported again such as major pieces of hardware and supplementary livestock. During this early age, however, Icelanders' sheep
had not yet grown numerous enough to provide all the woolens
needed in exchange for numerous imports. To make up the difference between what they needed from overseas and what woolens
from their own island they could use in trade, Icelanders would

have to rely upon any silver, gold, or other valuables they might have acquired as marauders or merchants before their settlement, or upon a few luxury wares such as arctic-fox skins or falcons that their island furnished. Lacking these, colonists would have to depend upon the charity of friends and relatives who had remained behind.

Icelanders of the time could not rely on others to bring necessities to their recently established and isolated colony. The passage to Iceland was still too new and untested to be hazarded by more than a few of their fellow Scandinavians, adept as they were as navigators, unless they too came as permanent settlers. Not many of them would be willing to chance loss of their cargoes, ships, or even lives just for the sake of obtaining a small amount of woolens, gold, or the occasional fur or falcon, especially when most of these could be obtained in more abundance from trade or pillage in areas that were safer to reach. Still less would others risk the voyage for providing only charity. Icelanders, who needed foreign goods far more than foreigners needed theirs, and who had gained at least a rudimentary knowledge of the seas surrounding their island on their original voyages of settlement, had to assume the responsibilities of trade themselves.

Since most of them had originally come from Norway, it was natural that they would first consider that country as a source for what they needed. Not only were ties of kinship numerous and still strong, and not only was the route reasonably well known, but also the recent émigrés would have known that their former home would be a good market for what woolens and other goods they had to exchange.

Trade of the settlement period must have been barely sufficient for the needs of the colonists, but it pointed the way to prosperity the following century. Once the influx of new settlers declined rapidly after about 930, sheep would increase at a much faster rate than the island's human population. These animals provided each household with ever more ample woolens to exchange for necessities, as long as the amount of pasturage owned was sufficient. Furthermore, now that the colony had attained some maturity, it needed to import fewer durable goods and far fewer replacements of livestock than when the settlement was still new. Relative to population, then, the need for imports generally decreased at the very time when the means for gaining them generally increased; the luxuries of a civilized life became affordable.

If ample woolens were to be exchanged for necessities and some luxuries, there had to be a market capable of absorbing the exports and providing the imports. During the century following 930 Norway was reasonably capable of doing both, just as during the settlement period. That Norway remained Iceland's best customer for woolens throughout the Commonwealth is one indirect indication that there was in insufficiency of them in the island's mother country, a shortage that is impossible to prove directly because there is only unreliable and very incomplete information regarding Norwegian land use and population throughout the whole medieval period. In return for various kinds of woven cloth and cloaks made of woolen tufts—but apparently only rarely if ever at this time the raw wool itself—as well as a certain amount of other Icelandic products including luxuries, Norway could furnish, among other things, timber and usually grain, the two most necessary Icelandic imports. The first Norway had in abundance, thereby accounting for sizable shipments back to timber-starved Iceland. Grain imports were much more of an absolute necessity for Icelanders, but unfortunately Norway was able to grow it mainly only in eastern valleys and in Trøndelag. In later years the amount produced in Norway would become insufficient even for its own needs, but between about 930 and about 1022 when the populations of both Iceland and Norway were smaller, Norway's own grain surpluses were probably sufficient for at least Iceland's minimum requirements.

During this early period, Icelandic merchants did not depend primarily upon that occupation for their livelihood. Trade was carried out more from motives of necessity than of profit. Of course, the two drives were interwoven, but the more or less direct barter methods of the time emphasized the aim of immediately fulfilling needs and desires. On-the-spot acquisition of goods through barter was particularly important for an Icelander in his trade with Norway or with any other country. He would leave Iceland, isolated from Norway and the rest of Europe by considerable miles of often unpredictable waters, mainly because he had to, and if he arrived at his destination safely he would drive the best possible bargain in an exchange of goods. But it was the exchange itself, not the bargain or profit, that would be the more important. From the standpoint of need, an Icelander had to trade with other countries not just to gain imports, but also to dispose of his woolen surpluses. Because sheep were raised all over the island, local demand for woolens was very low; yet every year the sheep produced a new coat of wool to be made into cloth which, though it could be stored, eventually had to be sold abroad before the stockpiles became overwhelming.

Not all Icelanders had the need to get rid of woolens, because the amount of surpluses varied. Usually only when they had sufficient woolens and other wares to warrant trips abroad to fetch the foreign goods personally would they travel the wide seas to trade. Those who held the largest pieces of land, capable of supporting a large number of sheep, were most likely to have the largest surpluses to exchange abroad. These men, usually chieftains or members of their families, also were most likely to at least share the ownership of a vessel, one that was of the original settlement fleet that had been kept in good repair or had been purchased more recently with their abundant woolens. Icelandic commercial law also favored these men because they were mainly responsible for shaping it. Yet their involvement in Icelandic government and politics, not to speak of management of their lands and wealth, often would prevent them from devoting a great deal of time to commerce. Those who were not of this class were perhaps generally more free of the domestic cares that sometimes prevented chieftains and members of their families from leaving home, but also these men usually had less land on which to raise their sheep, hence their means for trading abroad was generally less. Nevertheless if they owned medium-sized parcels of land, they could eventually acquire a significant amount of surplus woolens for foreign sale, generally taking passage on someone else's ship as crewmen and being alloted their requisite shares of the cargo space. Those who possessed small amounts of land and sheep rarely if ever would be able to accumulate enough of a woolen surplus to warrant a voyage abroad.

The smallest landowners and the owners of large- and medium-sized parcels of land, during the intervals when they were not traveling overseas themselves, would form a body of customers for an Icelander who returned home with foreign goods his family personally did not need. The trader could accept in exchange for those imports such Icelandic products as cattle, oxen, horses, and other articles for his domestic use. Or he could accept some woolens to be added to his own on his next trading voyage. The large landowner who was a trader would be more likely to profit by exchanging his foreign wares in this way than the one holding a medium-sized parcel because he probably would have produced more woolens than were necessary for acquiring in Norway only the goods he personally needed.

Since the Icelandic economy was more productive during this period than the Age of Settlement, and since probably Icelandic merchants sometimes could not satisfy all the desires of their homeland for imports, more Norwegians came to Iceland than before, especially because the route would have become better known to them from the reports of Icelanders and from a few of their adventurous fellow countrymen. But participation in the trade by Norwegians would be limited because they as yet did not have a great need for it. As useful as Icelandic woolens were to them, they were not essential. Also, Norwegians had a significant local demand for their grain and their timber could be left standing until needed, so they did not feel an urgency to sell these products. Less compelling than that of need because they, like Icelanders, were not professional merchants most of this time, would be the desire to make profits, the best of which would come from the commodities in great demand that they produced themselves. Grain was the product fetching the highest return, and so when Norwegians did not sell it to Icelanders in Norway, it must have formed the most substantial part of their cargoes when they came to Iceland. Timber, because it was much less essential to Icelanders and bulkier to carry, was a less rewarding cargo. Luxury products would bring a high return but few Norwegians had them to sell and the Icelandic demand for them was limited.

Thus during this early period Icelanders played the principal role in the Icelandic-Norwegian trade. The Icelandic sagas dealing with the period c. 930–c. 1030 reflect, however unreliably, the degree of Icelandic participation in the trade: they mention approximately 100 Icelandic ships, all presumably engaged in trade, but only 47 Norwegian vessels that came to Iceland.[1]

Icelanders had been fortunate in finding Norway so satisfactory a trading partner during the century following the Age of Settlement. Yet, the very success of that trade also could lead to an unfortunate dependence. If unusually bad weather greatly reduced Norway's grain harvests, Norwegians might suffer from reduced supplies, but Icelanders, if they had no other source for grain than Norway, might undergo utmost deprivation with hardly any at all. Then too, there was the danger that at times all Icelandic merchants might be forbidden from leaving Norway for reasons of state. When Iceland was still being settled, King Harald the Fairhaired (c. 860–c. 933), fearing that his country would become depopulated, forbade anyone to leave the country for Iceland. This prohibition not only affected would-be settlers, but it must have caused extreme hardship for those who were already in Iceland because they were effectively cut off from their Norwegian lifeline at a time when they especially needed supplies. Necessary imports could not be brought by new settlers, and Icelanders could not go back to Norway for them with any assurance that they would be able to leave the country again. After King Harald made his prohibition, he reconsidered and replaced it with a fluctuating toll paid by those leaving Norway. The new colony had been lucky, but Icelanders still might fear that another Norwegian king would willfully lay another ban on communication between the two lands. That possibility came true about 999 when King Óláf Tryggvason, in an effort to demand an acceptance of Christianity, forbade Icelanders from returning to their island: Icelanders converted the following year. Although bans on travel are known to have occurred only once during the settlement period and once during the century thereafter, the threat always existed. This threat would have been almost as disturbing as the reality, and it, combined with the possibility of Norwegian crop failure, encouraged Icelanders to seek alternate lands for trade.

The Faeroes, Shetlands, and Greenland (once it was settled about 986) could not be considered as even temporary suppliers of grain or other useful products, for they relied upon much the same imports as Iceland. Other places that might have grain to spare might be dangerous places for Icelandic traders to visit. Unsettled political conditions in Ireland, particularly before 1014, meant an Icelandic ship might be confiscated, as is said to have almost happened during the tenth century. Icelanders would mainly have come to Ireland during this time only when the lure of Viking luxuries there caused the risks to seem worthwhile. Likewise in Denmark it must have been the lack of a commercial understanding that reportedly caused an Icelandic cargo to be confiscated about 970, resulting in much ill feeling between Icelanders and Danes. Aloofness of Hebrideans from the Scandinavian world that was quite evident later suggests that Icelandic trade there was insecure even during the tenth and early eleventh centuries. Sweden, the Orkneys, and Scandinavian settlements on the Continent and in England remained as prospects, although they offered Icelanders no certain commercial privileges. Untoward incidents for Iceland's merchants, however, are never known to have occurred in England and the Orkneys, nor was there ever a suggestion that they might, and so they must have been fairly well received in these places. The Orkneys were closer to Iceland, but England had more ample supplies of grain and other foodstuffs such as honey, as well as access to wine and various luxuries. Because of this greater variety and abundance of products that Icelanders wanted, more of them came to England than to the Orkneys during these years before 1022.

Although during the early period Icelanders relied mainly on only the Orkneys and England as suppliers of grain and other products when Norway's own supplies were inadequate or inaccessible, all of the non-Norwegian countries mentioned benefited Iceland's foreign trade. None of them competed with Iceland to any extent in supplying woolens to Norway. Woolens of Greenland, the Faeroes, Shetlands, Orkneys, and probably the Hebrides were comparable to those of Iceland, but their supplies, compared with Iceland's, were negligible. Similar cloth of Swedish or Danish manufacture probably would not find its way to Norway in any significant quantity either, because Norway could offer little in return that Denmark or Sweden wanted. Ireland, like Denmark and Sweden, seems to have manufactured mostly ordinary cloth for domestic use of a quality that probably would have been similar to Iceland's, but Ireland's trade with Norway was mainly in luxury goods until the eleventh century and afterward even that trade must have greatly declined because by then England provided a better trading partner for both Ireland and Norway. After the beginning of the eleventh century England provided a substantial market for Norway's dried fish and other products in return for grain, fine cloth, and other goods. But English fine cloth, though it eventually came to Norway in some amount, was not competitive with the more ordinary type from Iceland. Thus Iceland's main export product, upon which it relied so greatly for Norwegian imports, was safeguarded from foreign competition during this period.

Icelandic trade was also encouraged because merchants from these non-Norwegian countries would not come to Iceland in appreciable numbers. Even if the route to Iceland were equally well known by all of them, and if they all could count on a friendly reception once they arrived, Iceland would have little to offer these merchants, apart from luxuries upon which no strong, regular commerce could be based. Icelandic cloth was hardly attractive to merchants who still had a sufficiency of ordinary cloth in their own lands.

Finally, Iceland derived some economic benefit by acting for a while as commercial intermediary between Greenland and Norway. The foreign trade of the Greenlanders themselves had begun to decline sharply after the 1020s, and even before then it had never been strong. Probably Norwegian merchants did not begin traveling to the island until the second half of the eleventh century, and yet Greenlanders badly needed foreign goods and could pay for them with their ample luxuries, especially walrus ivory. A few enterprising Icelanders, familiar with the route to Greenland, could thus make good profits by acting as exchange agents for Norwegian foodstuffs in Greenland and Greenlandic luxuries in Norway.

These mainly negative commercial advantages, however, were benefits, after all, only so long as Iceland continued its trade with Norway. And the positive advantages of these non-Norwegian places were limited. Even with England and the Orkneys—which were reasonably nearby, where grain and other products Icelanders needed were available, and where the threat that their ships would be confiscated did not seem great—Icelanders could not establish a permanent trade to replace or even to significantly supplement that with Norway. The Orkneys had neither a strong need for Icelandic woolens nor the grain surpluses to keep the much larger population of Iceland regularly supplied. And not until after the beginning of the eleventh century would England become an important manufacturer of fine cloth; before then, like the Orkneys, it had little need for Iceland's ordinary woolens. It was clear that Icelanders had little choice but to be content with Norway as their main trading partner.

Icelandic merchants, then, had to make their trade with Norway as secure as possible. They would not be able to do much about safeguarding Norway's ability to always have harvests ample enough to provide them with grain and other foods, or even much about making sure that Norwegians would always want their woolens, but the threat that the Norwegian king might prevent them from leaving Norway might be negotiated. The opportunity came in or about 1022 when the king of Norway, St. Óláf, was amenable to an agreement. Among other privileges, Icelanders now were promised always to be free to leave Norway if that country was not at war. Obligations of serving Norway during wartime and of paying a toll upon entering the country seemed to be fair in return for benefits given to them. In fact, since the toll was now payable at a rate somewhat below what it usually had been before when leaving the country, and since it was now fixed rather than flexible, even this obligation had certain benefits. Nor, in view of their rights in Norway, could Icelanders complain about allowing Norwegians in Iceland much the same rights as themselves, especially because even the king would not be allowed any special consideration in prosecuting a case.

When Icelanders made this agreement they might well have felt triumphant, overcoming as they did at least one of the major difficulties that had marked their previous trade with Norway. Yet even then or soon afterward their participation in the trade would begin to decline and that of Norwegians to advance. Thus, Norwegians were to become the true beneficiaries of the agreement.

THE MIDDLE PERIOD: c. 1022–c. 1180

As Icelanders became less active as merchants trading abroad and yielded their dominance in the trade to Norwegian merchants, they also entrusted most of the responsibility of their vital trade to these Norwegians. When Icelanders did this, not just their economic health, but also their political independence was endangered. These threats were manifested during the final decades of the Commonwealth. During this middle period the dangers of commercial dependence were muted because Norwegian monarchs were often diverted by political difficulties in their own country and because no insurmountable economic problems prevented Icelandic foreign trade from being well maintained by Norwegian merchants.

One reason Icelanders became less active in foreign trade during the earlier eleventh century was that investment opportunities at home were growing more attractive. Though Icelanders in the early period had acted as merchants mainly because of their own needs, they might have obtained more foreign products than they could directly use themselves, particularly if they took a large amount of woolens overseas. They therefore would have desired to invest those excess foreign goods for future profit. But at that time there had been significant disadvantages to the available investments. An Icelander could have exchanged his surplus imports for woolens to be added to his cargo for his next trip abroad, but since he already had obtained more foreign goods than he needed, he probably had a large enough woolen surplus of his own for trading overseas, particularly if he was a large landowner. Instead, the

Icelander might have lent either imports he did not need himself, such as farm equipment, or extra domestic products, such as livestock that he had acquired from imports, in return for a payment of annual interest. But since silver was mainly used for abstract reckoning of values rather than actually spent for transactions—at least from the latter tenth century onward—this return was often paid in woolens, and so this form of interest had the same disadvantages as extra woolens obtained more directly. A better investment for the Icelander's accumulated surpluses might have been more land on which to raise more sheep; at least the additional woolens he then obtained would be acquired at the lowest possible cost. But the disadvantage of this investment was a shortage of economical labor. If the Icelander already had a sizable amount of land, most of the work had to be done by thralls. Free laborers, being employed only when needed and working adequately in order to keep their jobs, were preferable, but such men were hard to find as long as almost all had land of their own, as was usually the case when land was still abundant and cheap. The disadvantages of these major investments had strongly deterred Icelandic participation in trade during the early period.

Around the beginning of the eleventh century, land probably became a better investment because the shortage of free labor would have grown less extreme as the population expanded. Most increasing families would not be able to easily support themselves by acquiring more farmland because after about 1000 it was rapidly becoming limited and expensive. Previously the small landowner usually found the produce from his farm scarcely more than adequate for his family's needs. As population increased, most of those holding medium-sized parcels were in much the same position. Lacking sizable surpluses, even saved over a prolonged period, the small landowner had not previously engaged in foreign trade; the same became true now for those holding somewhat more land. As greater demand increased the price of land, neither group had the means to buy more: they lacked either enough surplus domestic products or profits derived from trade. As their holdings grew increasingly inadequate to feed their growing families, some Icelanders had to seek employment elsewhere to support themselves. And some of these poor families would deplete their already small landholdings by succumbing to the temptation of selling part of their land for high prices. This would be only a temporary stopgap, however, and it would cause their descendants to feel the pinch of poverty even more strongly than they. The owners of extensive lands, on the other hand, better able to support their growing families on the lands they already held, with sizable surpluses of their own products, and the means of increasing their wealth by occasionally trading abroad, would be able to afford to buy expensive additional land. Furthermore, investment in more land would seem especially attractive to them now that nonslave labor recruited from poor families could be used. But just as the increasing poverty of owners of medium-sized parcels caused them to trade abroad much less often than before, now the acquisition of greater amounts of land by these wealthy men also would further hinder them from engaging in foreign trade: their responsibilities at home would increase with every additional acre they gained. Though the beginning of these effects of rising population might have started soon after 1000, it would take time for the consequences to become fully developed. Only during the last half century of the Commonwealth did the process lead to a great differentiation between a few rich and numerous poor.

The process might have taken even longer to reach this end had Norwegians not become more active in the Iceland trade. Since Icelanders needed certain vital imports, large landowners might have hesitated investing in more land even when free labor became more abundant had they not been sure the Norwegians would bring essential imports to them. If already high prices for acreage had not been driven up further by the rich, smaller landowners might have hesitated from selling their lands, especially while their families were growing larger. Or alternately, if smaller landowners sold part of their holdings to the wealthy, they might have used that capital for establishing as merchants at least some of their family members, rather than allow them to work as laborers. These men might have acted as agents for the wealthy—selling their woolens abroad, bringing back imports for them, and keeping part of the profits for themselves. But the increased activity of Norwegians provided more and more of the imports Icelanders needed, thereby encouraging a passiveness in trade on the part of Icelanders of all classes.

As in Iceland, population growth in Norway had a profound effect on its social and economic development. The piracy and plunder, trade and colonization of new lands that were the characteristics of the Viking Age were largely caused, at least in the case of Norway, by overpopulation at home accompanied by scarcity of land, especially in the western fjord districts of the country. Lacking enough land to farm, a good living could be made ransacking or exacting tribute abroad, but sooner or later the basic desire of acquiring new land gained the upper hand over these less savory occupations. Sometimes new land was gained easily, as was the case with Iceland and other sparsely inhabited or desolate North Atlantic islands; if need be, as with the more desirable agricultural lands in Ireland, England, and France, it was gained by conquest. About a century and a half after the beginning of the Viking Age, however, colonization as well as attacks quickly waned. By about 950 the established settlements abroad were no longer capable of absorbing many more immigrants. Furthermore, founding new settlements, whether by occupation of uninhabited lands or by conquest of others, was no longer practicable. Only Greenland would remain for the taking, but it was so remote and its habitable land so limited that it would not be of much use to Norwegians. Raids could not be carried out with as much ease as before because, honed by decades of Viking attacks, foreign defenses were sharpened, sometimes helped by older generations of Viking settlers. Even concerted Norwegian attempts to conquer new territory were much more of a gamble now that strong native armies were about to overtake old Scandinavian settlements in England and, sixty years later, in Ireland.

Norwegian population continued to expand after 950, but without as many of the earlier means of relieving the pressure. By the time forty years had passed, and perhaps two more generations, parts of Norway already may have become overpopulated again; if so, Óláf Tryggvason's attacks against England during the early

990s, before he became king of Norway, might have been at least partly caused by a desire to win some land for excess Norwegians. He was diverted by taking the Norwegian throne, but not many years later his Danish counterpart, Sveinn Forkbeard, succeeded in gaining the whole English kingdom. After Sveinn's descendants died out there and after the death of the last Anglo-Saxon king in 1066, a Norwegian monarch tried his hand at conquering England. Norway's population must have grown considerably during the previous century, so King Harald the Harsh-Ruler might have viewed England as a long-lasting refuge for his land-hungry subjects. But this last attempt to found a new Norwegian settlement ended in failure when Harald was killed at Stamford Bridge.

Though opportunities for colonization and pillage became much more limited after 950, trade was a solution to overpopulation that Norwegian Vikings had used earlier and that could be practiced even more assiduously. Trade in luxuries must have been accented at first, but beginning about 1050 the more important trade in necessities would have become more pronounced as Norwegians, not having been able to move away with ease during the previous century, became less able to supply all of their own agricultural needs.[2]

The pressures of overpopulation in Norway caused much the same results as it did in Iceland. There was a gradual increase in the size of individual land holdings—particularly those able to produce grain—owned by men who were already wealthy, with a corresponding decline in the size of lands owned by others. Large landowners in Norway often could not spare the time to trade abroad themselves, but the extra produce of their estates as well as other products gained from outside revenues gave them ample means for acquiring imports. Unlike Icelanders, however, many from families of medium and perhaps small landholdings, finding difficulty in making a living by farming, acted as transfer agents between the large landowners and foreign markets, depending thereby upon trade for at least part of their livelihood. Several reasons can be cited to account for the appearance of this merchant class in Norway, a class which did not develop in Iceland even though Icelanders found themselves in similar circumstances.

Merchants from more southerly parts of Europe, especially England, did not begin coming to Norway in appreciable numbers until the late eleventh and twelfth centuries, yet a Norwegian need for supplementary imports to supply an increasing population began to be felt before: Norwegians not only had to fetch all or most of those goods themselves, but they at first acted largely without competition. When Iceland grew short of usable land, those inhabitants who found themselves without adequate means to be independent farmers could not become part-time merchants as agents for the rich because they could not withstand competition from Norwegians who already engaged in trade to Iceland and were thus quite able to take over the major responsibility for it. Because Norway's population was larger than Iceland's, when a Norwegian need for gaining supplementary imports appeared, it could not be substantially satisfied by relatively few rich men, as had been the case with Iceland; Norway needed a significant body of men devoting a large part of their time to trade. Also, the development of a merchant class in Norway was aided by proximity to England and the Continent and by an abundance of timber for ships, both of which Iceland lacked.

Norway also had monarchs who actively encouraged the commercial activities of their subjects. Óláf Tryggvason did this at least indirectly. According to tradition soon before 1000 he established the town of Nidaros, situated just south of Hålogaland where the main fisheries of the kingdom were to be found and in one of the two main grain-growing areas of the country. The domestic and foreign needs of the administrative, military, and religious personnel of the town had to be provided for, a duty calling for a sizable number of at least part-time merchants. More importantly, the very location of the town furthered its commercial nature: directly to the west of the area's fertile grain fields lay Iceland, where much of that grain would have to be sent. Eventually, when Norway had to import supplementary grain as well as other products from places to the south for itself and for Iceland, the fish that was mostly used in exchange lay in convenient access to the town. Foreign commerce centered on Nidaros and provision for the needs of the town's populace could provide a good living to Norwegians as merchants.

More directly than his predecessor, St. Óláf Haraldsson promoted the interests of Norwegian traders in two important ways
when making his agreement with the Icelanders about 1022. By
insisting that Norwegians visiting Iceland be given the same
treatment as Icelanders themselves, he assured Norwegian traders
that their business on the island would not be hampered by unfair
Icelandic practices, legal or otherwise. The king also encouraged
Norwegian merchants by apparently giving them a financial privilege which allowed them to more advantageously trade with Iceland than Icelanders themselves. Before the agreement, a toll was
charged for everyone leaving Norway, including, of course, both
Norwegians and Icelanders. Now this arrangement was changed,
so that the toll was paid on entering Norway, not leaving it; it
seems that only Icelanders had to pay it, not Norwegians, because a
few years after the agreement, in the early 1030s, King Sveinn
Knútsson reinstituted the payment of the toll for Norwegians
leaving the country. Though it lasted only a short time, exemption
from this payment probably was responsible for a sharp increase of
merchants going to Iceland. In any case, by the time Sveinn re-
scinded it, he or his advisers must have thought that the volume of
Norwegian trade was already large enough to continue without
this inducement, yielding a significant addition to royal income.
Sveinn or his advisers must have been right, because his action
remained in effect even though many of his other unpopular laws
were eventually dispensed with.

Conditions were ripe during the early eleventh century not
only for the emergence of a Norwegian merchant class, but also, as
the rapid success of the exemption privilege of St. Óláf's agreement
helps to show, for a much stronger Norwegian participation in the
trade with Iceland than was possible before. For those Norwegians
who derived a major part of their living from commerce, the profits
to be gained from the Iceland trade were especially appealing;
unlike earlier, they thus were finding necessity alone less compelling as a motive for trade. Before the early eleventh century, men
who owned grain fields that were too small to produce surpluses
worthy of a voyage to Iceland had been willing to sell their small
excesses to Icelanders who had to come to Norway to collect the
grain themselves. Now, as more grain-producing land was being

accumulated by relatively few men, Icelanders would have more difficulty in finding small farmers willing to sell them grain, but, correspondingly, commercial agents of large landowners with substantial surpluses to sell would be able to trade grain in Iceland more frequently. Before, Icelandic commercial activity had deterred Norwegians from going to Iceland to trade. Now Icelandic competition was abating, not just because Icelanders were finding more difficulty procuring grain in Norway, but because of changed situations within Iceland. Taken as a whole, these overlapping changes must have greatly accelerated Norwegian participation in the Iceland trade during the eleventh century.

Before the early eleventh century Norway might have occasionally been short of grain for its own needs and would have had to import some additional amounts from more southerly lands for this reason alone. But once the country had assumed a large responsibility, and later on almost the whole of it, for providing grain as well as other goods to Iceland, Norway's trade with other countries had to become all the more frequent. Norwegian trade with Iceland also promoted trade with more southerly countries because returns from sales of imports to Iceland were realized primarily in woolens, all of which Norway, even with its expanding population, could not absorb itself. Of the possible trading partners that would be suitable for Norway's own needs and those resulting from its Icelandic commerce, England seemed to be most appropriate. Because of its urban development during the eleventh century and later, England had a large market for the dried fish that Norway could offer in return for grain and other supplies it needed. And England was particularly attractive during the eleventh century and later because it offered a good market for the ordinary woolens Norwegians were collecting from Iceland: England's own professional weavers mainly produced cloth that was too expensive for poor townsmen; common English cloth was not always available. Thus trade with England, which had both sufficient grain to sell Norwegians and a demand for excess Icelandic woolens, was the most important counterbalance to Norway's Iceland trade.

The increased volume of Norwegian foreign trade during the

eleventh century, especially with Iceland and England, was conducive to the development of Bergen, founded about 1075. Decently situated for the Iceland trade and better placed than Nidaros for the England trade, this new center rapidly became the most populous of Norwegian cities, eventually surpassing Nidaros in commercial importance, though the older city retained significance as a governmental and ecclesiastical center. The eastern towns of Oslo, Tønsberg, Sarpsborg, and Konungahella (mod.: Kungälv), almost all founded or promoted by various monarchs in the eleventh and twelfth centuries, were useful as defenses against Sweden and Denmark or as ecclesiastical centers, but by contrast to Bergen, they were of only secondary commercial significance. Their location, advantageous for trade with Denmark, Sweden, the northeastern Holy Roman Empire, and the eastern Baltic, was not convenient for the more important trade with Iceland and England.

While Norwegian urbanization in general encouraged Norwegian trade, it had deleterious effects as well. Because the towns were inhabited by considerable numbers of semiprofessional Norwegian merchants, royal officials and administrators, clergy, and some military—men who often were not raising sheep or crops themselves—these cities created an extra measure of demand for woolens and other goods from Iceland and foodstuffs, especially grain, from England and elsewhere. Also, the towns, particularly Bergen, provided convenient bodies of customers for merchants traveling from more southerly parts of Europe, such as England, who wanted to exchange their goods for Norwegian, Icelandic, or other products more advantageously than they could at home. While the visits of these foreign merchants who brought grain and other useful imports were helpful to Norway as a whole, their growing presence also deprived some Norwegian merchants of the profits that they would have gained by taking their goods to such a place as England themselves. But that loss could have more than compensatory rewards. More English merchants in Norway meant that correspondingly more Norwegians were freed from the necessity of providing their country with vital goods; they could devote more of their energy to trade with Iceland, particularly attractive to them because it offered undoubtedly greater profits than could ever be gained by trading with England: unlike the English trade, Norwegians by the twelfth century were unhampered by much competition from native merchants and by virtually none from other foreign merchants who seldom if ever went to that island.

Once Norwegians were able to dominate the Icelandic trade,[3] it would have been very difficult for the few Icelanders who still had the inclination and means to trade abroad to do so in an independent manner. The far larger numbers of Norwegians engaged not only in the Iceland trade but also in commerce elsewhere, their greater familiarity with the vagaries of foreign markets, their privileges in those markets gained by frequent visits, and their far greater ease of access to ocean-going ships, would make any continued strong Icelandic competition against them almost unthinkable. The usual arrangement for the chance Icelander wanting to trade abroad during this period would be either to become an occasional partner of a Norwegian merchant or to take passage on his ship as a crewman.

While most Icelanders consequently did not gain the financial rewards that the extended market area of the eleventh and twelfth centuries brought to Norwegian traders, that wider market still gave them certain important advantages. They could be reasonably sure that sufficient grain and other necessary imports would continue to be brought to them, and that their woolens would continue to be accepted in exchange because Norwegians had access to English grain and because they found markets in England for Icelandic woolens that they could not use themselves. In return for these advantages, stay-at-home Icelanders might have to pay somewhat more for imports than in the earlier period to assure Norwegians good profits—their main incentive for traveling to the isolated island. The rich with their more extensive acres could afford those prices, and the more numerous poor at least might have enough woolens or other goods to pay for the essentials.

Tempered as they probably were by higher prices, even these conditional advantages began to turn sour for Icelanders toward the end of the twelfth century. At that time, there were signs that grain and other foods were starting to become scarce even in non-Norwegian lands and that the desire for Icelandic woolens was beginning to decline in Norway and elsewhere. Icelanders were about to enter a period of severe economic distress.

THE LATE PERIOD: c. 1180–1264

About 1186 a local spring assembly for a district in southern Iceland changed the value of vathmál, the most common woolen cloth and the basic practical standard of foreign exchange. Compared to other frequently traded goods of both domestic and foreign origin, it was placed at a value 35 percent lower than had existed for at least the previous century and a half, a change that caused the comparative value of those other goods to rise correspondingly. Even though there is no record of similar price changes elsewhere at the time, it is quite unlikely that a lower price for vathmál and a higher price for other goods in terms of that medium were found only in the district for which the Árnes Thing, the assembly in question, had jurisdiction. Unless comparable values were found elsewhere, one living in the Árnes Thing district could merely exchange his vathmál someplace else in return for readily movable necessities such as grain, though he would not be able to exchange his cloth so easily elsewhere for domestic livestock such as cattle. It is improbable that the chieftains of the Árnes Thing district would have sacrificed their customary right of setting prices on incoming foreign goods themselves had there not been urgent need shared by them all to try to stabilize prices. Somewhat before about 1186, perhaps about 1180, a strong trend toward inflated prices for nonwoolen goods or toward a lower price for vathmál and probably other woolens must have begun in wide areas of Iceland or, as seems likely, in the whole country. In fact it appears that beginning about 1180, because of conditions abroad and to some extent in Iceland itself, simultaneously and mostly independently essential imports and nonwoolen domestic products were rising in price on the one hand, and, on the other, the value of vathmál and most other woolens was falling. These tendencies were to continue throughout the remaining decades of the Commonwealth, becoming ever more noticeable as time went by.

Because of population growth abroad, particularly in urban areas, and other reasons, the price of grain, Iceland's most consequential import, began to increase significantly toward the end of the twelfth century, even in places where it was being grown in relatively large amounts. As we know, Norway, Iceland's main direct supplier, depended mostly on England for grain supplements, an arrangement that was finally safeguarded by a mutual trade treaty in 1223. But by the time the treaty was made, prices of wheat, barley, and rye in England had doubled or tripled compared to what they had been a half century earlier.[4] Prices of English grain when brought to Norway would have been still higher, particularly because Norway had to face competition from such places as the Low Countries. By the time grain from England reached hungry Iceland, having been passed on by almost as needy Norway, its price would have been very much greater than in England itself.

Thus Icelanders stood to benefit almost as much as Norwegians themselves if the latter had success in finding cheaper sources for grain. The most likely possibility was northern Germany, where urban development was much less extensive than on the western Continent, where the populations of those towns that did exist were smaller, and where grain was grown in large amounts. The even more significant grain supplies of Poland were also of convenient access. During the late twelfth and thirteenth centuries any grain brought to Norway from such towns as Lübeck should have been priced much lower than that from England. Norwegian success in obtaining German grain seems to have been limited, however. About 1186 King Sverrir of Norway castigated German merchants, probably from the Rhineland, for not bringing useful products to Norway, and we may well believe that he was thinking primarily of grain. Rhenish merchants had less surplus grain to bring than those from Baltic Germany, and the latter apparently began to import it somewhat later. But even they apparently did not bring enough: during the winter of 1247–1248 King Hákon IV Hákonarson had to remind merchants from Lübeck to bring to Norway, "according to custom, . . . grain and malt, and allow our merchants to buy the same [in Lübeck] as long as scarcity exists in our kingdom. In return, we will not prevent your merchants from buying from us what they find most useful. But we do not wish our merchants to take [from Lübeck] more Lübeck ale than what they need to drink on the voyage, because it is not at all necessary for our land."[5] While it seems evident that a cheaper German alternative to expensive English grain still did not form a major part of Norwegian grain imports during the late twelfth and the first half of the thirteenth centuries, it, together with what Norway was able to produce itself, may have sufficed to absorb some of the increased cost of English grain. And if Norwegian merchants were not too greedy, a portion of that limited savings might have been passed on to Icelanders.

Regardless, though, of any benefit Icelanders ultimately might have gained from Norwegian commerce with Germany, grain imported to Iceland remained extraordinarily expensive during this late period. And the distress of those high prices was felt all the more because some Icelanders, who before had been able to grow small amounts themselves, now were able to grow even less because the climate of the island was beginning to grow cooler, from all indications, after about 1200. More importantly, shorter and less warm summers meant that grass grew less, so that the islanders could maintain fewer cattle than before; they had to replace them with sheep which could better use the shorter summer grass and which also could better cope with the longer, more severe winters. Consequently there were increased prices for cattle and their products, which were among the most important items for Iceland's domestic economy, equalling or exceeding the significance of woolens for home use.

Icelanders also probably raised more sheep during this late period than before because they would have looked upon more woolens, their time-honored export, as a good way of meeting the higher costs of essential imports such as grain. It is quite likely, though, that foreign demand for Icelandic woolens did not increase sufficiently to keep pace with the greater abundance. In fact that demand even must have diminished compared with earlier times. Only during the early period of Icelandic foreign trade had Norway alone been capable of absorbing all Icelandic cloth production. Afterward, even though Norway's population had been increasing, Norwegians had to resell many of those woolens to others, particu-

larly to the English. Now between about 1180 and 1264 Englishmen probably grew less willing to absorb their former share of
Icelandic cloth because of an increased manufacture of inexpensive cloth on their part. The spinning wheel, invented during the
thirteenth century or somewhat earlier, must have greatly accelerated the expansion of the English weaving industry, for with it
wool could be spun more quickly than with the age-old distaff and
spindle, thereby providing yarn to keep pace with the pedal-loom,
in use in England by the end of the twelfth century. Increased
production meant that cloth of high quality could be sold for
somewhat less, and that weavers would be able to more profitably
produce even common, inexpensive cloth. A greater availability of
fine cloth in England because of lower prices and of ordinary cloth
due to its increased production must have made serious inroads on
English demand for Icelandic vathmál. This lower demand would
have been very harmful to Iceland inasmuch as England was,
because of the intermediation of Norwegian merchants, the most
important market after Norway itself for Iceland's woolen exports.
Though there is no direct record of it—except if one considers
Normandy until its conquest by the French king in 1204 as part of
the English market—Iceland, like Germany and Spain,[6] now probably began to furnish England some wool instead of cloth to feed
hungry English spinning wheels and pedal-looms, for even growing
numbers of English sheep were becoming insufficient for the needs
of both the native English cloth industry and that of the Low
Countries. But English demand for Iceland's raw wool probably
was much less than there once had been for its low-cost finished
cloth, and in any case Icelanders would have gained less in exchange by exporting wool rather than the cloth woven from it.

As prices for imports and nonwoolen domestic products became quite high for Icelanders after the end of the twelfth century,
and prices for their woolen exports declined, the one magnified the
other. But these price movements were probably only largely ir-
relevant abstractions to many Icelanders. More tangibly, they
might have been unable to acquire what they needed because of the
shortages of domestic and foreign essentials and the overabundance of their woolens which the high and low prices represented.

During the early and middle periods of their trade, Icelanders had been almost totally dependent upon Norway as the direct supplier of its foreign needs and as the direct market for its own goods in return; moreover, during the middle period they had learned to depend essentially upon Norwegian merchants to come to their island to make those exchanges, for they ever more rarely went abroad themselves, and then usually on Norwegian ships. Later, as Norwegians were less able to acquire, even for themselves, enough of the grain and other goods that Icelanders needed, they naturally came to Iceland less often. Even though a severe Icelandic shortage of an important product such as grain might insure Norwegian merchants a good profit, if they did not have enough to sell they could not realize that profit. And even if they had some grain to sell at a high price, because they had to take their profits mainly in cloth that was harder to resell than before, or in wool that would be less profitable than cloth to resell, they still would be discouraged from coming to the island with their essential imports.[7] The infrequency of visiting merchants, in turn, caused the price of imports, when available, to rise still further and the price of woolens, when exchanged, to drop still lower.

Lacking sufficient cereals and dairy products or being unable to afford them, many Icelanders during these years must have suffered from malnutrition at best, starvation at worst. In 1192 a famine occurred, accompanied by a plague that itself may have been encouraged by undernourishment of its victims. Though a particularly severe food shortage such as this drew the attention of annalists, hunger must have been almost a daily companion to most Icelanders. That circumstance alone might have gone far in causing a general population decline, even without taking into consideration the occasional widespread famine and plague. By 1311 Iceland's population apparently dropped somewhat more than 15 percent compared with what it was two centuries before. The population figures for both about 1095 and 1311 are imprecise, and a comparison of these two figures does not reveal the full extent of the decline in population that must have occurred after about 1180. From then until the end of the Commonwealth, the decline surely was dramatic. The only good aspect to the population decline was that it would help to lower overall demand, and thus the price, for basic foods. But those effects took time to achieve and they probably would be of minimal significance anyway, considering that shortages of domestic and foreign food supplies probably increased at a faster pace than this drop in demand and that the market abroad for Icelandic woolens continued to weaken.

During this period of personal sacrifice caused by a sick economy, Icelanders attempted some remedies. One of them was imposition of maximum prices on certain vital goods. We already have encountered the first known experiment of this nature, that of the Árnes Thing. Another list of controlled prices followed about 1200, issued by the Althing. It was more comprehensive both in the number of products it listed and in the extent of its applicability, for it was in force for one year over the whole island, rather than a single district. It also took a different approach toward pricing controls. Whereas the Árnes Thing had lowered the usual value of vathmál 35 percent, thereby allowing a price rise of that much, but no more, for other products in terms of vathmál, the Althing's controls were much more severe. The Althing raised the value of vathmál by 6 percent compared to its traditional value and by 31 percent compared to the value given it by the Árnes Thing. The net effect was to lower other prices by the same amounts. By acknowledging both a higher value for nonwoolen goods and a lower one for vathmál, the Árnes Thing had been realistic in its attempt to impose price limits. During the interval between the Árnes Thing price list and that of the Althing, nonwoolen prices in general could only have increased while that for vathmál could only have declined; so when the Althing made its price limits run counter to these trends, it was being most impractical. For this reason the Althing's prices must have been almost impossible to enforce, even though there was a severe penalty for failing to observe them.

Perhaps it was fortunate that these prices could not be enforced. Had they been, even the increasingly fewer merchants who were coming from abroad by then would have been further discouraged from coming. Thus by instituting controls that were not enforceable and that would have been further injurious to trade had they been, the Althing encouraged lawlessness both among Icelanders and foreign merchants. Both in its intent and in its practical result, the Althing remedy was more harmful than beneficial. It must be admitted, however, that the approach toward pricing taken by the Althing probably was not unusual for the time. When the chieftains, who were fewer in number than in previous years, resumed their traditional right of pricing for their districts the goods on an incoming ship, no doubt they often either placed a value on their own vathmál or other woolens that was too high to please the ship's captain, or they valued the captain's cargo of imports too low to suit him. Disagreements over prices between chieftains and Norwegian merchants must have abounded, and one of them became so heated that it almost led to war with Norway in 1219. Soon afterward the chieftains' pricing duties were supplemented or replaced by local committees. This innovation made certain that ships landing at any harbor always, even in the absence of a chieftain, would have prices set on their cargoes, thereby depriving a foreign merchant of the excuse used earlier that he was not used to the practice of having his goods priced by others. And, more importantly, since a committee now set the prices rather than a single chieftain, a greater objectivity was attained which in turn might have meant fairer prices for both buyer and seller.

Control of prices by a local assembly, the National Assembly, chieftains or committees, struck not at the roots, but only at the most visible signs of the basic twin problem of shortage of imports and domestic foodstuffs and lack of a sufficient market abroad for Icelandic woolens. Since price regulation, unfair in the eyes of foreign merchants, only intensified a shortage of imports and an overabundance of exports, another approach altogether was required—and attempted. If Icelanders went abroad themselves, particularly to places other than Norway, they might be able to acquire more of the grain and other foreign products they needed, and they even might find equally satisfactory or better markets for their cloth or wool. In any case, by eliminating the intermediation of Norwegians they should be able to acquire those foreign products for less and to sell their own goods for more than if they merely waited at home to make exchanges with Norwegians. A few Icelanders during the years shortly before and after 1200 are known to have engaged in direct trade with places other than Norway, either independently or in partnership with Norwegian merchants. In 1188, a year following one when no ships at all came to Iceland from Norway, an Icelander went to Ribe, a port significant for its grain exports and other Danish agricultural goods; he returned not the next year as was customary, but during the same sailing season that he went. The apparent success of that voyage, so unlike the reputed Icelandic experience with Denmark during the tenth century, was not always repeated when Icelanders went to other places during this period. Though a few went apparently without incident to the Orkneys and England for grain, when they went to Normandy, as they may have in 1198, their ship and their sacks of wool were confiscated, and when they went to the Hebrides about 1202 they faced tolls that were so extraordinarily high that they could not do business there.

In general, the difficulties of finding suitable places other than Norway to trade with and, even more so, of reestablishing a sizable trade of their own with any country, were very great for Icelanders of the period and perhaps, in the long run, insurmountable. Even if they had been able to enjoy the same commercial privileges abroad as Norwegians, and even if they had been able to find good sources for grain and markets for their woolens, problems of a more domestic nature would greatly hinder a revival of trade on their part. One difficulty was their lack of ocean-going ships—only two Icelanders are known to have owned ships between about 1200 and 1264.[8] Because Norwegians had come to dominate their commerce during the middle period of their foreign trade, Icelanders had allowed their old ocean-going ships to fall into disrepair, and they had had little reason to acquire new ones. If they wished to start trading abroad again in considerable numbers they would have had to do so on Norwegian ships. Thus, at least at the outset, their trade could not be any more frequent than allowed by the insufficient Icelandic visits of Norwegian merchants. But a far more basic difficulty in renewing a strong commerce of their own, not to mention one that would last for some time, was that there were very few Icelanders of means who had the desire to engage in frequent commercial voyages abroad, despite the compelling economic reasons for doing so. The process of land accumulation by the wealthy that had started somewhat after 1000 had reached a point by about 1220 whereby Iceland was politically controlled by only five leading families. In efforts to retain or increase their power, prominent families both before and after that time were engaged either in sharp conflict among themselves or with the church, at first with Bishop Thorlák Thórhallsson of Skálaholt (1178–1193) and then with Bishop Guthmund Arason of Hólar (1203–1237). Civil disorders grew ever more frequent and violent during the thirteenth century, involving ever larger numbers, culminating at the Battle of Örlygstathir in 1238 when almost 2,000 men fought against each other, an enormous number for Iceland at that time. No doubt the economic ills of the period helped to intensify the selfishness, greed, and opportunism that were so much a mark of the period's political and military contests. Certainly the civil disruption, when power could be lost or won, prevented chieftains and their families—those who had the greatest financial ability for doing so—from engaging in more than rare commercial trips abroad.

Not only were these powerful Icelanders able to do nothing substantial about solving their country's grave economic problems, but by their fighting, so disruptive to the domestic economy, they aggravated those problems. Even more seriously, Iceland's economic agony was intensified by the interference of the king of Norway, anxious to annex the island. The last serious efforts to do so had been during the reign of St. Óláf, but after his death in 1030 disruptive political circumstances in Norway had diverted the attention of its monarchs from the island. Now in the thirteenth century, a time of generally more political stability for Norway, King Hákon IV Hákonarson (1217–1263) renewed those efforts, at first under the tutelage of Jarl Skúli Bártharson, afterward more overtly on his own. Because of the internal political and economic weakness of Iceland, his goal eventually might have been attained with little interference on his part, but, not a man to bide his time, he actively encouraged the troubles. While the archbishop of

Nidaros had urged at times since the late twelfth century the bishops of Skálaholt and Hólar to stand up to argumentative chieftains for the sake of Gregorian reforms, the king now did his part to intensify political jealousies among the chieftains themselves. He also encouraged for his ultimate advantage the poverty of the island which depended so greatly upon Norwegian merchants for vital imports. In 1219 no ships at all came to Iceland from Norway,[9] a circumstance that hardly seems fortuitous in view of the disputes Icelanders had been having with Norwegian merchants since 1215. And Skálholts annáll directly mentions a ban of Norwegian commerce with part of Iceland in 1243.[10] These royal efforts to impede commerce in order to remind Icelanders—though reminding hardly seemed necessary—that they were dependent upon good relations with Norway if they expected to be supplied with at least some foreign goods were seconded by the claims of nature, for consistently during the first half of the thirteenth century shipwrecks or other misfortunes occurred at sea.[11]

By 1262 Iceland was to so weakened by economic distress and internal political disputes that it was finally persuaded to allow the Norwegian annexation that King Hákon had been attempting for the past several years. In the Gizurarsáttmáli (Covenant of Gizur), so called because of the leading role played by the Icelander Gizur Thorvaldsson in arranging the annexation, men from both the North and South Quarters of the island agreed to become Norwegian subjects, yielding Iceland to the king. They also agreed to pay a tax to the Norwegian monarch amounting to twenty alnir of vathmál per year for each Icelander who previously had been responsible for paying the thing-tax. In return the king agreed to preserve the domestic tranquillity of the island and not to introduce new laws for Icelanders without their consent. Furthermore, he agreed that six ships were to sail to Iceland during each of the next two years, and afterward as many were to come as both the king and notable Icelanders should decide. In addition, certain items in the agreement of c. 1022 that Icelanders had made with St. Óláf were changed or confirmed: Icelanders or their heirs could claim inheritances in Norway without any time limit; the landaurar was abolished; and Icelanders were to have as advantageous rights in Norway as they had ever had before, as well as those which King Hákon had previously promised. The *Covenant* was to be binding only so long as Icelanders were satisfied that none of its terms was broken.[12] This agreement, marking the end of the medieval Icelandic Commonwealth, was sworn to by only a minority of Icelandic leaders, for neither the West nor East Quarters were represented, and a leading family of the South Quarter, the Oddaverjar, also refused to participate. But in 1263 and 1264 these holdouts agreed to the same terms.[13]

By thus surrendering their independence, Icelanders finally gained in some measure a remedy to the problems that had plagued them since about 1180. By replacing the authority of rival and jealous chieftains with the single authority of the Norwegian monarch, earlier civil disorders were put to rest. Though there was no assurance that prices of exports or imports would improve for Icelanders, they could hope that the destitution they had suffered earlier because few Norwegian merchants would come to their island would no longer exist. Although the agreement made in 1262 called for six ships to visit Iceland in the course of only the following two years, the two subsequent confirmations of the agreement in 1263 and 1264, together with one made in 1302 with King Hákon Magnússon—a treaty known as the *Gamli Sáttmáli (Old Covenant)*[14]—left no doubt that in ensuing years six ships always were to come annually from Norway. As the 1264 agreement put it, "for the sake of the need of the land and the poverty of the people who inhabit the land, we desire that such ships come here to the country laden with those goods which are useful for the country and useful for the people and which cannot be found here."[15] So far had Icelanders fallen from their days of earlier prosperity that the six ships that they insisted were to come yearly to their island without fail—by which they implied that they were to come regardless of adverse conditions in Norway[16]—probably represented more commerce than they had had for many years.

As the circumstances of this last period of the Icelandic Commonwealth's foreign trade plainly reveal, the economic misfortune in which Iceland found itself was due at least as much to general trends in Europe as to its own weaknesses. The development of new techniques of weaving, possibly coupled with some change in fashionable taste, greatly reduced the market for Icelandic woolens just at a time when growing populations abroad permitted fewer foodstuffs to be shipped to Iceland. Though Iceland, because of its very great dependence upon imports and its isolation from important trade routes, was among the first of European countries to feel the effects of a growing general shortage of food supplies, and, because of its narrow export base of inexpensive woolens, was among the first to suffer from a contraction of foreign markets for manufactured goods, other countries of western Europe, larger and economically much more fortunate than Iceland, were to suffer in varying degrees from those same problems during the fourteenth and fifteenth centuries.

Of course, even before this last period of the Commonwealth's foreign trade, Icelandic commerce was less than ideal; among other things, its geographical isolation, its poor endowment of natural resources, and its lack of a true merchant class militated against it. But Icelanders had efficiently exploited what assets they possessed so that they could be as self-sufficient as possible while still providing for themselves a sizable export product which they were long able to exchange for the imports they needed. Rather than submit to natural loneliness and a life of almost bare subsistence, members of Icelandic chieftain families and others had not only initiated a trade with Norway, but they also had explored commercial opportunities from Greenland to possibly Byzantium. Later, more professional Norwegian merchants had assumed most of the responsibility for maintaining Iceland's trade, thereby achieving their first regular participation in foreign commerce on a wholesale level. This had encouraged in turn a significant expansion of their trade with other parts of Europe, especially England. In return for surrender by the few of commercial profits to Norwegians, Icelanders as a whole had long been well served by them.

What is remarkable about the Icelandic Commonwealth's foreign trade is not that it ended in failure but that it persisted, despite limitations, for almost four centuries.

Icelandic Foreign Trade from 1264 to the End of the Middle Ages

The most important change in the nature of Iceland's foreign trade after union with Norway was replacement of woolens by dried fish, mostly cod, as the island's basic export. This exchange of an increasingly less desirable export for one that was growing more attractive abroad was made possible because of a continued shortage of meat and cereals in much of Europe.[1] A stricter and more widespread adherence to duties of Christian fasting, due as much to scarcity of meat as to religious considerations, also would have contributed to a larger amount of fish in the diet of Europeans. Regardless, however, of these general reasons for the increased popularity of fish in the late Middle Ages, it is doubtful that the export trade of Iceland would have been altered as significantly as it was had it not been for the mostly indirect but nonetheless decisive role of the Hanseatic League.

During the Commonwealth period the only dried fish ("skreith") taken from Iceland was for the meals of crewmen on ships that were carrying more lucrative cargoes. There was, of course, no market for fish in Norway, Iceland's main trading partner, as long as its own extensive fisheries, particularly in the

181

northern waters of the Lofotens and Vesterålens, remained more than adequate for its export needs. They remained quite sufficient as long as Norwegians depended primarily upon England to provide them with supplementary grain. But during the thirteenth century England was less able to supply grain and other foods as openhandedly as before. When Norway turned to Baltic and north German cities, especially Lübeck, as alternate suppliers, Norway found a market for dried fish that, even with its extensive fisheries, it could not completely satisfy. An overseas market was thus eventually created for Icelandic fish.

A sketch of the early Baltic German commercial presence in Norway will show more clearly the cause of these circumstances. As leaders of a commercial consortium which included merchants from Danzig, Riga, Dorpat, and Reval, Lübeckers had abundant grain from the hinterlands of these cities and others, but during the first half of the thirteenth century they were reluctant to bring it to Norway because they had as yet little need for Norwegian fish: that from the Danish Sound between Sjælland and Scania was more than sufficient as long as their trade was mainly confined to the Baltic area itself. This attitude underwent a dramatic and permanent change when in 1252 and 1253 privileges were first extended to Lübeckers and others from German Baltic ports to trade in Bruges, one of the most active commercial centers in northwestern Europe.[2] Maximum advantage was to be gained from this widely connected market by bringing there Norwegian not Scanian fish, for the latter would have to be transported less conveniently and hence less profitably across the lower Danish peninsula or by sea around it in dangerous waters, whereas the former could be brought directly from Bergen by an all-sea route in relatively calm summer waters. Useful as Norway became for Lübeckers, they now reciprocated by bringing plentiful amounts of Baltic grain to the country, thereby honoring the spirit of an agreement they had been forced to make—under an imperial threat of transferring their city to Norwegian jurisdiction—with King Hákon IV Hákonarson even somewhat before the Bruges privileges were secured.[3] But their motive in bringing abundant grain was not without a sinister side. By doing so, they would encourage Norwe-

gian commercial passivity; and they would discourage competition from other outsiders like themselves because such merchants
as the English could not bring so much grain nor sell it at so low a
price as they. Eventually Lübeckers and other German merchants
thus would be able to secure a virtual monopoly of Norwegian
foreign trade much like that which had already proved so profitable
for them in the Baltic; when that happened they could of course
raise prices for their imports and lower those they would pay for
Norwegian exports, which is to say they could demand more fish
for less grain. By 1284 the time had come for testing their success
in attaining that goal. King Eirík Magnússon had tried to curb
certain of their illegal practices in his kingdom; in return they now
placed an embargo upon the grain, flour, vegetables, and beer that
they previously had been bringing to the country. Native commerce had so declined and English participation in the trade had so
weakened that, in the words of a German chronicler, there "broke
out a famine so great that they [the Norwegians] were forced to
make atonement."[4] When the embargo was lifted in 1285, Norway
delivered itself to the mercy of its oppressors. It became an economic dependency of northern and Baltic Germans, who, in the
mid-fourteenth century, would replace their loose personal
partnership with a more substantial association of their towns,
well known in this form as the Hanseatic League.[5]

But the Hanseatic stranglehold upon Norwegian commerce in
general did not prevent some Norwegian mercantile activity; in
fact it helped to encourage Norwegian commerce where Hanseatic
competition was not encountered. Until nearly the end of the
Middle Ages, Hanseatic merchants were not permitted to sail to
Iceland,[6] and they showed no interest in violating that prohibition.
Suffering competition from the Hanseatics elsewhere, having to
exchange large quantities of their own fish for German grain and
other goods, and facing an apparently insatiable Hanseatic appetite
for still more fish, Norwegians would channel a considerable
amount of their commercial energy to Iceland, thereby gaining
profits by selling at particularly high prices their imports for fish or
by acquiring fish directly themselves, either of which would offset
some of their losses to the Hanseatics. In 1294—the same year that

King Eirík Magnússon was forced to allow extensive new privileges to the Germans in his kingdom—appeared the first indication that Norwegians were taking large amounts of dried fish from Iceland. The islanders wrote to the king that "we do not want much skreith exported from here while there is famine in the land."[7] Despite this plea, the amount of dried fish exported from Iceland during the first half of the fourteenth century must have sharply increased, so that at least by 1340 dried fish had replaced wool products as the major export of the island.[8] This Norwegian interest in the Iceland trade, however, would slacken considerably in the latter half of the century. The onset of the Black Death in Norway during 1349 and its recurrences afterward must have been primarily responsible, but some measures of the Norwegian government, either more vigorously enforced or newly invoked probably as a result of the Death, may have added to the decline of Norwegian trade to Iceland. It was during the reign of King Magnús Eiríksson (1319–1343) that a sekkjagjald ("sack-tax") of 5 percent is first known to have been imposed on all incoming goods from Iceland, but only after about 1350 was it rigorously enforced as a means of increasing royal revenues, so badly needed now that other sources of income had declined because of the depleted population.[9] And in 1361 the trade with Iceland was reserved exclusively for merchants of Bergen.[10] This restriction could have been an effort to maintain the prosperity of that city, even with its reduced population, at the expense of others such as Nidaros which previously had engaged in trade with Iceland; transporting Icelandic skreith directly to Bergen, where it would be reexported by the Hanse, also would save the labor, now in shorter supply, of bringing it to that point from elsewhere in Norway.

The rise of Norwegian shipping to Iceland during the first half of the fourteenth century and its decline during the last half can be seen in data presented in the Icelandic annals. Compared with earlier and later periods, the annals are quite extensive for the period 1250–1399. Of course, in spite of the comparative richness of the annals for this century and a half and thus their usefulness as sources for the period, not all shipping activity can be expected to have been recorded in them, but instead only what was noteworthy for some reason; it might be that important persons arrived or departed, or that an unusually large or small number of ships arrived in one year, or that a mishap at sea occurred. Compared with both arrivals and departures, the number of accidents recorded is unusually prominent, and so it may be assumed with some justification that these mishaps consistently occurred, that they were virtually always noted, and that consequently they provide a useful index of total shipping activity during various periods of this century and a half. As Chart 1 shows, during the first half of the fourteenth century the number of recorded accidents increased to about sixty-six from about fourteen during the latter half of the thirteenth century, an increase of 371 percent; and from about sixty-six the number declined to about thirty-six during the latter half of the fourteenth century, a drop of 45 percent.[11] Almost as telling, though less trustworthy because of the smaller numbers involved, are the greater numbers of years during the last half of the fourteenth century, compared with the first half, when no ship or only one came to Iceland from Norway. In 1350 and 1355 no ships arrived; in each of the years 1357, 1362 (?), and 1367 only one ship came; in 1374 and 1389 there were no ships; and in 1392 only one ship arrived. In the first half of the fourteenth century only in 1325 did just one ship come and in 1326 or 1327 none at all.[12] Finally, there are no years during the last half of the fourteenth century when unusual numbers of ships came to the island, but in 1337 three ships came to Eyrarbakki, and in the winter of 1340–1341 ten ships were in Hvalfjörth—both of these harbors were most convenient to the best fishing areas.[13]

Another indication of the growing demand abroad for skreith is its increase in value in Iceland. That rise is illustrated in Table 3.[14] Based on that table, another can be made. Table 4 depicts the decreasing number of fish per legal eyrir, thereby illustrating in a different way the rising value of dried fish. Before about 1200 and thus during most of the Commonwealth, while Icelanders no doubt consumed large amounts of fish, it probably was not unduly emphasized in their diet as long as they had plentiful domestic livestock and adequate imported foods. During the two-and-a-half centuries after the settlement period its price must have been both

CHART 1 *Approximate Arrivals, Departures, and Ship Accidents
Recorded in the Icelandic Annals*

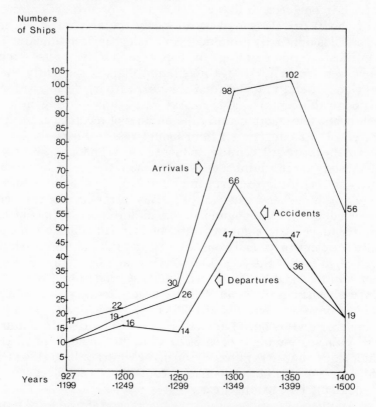

Source: *Ann.* The number of arrivals, departures and ship accidents for the
various periods are determined in the following manner: 1) clearly repetitive
inclusions are counted as one incident; 2) if several men are noted leaving or
arriving in Iceland, it is assumed that they traveled on the same ship; 3) if ship
accidents are recorded only in general numbers, such as "several ships were
wrecked," three ships are counted.

fairly low and fairly stable because Icelandic demand could easily
be satisfied by local fishermen, even when that demand was probably increased after per capita land holdings began to be reduced
about 1000. Probably by about 1186, certainly after 1200, its price,

TABLE 3   VALUE OF SKREITH IN TERMS OF VATHMÁL

	Vættir of skreith per *hundred* [120] *alnir of vathmál*	*Rise in* *percent*
Until c. 1200	10	(100)
Until c. 1300	8	125
1350–1400	6	167
1420–1550	3.5	286

Source: Thorkell Jóhannesson, *Die Stellung der freien Arbeiter in Island*, p. 63n 1. The period before 1200 is taken as the standard against which succeeding price increases are measured.

however, would have increased significantly because almost all Icelanders would have found cattle raising a great deal more difficult and importations of foods much less ample than before. After Norwegians grew interested in exporting dried fish toward the end of the thirteenth century, its price would have climbed even more, until a high point was probably reached about 1350. Shortly after 1412, the price of skreith again began to increase substantially because of visits of English and then Hanseatic merchants to Iceland.

Because skreith superseded vathmál and other wool products as Iceland's most important export, skreith also replaced vathmál as the island's most important practical monetary standard, though nominally a legal eyrir continued to be calculated in terms of six alnir of vathmál. Certainly by the fifteenth century the transition had been made,[15] but there is good reason to believe that

TABLE 4   NUMBER OF FISH PER LEGAL EYRIR

	Pounds per *20 aurar*[a]	*Total number* *of fish*	*Number of* *fish per* *legal eyrir*
Until c. 1200	766.40	306.56	15.33
Until c. 1300	613.12	245.25	12.26
1350–1400	459.84	183.94	9.20
1420–1550	268.24	107.30	5.37

[a]The average weight per fish is considered to be 2.5 lbs.

the change occurred much earlier. With the full consent of the Norwegian monarch, a new price list, similar to that of a century before, was issued for Iceland about 1300,[16] except that the rate of legal aurar to an eyrir of pure silver was set at 6:1. Vathmál had been raised in value, probably artificially, about 1200 by the Al-thing so that the relationship of legal aurar to one of pure silver was set at 7.5:1 instead of the earlier 8:1 or even 10.83:1. Probably that had been done to make foreign goods cheaper for Icelanders, which meant of course that Norwegian merchants who accepted vathmál got less of the cloth than before for the same amount of imports. It is understandable that Icelanders would have tried to better their economic position at the expense of Norwegians while the island-ers were still politically independent. But about 1300 why would the Norwegian king allow another increase in the value of a legal eyrir if it meant a significant loss for Norwegian merchants? The answer must be that they would not suffer a loss because, although the legal eyrir was based on vathmál in theory, in actuality it was based on skreith. When the relationship between legal aurar and an eyrir of pure silver had been 8:1 before c. 1200, there had been about 15.33 fish per legal eyrir and by c. 1300 it took only about 12.26 fish to equal a legal eyrir, a rise in its value of 25 percent—as Tables 3 and 4 indicate. It does not seem a coincidence, then, that the value of a legal eyrir was also increased 25 percent about 1300 compared to its old 8:1 ratio with pure silver. The problem with raising the value of a legal eyrir to make it correspond to the rising value of skreith, while logical enough in itself because of skreith's new commercial significance, was that it also caused the value of vathmál to increase even though in actuality vathmál had lost much of its earlier value and no longer was so important an export. Afterward, therefore, the value of a legal eyrir was not increased beyond the 6:1 relationship to pure silver: while an increase would have caused the legal eyrir to reflect faithfully a continuing rise in the price of skreith, it would not reflect well the value of vathmál. The price of skreith could still be expressed in terms of a legal eyrir, except that less fish would be needed to make up that eyrir as the price of skreith increased. Assuming, however, a theoretical in-crease in the value of a legal eyrir against an eyrir of pure silver to match the increasing value of skreith, Table 5 and Chart 2 can illustrate the general price fluctuations during the Middle Ages for Iceland's two main exports, at first vathmál, later skreith.

Once Norwegians found trade with Iceland attractive because of the island's dried fish, as attested by the increased volume of traffic and the increased price of fish, it might be expected that Icelanders would benefit significantly. But the Icelandic plea of 1294 asking that skreith not be taken from them in quantity while they were suffering famine is as much a sign that the islanders were being inadequately provided with necessary imports as it is that Norwegians were beginning to take large amounts of fish from Iceland. Despite the increased volume of Norwegian trade to their island, and despite the increased price for skreith, later on during the fourteenth century it is doubtful that Icelanders were much better off than they had been in 1294 or even during most of the previous years of the thirteenth century. In 1320, in fact, they repeated with almost the same words their complaint of 1294.[17]

One of the main reasons Icelanders had allowed the union of their country with Norway between 1262 and 1264 was that they had been promised by the king that he would be responsible for

TABLE 5 MEDIEVAL ICELANDIC PRICES FOR VATHMÁL AND SKREITH IN RELATIONSHIP TO PURE SILVER

	Price index of skreith	*Legal aurar:* pure silver eyrir[a]
c. 875	——	2:1
by c. 930	90[-b]	8:1
c. 1186	100[-b]	10.83:1
c. 1200	100	7.5:1
c. 1300	125	6:1 [6:1]
c. 1350	167[b]	[2.64:1][b]
1350–1400	167	[2.64:1]
1420–1550	286	[1:6.88]

[a]Ratios without brackets are those between legal aurar and one eyrir of pure silver, the legal aurar being based upon vathmál. Ratios with brackets are theoretical, the legal aurar being based upon skreith.
[b]Assumed.

CHART 2 *Fluctuations in the Price of Vathmál and Skreith in Terms of Known Ratios between the Legal Eyrir and the Pure Silver Eyrir, c. 870–1500*

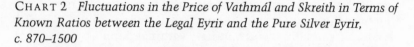
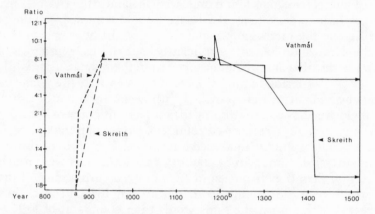
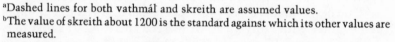

[a]Dashed lines for both vathmál and skreith are assumed values.
[b]The value of skreith about 1200 is the standard against which its other values are measured.

sending six ships laden with necessities every year to Iceland, a promise that was confirmed by subsequent agreements. Icelanders thought they could rest assured that they would not suffer the deprivation they had experienced during the earlier part of the century. It was not an unnatural expectation that the king would be responsible for providing their basic imports. Two centuries before, even when Iceland was politically independent, King Harald the Harsh-Ruler had assumed an obligation for the welfare of the islanders by insisting that the four shiploads of grain he allowed to be sent to Iceland during a period of shortage on the island be sold only at the usual price and no higher. Also before Iceland's annexation, Norwegian kings had insisted that royal permission be granted before Norwegians take such a necessity as grain to the island. Following Iceland's union with Norway, the king extended his direct participation in the Iceland trade and his indirect influence on the commerce of other Norwegians with the island: at least by about the middle of the fourteenth century the king was reserving for himself a quarter of the cargo space on all ships headed for Iceland, and, at about the same time, he confined the trade to Bergen merchants exclusively. Yet despite the profits that he himself could obtain from the trade and despite his responsibility for sending essential imports to Iceland, a responsibility pledged directly to the islanders by agreement and indirectly assumed by his commercial participation and influence, it became almost impossible for the Norwegian monarch to make certain that six shiploads of basic provisions were sent to Iceland every year. There had to be enough food supplies in Norway itself before any could be spared for Iceland; that had been the reason for the requirement of obtaining royal permission before 1262 for sending some or any grain to Iceland. When Norway became heavily dependent upon Hanseatic merchants to bring basic foodstuffs and when there was little chance, due to Hanseatic competition, for Norway to gain more from the southerly trade of its own merchants or from the Norwegian trade of non-Hanseatics, often Norway would have a barely sufficient amount of imported foodstuffs for its own requirements, with very little or none to spare for Iceland. When a market for Icelandic fish developed, Icelanders had a more appealing product to offer in exchange for Norwegian imports than woolens had become. But unlike woolens, Norwegians could obtain fish directly themselves. The more frequent visits of Norwegian merchants therefore did not necessarily mean that they brought correspondingly more imports to Icelanders. During the last half of the fourteenth century when the number of Norwegian ships visiting Iceland sagged, the amount of imports for Icelanders must have been even less adequate. It almost goes without saying that when Norwegians did bring imports and when Icelanders traded for them the skreith they had caught and cured themselves, the prices of those imports they gained at least must have kept pace with increases in the price of skreith. Consequently not even the rising value of skreith would have been of much benefit to Icelanders on the whole.

Soon after the beginning of the fifteenth century a change occurred, to the dismay of the Dano-Norwegian king (the joint monarchy was established in 1380) and to the good fortune of

Icelanders. English merchants began coming directly to Iceland in ever increasing numbers beginning in 1412, a year when no ships at all came to Iceland from Norway.[18] English merchants, who found the fisheries of their own island inadequate for their country's needs, who had been effectively excluded from much of the trade with Norway and the Baltic by the Hanse, and who had the necessary ships and technical navigational skills, looked to Iceland as a rich source for the skreith they desired.[19] Icelanders must have considered themselves fortunate, because English merchants now could bring the foods, especially grain, which they, even with a continuing shortage themselves, still had in more plentiful amounts than Norwegians. Of course such trade was not only illegal from the viewpoint of successive Dano-Norwegian monarchs, but also it caused them the loss of significant revenue, for the English did not pay the sekkjagjald when they traded with Iceland directly; moreover Bergen merchants were being hurt in their own sanctuary by English competition for fish and by English sale of imports to Icelanders. The kings repeatedly objected to the English infringement of their prerogatives, both to the English monarch and to their Icelandic subjects, but without much effect. The trade was too beneficial for both England and Iceland for it to be ended merely because of legal considerations. Icelanders acquitted themselves well in 1419 when Eirík of Pomerania, king of all three Scandinavian lands, objected to their trade with the English:

> Your letter has arrived here in which we are forbidden to trade with certain foreigners. But our established law says that six ships shall come to us every year from Norway. That has not happened for a long time, wherefore Your Grace and this poor land have suffered deep injury. Thus in God's grace and your trust we have been trading with foreigners who have come in peace. . . . But we have punished those men on doggers and fishing boats who have robbed and created a disturbance in the harbors.[20]

Icelanders or royal governors and other officials were not always able to control English depredations on the island, however well the Icelanders claimed to have done so in 1419. But though the atrocities were many, Icelanders probably were able to benefit from the higher price that their skreith commanded, now that

Englishmen were able to bring a greater amount of necessities than had Norwegians, and now that Englishmen were coming in greater numbers and more regularly than Norwegians.

Led by Lübeck, the Hanseatic League for many years did not seriously object to the English trade with Iceland because Lübeck did not sell much skreith directly to England anyway, and most of what the English brought from Iceland was consumed in England and did not compete with that the Hanse was selling on the Continent.[21] Without the aid of Hanseatic seapower, the protestations of the Dano-Norwegian monarchs concerning the Iceland trade of the English could not have had much practical result. But after 1448, when Christian I assumed rule of Denmark and Norway, a greater degree of cooperation with the Hanseatic League in general came about when he took a strong stand against English illegalities in the Baltic which it was to the interest of the Hanse to suppress. When the English murdered the governor of Iceland in 1467, bad feelings were intensified, and a five-year war broke out between England and its enemies Denmark, Norway, and the Hanse. In 1468 members of the league were allowed to trade directly with Iceland,[22] no doubt so that they would be encouraged to put down English illegalities there. But though Hamburg and Bremen merchants took advantage of this new privilege, it was not to the interest of Lübeck to make use of the right itself or to allow the other Hanse cities to do so. Lübeck had Bergen under its control and therefore it had ample amounts of skreith from Norway and Iceland for its own markets and for selling to other members of the league for their markets. The direct acquisition of Icelandic skreith by other Hanse cities therefore undermined Lübeck's profits when the fish was sold in continental markets without Lübeck's intermediation. In 1482 the Hanse Council, which was headed by Lübeck, prohibited any members of the league from sailing to Iceland even though they had been given permission by the Dano-Norwegian king to do so. The league was already beginning to lose its earlier cohesiveness, partly due to a jealousy of other Hanse cities—probably justified—over what they considered to be Lübeck's inordinate share of league profits. Hamburg and Bremen ignored the council's prohibition of 1482, and though it was tiresomely repeated the following year and thereafter until the 1520s,[23] it similarly had no effect. Because Hamburg merchants, who were especially active in the Iceland trade, now supported the royal governor on the island, and because the Germans' presence made possible a more effective enforcement of law and order, the Dano-Norwegian monarch in 1490 finally permitted Englishmen to visit the island to trade and to take away skreith, provided they paid the sekkjagjald to the proper royal official who was now established on the island.[24] But Englishmen began to grow less interested in coming to Iceland because of the export toll and strong German competition for the best fisheries. After equally rich fisheries in the New World were discovered in 1497, which were freely open to them, they began traveling there instead.[25]

Hamburg merchants thus mainly provided Icelanders with necessary imports at the conclusion of the fifteenth century, as they would until the reestablishment of the Danish trade monopoly at the beginning of the seventeenth century. During that time, though Icelanders could not be called prosperous, at least they were as well off economically as they had been during the time of English dominance in the trade without, however, suffering from depredations on their island: in contrast to English practices and even to their own earlier habits in Norway, the German merchants were generally respectful of the laws, commercial and otherwise, while they traded in Iceland.

By the end of the Middle Ages, Icelanders had found that economically speaking the loss of their political independence ultimately had come to mean a law-abiding commercial exploitation by others in return for a reasonably reliable and adequate provisioning of their basic needs. Although even this rather ignominious security was beneficial compared to the dark years at the end of the Commonwealth, some might have questioned whether the price paid for it had been too high. Now that fish had replaced woolens as their island's basic export, some might have believed that the spirit of Icelandic commercial enterprise, if they were still free to exercise it, would have yielded them more satisfactory results.

⅄ Glossary of Frequently Used Icelandic Words and Terms

Alnir	See Öln
Althing	The Icelandic "National Assembly," established c. 930, meeting in summer at Thingvöll in southwestern Iceland
Aurar	See Eyrir
Eyrir, pl. aurar	"Ounce," a term of weight and of value; its weight was slightly less than an ounce, equalling about 27 g. The value of a legal eyrir usually consisted of six alnir of vathmál.
Hafnarvathmál	"Vathmál for clothing," probably of a finer grade than ordinary vathmál
Hafskip	Any sea-going ship
Knörr, pl. knerrir	A rather large sea-going cargo ship
Kúgildi	The value of a "standard" cow, 3–10 years of age that could bear calves and give milk; was to be horned and faultless; was no worse than average; and could give enough milk for one calf. Its value varied, although at least between c.1100 and 1300 its value was 2–2.5 aurar of pure silver.
Landaurar	"Landing fees": during the Commonwealth, a toll

195

paid by Icelanders (and by Norwegians engaged in the Iceland trade except c. 1022–c. 1030) when entering Norway (before c. 1022 when leaving Norway); after c. 1022 payable instead in the Shetlands or Orkneys if visited prior to arrival in Norway. It consisted of either six alnir of vathmál and six cloaks or ½ mörk of impure silver.

Lest, pl. lestir — "Last," a term of weight, equalling in Iceland 3,310.848 lbs. (1.5 metric tons), or perhaps, as in Norway, 2,759.04 lbs. (1.25 metric tons)

Lögeyrir, pl. lögaurar — "Legal eyrir," usually six alnir of vathmál

Merkur — See Mörk

Mórent — Brown-striped vathmál

Mörk, pl. merkur — A term of weight and of value: its weight was 217 g or about ½ pound, eight times the weight of an eyrir. It also was eight times the worth of an eyrir.

Öln, pl. alnir — A basic unit of measurement; at least by c. 1100 the "long öln" was about 22″ (c. 56 cm); the "short öln" was 18″ (c. 46 cm)

Sekkjagjald — A Norwegian toll of 5% on cargoes of ships engaged in the Iceland trade, established by the earlier 14th century

Skarlat — A type of foreign cloth of various colors such as red, yellow-brown, blue, green, and white

Skreith — Dried fish, usually cod

Stika, pl. stikur — "Stick," a term of measurement equalling two short alnir or 36″ (c. 92 cm)

Tháttr, pl. thættir — An anecdotal story or short saga

Thing — An assembly

Vathmál — A coarse woolen cloth resembling tweed

⚓ Abbreviations

Ann.	*Islandske annaler indtil 1578.* Edited by Gustav Storm. Christiania, 1888.
Bisk. 1, 2	*Biskupa sögur.* Edited by Jón Sigurthsson and Guthbrandur Vigfússon. 2 vols. Copenhagen, 1856–78.
DI	*Diplomatarium Islandicum: Íslenzkt fornbréfasafn.* Edited by Jón Sigurthsson et al. Copenhagen, 1857–.
Gesta	Adam of Bremen. *Gesta Hammaburgensis ecclesiae pontificum.* Edited by G. Waitz. *Monumenta Germaniae historica. Scriptores rerum Germanicarum in usum scholarum,* vol. 2. Hanover, 1876.
Grágás 1a, 1b	*Grágás: Elzta lögbók íslendinga [Konungsbók:* Royal Library of Copenhagen 1157 fol.]. Edited by Vilhjálmur Finsen. First part: 1a; second part: 1b. Copenhagen, 1852.
ÍF	*Íslenzk fornrit.* Edited by Sigurthur Nordal et al. Reykjavík, 1933–.
ÍS	*Íslendinga sögur.* Edited by Guthni Jónsson. 13 vols. Reykjavík, 1953.
Íslb.	*Íslendingabók.* Edited by Jakob Benediktsson. *Íslenzk fornrit,* vol. 1, pt. 1:1–28. Reykjavík, 1968.

197

KLNM   *Kulturhistorisk leksikon for nordisk middelalder.* 22 vols. Copenhagen, 1956–78.

KS   *Konungs skuggsiá.* Edited by Ludvig Holm-Olsen. Oslo, 1945.

Land.   *Landnámabók.* Edited by Jakob Benediktsson. *Íslenzk fornrit,* vol. 1, pt. 1:29–210, pt. 2. Reykjavík, 1968. Unless otherwise stated, all references are to the version known as *Sturlubók* (c. 1275).

NK   *Nordisk kultur.* 30 vols. Copenhagen, Oslo, Stockholm, 1931–56.

s.   *saga.*

Stur. 1, 2   *Sturlunga saga.* Edited by Jón Jóhannesson, Magnús Finnbogason, and Kristján Eldjárn. 2 vols. Reykjavík, 1946.

th.   *tháttr.*

⚓ Notes

Preface

1. Kristján Eldjárn, *Kuml og haugfé*, p. 435.

2. See Bibliography of Cited Works for full bibliographical information of this collection and that of other sources mentioned in the Preface.

3. Mainly nonhistorical are the "Heroic Sagas," relating adventures of Scandinavian heroes of a dim, early past, and the "Knights' Sagas," dealing with the adventures of non-Scandinavians; none of the former is used here, and, of the latter, only *Tristrams s. ok Ísöndar* (1226) has been cited.

4. *ÍF* 26:5–7.

5. In an article that is essentially a critique of M. I. Steblin-Kamenskij, *The Saga Mind*, Peter Hallberg makes several convincing points about the degree of truthfulness of saga writers in general, and he defends the historical acumen of Snorri in particular ("The Syncretic Saga Mind," *Mediaeval Scandinavia* 7[1974]:102–17, especially pp. 105–6).

6. The "freeprose" school can be exemplified by Andreas Heusler in his *Die Anfänge der isländischen Saga*. The "bookprose" school is exemplified by Björn M. Ólsen, "Um Íslendingasögur," *Safn til sögu Íslands* 6(1937–39):1–427. The arguments of both sides are summed up by Theodore M. Andersson, *The Problem of Icelandic Saga Origins*.

7. See Anne Stine Ingstad et al., *The Discovery of a Norse Settlement in America*. Other independent evidence which also could have further supported the general historical element in the two sagas, the Vinland Map, must be relegated to this footnote because on 26 January 1974 Yale University announced that certain tests proved that it was drawn no earlier than the 1920s, rather than about 1440 as was previously believed. Nevertheless, the map was useful for provoking a great deal of still valuable commentary concerning northern geographical knowledge during

the Middle Ages; see in particular *The Vinland Map and the Tartar Relation* and *Proceedings of the Vinland Map Conference.*

8. The scholarly literature on the Icelandic sagas is abundant. Several interesting volumes recently published in English that bear at least in part upon the problem of historical reliability may be cited here: Richard M. Allen, *Fire and Iron: Critical Approaches to Njáls saga;* Peter Hallberg, *The Icelandic Saga;* Lars Lönnroth, *Njáls Saga;* Sigurdur Nordal, *The Historical Element in the Icelandic Family Sagas;* Einar Ól. Sveinsson, *Dating the Icelandic Sagas;* idem, *Njáls Saga.*

9. Approximate dates of the composition of sagas are listed in Bibliography of Cited Works.

10. The first treatment of Icelandic trade in English was a chapter entitled "The Iceland Trade" by Eleanora M. Carus-Wilson, in *Studies in English Trade in the Fifteenth Century* (1933). This investigation's arguments are convincingly presented, but it was not basically concerned with the period before 1412. A mainly noninterpretative study of Commonwealth trade was undertaken in English by O. Tønning in his *Commerce and Trade on the North Atlantic* (1936). This work is not dependable: Tønning misquotes the evidence or incorrectly describes it, quite apart from making incomplete or wrong citations. It should be mentioned that even quite scholarly works are not always accurate concerning Iceland. For instance, Archibald R. Lewis, in his *The Northern Seas,* bases most of his statements concerning the Iceland trade on Tønning's unreliable work, and Michael M. Postan, in his otherwise excellent chapter in the second volume of *The Cambridge Economic History of Europe* entitled "The Trade of Mediaeval Europe: The North," errs when he mentions Iceland twice in passing.

11. See Jón Jóhannesson, *Íslendinga saga* 1:337–38.

CHAPTER ONE

1. The sources vary concerning the first Scandinavian discoverer of Iceland: cf. *Sturlubók,* chs. 3, 4, and *Hauksbók,* chs. 3, 4, in *Land.,* pp. 34–37. Both of these versions of *Landnámabók* agree that the third man to arrive was Flóki Vilgertharson *(Sturlubók,* ch. 5; *Hauksbók,* ch. 5: *Land.,* pp. 36–38), who came c. 868. The earliest voyages were exploratory only, the first permanent resident supposedly being Ingólf Arnason, who, about 870, settled in Reykjarvík *(Íslb.,* ch. 1, p. 5). On the discovery of Iceland, see Trausti Einarsson, "Nokkur atrithi varthandi fund Íslands," *Saga* 8(1970):43–63.

2. "Liber de mensura orbis terrae," in *Sources for the Early History of Ireland,* pp. 546–48.

3. *Íslb.,* ch. 1, p. 5; *Land.,* ch. 1, pp. 31–32.

4. The pre-Norse Irish habitation of Iceland is disputed. For discussions that emphasize its probability, see T. C. Lethbridge, *Merlin's Island;* idem, *Hermits and Herdsmen.* For the contrary opinion, see Matthias Thórtharson, "Manngerthir hellar í Árnessýslu og Rangárvallasýslu," *Árbók hins íslenzka fornleifafélags* (1930–31), pp. 1–70. See also Einar Ól. Sveinsson, "Papar," *Skírnir* 119(1945):170–203. A summary of the problem is found in Kristján Eldjárn, *Kuml og haugfé,* pp. 12–13, 22n5.

5. Cf. P. A. Munch, *Det norske folks historie* 1(Christiania, 1852):556, cited by Ólafur Lárusson, "Island," *NK* 1:123; Lárusson, "Island," p. 124.

6. Barthi Guthmundsson, in his *Origin of the Icelanders,* contends that various ties Iceland had with Denmark and Sweden rather than with Norway prove the important role that eastern Scandinavia had in the settlement of Iceland. This view is contradicted by the most important Icelandic source, *Landnámabók,* which stresses that most settlers came from Norway: Guthmundur Hannesson has calculated that according to *Landnámabók's* information 84.3% of the settlers came from Norway, 3% from Sweden, and 12.6% from the British Isles ("Körpermasse und Körperproportionen der Isländer," *Flygirit árbók háskola Íslands*). Most settlers from Norway seem to have come from the southwest: cf. *KLNM,* s.v. "Landnám I" and Kenneth G. Chapman, *Icelandic-Norwegian Linguistic Relationships.*

7. See for example, *Land.,* chs. 13, 84, 95, 97, pp. 50, 122, 136, 138–40.

8. Today only about 13% of the land area is inhabited (Albert Nilsson, "Den sentida bebyggelsen på Islands landsbygd," *Forntida gårdar i Island,* pp. 271, 325).

9. *Guthmundar s. Arasonar,* ch. 2, *Bisk.* 2:5.

10. *Ann.,* pp. 134, 154.

11. Ibid., pp. 111, 262–63.

12. *KLNM,* s.v. "Klimat, Island och Grönland." Toward the end of the 14th century and for at least part of the 15th, the climate began to improve, but from the period after 1430 nothing is known except that there may have been drift ice in 1470 and in 1479 (ibid.). On climatic conditions, see also *The Vinland Map and the Tartar Relation,* p. 170; Edvard Bull, "Islands klima i oldtiden," *Geografisk tidsskrift* 23(1916):1–5; Jón Eythórsson, "Um loftslagsbreytingar á Íslandi og Grænlandi síthan á landnámsöld," *Skírnir* 100 (1926):113–33; and Sigurdur Thorarinsson, *The Thousand Years Struggle Against Ice and Fire.*

13. Lárusson, "Island," p. 135.
14. *Haralds s. gráfeldar*, ch. 16, *ÍF* 26:221–22.
15. "Um skattbændatal 1311 og manntal á Íslandi fram ath theim tima," *Safn til sögu Íslands* 4(1907–15):359–84.
16. *Íslb.*, ch. 10, pp. 22–23; cf. *The Book of the Icelanders*, Islandica 20(1930):56, 70; see also *Kristni s.*, ch. 13, *Bisk.* 1:28.
17. This is the opinion held by Magnús Stephensen, *Island i det attende aarhundrede* (Cophenhagen, 1808), cited by Lárusson, "Island," p. 126.
18. A population of almost 80,000 is in accord with the estimate of B. M. Ólsen, who places it at 77,520 in c. 1095 ("Skattbændatal," pp. 342–56). Sturla Frithriksson ("Gras og grasnytar á Íslandi" unpublished MS made available by courtesy of Björn Thorsteinsson, pp. 10–16) has calculated the population that medieval Iceland was capable of supporting maximally, based on the amount of grassland available for sheep. His figure of c. 76,190 confirms by valuable independent means that there were approximately 80,000 Icelanders in c. 1095 when their numbers attained their known maximum during the Middle Ages. Frithriksson's argument needs to be summarized here: Based upon reasonably accurate census figures at the beginning of the 18th and 19th centuries, the population of Iceland was c. 50,000, the number of sheep c. 300,000, and the number of cattle, c. 25,000. Considering that sheep and cattle were basic to the needs of the population, and that the numbers of people, sheep, and cattle were fairly stable during these two centuries, a basic ratio may be established: for the support of each person, an average of 6 sheep and ½ a head of cattle were required. Or, since one head of cattle was legally equal to 6 sheep (and, though Frithriksson does not say so, presumably consumed as much as 6 sheep), an average equivalent of 9 sheep per person were needed. According to Halldór Pálsson ("Avl og brug af får i Island," *Norræna búfræthifélagith*, N.J.F., Landbrugsmötet, July 1954), each sheep needs about 700 kg of hay per year, or, for 9 sheep, 6,300 kg. A minimum of 300 kg of hay can be produced yearly in Iceland from one hectare (2.471 acres) of noncultivated land, of which a sheep would use only 120 kg (it is estimated that an average of 40% of the available grass is eaten each year before the land is put to other uses). Therefore to yield 6,300 kg of hay, supporting 9 sheep, or the living of one person, 52.5 hectares of uncultivated land would be needed. The total amount of land suitable for vegetation in Iceland c. 1700 was about 2,500,000 hectares, but during the period of settlement there were about 4,000,000 hectares available, capable therefore of ultimately supporting 76,190 people. Though Frithriksson does not say so, it should be added that by c. 1095 a

few hectares would be lost because of erosion, etc., but this would make no appreciable difference in number of sheep (and human population) that could be supported. The factor of climate, which might have been somewhat better c. 1095 than now, is not taken into consideration; therefore possibly each hectare produced, at the minimum, a larger amount of hay at that time, supporting in turn more sheep and consequently more people.

19. The calculation is contained in a mid-16th-century document; the original has been lost. It is printed by Ólsen, "Skattbændatal," pp. 297–98.

20. Ólsen thinks the "C" meant the Old Icelandic "hundrath" or 120 (ibid., p. 298). Basing his calculations on this assumption, he gives a total number of those paying the tax in the whole land of 3,812. He compares the total number of those who paid the tax and those who did not in the 19th century and arrives at the ratio of 1:19; thus he calculates a population of 72,428 by 1311 (ibid., pp. 295–341). Thorkell Jóhannesson says that this figure is too high ("Plágan mikla 1402–1404," *Skírnir* 102[1928]:86). For a discussion of Icelandic population with lower estimates than those suggested above for c. 930, 1000, and 1100, see *KLNM*, s.v. "Population, Island": those estimates are all based essentially on only *Landnámabók*'s c. 400 named settlers.

21. *Ann.*, pp. 61, 71, 75, 202, 274–75; *Annales Islandici posteriorum saeculorum* 2:2.

22. *Guthmundar s. Arasonar*, ch. 22, *Bisk.* 2:44. The sagas and annals give further evidence of famines. For instance, cf., for the period just after 985, *Svatha th. ok Arnórs kerlingarnefs*, ch. 2, *ÍS* 8:337; for 1197, 1306, 1309, 1310, 1321, and 1331, *Ann.*, pp. 121, 74–75, 267, 154. Severe as famine and plague had been before, Icelanders escaped the first phases of Europe's Black Death during 1347–51. But when it reached their island between 1402 and 1404 it was devastating. In 1403, 640 dead bodies were delivered to Kirkjubær monastery alone before the count was stopped. The once flourishing monastery at Thykkvabær was visited three times by the plague, so that only two brothers and a servant remained (*Ann.*, p. 286). Altogether, it has been estimated that during the first 919 years of Iceland's history, there were 45 years when a famine is known to have occurred (Hannes Finnsson, "Um mannfækun af hallærum á Íslandi," *Rit thess konúnglega íslenzka lærdóms- lista félags* 14[1796], cited by Lárusson, "Island," p. 133).

23. *Guthmundar s. Arasonar eptir Arngríms ábóta*, ch. 2, *Bisk.* 2:5; cf. Helge Ingstad, *Land under the Pole Star*, p. 68.

24. B. M. Ólsen, "Kornyrkja á Íslandi," *Búnatharrit* 25(1910):81–152, cited by Eythórsson, "Loftslagsbreytingar," p. 121.

25. *Thorgils s. ok Haflitha*, written c. 1200, says of Reykjahólar in western Iceland that "at that time [c. 1119] agricultural conditions were very favorable" (ch. 10, *Stur.* 1:27), implying that they were not at the time of the saga's composition. See also Thorarinsson, *Thousand Years Struggle*, p. 16.

26. *Svínfellinga s.*, ch. 8, *Stur.* 2:95; Kristján Eldjárn, "Two Medieval Farm Sites in Iceland and Some Remarks on Tephrochronology," *The Fourth Viking Congress*, pp. 15–17. Adam of Bremen, writing about 1075, the earliest author to give an account of Iceland, says "no crops are grown there" (*Gesta*, bk. 4, ch. 35, p. 184). This statement seems exaggerated in view of the Icelandic evidence. Sigurdur Thorarinsson mentions that pollen analyses from the farms of Thjórsárdal in southern Iceland, farms preserved since the eruption of Mt. Hekla in 1104, show that barley was cultivated there then, and traces of oats show that this grain also grew there, though perhaps only accidentally (*Thousand Years Struggle*, pp. 15–16).

27. Ch. 8, *Stur.* 2:95. Saemund's share of the livestock, excluding the geese, was worth perhaps about 1,630 legal aurar or perhaps about $65,200 in present-day values, counting each eyrir as worth about $40.00 (see below, ch. 2, n62). In spite of the apparent prosperity of this farm in the mid-13th century, it would not last. Already during the 13th century the nearby glacier, Vatnajökull, was advancing closer to the farm. Presently it is on the point of engulfing the home-field (Thorarinsson, *Thousand Years Struggle*, p. 37, plate IVb). Although not mentioned in *Svínfellinga s.*'s list of property, goats were raised on Iceland. Remains of large horns of rams found at Hölstathir on Lake Mývatn in the north dating from c. 1000 have been excavated (Magnus Degerbøl, "Nogle bemærkninger om husdyrene paa Island i middelalderen," *Forntida gårdar i Island*, pp. 268, 325; see also *KLNM*, s.v. "Geiteavl, Island"). At Stöng, a farm in the south that had been destroyed and covered with volcanic ash in 1300 after an eruption of Mt. Hekla, excavations have brought to light remains of the kinds of livestock that Saemund Ormsson had at Svínafell; bones of horses, sheep, cattle, pigs, and geese have been found there (Degerbøl, "Husdyrene," pp. 261–68, 324–25). In Iceland "the conditions for raising pigs certainly were not especially good" (ibid., pp. 268, 325), but still evidence from the sagas such as *Svínfellinga s.* support their existence in more than nominal numbers (see also *Grágás* Ib:121–22; Konrad Maurer, *Island von seiner ersten Entdeckung bis zum Untergange des Freistaats*, p. 394). Chickens apparently were only rarely raised in Iceland; neither literary sources nor

archaeological evidence indicate their presence in large numbers. A man called Hen Thórir, however, was supposed to have gained his nickname because he sold them (*Hœnsa-Thóris s.*, ch. 1, *ÍF* 3:6); chickens are also mentioned in *Flóamanna s.*, ch. 31, p. 63.

28. Adam of Bremen states that Iceland "has on it many people, who make their living only by raising cattle [or "sheep"] and they clothe themselves with their pelts [or "fleeces"]" (*Gesta* 4:35:184).

29. Richard Cleasby and Gudbrand Vigfusson, *An Icelandic-English Dictionary*, s.v. "gler."

30. *KLNM*, s.v. "Fåreavl, Island."

31. Ibid.

32. There are many instances of hay gathering in the sagas: see, for instance, *Brennu-Njáls s.*, ch. 75, *ÍF* 12:182; *Thorgils s. skartha*, ch. 67, *Stur.* 2:209.

33. *KLNM*, s.v. "Fåreavl, Island."

34. Ibid. Icelandic sheep during the Middle Ages may have been especially suited to the climate because apparently they were sturdier than contemporary Danish sheep: see Degerbøl, "Husdyrene," pp. 263–64, 325. Sturla Frithriksson ("Gras," p. 12) points out that although cattle and sheep were the most important livestock, cattle were usually kept in the homefield, while sheep made use of more outlying areas. Therefore with more ample space, sheep would be emphasized more than cattle.

35. Eggert Olafsen, *Riese igiennem Island* 2(Sorø, 1772):943, cited by Ingstad, *Land under Pole Star*, p. 69.

36. Ingstad, *Land under Pole Star*, p. 68.

37. *Guthmundar s. Arasonar*, ch. 54, *Bisk.* 2:111; see also *Grágás* 1b:122–23.

38. On the significance of whale meat and dried fish, especially during times of fasting, see *Íslendinga s.*, ch. 104, *Stur.* 1:379–80.

39. *DI* 2:78–80; see also *DI* 1:414–15 [c.1220], 476 [1224], 507 [1234], 580 [c. 1250]; *Grágás* 1b:125–31. In Iceland whaling consisted of driving whales ashore with harpoons (*KLNM*, s.v. "Hvalfangst, Island").

40. *Guthmundar s. Arasonar eptir Arngríms ábóta*, ch. 2, *Bisk.* 2:5.

41. Ibid., ch. 87, *Bisk.* 2:179. Pope Alexander III wrote (c. 1170–72) to the archbishop of Nidaros, who had jurisdiction over the Icelandic church, that those who depend on fishing for a livelihood may fish on Sundays and other holy days if the fish come near shore, except on the holiest days; but they must give the greater part of their catch to the local church and to the poor (*Latinske dokument til norsk historie*, p. 21).

42. *Land. (Melabók)*, p. 87n10 says that Björn was a Norwegian who

settled at Dalsmynni before 930; he was supposedly the first to forge iron in Iceland and because of this, he was called Rauthabjörn (Red-Björn, or Red-ore Björn). On Icelandic bog iron and the smelting of it, see also *KS*, p. 21.

43. Thorkell Jóhannesson, *Die Stellung der freien Arbeiter in Island*, pp. 87–88. Another instance is in Thjórsárdal: at Gjáskógar, which was destroyed by volcanic eruption in 1104 but had been deserted before then, there is much evidence of bog iron being smelted at a time well before 1100. Apparently this was an iron extraction area for several prosperous farms in the vicinity (Eldjárn, "Two Medieval Farm Sites," p. 14).

44. Jóhannesson, *Der freien Arbeiter*, p. 89.

45. There may have been some significant woods on Iceland in the earliest years of settlement, for *Land. (Hauksbók)*, ch. 20, p. 59, states "Ávang was an Irishman who was the first to settle at Botn, and he lived there his whole life. At that time there was so large a forest there that he built an ocean-going ship." Although the story itself might be regarded as apocryphal, it does illustrate the tradition that Iceland had more woods when it was first settled than later.

46. *Gesta* 4:35:184. Houses of cut stone were unknown. Most were built with a mixture of stones, lava, earth, and sod, and sometimes with just the sod alone (*KLNM*, s.v. "Husbygge, Island"). On private dwellings in Iceland in general, see V. Gudmundsson, *Privatboligen på Island i sagatiden*.

47. Björn Thorsteinsson, *Ný Íslandssaga*, pp. 142, 145; Jón Jóhannesson, *Íslendinga saga* 1:369.

48. See Oscar Albert Johnsen, *Norwegische Wirtschaftsgeschichte*, p. 33; J. Jóhannesson, *Íslendinga saga* 1:372.

49. Alexander Bugge, "Handelen mellem England og Norge indtil begyndelsen af det 15de aarhundrede," [*Norsk*] *Historisk tidsskrift*, 3rd ser. 4(1898):136.

50. See Johnsen, *Wirtschaftsgeschichte*, p. 33.

51. *Topographica Hibernica*, bk. 2, ch. 13, pp. 95–96; *The Art of Falconry*, bk. 2, ch. 4, p. 111.

52. On Icelandic falcons and falconry abroad, see G. Hofmann, "Falkenjagd und Falkenhandel in den nordischen Ländern während des Mittelalters," *Zeitschrift für deutsches Altertum* 88(1957):115–49; *KLNM*, s.v. "Falkar, Island"; and Björn Thórtharson, "Íslenzkir Falkar," *Safn til sögu Íslands*, 2nd ser., 1(1957).

53. T. J. Oleson, "Polar Bears in the Middle Ages," *Canadian Historical Review* 31(1950):49.

54. *Ann.*, pp. 152, 205, 345, 395. Polar bear skins are noted in many

church inventories (for examples, see DI 3, index, s.v. "Kirkja, búnathr: bjarnfell"); some of these may have come from polar bears killed on Iceland.

55. *Grágás* [*Statharhólsbók:* Arnamagnaean Collection, AM 334 fol.] (Copenhagen, 1879), pp. 372–73, cited by Oleson, "Polar Bears," p. 49; see also *Grágás* 1b:188–89; *KLNM*, s.v. "Import- och exportsförbud, Island."

56. Like polar bears, Icelandic horses were probably sent abroad mainly as gifts. This is the case with the only known instance: *Sneglu-Halla th.*, ch. 10, *ÍF* 9:294. On horses as an occasional article of export, see J. Jóhannesson, *Íslendinga saga* 1:344, 372; cf. however *KLNM*, s.v. "Hestehandel, Island."

57. Bugge, "Handelen mellem England og Norge," p. 148; see also *KLNM*, s.v. "Svovl."

58. Sulphur's military function appeared after the Third Crusade (1187–92) when Europe discovered how to manufacture Greek-fire, requiring sulphur, naphtha, and saltpeter. For the probable use of Icelandic sulphur for military defense and weaponry, see *KS*, pp. 60, 63; *Laurentius s.* ch. 8, *Bisk.* 1:798–99.

59. *Grágás* 1b:72.

60. Though Icelanders could grind the imported whole grain barley themselves, it usually seems to have been brought already ground, perhaps because it would make more economical use of cargo space in that form. For malt, see *KLNM*, s.v. "Malt och malthandel, Island"; for the grain trade in general, see *KLNM*, s.v. "Kornhandel, Island."

61. *Ann.*, p. 270.

62. *Egils s. Skallagrímssonar*, ch. 29, *ÍF* 2:75, implies that Skallagrím built at least some of his farm buildings at Álptanes from the abundant driftwood found nearby at Mýrar.

63. See *Grágás* 1b:123–25.

64. An exception may be "broad linen," possibly from the Low Countries.

65. Alexander Bugge, *Den norske trælasthandels historie* 1:50.

66. *Gunnlaugs s. ormstungu*, ch. 7, *ÍF* 3:71; *KLNM*, s.v. "Klede, Island."

67. H. Falk, *Altwestnordische Kleiderkunde*, pp. 58–59. If any cloth was colored, it was likely to be foreign because Icelandic vathmál was probably not dyed. Besides red, skarlat came in yellow-brown, blue, green, and white (*Laxdœla s.*, *ÍF* 5:60n1). "Sæi" (or "særi"), a cloth of uncertain nature, though perhaps the English cloth known as "say," is mentioned as being red, yellow, blue, and green (*DI* 4:180; *DI* 2:635; *DI* 5:410, cited by Falk, *Kleiderkunde*, p. 55). Suggesting that it was not until late in the

Commonwealth that foreign cloth was often imported for the rich, reference to dyed cloth is especially frequent only from the beginning of the 13th century when one of the best records for everyday life at that time, the saga collection known as *Sturlunga s.*, makes several references to green and red kirtles.

68. In 1203 at least some imported grape wine was replaced by that made from local berries (*Ann.*, p. 122); on 11 May 1237 Pope Gregory IX forbade this innovation (*DI* 1:514).

69. *DI* 1:597. Glass windows were probably first imported by Bishop Páll of Skálaholt, who brought two of them in 1195 (*Páls s. biskups*, ch. 5, *Bisk.* 1:131; see, however, *Thorláks s. hins ýngri*, ch. 12, *Bisk.* 1:275). Glass panes were generally small, as must have been the case with the church at Skarth because the inventory makes no mention of unusual size. Some relatively large panes are mentioned in other church inventories: at Setberg one was a "stika" high (about one yard, *DI* 4:173); at Melar one was one and a half "alnir" high (about 27", *DI* 4:193); one at Torfastath was of the same height and one "öln" (18 ") broad (*DI* 4:217). See also *Íslendinga s.*, ch. 33, *Stur.*, 1:265.

70. See Kristján Eldjárn, *Um Hólarkirkja*; Matthías Thórtharson, "Island," *NK* 23:288–316. For a splendid example of a chalice from the cathedral of Skálaholt dating from the mid-14th century, see the frontispiece to *KLNM* 8(1963). *Skálholts annáll* (*Ann.*, p. 206) notes that in 1329 a "likeness" of Bishop Guthmund was brought to Iceland and taken to Hólar. Not all icons apparently were imported as finished products. An Old Icelandic manuscript printed as "Líknesjusmith," ed. Kr. Kålund, in *Alfrœthi íslenzk* 1(1908):89–91, gives elaborate directions for making icons of saints and holy men with gold and silver. A stained glass window is mentioned in *DI* 3:87 in which was depicted Bishop Páll and St. Thorlák. For Icelandic artists, see *Páls s. biskups*, ch. 16, *Bisk.* 1:143–44; for an Icelandic goldsmith, see *Guthmundar s. dýra*, ch. 12, *Stur.* 1:186; for the art of working in gold generally, see Björn Th. Björnsson, *Íslenzk gullsmithi*.

71. The inventory of the church at Múli of 1318 (*DI* 2:435) mentions three English graduals and an English psaltar; see also inventory of the church at Háls of 1318 (*DI* 2:439).

72. Inventory of 1318, *DI* 2:435. Aside from its usual furnishings, a church, by at least the 14th century, might have had an organ as well. A priest named Arngrím Brandsson, who, it seems more than probable, was the same cleric who later became abbot of Thingeyrar monastery and who wrote the life of Bishop Guthmund of Hólar, was sent on an errand to the

archbishop of Nidaros in the earlier 14th century by Bishop Lárentíus of Hólar; he did not perform his duties very well, for he spent most of his time in Norway learning to play the organ from an old master. So devoted apparently was he to the instrument that when he returned to Iceland in 1329, he brought one back with him (*Ann.*, p. 397; *Laurentius s.*, chs. 61, 78, *Bisk.* 1:868, 908). In 1394 or somewhat afterward another organ, or possibly the same one that Arngrím had brought to Iceland 65 years before, was noted in an inventory of a church at Myklabær in Blönduhlíth (*DI* 3:565).

CHAPTER TWO

1. The sacred function of a chieftain ("gothi") can be seen in the origin of the Icelandic word itself as well as in that of "gothorth" ("chiefdom"), for both are related to "goth" (or "guth": "god"). By c. 965 when Iceland was divided into quarters, each quarter was supposed to have three (or four) main temples, one for each local assembly district ("thingsókn"). Whether this was actually implemented is unknown.

2. Usually a chiefdom had geographical limits because a follower of a chieftain would wish to use the site of pagan worship where his chieftain presided and for which he would pay a tax; and similarly during the Christian period, he probably would want to avail himself of a church his chieftain often built and of services there, for both of which he also paid a tax. The chieftain in turn would wish his followers to be in reasonable proximity to his own residence so that he could count on them to help keep the peace and to support him during times of conflict. Attendance at a local assembly, which came to be compulsory, would also imply residence in the vicinity. The fact that men had to live in the same quarter as their chieftain by c. 965 shows that at least by then nine (or twelve) chiefdoms were geographically confined to the area within a quarter.

3. Every farmer or landowner had to accompany his chieftain to at least one of three assemblies, the spring assembly ("várthing"), the late summer assembly ("leith"), or the Althing. Those who held a certain minimum of possessions in relationship to family size had to pay a tax to support men going to the Althing ("thingfararkaup"). At the spring assembly the chieftain picked every ninth man (in fact sometimes more) to accompany him to the Althing, for the expenses of which the thingman was paid his share of the thingfararkaup.

4. The written codification is known as *Grágás*. Parts of it survive in two main manuscripts, mostly overlapping in content, *Konungsbók* and *Statharhólsbók*. Because both date from the 13th century, it is impossible

to know for certain which material in these manuscripts is from after 1117–18 and which from before. For a discussion of *Grágás*, see Jón Jóhannesson, *Íslendinga saga* 1:109–13.

5. See *Íslb.*, ch. 5, pp. 12–13.

6. For more detailed discussions of Icelandic government, see Jóhannesson, *Íslendinga saga* 1:53–113; Björn Thorsteinsson, *Ný Íslandssaga*, pp. 84–105; and Simon Kalifa, "L'Etat et l'organisation sociale dans l'Islande médiévale," *Etudes germaniques* 22(1967):404–26. Older, but more extensive treatments are Konrad Maurer, *Altisländisches Strafrecht und Gerichtwesen*; idem, *Die Entstehung des isländisches Staats und seiner Verfassung*; Vilhjálmur Finsen, *Om den oprindelige ordning af nogle af den islandske fristats institutioner*; and Aa. Gregersen, *L'Islande: son statut à travers les âges*. The most important primary sources are *Thingskapa th.* (*Grágás* 1a:38–143) and *Lösögumanns th.* (*Grágás* 1a:208–17).

7. See Bjarni Einarson, "On the Status of Free Men in Society and Saga" (*Mediaeval Scandinavia* 7[1974]:45–55), for an argument somewhat contrary to that offered here. He says that Icelandic society in earliest times consisted of individuals who as free men considered themselves all as essentially equal, though they looked to the chieftains for religious and political leadership; it was only later, after the Christian tithe was introduced and when chieftains consequently were able to achieve more wealth that there was a greater social imbalance, causing in practice unequal behavior on the part of chieftains toward the less prosperous, though theoretical equality remained. While Einarsson's estimation of the greater wealth and power gained by chieftains after the introduction of the tithe in 1097 should not be discounted, his arguments for an earlier essential equality among all free men seem acceptable only with reservations. Surely if we consider only the chieftains' governmental powers, which were well established before the end of the 11th century, it seems that even then they were more than just "first among equals" in practice, however much equality may have existed in theory.

8. The Svínfellingar, Oddaverjar, Haukdælir, Sturlungar, and Ásbirningar: see Jóhannesson, *Íslendinga saga* 1:274–79.

9. For the Icelandic conversion, see *Kristni s., Bisk.* 1:3–32; *Íslb.*, ch. 7, pp. 14–18; Konrad Maurer, *Die Bekehrung des norwegischen Stammes zum Christentum.* Until 1103 or 1104 when the archiepiscopacy of Lund was created, Iceland remained under the archbishop of Hamburg-Bremen; from 1152 or 1153 when the archiepiscopacy of Nidaros was established, Iceland obeyed it. For a general account of early Icelandic Christianity, the most important source is *Íslb.*, chs. 7–10, pp. 14–26. Modern works

treating Icelandic Christianity during the Commonwealth are Jón Helgason, *Kristnisaga Íslands*, vol. 1, and Jón Hnefill Athalsteinsson, *Kristnitakan á Íslandi*.

10. Jóhannesson, *Íslendinga saga* 1:198.

11. Instead of employing others to be priests, a church owner could assume the duties himself, as did for instance the historian and chieftain, Ári Thorgilsson. This economical arrangement was effectively stopped in 1190 by the archbishop of Nidaros (Jóhannesson, *Íslendinga saga* 1:198, 224).

12. *Húngrvaka*, ch. 6, *Bisk.* 1:68.

13. *Íslb.*, ch. 10, p. 22.

14. *Ann.*, pp. 19, 110; see also nine versions of the decision of the Althing to adopt the tithe in *DI* 1:73–162. For a thorough discussion of the tithe, see Jóhannesson, *Íslendinga saga* 1:177–80, 202–9; see also *KLNM*, s.v. "Tiend, Island."

15. In the latter 13th century Bishop Árni Thorláksson of Skálaholt defended the Icelandic tithe from the charge that it was based upon the condemned practice of usury by stating that permission for the Icelandic method had been given by a Pope Innocent, perhaps Innocent IV (1243–54) (Jóhannesson, *Íslendinga saga* 1:204–6).

16. Ibid. 1:75–76, 202.

17. See ibid. 1:178.

18. It is doubtful that the chieftains profited from the thingfararkaup to any extent if at all, for they had to pay at least part, perhaps all, of the collected amount to the thingmen who actually accompanied them to the Althing; if they had any of the total amount remaining, no doubt it often would be needed to provide their followings with weapons and with lodging at the Althing (see Jóhannesson, *Íslendinga saga* 1:80–82). Other less regular income included the collection of the "fjörbaug," a fine levied against an outlaw under a chieftain's jurisdiction when the outlaw's property was seized for three years; and eventually, in some districts, a sheep tax ("sauthatoll") was levied against the chieftain's men (Einar Ól. Sveinsson, *The Age of the Sturlungs*, p. 10).

19. See *Thorláks s. biskups hins elzta*, chs. 11–16, *Bisk.* 1:100–109.

20. For the life and career of St. Thorlák see ibid., pp. 87–124, and *Thorláks s. biskups hins ýngri, Bisk.* 1:261–332. For a full discussion of St. Thorlák's reforms and reaction to them, see also Jóhannesson, *Íslendinga saga* 1:202–24.

21. See *Guthmundar s. Arasonar, Hóla-biskups hins elzta, Bisk.* 1:405–558; *Guthmundar s. dýra, Stur.* 1:160–212; *Guthmundar s. Arasonar, Hóla-biskups, eptir Arngríms ábóta, Bisk.* 2:1–184. The litera-

ture concerning the still controversial figure of Bishop Guthmund is very large. The discussion of Jóhannesson (*Íslendinga saga* 1:236–53) is well balanced; for a discussion of Guthmund that is mainly favorable and that also indicates the major interpretations of his life, see Régis Boyer, "L'Evêque Guthmundr Arason: Témoin de son temps," *Etudes germaniques* 22(1967):427–44. It was not until after annexation that the Icelandic clergy won independence from secular influence, beginning with Bishop Árni Thorláksson of Skálaholt (1269–98). By that time the church became the most important force in Iceland itself because the power of the chieftains had been totally broken. For a discussion of the attempted reforms of both Guthmund and Thorlák and the results, as well as a consideration of church-state relationships in Norway during the latter 12th century, see Peter Foote, "Secular Attitudes in Early Iceland," *Mediaeval Scandinavia* 7(1974):36–44, especially pp. 39–44.

22. *Land.*, chs. 9, 97, 113, 115, pp. 45, 139, 152–56.

23. Ingólf gave at least one of his thralls freedom and his own farm (*Land.*, ch. 9, p. 45). Auth gave four freed thralls sizable parcels in Laxárdal (*Land.*, chs. 100–103, pp. 141–42).

24. Most of the large household of 20 persons who accompanied Auth to Iceland, even those who were not thralls, may have been intended to labor for her (*Land.*, ch. 95, p. 138). Geirmund had a following of 80 freedmen, most of whom must have been laborers. He also had four farms directed by freedmen or thralls (*Land.*, chs. 113, 115, pp. 153–54).

25. Jóhannesson, *Íslendinga saga* 1:420.

26. About 1100 it has been estimated that most Icelandic farmers still owned their own land. But a possible indication that many were tenants even then may be seen in the tithe arrangement, which was established a few years earlier, for it was based by implication upon rents received. There are a number of indications that during the next two centuries poverty among freeholders increased, accompanied by a corresponding rise in numbers of tenants (see Jóhannesson, *Íslendinga saga* 1:411–13).

27. *Grágás*, begun in 1117–18, still mentions slaves, and thus if these references are not to be regarded as holdovers from an earlier period some slave labor must have still existed at the beginning of the twelfth century. Nevertheless the last known thrall belonged to Thorsteinn Síthu-Hallsson about or somewhat after the middle of the 10th century (*Draumr Thorsteins Síthu-Hallssonar*, ÍF 11:323–26; Jóhannesson, *Íslendinga saga* 1:419). On Icelandic slavery, see Árni Pálsson, "Um lok thrældoms á Íslandi," *Skírnir* 106(1932):191–203.

28. *Grágás* 1b:135–39; ibid. (Vithbœtir IV [AM 347, fol.]), p. 248; Jóhannesson, *Íslendinga saga* 1:412–14. Loans of money could draw the

criticism of usury. Therefore it is not certain that legal recognition of interest-bearing loans involved money or livestock (see, for example, *Brennu-Njáls s.*, ch. 6, *ÍF* 12:22).

29. Chs. 10, 53, *Stur.* 1:237, 304.

30. That land was considered a safer investment can be seen when the father in *Konungs skuggsjá* tells his son, "And if you see that your trading profits grow quite large, take two thirds and invest it in good farm land because such an investment is thought to be the best, whether a man uses it for himself or for his relations. And then you should do as you wish with the third part—keep it longer in business or put it all in land" (*KS*, pp. 6–7). This Norwegian work written about 1250 refers, of course, to circumstances there at that time. Earlier, however, such advice might well have been followed by Icelanders. Once a fortune had been increased by hazardous foreign trade, a more conservative but profitable investment in land would have been especially attractive.

31. *Grágás* 1b:67–68. Whether ownership of a vessel was singular or plural, the ship could be lent for a fixed fee. In this case the borrower had to take full responsibility for the ship; he could not go any farther than had previously been agreed upon; he was limited to carrying the same cargo that was previously promised; and the borrower in turn could not lend the ship for a profit (ibid.). Most Icelandic shipowners actively participated in voyages themselves, although by the 12th and 13th centuries some Icelanders who still owned a ship might send substitutes on a voyage, the owner gaining profits from that portion of the cargo that belonged to him (Oscar Albert Johnsen, "Le Commerce et la navigation en Norvège au moyen âge," *Revue historique* 178[1936]:394). There is no reason to doubt that trading activity could be carried on by passengers as well as owners and crew. Whenever a ship arrived in a district anyone could take passage; but if the ship became overloaded, the cargo of the captain had to be taken off first, then that of the passengers. If the ship still was overloaded, those taking passage last had to get off and the skipper had to pay each six aurar for breach of contract. These details are found in the Icelandic code, *Járnsítha* (ch. 129, *Norges gamle love* 4:298), which was issued in 1271. However, these stipulations probably reflect similar conditions existing since before the annexation of 1262–64.

32. *KLNM*, s.v. "Geistlighetens handel, Island."

33. *Latinske dokument til norsk historie*, p. 48.

34. That some parish priests traded abroad, at least for their bishop, is suggested by the fact that Bishop Páll of Skálaholt made a count, c. 1200, of the number of priests in his diocese, "because he wanted to let priests go abroad if enough remained behind" (*Páls s. biskups*, ch. 11, *Bisk.* 1:136).

35. See Johnsen, "Le Commerce," p. 394. As part of their duties, the crew had certain cooking responsibilities as described in *Eyrbyggja s.*, ch. 39, *ÍF* 4:104–6. The success story of Odd Ófeigsson is exceptional: though once a relatively small landowner, he eventually was able to buy several trading ships as well as a chiefdom because of his astute trading practices (*Bandamanna s.*, *ÍF* 7:291–363).

36. For the results of excavations at Gásir, see Finnur Jónsson and Daniel Bruun, "Det gamle handelssted Gásar (at Gásum), yngre Gæsir, ved Øfjord (Eyjafjörthur)," *Kongelige danske videnskabernes selskabs forhandlinger*(1904), pp. 95–111. Magnús Már Lárusson (*KLNM*, s.v. "Handelsplasser, Island") says that the largest markets during the Commonwealth were Eyrar and Hvítárvellir (at the mouths of two rivers named Hvítá in the South Quarter), Straumsfjörth, Dögurtharnes, and Vathill in the west, Bortheyri, Blönduóss, Kolbeinsáróss, and Gásir in the north, Krossavík in the northeast, Gautavík in the east, Hornafjörth in the southeast. Many other but less important markets and fairs are mentioned in the saga literature. Numerous as they were before, by the 13th century only ten are known to have been in use (Jóhannesson, *Íslendinga saga* 1:384–85).

37. According to *Grágás* (1b:69–71) a harbor was defined as a place where ships had previously come. At harbors merchants or traveling buyers had the right to water and pasturage, the latter for no more than three days. In return the landowner was paid by each merchant and passenger a toll ("hafnartoll" or "skiptoll") of one öln of vathmál, or one woolen cloak, or as much raw wool that, spun, would be ⅙ of a skein. For landing fees, the captain had to pay the landowner nine alnir; in return he had the right to protect his ship with turf and stone provided there was a field or meadow. The landowner had to house the ship's crew. If the merchant stayed over for the winter, he might stay on the farm by signing a contract ("forgift"), outlining definite conditions (*KLNM*, s.v. "Handelsafgifter, Island"). Because Norwegian merchants were exempt from these tolls, though entitled to the benefits, it is reasonable to suppose that Icelanders themselves did not have to pay these fees: see Jóhannesson, *Íslendinga saga* 1:384.

38. *Thorgils s. ok Haflitha* (written c.1200), speaking of 1119, ch. 10, *Stur.* 1:27; *Sturlu s.* (written shortly after 1200), ch. 4, *Stur.* 1:66; *Prestssaga Guthmundar gótha* (written first or second decade of 13th century), ch. 7, *Stur.* 1:130.

39. As originally those in Norway seem to have been: cf. *Óláfs s. kyrra*, ch. 2, *ÍF* 28:204–5; see also Jóhannesson, *Íslendinga saga* 1:108–9.

40. *KLNM*, s.v. "Gilde, Island"; see Oscar Albert Johnsen, "Gil-

devæsenet i Norge i middelalderen: oprindelse og utvikling," [Norsk] Historisk tidsskrift, 5th ser., 5(1924):29.

41. Magnús Már Lárusson, "Íslenzkar mælieiningar," *Skírnir* 132(1958):243.

42. *DI* 1:311; *Grágás* 1b(Vithbœtir IV[AM 347 fol.]):249.

43. The weight of an örtug would be 9 grams (⅓ that of an eyrir); the weight of a penning was ⅒ that of an örtug. These weights were probably seldom used, and thus they are largely theoretical.

44. Asgaut Steinnes, "Mål, vekt og verderekning i Noreg i millomalderen og ei tid etter," *NK* 30:153, s.v. "skålpund."

45. See Lárusson, "Íslenzkar mælieiningar," p. 243; *KLNM*, s.v. "Lispund, Island." For the definition of a lest the sources vary. The Norwegian Gula Thing law stated that there were 10 skippundar in a lest; however the Icelandic source (*Guthmundar s. Arasonar hins elzta*, ch. 94, *Bisk.* 1:545) probably should be regarded as the more trustworthy for Icelandic usage: instead of 10 skippundar to a lest, it has 12: "*xij skippund í lest.*" If, however, there were only 10 skippundar to a lest in Iceland, then the lest would be 2,759.04 lbs. (1.25 metric tons) and the áhöfn would be 33,108.48 lbs. (15 metric tons).

46. Gold did not play a significant role as an exchange medium in Iceland. When mentioned as a value of account, it was usually to avoid confusion with pure and impure silver. It was worth eight times the same weight of pure silver. Gold itself was rare in Iceland, and it was used mainly for ornamental purposes.

47. *KLNM*, s.v. "Alen, Island."

48. As will be discussed in Chapter 6, the use of the stika in Iceland was probably related to English practice. Conceivably a stika measurement, composed of two alnir, either "long" or "short," was occasionally used before c. 1100 to achieve greater exactitude for the measurement of a single öln; in this case the stika per se may not have been introduced because of English measurement reforms. Nevertheless, when the standard stika was adopted by law c. 1200, this regulation must have been due to English usage; probably it had conformed to English measurement ever since shortly after 1100.

49. *DI* 1:307–9; *Grágás* 1b(Vithbœtir IV[AM 347 fol.]):250.

50. In addition, vathmál 4 alnir in length by 2 wide, and 1.5 alnir in length by 1 wide was sometimes used in certain districts of Iceland as being equivalent to 1 "legal" eyrir for only those districts ("thinglagseyrir").

51. Björn M. Ólsen, "Um skattbændatal 1311 og manntal á Íslandi fram ath theim tíma," *Safn til sögu Íslands* 4(1907–15):366–71; Thorkell

Jóhannesson, *Die Stellung der freien Arbeiter in Island,* pp. 38–40; J. Jóhannesson, *Íslendinga saga* 1:396.

52. Cf. the discussion below in Chapter 4 of comparative values of woolens and impure silver in Iceland and Norway, values which must have existed by c. 1022; J. Jóhannesson says that the new ratio certainly occurred by the mid-11th century (*Íslendinga saga* 1:395).

53. It thus took 24 alnir of vathmál to equal 1 eyrir of impure silver and 48 alnir for 1 eyrir of pure silver. Just as the eyrir as a weight was divided into smaller units, so it was as a monetary designation: there were 3 örtugar to an eyrir; and there were 20 penningar (at an early time only 10) to an örtug. *Grágás* (lb:192) gives an exact if confusing definition of the value of vathmál in terms of impure silver: "When Christianity came out here to Iceland impure silver was used in all large transactions; it should withstand cutting, and the greater part should be silver and so struck that sixty pennies make an eyrir. . . . It was proclaimed that the following were equal: one hundred [i.e., 120 alnir of vathmál valued in aurar] of [impure] silver and four hundred [i.e., 480] and 20 alnir of vathmál; and then an eyrir [of impure silver] equals ½ a mörk of vathmál" (*"That var iafn micit fe callat .c. silfrs. sem iiii. hundroth oc xx. alna vathmala. oc varth tha at halfri mörc vathmala eyrir"*). If the latter part of the statement is translated in this way, the 4:1 ratio of legal aurar (of vathmál) to an eyrir of impure silver is exact if one ignores the extra 20 alnir of vathmál; for this reason the 20 alnir is thought by Finnur Jónsson to be a scribal error ("Islands mønt, mål og vægt," *NK* 30:156); G. W. Dasent (*The Story of Burnt Njal* 2:403) says that the extra 20 alnir corresponded to the extra 6d. in the pound when payment to the English Exchequer was made by weight, "as so much thrown in to turn the scale." In criticizing Jónsson's interpretation, Svend Aakjær says (in Jónsson, "Islands mønt," p. 161n4) that "four hundred and 20 alnir of vathmál" should be read as "twenty-four hundred [i.e., 2,880] alnir of vathmál" and that one hundred (i.e., 120) of silver should be understood as 120 aurar of impure silver. In this case the 4:1 ratio between legal aurar and an eyrir of impure silver is still upheld. Aakjær unnecessarily weakens his argument by combining two ratios of legal aurar to an eyrir of pure silver, 8:1 and 7.5:1. Magnús Már Lárusson ("Nokkrar athugasemdir um upphæth manngjalda," *Saga* 1[1960]:76–91) tries to prive that the author of this clause attempted to describe conditions for 1000, but that he reflected conditions pertaining to 1200 or afterward. Lárusson suggests that instead of the literal "four hundred and twenty alnir of vathmál," 624 were actually intended; and he suggests that the "hundred of silver" ought to be read as "120 örtugar of silver." Lárusson's argument is difficult to follow in places, especially because it is not

readily apparent how he arrives at the figure of 624. In any case his reasoning is weakened by two erroneous statements on p. 78: that when a legal eyrir that varied from the standard 6 alnir legal eyrir was instituted for a district, the amount of cloth concerned apparently remained the same, and that the Althing price list of c. 1200 considered the value of a kúgildi as being 120 alnir. For these reasons it has seemed preferable to continue to consider this clause in *Grágás* as testimony to an 8:1 ratio between legal aurar to an eyrir of pure silver.

54. Ólsen, "Um skattbændatal," pp. 366–71; Th. Jóhannesson, *Der freien Arbeiter,* pp. 38–40; J. Jóhannesson, *Íslendinga saga* 1:396.

55. The manner followed here of writing the ratio may cause confusion, for it could be written 1:8 instead; the legal eyrir, in either way of writing the ratio, was worth ⅛ the pure silver eyrir.

56. See J. Jóhannesson, *Íslendinga saga* 1:394–95.

57. Reasons for the 10.83:1 ratio will be discussed shortly. Jón Jóhannesson favors a decrease in the value of silver as being the cause of the changes to 7.5:1 and 6:1. He cites a significant increase of silver mining in Germany and the beginning of it in Sweden and possibly other places in Scandinavia during the latter part of the 12th century (*Íslendinga saga* 1:395). However, the silver and copper mining industry of Saxony, especially near Goslar, had already peaked in productivity by c. 1200 (Michael Postan, "The Trade of Mediaeval Europe: The North," *The Cambridge Economic History of Europe* 2:202) and the silver mines of Sweden could have furnished only a relatively small amount of the metal compared with Saxony by 1200; during the 14th century the Swedish mines already had become exhausted (John U. Nef, "Mining and Metallurgy in Mediaeval Civilisation," *Cambridge Economic History* 2:458). It seems doubtful that either of these sources of new silver could have been responsible for a drastic fall in the value of this metal in Scandinavia. By comparison, during the Viking period very large amounts of silver were brought to Scandinavia from abroad. Yet the resulting decrease in its value seems to have been only about 17% even in places in Norway such as Rogaland that received particularly large amounts of the metal (Steinnes, "Mål, vekt og verderekning," p. 130; *KLNM* s.v. "auralag"; Jan Petersen, "Handel i Norge i vikingetiden," *NK* 16:44). When the devastations of the Vikings ceased and they were converted to Christianity, this allowed a fuller Scandinavian participation in trade with western Europe. Their accumulated silver supplies consequently began to dwindle, causing the value of silver to rise again in Scandinavia. As reliance upon foreign imports increased, especially during the 13th century in Norway, more silver would have been drawn away, resulting in a higher price for it, particularly

in Norway. Even if silver mined in Sweden and possibly in Norway had helped to offset this growing scarcity, it is not probable that the new mines could have so completely reversed the price trend that silver was worth 25% less by c. 1300 compared to what it had been worth somewhat before 1200—even during the Viking Age the decline in value had been less. In Iceland from c. 930 until almost 1200 the number of legal aurar compared to an eyrir of pure silver must have been approximately the same, 8:1. In light of diminished supplies of silver in 13th-century Norway, Iceland's most important trading partner, it is most unlikely that the silver supply increased in Iceland at that time. The alternative explanation must be favored: the value of vathmál was artificially increased, both in c. 1200 and in c. 1300.

58. *DI* 1:165.

59. J. Jóhannesson, *Íslendinga saga* 1:396.

60. Steinnes, "Mål, vekt og verderekning," p. 134.

61. J. Jóhannesson, *Íslendinga saga* 1:397. This document of c. 1186 is a price list of a spring assembly, the Árnes Thing. While the listed price for a kúgildi must reflect an earlier common price of 2.5 silver aurar—which is the equivalent of 20 legal aurar using the common ratio of 8:1—in this particular case the price was actually somewhat higher. In this list the value of vathmál and correspondingly that of a legal eyrir had declined exceptionally in relationship to an eyrir of pure silver, so that it now took 10.83 legal aurar to equal one eyrir of pure silver. Therefore if 20 legal aurar is regarded as the constant price, a kúgildi would cost only 1.85 aurar of pure silver in this case; if 2.5 pure silver aurar is the constant, though it is not expressed this way on the price list, a kúgildi would actually be 27 legal aurar.

62. See J. Jóhannesson, *Íslendinga saga* 1:396–97. These valuations permit very approximate estimates of present purchasing power of one legal eyrir; these estimates, however, can be accepted only with the greatest caution because, quite apart from the very different conditions of the Middle Ages compared with those at present, a cow's value varies a great deal today, just as it did in medieval Iceland. If presently (1980) in the U.S. a cow described above as "standard" is worth about $600.00, then the 20 aurar kúgildi would mean the eyrir would be worth about $30.00 today; the 16 aurar kúgildi about $37.50 per eyrir; the 15 aurar kúgildi about $40.00 per eyrir; the 12 aurar kúgildi about $50.00 per eyrir. The value of a kúgildi, in terms of aurar, given by the Árnes Thing price list probably was actually 27, thus the legal eyrir in that case would equal about $22.22 today.

63. See J. Jóhannesson, *Íslendinga saga* 1:379.

64. For examples of this practice, see *Hœnsa-Thóris* s., ch. 1, *ÍF* 3:6; *Gunnars* s. *Keldungnúpsfífls*, ch. 4, *ÍF* 14:354; *Brennu-Njáls* s., ch. 101, *ÍF* 12:258; *Ljósvetninga* s., *ÍF* 10:21; *Íslendinga* s., chs. 15, 35, *Stur.* 1:240–41, 269, 270; *Reykdœla* s. *ok Viga-Skútu*, ch. 9, *ÍF* 10:172–73. See also J. Jóhannesson, *Íslendinga saga* 1:379–80.

65. *DI* 1:316; *Grágás* 1b(Vithbœtir IV[AM 347 fol.]):246. The size of each öln of vathmál used for this list's computation was to be 3 spans ("spannir") long by 2 wide. Because 2 spans equalled 1 legal öln, the measurement used here could be expressed as 1.5 alnir in length by 1 öln in width for each piece of vathmál that was to equal an eyrir. The usual measurement for each piece of vathmál used for this purpose was 1 öln in length by 2 in width. Thus the square measurement of the material in the usual piece was 25% more than in that of the Árnes Thing. One purpose of this Árnes Thing price list obviously seems to have been to allow a variant size of vathmál to be exchanged. The quantity of vathmál given by the Árnes Thing for 120 legal aurar and the usual amount of vathmál for 120 legal aurar may be summarized in the following manner:

ÁRNES THING STANDARD	USUAL STANDARD
Quantity:	
360 alnir = 120 legal aurar	720 alnir = 120 legal aurar
(or 3 alnir = 1 legal eyrir)	(or 6 alnir = 1 legal eyrir)
Expressed in measurement:	
2 spans wide x 1080 spans long = 120 legal aurar	4 spans wide x 1440 spans long = 120 legal aurar
(or 1 öln wide x 540 alnir long = 120 legal aurar)	(or 2 alnir wide x 720 alnir long = 120 legal aurar)
Therefore:	
2160 spans² = 120 legal aurar	5760 spans² = 120 legal aurar
(or 540 alnir² = 120 legal aurar)	(or 1440 alnir² = 120 legal aurar)

Because the square measurement of material in each usual piece of vathmál that was used to correspond to a legal öln was 25% greater than that used by the Árnes Thing, for the sake of consistency 25% must be deducted from the usual square measurement per 120 legal aurar when comparing it to the amount of vathmál for 120 legal aurar given by the Árnes Thing:

ÁRNES THING STANDARD	USUAL STANDARD
2160 spans² = 120 legal aurar	5760 spans² - 25% = 4320 spans = 120 legal aurar

(or 540 alnir² = 120 legal aurar)   (or 1440 alnir² - 25% = 1080 alnir²
                                          = 120 legal aurar)

Thus the usual amount of vathmál for 120 legal aurar, in terms of the Árnes Thing measurement, is exactly twice as great, just as was the value of a usual legal eyrir compared to one of the Árnes Thing.

66. This date for the Althing price list is disputed. It is set at c. 1100 by Jón Sigurthsson, the editor of the volume of *Diplomatarium Islandicum* in which it is included (*DI* 1:164) and at c. 1200 by J. Jóhannesson (*Íslendinga saga* 1:397–98). The latter's main argument for this date is the ratio of 8:1 being changed to 7.5:1. In addition to the generally urgent need for price regulation at this time (ibid., p. 382), the very serious inflation reflected by the regulations of the Árnes Thing made some action for the island as a whole imperative. The regulations of the Árnes Thing must have occurred before c. 1200 because the stika law regulating cloth measurement in perpetuity was made at that time: the measurement of cloth in the Árnes Thing list does not correspond to this legal measurement. Jón Sigurthsson gives the date of the Árnes Thing list as c. 1200 (*DI* 1:316), but it must have been somewhat before then.

67. Most of the goods mentioned in the list concern domestic agricultural products, products derived from them, or products of wild animals; these items mostly concerned only domestic trade, with the exception of vathmál and other woolens. Some of the listed items, however, would have to be imported: most grain meal, broad linen, English linen, and wax, as well as gold and silver and perhaps some of the iron products. That imported products are mentioned in this list with fixed prices indicates that they must have been commonly traded.

68. England obviously furnished Icelanders with this English linen, though not necessarily directly. England, too, with its rich mines may have been the origin of some of the iron products mentioned. Because it is mentioned as a type of broad linen distinct from the English linen, it may have been of Flemish origin.

69. *DI* 1:164–67; *Grágás* 1b:192–95.

70. *DI* 1:166–67; *Grágás* 1b:194.

71. *DI* 1:167; *Grágás* 1b:194.

72. *Íslendinga s.*, ch. 37, *Stur.* 1:274,277; Sveinsson, *Age of the Sturlungs*, p. 50.

73. *Íslendinga s.*, ch. 15, *Stur.* 1:240–41.

74. In revenge, during the summer of 1216, merchants in Bergen set out against Sæmund's son, Páll, who had to flee to Nidaros; on his way he

drowned. Icelanders from the district that Sæmund and Thorvald controlled blamed the Norwegians for Páll's death. In retaliation, in the summer of 1217, Sæmund led an army of 600 against some Norwegian merchants on Iceland, taking from them 43,200 alnir of vathmál or its equivalent. In return, the Norwegians killed Sæmund's brother Orm during the summer of 1218. Then, in 1219, Orm's son-in-law dragged a Norwegian from a church and killed him. Norway contemplated war with Iceland, using this feud as an excuse, but Snorri Sturluson, who was in Norway at the time, exercised his powers of diplomacy to prevent it, promising, insincerely as it turned out, to bring Iceland under Norwegian control more peaceably. See *Ann.*, pp. 124–25; *Íslendinga s.*, chs. 35, 38, *Stur.* 1:269–70, 277–78; Jón Sigurthsson ("Introduction" to no. 152), *DI* 1:602–3; Sveinsson, *Age of the Sturlungs*, pp. 29–30; Halldor Hermannsson, *Sæmundr Sigfússon and the Oddaverjar*, p. 19; J. Jóhannesson, *Íslendinga saga* 1:283–91.

75. J. Jóhannesson, *Íslendinga saga* 1:380.

76. *Grágás* 1b:72–73; see also J. Jóhannesson, *Íslendinga saga* 1:380–81; *KLNM*, s.v. "Marked, Island."

77. After the loss of Icelandic independence, the former "first-buying" and pricing rights that had been held by the chieftains on incoming cargoes were then assumed by the Norwegian king. Every ship that came into the district of jurisdiction of the king's representative, the "sýslumath," now had its cargo priced by that official (Sigurthsson, "Introduction to no. 152," *DI* 1:602–3). On the "first-buying" rights of the sýslumath, acting for the king, see *DI* 2:163.

CHAPTER THREE

1. One of the few rulers to provide effective opposition for a time to Viking attacks by sea was King Alfred the Great: see *The Anglo-Saxon Chronicle*, p. 90.

2. See Magnus Andersen, *Vikingefærden 1893*.

3. See N. Nicolaysen, *The Viking Ship Discovered at Gokstad*; A. W. Brøgger and Haakon Shetelig, *The Viking Ships*; Thorleif Sjøvold, *The Oseberg Find and the other Viking Ship Finds*; Haakon Shetelig and Hjalmar Falk, *Scandinavian Archaeology*, pp. 371–75. On Norse ships and navigation in addition, see *KLNM*, s.v. "Skibstyper, archæologiske vidnesbyrd" and "Skibstyper, skriftlige kilder"; Hjalmar Falk, "Altnordisches Seewesen," *Wörter und Sachen* 4(1912):1–122; and Uwe Schnall, *Navigation der Wikinger*.

4. The remains of another ship dating from about 1100 was excavated in 1948; it may have been a knörr. See Bernhard Færøyvik, "Eit kjøp-

mannskip fra elleve hundred ári," *Bergens tidende,* 29 May 1948 and his "Leivdar av eit kaupskip på Holmen, Bergenhus," *Bergens sjøfartsmuseets årbok* (1948) (both cited by Lúthvík Kristjánsson, "Grænlenzki landnemaflotinn og breithfirzki báturinn," *Árbók hins íslenzka fornleifafélags* [1964], p. 25).

5. Tryggvi Oleson, *Early Voyages and Northern Approaches,* p. 13.

6. *Ann.,* p. 278, s.v. 1361, records a ship having at least 90 passengers and crew. This ship was probably a búza, which was similar to the knörr, though larger. Still, the number aboard seems excessive. The knörr, though usually a transoceanic vessel, apparently was used sometimes for coastal shipping. The Icelandic trader Odd Ófeigsson used two knerrir though he did not travel "north of Eyjafjörth or west of Hvítá" (*Bandamanna s.,* ch. 1, *ÍF* 7:297).

7. Shetelig and Falk, *Scandinavian Archaeology,* p. 375; G. J. Marcus, "The Navigation of the Norsemen," *Mariner's Mirror* 39(1953):115; *KLNM,* s.v. "Handelssjöfart."

8. *Hákonar s. Hákonarsonar,* ch. 283, p. 545; see also Bruce E. Gelsinger, "Some Unusual Norwegian Thirteenth-Century Ships," *Mariner's Mirror,* forthcoming.

9. It has been calculated that a keelboard for the Gokstad Ship would have required a straight growing oak about 82′ (c. 25 m.) high (Sjøvold, *Oseberg Find,* p. 58), an exceptional height even during the Middle Ages. Ships intended for coastal navigation or for generally placid waters, such as the longship, could use a jointed keel (e.g., Skuldelev II) and thereby achieve length for greater than the Gokstad Ship, but the great stress of heavy winds on open seas against the sail, transferred to the keel where the mast was anchored, would have made such vessels too dangerous to sail open waters (see P. H. Sawyer, *Age of the Vikings,* p. 78). Snorri Sturluson says that King Harald Gormsson of Denmark was discouraged in the 10th century from invading Iceland because of the longship's unsuitability for open seas (*Óláfs s. Tryggvasonar,* ch. 33, *ÍF* 26:270–72); these remarks may allude to similar plans of the Norwegian jarl that had to be discarded in 1218 or 1219, perhaps partly for similar reasons: see *Íslendinga s.,* ch. 38, Stur. 1:277–78.

10. Shetelig and Falk, *Scandinavian Archaeology,* p. 375.

11. By 1498 a ship called a "ferja" apparently was used for traveling overseas, because in that year King Hans of Denmark-Norway granted permission to the bishop of Skálaholt to trade everywhere in his kingdom with the *Skálholtferja* (*DI* 7:408). An earlier ship of the bishop, however, might have been a true ferry, and this later one may have kept the former name even though it may not have been the same type of ship. Cf. the

Hólaferja belonging to the northern Icelandic bishop mentioned for 1394: *Ann.*, p. 426.

12. Marcus, "Navigation," p. 115.

13. Shetelig and Falk, *Scandinavian Archaeology*, pp. 375–76.

14. Ibid., p. 376.

15. Or a little farther forward, as in the Oseberg Ship (Shetelig and Falk, *Scandinavian Archaeology*, p. 362).

16. Ibid., p. 363.

17. *KS*, p. 6. He should also have a "good supply of nails, . . . both spikes and rivets, . . . good grapnels and hardware, chisels and augers, and all those other tools which ships' carpenters need to have."

18. Shetelig and Falk, *Scandinavian Archaeology*, pp. 363, 370.

19. As on the Gokstad Ship: Sjøvold, *Oseberg Find*, p. 24.

20. As on Skuldelev I: Olaf Olsen and Ole Crumlin-Pedersen, "The Skuldelev Ships (II).," *Acta Archaeologica* 38 (1967): 100.

21. See Bruce E. Gelsinger, "The Norse 'Day's Sailing'," *Mariner's Mirror* 56(1970):107–9; idem, "The Mediterranean Voyage of a Twelfth-Century Icelander," *Mariner's Mirror* 58(1972):164.

22. See, for example, *Guthmundar s. Arasonar hins elzta*, ch. 3, *Bisk.* 1:411.

23. For an example of a ship purchased in Iceland, see *Svarfdœla s.*, ch. 26, *ÍF* 9:200. The typical cost of a hafskip cannot be determined accurately because of lack of necessary data as well as undoubted variability in the price. However, the value of one ship in the earlier 13th century may be approximated. A fine of 90 "hundred" of vathmál (10,800 alnir) was paid by the exchange of a knörr, 18 "hundred" (2,160 alnir of vathmál) worth of either driftwood or other valuables cast ashore, and some gold and silver (*Íslendinga s.*, ch. 79, *Stur.* 1:341). If the metal amounted to no more than 2 "hundred" worth of vathmál (240 alnir), then the cost of the ship would be 70 "hundred" (8,400 alnir). Either of two ratios of legal aurar to one of pure silver could have been in use at the time. If the ratio was 8:1, the cost of the ship would be 175 pure silver aurar. If the ratio was 7.5:1, which seems more likely, the cost would be 187 silver aurar. Another ship in 1394, purchased by the bishop of Hólar, cost him 60 "hundred" (7,200 alnir of vathmál) (*Ann.*, p. 426). At that time the ratio of legal aurar to one of pure silver was 6:1; therefore this amount was the equivalent of 200 aurar of pure silver. Even though these two instances are widely separated in time, and there is no way of comparing the ships in each transaction, it may not be far from the truth to state that the cost of a knörr was usually between 175 and 200 aurar of pure silver. More generally, the cost of a good merchant ship seems to have been the equivalent of

one good farm or two smaller ones: see *Laxdœla s.*, chs. 38, 69, *ÍF* 5:111, 203; *Gísla s. Súrssonar,* ch. 38, *ÍF* 6:118; *Hallfrethar s.*, ch. 2, *ÍF* 8:140; see also Kristjánsson, "Landnemaflotinn," p. 29.

24. For a supposed instance of building a ship from local forests in Iceland during the Settlement Age, see *Land.*, p. 34. Other ships built in Iceland, whether of imported timber or of driftwood, and of uncertain type, are noted: in 1359 a Norwegian, Ívar Holm, departed Iceland on a ship he had built himself, perhaps in Iceland (*Ann.*, p. 358); in 1388 one was built at the busy marketplace of Eyrar in southern Iceland (*Ann.*, p. 208); and *Lögmanns annáll* (*Ann.*, p. 292) mentions that Bishop Árni Ólafsson built a large vessel in 1416 and that he had many others built, presumably in Iceland. See also *Ann.*, p. 360, s.v. 1362; *Svarfdœla s.*, ch. 13, *ÍF* 9:156.

25. Kristjánsson, "Landnemaflotinn," pp. 20–49, 53–54, 62, 64–66, 67–68.

26. *KS*, p. 6.

27. Ibid.

28. A. W. Brøgger and Håkon Shetelig, *Vikingeskipene* (Oslo, 1950), p. 253, cited by Kristjánsson, "Landnemaflotinn," p. 36.

29. G. J. Marcus, "Norse Traffic with Iceland," *Economic History Review*, 2nd ser., 9(1957):412.

30. *KS*, pp. 36–37. According to *Jónsbók* (c. 1280 or c. 1300) a ship could come to Iceland as late as 8 September—a time that is formally designated in 1531 as the last possible time in the year to arrive on the island (*DI* 4:461). The beginning of the period when ships may come to Iceland was set in 1530 as 1 May, but it is not known whether this limit was an innovation of that year or only a reiteration of previous practice: *KLNM*, s.v. "Handel, Island"; see also E. Baasch, *Die Islandsfahrt der Deutschen*, p. 63.

31. For an instance of ice blocking access to Iceland all of 1233, see *Ann.*, p. 129. The year 1183 was stated to be bad for traveling: 500 or 600 men were lost from hafskip (ibid., p. 180). In 1209 four ships were driven to Greenland (ibid., p. 182). In 1223 a certain Authbjörn's ship was lost and 63 men were drowned (ibid., pp. 24, 63, 126, 186). In 1232 four ships were wrecked and 47 men were lost (ibid., p. 25). In 1256 three ships were wrecked at Eyrar (ibid., p. 66).

32. *Land.*, ch. 5, p. 36.

33. Ibid., ch. 2, p. 33.

34. Ed. P. A. Munch (Christiania, 1850), cited by Thorvald Thoroddsen, *Landfrœthissaga Íslands* 1:69.

35. This route was established by Eirík the Red about 982 (*Grœnlen-*

dinga s., ch. 1, *ÍF* 4:242). Returning to Greenland from Vínland, Leif, Eirík's son, sighted the ice-capped mountains of his homeland (ibid., ch. 4, *ÍF* 4:253). The route to Greenland from Iceland was changed by the 14th century from a westerly to a more southerly direction, probably because of worsening climate.

36. *KS*, pp. 7–9.

37. Ibid., p. 36.

38. Ibid., p. 10.

39. Ibid.

40. These directions are only approximate for most of the year, for only twice a year, on the vernal and autumnal equinoxes, does the sun rise due east and set due west. In the 12th century Star-Oddi (Oddi Helgason) recorded the day of the year on which he could see the sun rise or set at each of the eight main points of the horizon, and at each point between them (E. G. R. Taylor, *The Haven-Finding Art*, pp. 90–91). As she points out, there is no direct evidence that seamen knew or made use of Star-Oddi's findings.

41. *Land.*, ch. 2, p. 32. In his version of the book about thirty years later, Hauk Erlendsson changed this information slightly, saying that one should sail due west from Hernar (just north of Bergen) to reach Hvarf (ibid., ch. 2, p. 33). The magnetic compass, known in Hauk's day, and possibly in Sturla's as well, could not be depended upon for holding the same course over more than a thousand miles of open sea, as G. J. Marcus has pointed out ("Navigation," p. 124).

42. The "sol-skuggjáfjöl" ("sun-shadow board"), more sophisticated than a simple stick, might have been used instead, though it served essentially the same function (see Marcus, "Navigation," p. 126). The quadrant is mentioned in *Rím*, an astronomical and geodetic treatise in Old Icelandic dating from the late 13th century, though this reference may be a later insertion (*Alfræthi íslenzk* 2:107). The quadrant referred to by *Rím* seems to have been used for measuring the height of Polaris only on land; there is no proof that this instrument was used at sea by this time. In the 14th century the astrolabe may have been known by Scandinavians. In a lost account of the North by Jacob Cnoyen there was supposed to be contained the so-called *Inventio fortunata*. Gerard Mercator wrote of the contents of the book to his friend, Dr. John Dee. According to Mercator's report, Cnoyen said that in 1364 eight people came to Norway from "northern islands." One was a priest with an astrolabe who told the king that four years before an English Minorite from Oxford, a good astronomer, had journeyed all the way to the North Pole, describing what he saw in a book called *Inventio fortunata*. John Dee thought the English friar

was Nicholas of Lynn, which is now generally accepted. If this report is true, concerning the instrument it gives the only evidence for the use of the astrolabe in the North before the end of the 15th century. However, as early as 1589, Thomas Blundeville (in *A Briefe Description of Universalle Mappes and Cardes*) said that he did not believe that the friar went so far north and that he measured with an astrolabe in those areas (*The Vinland Map and the Tartar Relation*, pp. 179–82). T. J. Oleson also takes a dim view of the validity of the monk's voyage ("Inventio Fortunata," *Annual of the Icelandic National League* 44 [1963]:64–76).

43. Both *Sturlubók* (ch. 2) and *Hauksbók* (ch. 2) (*Land.*, pp. 32–34) state that one should sail to Ireland from Reykjanes in the southwest of Iceland. Thus Reykjanes may be assumed to be the usual port of embarkation for Ireland, and the prevailing westerlies were counted upon to bring a ship to Ireland during the period of its southerly voyage. If the ship left from the southeast tip of Iceland, as superficially seems more logical because Iceland is closer to Ireland at that point, the westerlies might blow the ship too far to the east to hit Ireland.

44. Until sand clocks were invented during the 13th century, water clocks were mainly used to determine time; until the chronometer was invented in the mid-18th century, there was no accurate way to determine longitude. In the Middle Ages relative longitude was determined, on land, by observing celestial phenomena from two parts of the world at the same time. But sparse data collected this way undoubtedly was not used by mariners: see J. K. Wright, "Notes on the Knowledge of Latitudes and Longitudes in the Middle Ages," *Isis* 5(1923):83–84; and Gelsinger, "Mediterranean Voyage," p. 160.

45. The meaning of the term "day's sailing" ("dœgra sigling") is debatable. According to *Rím*, the word "day" ("dœgr") alone means twelve hours (*Alfrœthi íslenzk* 2:7, 77, 85, 174), but the term "day's sailing" signifies a distance of two "twelfths" or 144 nautical miles. Defined accordingly, the term would mean a distance, not a period of time: see Roald Morcken, "Norse Nautical Units and Distance Measurements," *Mariner's Mirror* 54(1968):396, 396n2; idem, "The Norse 'Day's Sailing' (Doegr Sigling)," *Mariner's Mirror* 56(1970):347–49; "Old Norse Nautical Distance Tables in the Mediterranean Sea," *Sjøfartshistorisk årbok 1971* (1972), pp. 187–90, 214. In spite of *Rím's* definite statement, there is too much controverting evidence to believe that the term meant in fact merely distance; instead it usually must have meant a period of time. But the two meanings are not irreconcilable, for if a ship went six knots as an average good speed, in twenty-four hours it would travel 144 n.m.: see Gelsinger, "Norse 'Day's Sailing' "; idem, "Mediterranean Voyage," p. 164n38.

46. See Frederic C. Land, "The Economic Meaning of the Invention of the Compass," *American Historical Review* 68(1963):611–12.

47. In his version of *Landnámabók*, Hauk Erlendsson, about 1307, mentions the lodestone, the earliest direct reference to it in Scandinavia: *Land.*, ch. 5, p. 37. Earlier it was described by the Englishman Alexander Neckham about 1187: *De nominibus utensilibus*, in *A Volume of Vocabularies*, p. 183. Neckham's is the first reference to the instrument in Europe.

48. Bruce E. Gelsinger, "Lodestone and Sunstone in Medieval Iceland," *Mariner's Mirror* 56(1970):223–26.

49. An inventory of the church at Hrafnagil made in 1394 mentions a "cased sunstone" (*DI* 3:560), which must have been a mariner's compass (Gelsinger, "Lodestone," pp. 225–26); for the year 1362 *Gottskálks annáll* mentions that Thorsteinn Hallsson, who was the priest of the church at Hrafnagil, went on his ship to Norway (*Ann.*, p. 360; see also *Ann.*, pp. 226, 279, 408). Because the mariner's compass was known to have been at his church in 1394, it is possible that Thorsteinn had that instrument with him in 1362.

50. Thorkild Ramskou, *Solstenen*; see also my review of this work in *Scandinavian Studies* 42(1970):362–63.

51. Gelsinger, "Lodestone," p. 223.

52. A type of sun compass, working on the same principle as the sundial, useful for getting a bearing by the sun, may also have been known as a navigational instrument. A sundial is mounted, using a compass, with its gnomon pointing due north, or 12 o'clock; the sun, when due south, will be exactly aligned with the gnomon, and at other positions during the day it will cast a shadow indicating the time. Thus, knowing direction, time can be determined. On the other hand, if noon is known, the dial can be placed in a position so that the shadow is cast to the proper time, and then the gnomon will be pointing due north—the sundial now becomes a sun compass, for, knowing time, direction can be determined. The Old Norse version of the sun compass, a precursor to the azimuth circle, may have been what Carl V. Sølver reconstructed from a fragment found in Greenland: see his "Leitharsteinn: The Compass of the Vikings," *Old Lore Miscellany* 10(1946):293–321. The sun compass he describes, however, would have had only very limited use at sea.

CHAPTER FOUR

1. *King Alfred's Orosius*, pp. 17–19.

2. See Charlotte Blindheim, "The Market Place in Skiringssal: Early Opinions and Recent Studies," *Acta Archaeologica* 31(1960):83–100.

3. Rye was less common than barley and was regarded as more of a

luxury. No direct literary reference is made to oats, though archaeology has yielded testimony to its use. Oats occasionally may have been mixed with barley (Oscar Albert Johnsen, *Norges bønder*, pp. 58, 66, 122–45; Knut Helle, *Norge blir en stat*, pp. 151–53).

4. Alexander Bugge, *Den norske trælasthandels historie* 1:60–61.

5. Cattle were the most important livestock in Vestlandet, though horses, sheep, goats, and pigs were raised as well (Johnsen, *Norges bønder*, pp. 151–53). The importance of livestock in this region can be seen in the probable greater use of shielings in the highlands, where cattle and sheep were driven in summer. The law of the Gula Thing, which was valid for Vestlandet, is much more detailed in its stipulations regarding use of these shielings than is the law of the Frosta Thing, valid for Trøndelag, where livestock was probably not as important. The number of medieval shielings is unknown, but in 1907 the three central districts of the old Gula Thing area contained about half of those in the whole country (ibid., pp. 153–55). For archaeological evidence of trade in Vestlandet during the Viking period, mainly scales, see Jan Petersen, "Handel i Norge i vikingetiden," *NK* 16:42–43.

6. *Egils s. Skallagrímssonar* confirms in broad outline Óttar's 9th century report of the commercial importance of Hålogaland and the district of Oslo Fjord (chs. 10, 17, 26, 57, *ÍF* 2:27–28, 41–42, 67, 164). But in specific details it gives a truer picture of the time it was written (c. 1200) than the time it purports to represent.

7. *Óláfs s. Tryggvasonar*, ch. 70, *ÍF* 26:318.

8. *Óláfs s. helga*, ch. 53, *ÍF* 27:70.

9. It is true that Óttar's account suggests that he brought his northern products first to Oslo Fjord and to Hedeby before going abroad to England. Undoubtedly others would have as often gone directly to western European destinations such as England: see Oscar Albert Johnsen, "Norges handel og skibsfart i middelalderen," *NK* 16:129, where he goes so far as to say "Hålogaland was the main emporium for Norway's export trade in the Viking period."

10. See Johnsen, "Norges Handel," p. 129.

11. For Nidaros's commercial importance in the Middle Ages, see Alexander Bugge, *Nidaros's handel og skibsfart i middelalderen*; Grethe Authén Blom et al., *Trondheims bys historie* 1. Nidaros remained an important center for the Iceland trade until the 14th century (*KLNM*, s.v. "Islandshandel").

12. *Óláfs s. helga*, ch. 61, *ÍF* 27:28; *Haralds s. Sigurtharsonar*, ch. 58, *ÍF* 28:139; *Óláfs s. kyrra*, ch. 2, *ÍF* 28:204; *Magnússona s.*, ch. 19, *ÍF* 28:223.

13. As early as about 1130 the reputation of Norwegian towns had

already reached the Anglo-Norman historian Ordericus Vitalis, for he listed all six important centers, which he calls "cities" (*civitates*): Bergen, Konungahella, Kaupang (as it was known before it received the name of Nidaros), Borg (Sarpsborg), Oslo, and Tønsberg (which by then had replaced or absorbed Skiringssal): *Historia ecclesiastica* 4:27. Other less important towns founded during the 12th century were Stavanger and Hamar (mainly significant as episcopacies only), Vågen, Veøy, Borgund, and Lusakaupang (all hardly more than marketplaces); the markets of Skein and Marstrand became significant in the 13th century (Helle, *Norge,* pp. 166, 170–71). On the importance of royal and clerical residence in towns for furthering their development, see *KLNM,* s.v. "Stad, Norge."

14. Accurate and fairly well-spaced population figures for medieval Norway are not available. Oscar Albert Johnsen estimates, however, that Norway's population quadrupled during the six centuries after about A.D. 400; about 1300 he thinks it must have reached a total of about 400,000 ("Norges folk i middelalderen," *NK* 2:66, 88–89). Surely after about 1050 population in more fertile Østlandet and in Trøndelag must have begun to grow faster than in Vestlandet because during the three centuries following the Viking period new clearings were least common in the latter but quite prevalent in the east and to a lesser extent in Trøndelag (cf. ibid., 67–68; Helle, *Norge,* p. 148). Yet population in Vestlandet still would have continued to be significant, and it thus would have represented a major area to be supplied with supplemental grain from elsewhere. As early as the reign of St. Óláf in the early 11th century, in fact, there seems to have existed at times a shortage of grain in the west and far north in relationship to population: the king is said to have sent word to all the districts from the south coast to Hordaland that grain, malt, and flour were not to be sold abroad. Presumably he had to take this drastic step because only in that way could he be assured that there would be enough grain for the support of his retinue when he came to these areas, as he planned. After this order was issued, a chieftain living in Hålogaland ran short of grain because of poor seasons and crop failures. The Hålogalander sailed south to Rogaland, where St. Óláf's order was in effect, and illegally bought some, pleading famine conditions in the north. The grain was later confiscated by a king's man (*Óláfs s. helga,* chs. 115, 117, *ÍF* 27:191, 194–98). In light, then, of the heavy demand for grain in western and northern Norway, grain from new land cleared in Østlandet and Trøndelag would have had to be supplemented, probably as early as c. 1050, with grain from abroad. For a somewhat different point of view, see Knut Helle, *Norge,* pp. 171–72; idem, "Anglo-Norwegian Relations in the Reign of Håkon Håkonsson (1217–63)," *Mediaeval Scandinavia* 1(1968):102–4.

15. Johnsen, "Norges folk," p. 68.

16. See Helle, Norge, p. 156.

17. Among other goods, the tithe was collectable in barley, rye, and wheat (Johnsen, Norges bønder, p. 142); the wheat must have been imported.

18. In the 12th century the church probably held less land than the monarchy, but churchmen's land holdings would rapidly equal and then exceed those of the king. By shortly before 1350 it has been estimated that of the total value of all Norwegian land about 40% was owned by the church and only about 7% by the crown. Because the secular nobility owned about 20%, there remained about 33% still in possession of nontenant farmers and city dwellers (Helle, Norge, pp. 158, 194; see also Johnsen, "Norges folk," pp. 78–79).

19. The eleventh article of the Canons of Nidaros (1152), which prohibited clerics from engaging in trade for personal profit, probably reflects a prejudice of the Church as a whole against trade, a bias beginning to become evident with the revival of European commerce in the 11th century; this view was shared in Catholic Europe by secular aristocrats: see Lester K. Little, "Pride Goes Before Avarice: Social Changes and the Vices in Latin Christendom," American Historical Review 76(1971):16–49. In Norway the prejudice on the part of men of high secular standing, who were not feudal aristocrats in the continental sense except when they assumed some of their superficial trappings in the 13th century, may not have been as great as elsewhere; the 13th-century author of Konungs skuggsjá seems to place a career as a merchant almost on a par with that of being a royal retainer.

20. Among a series of laws enacted during the reign of King Sveinn Knútsson (1030–35) was one that stated that a small amount of cargo space (one "rúm") on every ship leaving Norway had to be reserved for the king's use (Óláfs s. helga, ch. 239, ÍF 27:400); this law seems to be an early example of regular but indirect royal participation in trade. Whether Sveinn's law was repealed during the early 12th century when others were, is unknown. But it may have furnished a precedent for a mid-14th-century practice and probably before of royal reservation of a quarter of the cargo space on all ships traveling to Iceland (see KLNM, s. v. "Fiskehandel, Island"). The existence of a significant professional Norwegian merchant class is disputable. Such scholars as Alexander Bugge (e.g., Studier over de norske byers selvstyre og handel) uphold the theory; others do not (e.g., Michael Postan, "The Trade of Medieval Europe: The North," The Cambridge Economic History of Europe 2:169–70). The argument is neatly summarized by Aksel E. Christiansen ("Scandinavia and the Advance of

the Hanseatics," *Scandinavian Economic History Review* 5[1957]:90–91)
and by Knut Helle (*Norge*, p. 174).

21. Oscar Albert Johnsen, *Norwegische Wirtschaftsgeschichte*, pp. 103–4.

22. *Óláfs s. helga*, ch. 64, ÍF 27:83.

23. *Óláfs s. kyrra*, ch. 2, ÍF 28:204.

24. *Orkneyinga s.*, ch. 60, ÍF 34:131–32.

25. *Sverris s.*, ch. 104, p. 110.

26. *Historia de profectione Danorum in Hierosolymam*, in *Scriptores minores historiae Danicae medii aevi* 2:475–76.

27. Johnsen says that Norwegian urban population reached its zenith about 1300 when the non-rural population numbered about 20,000 or about 5% of the total in the country. Of this number, Bergen's population surely would have been about 7,000; Nidaros's, 3,000; Oslo's, 2,000; and Tønsberg's, 1,500 ("Norges folk," pp. 76–77).

28. This was true even in Vestlandet where sheep were preferred somewhat more than elsewhere because they were better suited to make use of the small amounts of grassland on the numerous, small, and uninhabited islands in fjords or along the coast. On the relative importance in Norway of cattle and sheep raising, see Johnsen, *Norges bønder*, pp. 151–53; *KLNM*, s.v. "Fåreavl [Saueavl], Norge."

29. See Johnsen, *Norges bønder*, pp. 151–52; Marta Hoffman, *The Warp-Weighted Loom*, p. 218.

30. Hoffman (ibid., p. 368n102) says "during the Middle Ages, large quantities of Icelandic wadmal were also imported [to Norway]; some of this was for use in Norway, but most was probably re-exported." She states further, "Alexander Bugge . . . assumed that the wadmal brought to England from Norway was of Icelandic origin": Bugge, "Handelen mellem England og Norge indtil begyndelsen af det 15de aarhundrede," [*Norsk*] *Historisk tidsskrift*, 3rd ser., 4(1898):146–47; idem, *Studier over de norske byers selvstyre*, pp. 220–21.

31. See Einar Ól. Sveinsson, *Age of the Sturlungs*, pp. 12–19; Hallvard Magerøy, *Norsk-islandske problem*.

32. *Óláfs s. helga*, ch. 125, ÍF 27:215–16. See Jón Jóhannesson, *Íslendinga saga* 1:268–69.

33. In 1026 St. Óláf made a less polite attempt to annex Iceland; but it too was unsuccessful: see *Óláfs s. helga*, chs. 136, 138, 141, 155, ÍF 27:240–41, 243–49, 255–61, 287.

34. Probably before 1024 as well St. Óláf had been careful in personal ways to show a friendly countenance toward Iceland. He sent various personal gifts to several Icelandic chieftains, allowed several Icelanders to

enter his service at the Norwegian court, and sent timber for some new churches in Iceland, including one built at Thingvöll. Snorri Sturluson says of these acts—though his words could have referred to the agreement as well—that "in this attempt at friendship, which the king made toward Iceland, there existed some considerations which became evident later" (*Óláfs s. helga,* ch. 124, ÍF 27:214).

35. The agreement's stipulations that follow are found in *Grágás* Ib:195–197; *DI* 1:54, 64–70. The agreement was first committed to writing some 60 years after it was originally made; the extant manuscripts probably follow the c. 1022 version quite closely: see Jóhannesson, *Íslendinga saga* 1:134–35.

36. *Norges gamle love* 1:71, cited by Jóhannesson, *Íslendinga saga* 1:135–36. See also *KLNM,* s.v. "Hauld." Björn Thorsteinsson (*Ný Íslandssaga,* p. 149) states that other foreigners had a rank only half that of an ordinary Norwegian farmer, with an infringement of honor payable at only ¼ that made to Icelanders in Norway. When the Bjarkeyjar Law was introduced to Norway at a later time, all foreigners, including Icelanders, held the same rank in Norway (see *Norges gamle love* 1:314, 321), and thus the earlier Icelandic privilege was no longer distinctive (Jóhannesson, *Íslendinga saga* 1:136).

37. Jóhannesson, *Íslendinga saga* 1:137.

38. *Óláfs s. Tryggvasonar,* ch. 81, ÍF 26:329.

39. For instance in 1219 no ships came from Norway to Iceland (*Ann.,* pp. 125, 185, 326). In 1243 there was a ban on Norwegian trade with part of Iceland (*Ann.,* p. 189).

40. Jóhannesson, *Íslendinga saga* 1:139.

41. St. Óláf's Danish successor, Sveinn Knútsson, introduced, among other unpopular laws, one stating that no man could leave Norway without royal permission (*Óláfs s. helga,* ch. 237, ÍF 27:399); if it affected Icelanders, the law might have limited Icelandic egress from the country even when their military help was not needed. It is not known how long after Sveinn's reign the law lasted, but according to one source it was apparently still in force during the time of King Magnús the Good Óláfsson (1035–47), and it was applicable to an Icelander. It seems to have been used as an attempt to regulate trade: "It is said that one time when Thorsteinn returned [to Norway] from a trading journey to Dublin, it [the journey] was not with the king's permission. And it was not at that time that men journeyed abroad on trading voyages without the king giving permission for it; and he was blamed by everyone for leaving [Norway in the first place] without permission" (*Thorsteins th. Síthu-Hallssonar,* ch. 1, ÍS 10:407).

42. *Íslb.,* ch. 1, pp. 5–6.

43. *Óláfs s. helga* (ch. 72, *ÍF* 27:95) also confirms payment of the landaurar. See also *KLNM,* s.v. "Handelsafgifter, Norge."

44. *Óláfs s. helga,* ch. 239, *ÍF* 27:399–400; see also Laurence M. Larson, *Canute the Great,* p. 283.

45. *Óláfs s. helga,* ch. 239, *ÍF* 27:400–401.

46. *Magnússona s.,* ch. 17, *ÍF* 28:256; see also Jóhannesson, *Íslendinga saga* 1:138, and *KLNM,* s.v. "Handelsafgifter."

47. *KLNM,* s.v. "Handelsafgifter."

48. Probably dating from about the same time as the agreement, Icelandic law defined procedures should a Norwegian or other Scandinavian be killed: *Grágás* 1a:172–74. On inheritance in Iceland of property owned by Norwegians, as well as Danes, Swedes, English, and others, see *Grágás* 1a:228–29.

49. Ch. 7, *ÍF* 26:211–12.

50. On these cloaks, see Halfdan Koht, "Gråfelden i nordisk historie," [*Norsk*] *Historisk tidsskrift,* 5th ser., 11(1930):19–36.

51. In addition the archbishop had the right to collect the toll of one ship yearly: *DI* 1:228; *Latinske dokument til norsk historie,* p. 61. The most likely date of the letter is 1163 or 1164: see Eirik Vandvik, *Magnus Erlingssons privilegiebrev og kongevigsle,* for a thorough interpretation of the document as a whole, including its time of origin.

52. *Latinske dokument,* p. 101. The version in *DI* 1:293 says "faultless cloth."

53. Assuming 3 vættir of meal = 120 alnir: thus 480 merkur of meal = 120 alnir; 207,360 merkur = 30 lestir; thus 207,360 ÷ 480 = 432; 432 x 120 = 51,840. Most of the cloth must have been ordinary vathmál because even a slightly more expensive fabric such as brown-striped vathmál (mórent) probably would not have been found in such quantity.

54. *Haralds s. Sigurtharsonar,* ch. 36, *ÍF* 28:119. See also *Sneglu-Halla th.,* ch. 1, *ÍF* 9:264. Exactly the opposite opinion of King Harald was held by Adam of Bremen, whose informant for most matters relating to Scandinavia was Sveinn Estridsson, king of Denmark and Harald's enemy. Adam says, among other things, that Harald "extended his bloodstained power as far as Iceland" (*Gesta,* bk. 3, ch. 16, p. 107).

55. Jóhannesson, *Íslendinga saga* 1:141.

56. *Ann.,* p. 470.

57. See *Gesta* 3:15:106; Jóhannesson, *Íslendinga saga* 1:141.

58. *Haralds s. Sigurtharsonar,* chs. 28, 32, 34–35, 40–53, 58–69, 71, *ÍF* 28:104–6, 110–18, 122–35, 139–62.

59. Ch. 1, *ÍF* 5:265.

60. In the Althing price list of c. 1200 3 vættir of (barley) meal was worth 1 cow. Because the value of a "legal cow" was usually the equivalent to 120 alnir of vathmál probably from the period of settlement until late in the 12th century, a skippund of meal would cost 144 alnir. *Mörkinskinna*, a manuscript which contains a slightly different version of this story compared to Snorri's, states that the price was set at 144 alnir per skippund ([Copenhagen, 1932], p. 170, cited by Jóhannesson, *Íslendinga saga* 1:140), therefore exactly corresponding to the legal rate. This price is probably more accurate than Snorri's 120 alnir per skippund.

61. Henry Goddard Leach, "The Relations of the Norwegian with the English Church," *Proceedings of the American Academy of Arts and Sciences* 44(1909):543. Before this grant was made, there must have been English trade carried on by the archbishop even without special favor, just as afterward the archbishop of Nidaros did not limit his trade with England merely to his one privileged ship: ships of the archbishop in addition to the privileged one are mentioned in English records for 1223, 1225, 1226, 1233, and 1236 (ibid.).

62. In a letter of 1267, King Magnús Hákonarson specifically stated, however, that the archbishop could send 30 lestir of "Norwegian goods" from his rents and revenues from Hedemark and Oslo to Iceland (*DI* 9:81). If these "goods" meant grain, then it would appear that this was a confirmation of the earlier privilege given by King Magnús Erlingsson to the archbishop and that now the grain came mostly or exclusively from eastern Norway. Perhaps the king believed that this native grain could be spared because by now Hanseatics were importing significant quantities. But even if the 1267 privilege is interpreted as a revision of the one of c. 1164, the amendment did not last long, for in 1277 the king confirmed the mid-12th century privilege in almost the same words as the original, that is without specifying the origin of the grain (*Norges gamle love* 2:462–67). As before, presumably the archbishop at least occasionally would have to import some grain to Norway in order to be able to send his annual allotment to Iceland.

63. In Iceland three rafters were legally set at a price of 6 alnir of vathmál or one legal eyrir somewhat before 1200 (*DI* 1:318); this price is relatively inexpensive, but had the size of the rafters been given, a more accurate estimation of value could have been obtained.

64. *Reykdœla s. ok Víga-Skútu*, ch. 9, ÍF 10:172–73.

65. *Gísla s. Súrssonar*, ch. 7, ÍF 6:24–25.

66. For instances of trade in these less important items (or at least gifts made of them) specifically between Norway and Iceland, see, for "Russian hats" and tapered axes, *Ljósvetninga s.*, ch. 2, ÍF 10:6; for "a

stained saddle with bit," *Grettis s.*, ch. 24, *ÍF* 7:87; for religious articles, *Páls s. biskups*, ch. 16, *Bisk.* 1:143; for falcons, reexported from Norway, *Diplomatarium Norvegicum* 19:pt.1:66, 86, 89, 127, 317, 139, 141–43, 145, 150, 157, 160–61; for polar bears, *Land.*, ch. 179, p. 219, *Vatnsdœla s.*, ch. 16, *ÍF* 8:44, and cf. Ernst Kantorowicz, *Frederick the Second*, pp. 196, 358; for sulphur, *Arna s. biskups*, ch. 24, *Bisk.* 1:713, and cf. *KLNM*, s.v. "Handelsprivileger."

67. *Óláfs s. Tryggvasonar*, ch. 33, *ÍF* 26:270.

68. *Svarfdœla s.*, ch. 27, *ÍF* 9:202; *Thorsteins s. uxafóts*, ch. 3, *ÍS* 10:346. In the 10th century Gunnar Hámundarson went to Denmark after a Viking expedition; there is no hint that he went there specifically to trade. However his trip indicates some of the luxuries reputedly available in Denmark. King Harald Gormsson gave Gunnar not only his own robes, but also his gold-embroidered gloves, a headband with gold, and a Russian hat (*Brennu-Njáls s.*, ch. 31, *ÍF* 12:82–83). Fur-Björn Skútathar-Skeggjason of Iceland was also in Denmark in the 10th century, but whether before he settled in Iceland and whether for trading purposes is uncertain (*Land.*, ch. 174, p. 212). Hallfreth the Troublesome Skald Óttarsson, an Icelander, about 997 went from Norway on a buying trip to Eyrar: this place may have been in Scania, then part of Denmark; but it was more likely to have been the neutral territory of the Brenneyjar (*Hallfrethar s.*, ch. 7, *ÍF* 8:167).

69. *Laxdœla s.*, ch. 73, *ÍF* 5:212–14.

70. *Gesta* 4:36:184, schol. 148; Jóhannesson, *Íslendinga saga* 1:386. Reference to Ålborg is also made in a guidebook for Icelandic pilgrims: "Leitharvísir," in *Alfrœthi íslenzk* 1:13.

71. *Ann.*, p. 120.

72. See *Vita Anskari*, ch. 30, in *Monumenta Germaniae historica*, *Scriptores* 11, cited by Archibald Lewis, *The Northern Seas*, p. 308; Aksel E. Christensen, "Danmarks handel i middelalderen," *NK* 16:114.

73. Christensen, "Danmarks handel," p. 114; Sture Bolin, "Mediaeval Agrarian Society in its Prime: Scandinavia," *The Cambridge Economic History of Europe* 1:649.

74. *De med jydske Love beslægtede stadsretter*, ed. P. G. Thorsen (Copenhagen, 1855), p. 10, cited by Bogi Th. Melsteth, "Ferthir, siglingar og samgöngur milli Íslands og annara landa á dögum thjóthveldisins," *Safn til sögu Íslands* 4(1907–15):750. In 1236 Órækja Snorrason went from Eyrar in southwestern Iceland to Denmark; his journey was not, however, made specifically for trade (*Íslendinga s.*, ch. 115, *Stur.* 1:397).

75. Christensen, "Danmarks handel," p. 110.

76. Although Saxo Grammaticus includes in his *Gesta Danorum* (Praefatio 2, pp. 7–8) a description of Iceland, he limits himself to natural

phenomena. His treatment reflects what must have been little direct Danish knowledge of Iceland during the time his preface was written, the early 13th century.

77. *Ann.*, pp. 119, 180, 324.

78. Like Magnús, the Icelanders who are mentioned in the laws for the city of Schleswig of c. 1201 were probably there to purchase foods and other supplies that were becoming increasingly scarce in Norway.

79. See *KLNM*, s.v. "Handelsafgifter, almindelig og Danmark."

80. 1a:172, 229, 238–39.

81. *Ólafs s. helga*, chs. 68, 71, 80, *ÍF* 27:86–87, 92, 114–17.

82. *Gunnlaugs s. ormstungu*, ch. 9, *ÍF* 3:78–79.

83. As will be mentioned in Chapter 6, Sighvát is said to have traded when he was in Normandy. Reference should also be made to Gizur Ísleifsson, who became bishop of Skálaholt in 1082: he spent one of the previous two years in Swedish Gautland (*Íslb.*, ch. 10, pp. 21–22); there is no indication that trade was involved, but some might have been.

84. *Flóamanna s.*, chs. 12–17, 18, pp. 16–29. Better known is a journey undertaken by Höskuld Dala-Kolsson about thirty years earlier to the flourishing marketplace at the neutral and thus toll-free Brenneyjar. The market there must have enjoyed widespread commercial contacts because Höskuld is said to have been able to purchase an Irish slave to be used as his concubine from a certain wealthy slave-trader, Gilli, nicknamed "the Russian," presumably because of his trips there. Höskuld took his slave back to Iceland (*Laxdœla s.*, ch. 12, *ÍF* 5:22–25).

85. *Land.*, ch. 3, p. 35. In addition, several other of his countrymen are mentioned as settlers: see *KLNM*, s.v. "Islandshandel, Sverige."

86. *Jóns s. helga eptir Gunnlaug múnk*, ch. 23, *Bisk.* 1:235.

87. 1a:172, 229, 239.

88. *Fornmanna sögur* 5:314–20, 325; *Ólafs s. mágri*, chs. 34–41: cited by Melsteth, "Ferthir," p. 721.

89. *Ólafs s. helga*, ch. 67, *ÍF* 27:85–86.

90. See *Ynglinga s.*, chs. 41–50, *ÍF* 26:72–83; *Hálfdanar s. svarta*, chs. 1–5, *ÍF* 26:84–89; *Haralds s. hárfagra*, chs. 1–19, *ÍF* 26:94–118.

91. *Ólafs s. helga*, ch. 72, *ÍF* 28:95, 97.

92. Haakon Shetelig ("Islenzkar dysjar og fornleifar fra víkingaöld," *Árbók hins íslenzka fornleifafélags* [1937–39], pp. 12–16) thinks that certain objects dating from the 10th century found in Iceland show a Swedish-Baltic style that was hardly ever practiced in Norway. He therefore suggests that a direct trade existed between Iceland and Sweden and/or the southern Baltic area, by-passing Norway (from Jóhannesson, *Íslendinga saga* 1:363). It seems more likely that these objects came only indirectly to Iceland via Norway.

CHAPTER FIVE

1. Helge Ingstad, *Land under the Pole Star*, p. 24.

2. See *KS*, p. 30; *Grœnlendinga th.*, ch. 6, *ÍF* 4:290. For archaeological testimony, see *KLNM*, s.v. "Fåreavl, Grønland" and "Geitavl, Grønland"; Ingstad, *Land under Pole Star*, p. 61.

3. *KS*, p. 30. This work must reflect conditions on Greenland c. 1250 when it was written, because the climate of the island probably began to deteriorate after c. 1200, just as it did in Iceland. Efforts to grow grain then would have been even less successful than before. For other foods cultivated by Greenlanders, or which they made use of in a wild state, see *Páls s. biskups*, ch. 9, *Bisk.* 1:135; Ingstad, *Land under Pole Star*, pp. 68–69.

4. *KS*, p. 30. Archaeological evidence also gives weight to this statement. Reindeer bones have been found in large numbers in both the Eastern and Western Settlements (Tryggvi Oleson, *Early Voyages and Northern Approaches*, p. 17). According to Magnus Degerbøl, more than half the bones found at Brattahlíth in the Eastern Settlement are seal (*Meddelelser om Grønland* 88[1934], cited by Ingstad, *Land under Pole Star*, p. 42).

5. *KS*, p. 29.

6. On walrus tusks, see *Grœnlendinga th.*, ch. 1, *ÍF* 4:273–74; *Pavelige nuntiers regnskaps-og dagbøker*, p.19; Henry S. Lucas, "Medieval Economic Relations between Flanders and Greenland," *Speculum* 12(1937):174. Some ivory may have been carved before being exported: see *KLNM*, s.v. "Benskurd."

7. For falcons, see *KS*, p. 30. For polar bears, see Ingstad, *Land under Pole Star*, p. 234; T. J. Oleson, "Polar Bears in the Middle Ages," *Canadian Historical Review* 31(1950):47–55.

8. *KS*, p. 29.

9. Although these voyages will be referred to later, they do not come under the scope of this study of Icelandic commerce: Greenlanders and Icelanders made trips to North America in an attempt to acquire necessary goods and to establish new settlements but not primarily for trade.

10. Ch. 3, *ÍF* 4:248.

11. See Erik Wahlgren, "Fact and Fancy in the Vinland Sagas," in *Old Norse Literature and Mythology*, pp. 43–44.

12. Ch. 5, *ÍF* 4:210.

13. See *Grœnlendinga s.*'s more plausible account, chs. 3–4, *ÍF* 4:248–54. See also Wahlgren, "Fact and Fancy," pp. 29–30; Jón Jóhannesson, "The Date of the Composition of the Saga of the Greenlanders," *Saga-Book of the Viking Society for Northern Research* 16(1962):54–66.

14. Chs. 16–18, 24, *ÍF* 6:201–11, 214, 257.

15. *Gesta*, bk. 3, ch. 24, and addition to bk. 3, pp. 112, 149. During the 11th century the archiepiscopal see of Hamburg-Bremen still had jurisdiction over all Scandinavia, including Greenland.

16. The first bishop for Greenland, Eirík upsi Gnúpsson, evidently did not make his permanent residence there. Probably an Icelander (see *Land.*, ch. 17, p. 56 where he is called the "Greenlanders' bishop"), he is known to have gone to "seek" Vínland in 1121 (*Ann.*, pp. 19, 59, 112, 252, 320, 473); presumably he did not return.

17. *Grœnlendinga th.*, ch. 1, *ÍF* 4:273–75.

18. See ibid., ch. 6, p. 288.

19. *Scriptores minores historicae Danicae medii aevi* 2:476. The gap in the evidence includes King Sverrir's significant omission of Greenlanders among the foreign merchants in Bergen about 1186 whom he praised or criticized: see *Sverris s.*, ch. 104, p. 110.

20. See in particular his statement, " 'in return for their [foreign] wares men bring from there [many Greenlandic products]' " (*KS*, p. 29).

21. Lúthvík Kristjánsson, "Grænlenzki landnemaflotinn og breithfirzki báturinn," *Árbók hins íslenzka fornleifafélags* (1964), pp. 30–38, 61–62, 65, 67.

22. One of the earliest immigrants after the original settlement was Bjarni Herjólfsson, arriving with his ship about 987. Like him, all settlers before c. 1000 were Icelandic. Thorbjörn Vífilsson came with 30 others (*Eiríks s. rautha*, ch. 3, *ÍF* 4:205); according to *Eyrbyggja s.* (ch. 48, *ÍF* 4:135), Snorri Thorbrandsson and his brother Thorleif kimbi came, but according to *Grœnlendinga s.* (ch. 1, *ÍF* 4:243) only one son of Thorbrand came, and he was not either of the two mentioned by *Eyrbyggja s.*, rather a son named Helgi. *Eiríks s.* mentions Snorri Thorbrandsson coming to Greenland with Thorfinn Karlsefni, but as a merchant not a settler (chs. 7, 8, pp. 219, 221). An attempt at settlement was made by Thorgils örrabeinsstúp with 20 others (*Flóamanna s.*, chs. 20–26, pp. 32–56). One of the last attempts at settlement occurred in 1125 when a group of Norwegians led by someone named Arnbjörn were driven to the desolate eastern coast of Greenland where they all died. About 1130, Greenlanders found and retrieved their ship (*Grœnlendinga th.*, chs. 1–2, *ÍF* 4:275–76, 278).

23. An important place for gathering driftwood as well as for hunting walrus was at Northrsetur, in the vicinity of modern Holsteinborg, north of the old Western Settlement. It was not permanently inhabited, but summer trips there seem to have been frequent; see *Greenland Annals* (17th century), in *Grønlands historiske mindesmærker* 3:242–43, from Ingstad, *Land under Pole Star*, p. 81. On driftwood, see also Finn Gad, *History of Greenland* 1:85. Lúthvík Kristjánsson says that the majority of

the 25 ships used by Eirík the Red and his followers to cross from Iceland to Greenland about 986 were cargo and fishing boats of ten or twelve oars each, built of driftwood ("Grænlenzki landnemaflotinn," pp. 20–49, 62, 64–66, 67–68). Yet even on such a relatively short passage 11 of the 25 ships did not make Greenland, and even if they could cope with open seas the cargo space on such small boats would have been very limited—for this reason alone the boats would not have been usually taken on distant voyages for trade. In 1347 a small Greenlandic boat, perhaps built of driftwood, was driven to Iceland on its way back to Greenland from North America with several men aboard (*Ann.*, p. 213). This was clearly an exceptional circumstance, and the boat had come to Iceland only involuntarily. The ordinary sailing of this boat, even to "Markland" (i.e., probably to Labrador or possibly Newfoundland) would not have involved a distant sea crossing, for the route to North America was probably Northrsetur, Baffin Island (Helluland?), Labrador (Markland?), Newfoundland or New England (Vínland?).

24. About 1003, on returning to Greenland from North America, Leif Eiríksson is said to have rescued from a reef near Greenland some Norwegians whose leader was named Thórir; Thórir's ship had been carrying timber, which Leif retrieved (*Grœnlendinga s.*, ch. 4, *ÍF* 4:253–54). Undoubtedly Thórir's timber was not intended for shipbuilding because the large pieces of timber would have required an exceptionally large ship, a point not noted by the saga. Except for this example, specific Norwegians are not mentioned bringing timber to Greenland, certainly not for shipbuilding. Even in Thórir's case, Iceland may have been his original goal rather than Greenland.

25. *Grœnlendinga s.*, ch. 3, *ÍF* 4:248.

26. The earliest known purposeful voyages to North America undertaken by Norsemen occurred at the beginning of the 11th century; the last in 1347 (*Ann.*, p. 213). One area there, "Markland" ("Forest Land"), closer to Greenland than Vínland, seems to have been particularly valuable for timber: probably this is why it was visited (in 1347 for instance) long after the early 12th century when the exact location of Vínland already was becoming clouded, as the reference to the 1121 trip of Bishop Eirík Gnúpsson suggests. Even so, the timber brought back to Greenland from North America apparently was not large enough to build even small ships: one version of *Eiríks s.*, the redaction in *Hauksbók*, says in a tone of admiration that some of the trees with which Leif Eiríksson returned to Greenland "were so large that they were used for house-building" (ch. 5, *The Vinland Sagas*, trans. Magnus Magnusson and Hermann Pálsson, p. 86n2).

27. The scarcity of large Greenlandic ships during the early 11th century seems confirmed by the saga accounts of the earliest North American voyages. According to *Grœnlendinga s.*, Leif, son of Eirík the Red, apparently had no suitable ship available until he bought Bjarni Herjólfsson's (ch. 3, *ÍF* 4:248). On the other hand, if we can believe in the voyage of Freythís Eiríksdóttir and her companions (Wahlgren believes it to be fictional, "Fact and Fancy," pp. 58–61), she seems to have obtained her own ship, though smaller than the one owned by the Icelanders who accompanied her (ch. 8, pp. 264, 267). According to *Eiríks s.*, the voyages to Vínland subsequent to Leif's involved ships originating mostly from Iceland, even though Leif had brought back a little wood. The first voyage after Leif's expedition was by the ship Thorbjörn Vífilsson had sailed to Greenland from Iceland, but this expedition did not get to North America (ch. 5, *ÍF* 4:213). For the next voyage this ship was again used, captained by Thorvarth, Eirík's son-in-law, accompanied by three other ships. One, of unknown origin, seems to have been captained by Thorhall the Hunter. Both of the other two were Icelandic: one was owned and skippered by the two Icelanders Bjarni Grímólfsson and Thorhall Gamlason, the other by Thorfinn Karlsefni and Snorri Thorbrandsson (ch. 8, pp. 221–22): on these latter ships, see below, note 52.

28. There is no way of telling how large Eirík's farm was because today much of it has been covered by the sea. But his wealth, which must have been based upon a considerable land holding, is implied by the size and solid construction of his house and the number and size of his outbuildings; see Gad, *Greenland* 1:41–44. For descriptions of other early Norse buildings in Greenland and their contents, which also imply some degree of riches, see ibid., pp. 36–39, 45, 63–78, 111–18; Ingstad, *Land under Pole Star*, p. 34; Magnusson and Pálsson, *Vinland Sagas*, pp. 19, 92n1. *Eiríks s.* specifically says that at Brattahlíth goods of Icelandic traders were stored in large outbuildings and that there was no shortage of those buildings (ch. 7, *ÍF* 4:219).

29. Gad, *Greenland* 1:33–34.

30. *Grœnlendinga th.*, ch. 1, *ÍF* 4:274. Eventually the episcopal estate at Garthar came to be very large. For details of the size of the cathedral and the bishop's residence, as well as episcopal incomes, see Gad, *Greenland* 1:111–12; Ingstad, *Land under Pole Star*, pp. 187, 189.

31. See Ingstad, *Land under Pole Star*, p. 206.

32. Bishop Arnald (1125–1150) left Garthar c. 1150 and was appointed bishop of Hamar in Norway in 1152; Bishop Jón smyrill (1188–1209) was in Iceland during part of his Greenlandic term of office, and in Rome during 1202–1203; Bishop Óláf (1246–1280) was in Iceland during 1262–

1264 and in Norway until 1271; Bishop Thórth (1288–1314) went to Norway in 1309; Bishop Árni (1314–1343) was transferred to the Faeroes in 1348 (Ingstad, *Land under Pole Star*, pp. 355–56). A letter written by Pope Martin IV to the archbishop of Nidaros in 1282 says that levies forwarded to Rome from Greenland, as well as from Iceland and the Faeroes, must be in the form of silver or gold, because such goods as sealskins, walrus ivory, and ambergris are not convenient means of payment for Jerusalem or for the Holy See of Rome (*DI* 2:235–36). This communication suggests that some clerics traded their products abroad in order to gain the necessary silver or gold.

33. *Authunar th. vestfirzka*, ch. 1, *ÍF* 6:361. An Icelander named Authunn went along.

34. For a general discussion of navigational methods used in sailing to Greenland, see G. J. Marcus, "The Greenland Trade Route," *Economic History Review*, 2nd ser., 7(1954–1955):74–75. It is hard to estimate how much knowledge of the seas between Greenland and Norway was possessed by early Greenlandic seamen, who are said to have traveled between the two lands apparently before Norwegians did. Because current and winds were generally favorable going east, the voyage to Norway would not have often presented many unusual problems (though, according to *Eiríks s. rautha*, Leif Eiríksson had some). Concerning the much more difficult return trip, no details are given by *Grœnlendinga s.* for the voyage of Bjarni Herjólfsson between 1000 and 1015. *Eiríks s. rautha*'s description of Leif's supposed westerly trip would indicate his ignorance of the location of Greenland in relationship to Norway if particularly bad weather was not to blame (the saga says only that he ran into prolonged difficulties). On a return trip to Greenland, Skúf is said by *Fóstbrœthra s.* only to have had a long and stormy passage. All of these supposed direct voyages from Norway to Greenland may be anachronistically attributed. More believably Thorgrím Einarsson is said by *Fóstbrœthra s.* to have returned via Iceland; he would have done so because this non-direct route was less hazardous to the inexperienced navigator of the Greenlandic seas.

35. St. Óláf may have been particularly acquainted with the danger of a Greenland sailing because his nephew, Finn feginn, is said to have been shipwrecked on Greenland's eastern shore where he lost his life: *Grønlands historiske mindesmærker* 2:662–63, cited by Ingstad, *Land under Pole Star*, p. 99.

36. *Óláfs. helga*, ch. 85, *ÍF* 27:127. The voyagers did not make Greenland that time, but another attempt somewhat later succeeded. The purpose of these voyages was mainly political, though some incidental trade may have taken place. When the ship finally got through about 1023, it

was to deliver St. Óláf's messages to his supporters in Greenland (ibid., ch. 124, p. 214), probably asking them to allow his annexation of their island, a request which was refused.

37. Besides the example of Arnbjörn and his fellow Norwegians mentioned above, the Icelandic annals refer to many: in 1185 a "Greenland-farer" was lost (Ann., p. 180). In 1189 Ásmund kastanrazi, with 13 or 18 men, came to Iceland from the east coast of Greenland on a ship lashed together with animal tendons and wooden pegs (ibid., pp. 22, 61, 120); if Ásmund was a Norwegian, his original ship may have been wrecked, and he may have rebuilt it in this way; if a Greenlander, he may not have been able to obtain any better ship. The next year, leaving Iceland, his ship disappeared. In 1188 or 1189 a ship named *Stangarfoli*, probably from Norway, was cast up on the east coast of Greenland where it remained undiscovered for 14 years (ibid., pp. 120, 180; *Prestssaga Guthmundar gótha*, ch. 14, *Stur*. 1:138). In 1209 the *Hörvar-Garprinn* and the *Thjótt-Keptrinn* were driven to Greenland as well as two other ships belonging to Jón stámi ríki and Ketill stámi (*Ann*. pp. 123, 182); these were all probably Norwegian ships and Jón and Ketill do not seem to have been Icelanders; in 1212 Ketill returned to Iceland from Greenland (ibid., p. 124). In 1262 Bishop Óláf of Greenland was aboard a ship that had intended to go to Norway from Greenland, but it was wrecked at Herthísarvík in Iceland (ibid., p. 193). After this time accidents involving ships going or driven to Greenland are known to have occurred in 1266, 1381 or 1382, 1385, and 1406 (ibid., pp. 330; 282, 364–65, 413–14; 365, 414; 288).

38. Passim., *ÍF* 4:271–92: this work mentions two Norwegian merchants being in the Western Settlement about 1130, each with his own ship. At least one more ship, perhaps two, were owned by other Norwegians in the Western Settlement at the same time. Furthermore, several other voyages to Greenland from Norway are mentioned or implied in this work, all of which must have involved trade to some extent: the Greenlander Einar Sokkason traveled to Norway probably on a Norwegian ship and returned with Bishop Arnald on another or the same one; news of the wreck of the ship of Arnbjörn and other Norwegians and a claim by Bishop Arnald to their property reached Norway probably by way of another Norwegian ship; and relatives of Arnbjörn and his party came to Greenland to claim the confiscated property; they are specifically said to have brought goods to trade on their ship.

39. For examples of Norwegian ships engaged in voyages to Greenland not otherwise cited, see *Ann.*, p. 122 for 1202; ibid., p. 212 for 1346; ibid., p. 361 for 1361.

40. *KS*, p. 29.

41. Ibid.

42. When Greenland was eventually annexed by Norway in 1261, only two ships a year were to be sent there, and the Greenland trade became a strictly Norwegian prerogative (*Hákonar s. Hákonarsonar*, ch. 317, p. 567). Apparently even these two ships did not always come. The last known intentional medieval Norwegian voyage to Greenland took place in 1381: in 1383 the ship arrived back in Norway (*Ann.*, p. 414). That the voyage itself is in the annal as a noteworthy event suggests that by that time Norwegian ships did not usually go to Greenland.

43. See *Grœnlendinga s.*, ch. 2, pp. 246–47.

44. 1a:240.

45. *Grœnlendinga s.* ch. 1, *ÍF* 4:242; *Eiríks s.*, ch. 2, *ÍF* 4:200; *Land.*, ch. 2, p. 32. The c. 1307 version of *Landnámabók* (*Hauksbók*, ch. 2, *Land.*, p. 33) says that one sails from Iceland directly to the southern tip of Greenland (Hvarf). The reason for this alteration must have been the increasing amount of ice, due to the cooler climate, found in Denmark Strait farther to the north where sailings were made earlier.

46. As difficult as these westerlies in general were for Icelanders going to Greenland, one of these winds was useful for the return passage, making this voyage easier than if they had attempted to retrace the path they had taken to come there. Unless they caught the westerly winds that could drive them straight to Norway—the problem taken into account by the c. 1022 agreement with St. Óláf—they could pick up one coming from the southwest that would send them back to Iceland. Apparently this was what happened in 1262 when Bishop Óláf of Greenland, who probably intended to sail from his see to Norway, came instead to Iceland when the ship he was on was driven to Herthísarvík on the southwestern coast of Iceland. This same wind probably also accounts for the Norwegian "Greenland-farer" which was wrecked at Hítarnes on the western coast of Iceland in 1266 (*Ann.*, p. 330).

47. This is the view of some of the best recent discussions of the two sagas: Wahlgren, "Fact and Fancy"; Jóhannesson, "Date of the Composition of the Saga of the Greenlanders"; and Björn Thorsteinsson, "Some Observations on the Discoveries and the Cultural History of the Norsemen," *Saga Book of the Viking Society for Northern Research* 16(1963–1964):173–91.

48. Ch. 7, *ÍF* 4:260–61.

49. Ch. 8, pp. 264–65.

50. Ch. 7, pp. 218–20.

51. For the following events, see *Eiríks s.*, chs. 7, 8, pp. 219–22.

52. Whether Thorhall had his own ship is not certain; he may have

gone on the one sailed by Thorvarth. However, later in the saga (ch. 9, p. 225) Thorhall leaves the main expeditionary force on "his" ship. Admittedly the saga is ambiguous on this point, but since the writer says that the two Icelandic ships each had a crew of 40 and because he gives the total number of people as 160, he must have been thinking of four ships leaving Greenland.

53. Ch. 48, ÍF 4:135.

54. Chs. 14, 30, ÍF 7:36, 101.

55. Fóstbrœthra s., chs. 21–24, ÍF 6:224–29.

56. Íslb., ch. 6, p. 14.

57. Grœnlendinga th., chs. 2, 6, ÍF 4:279, 292. (See above note 33.) In addition to these men, another Icelander, Hrafn Sveinbjarnarson may have been to Greenland on a walrus hunt at the end of the 12th century; if so, he probably came with Norwegian merchants: see Hrafns s. Sveinbjarnarsonar, ch. 4, Bisk 1:641–42.

58. This period of short food supplies could have been due not just to a lack of foreign merchants coming to Greenlandic shores, but also to a temporary lack of game supplies that Greenland could usually provide for itself. A few years before the arrival of Thorfinn and the other Icelandic merchants, Eiríks s. says, there was a severe famine in Greenland because of a lack of success during hunting expeditions (ch. 4, p. 206). It should be mentioned here that Vínland probably did not provide much if any grain for Greenlanders, either before or after Thorfinn's visit there: "self-sown" wheat is much made of by Eiríks s., but neither wheat nor any other grain is directly mentioned being in Vínland by Grœnlendinga s.; Vínland's "wheat," if it existed at all, actually may have been wild rice, Zizania aqautica, which commonly grows now in coastal areas as far north as Newfoundland, but which is difficult to gather in significant amounts (see Wahlgren, "Fact and Fancy," p. 49). Since Eiríks s. stresses Vínland wheat, its references to Eirík's food shortage and Thorfinn's gift of grain possibly may be interpreted only as an effort of the saga's author to magnify the importance Vínland wheat would have had for Greenlanders. But even if we must be skeptical of the existence in Vínland of this foodstuff, we do not have to question Greenlanders' need for imported grain.

59. Thorfinn and the others may have had more reason to come to Greenland than merely to make high profits from their grain cargoes. Did they think of sailing to Vínland only after they were at Brattahlíth for the winter when there was "much talk" of the new lands (Eiríks s., ch. 8, p. 221; Grœnlendinga s., ch. 7, p. 261), or did they hear reports about the new land before they came to Greenland, and a voyage there was already in the back of their minds even before they left Iceland? More than Eiríks s.,

Grœnlendinga s. gives the impression that Thorfinn was convinced that he should go only after a great deal of Greenlandic persuasion; in this case he would not have had much resistance to the voyage from the others who would be on his ship, since, according to this account, they seem to have been mainly Greenlanders, and they must have wanted to go. But, as *Eiríks s.* says, there were 40 men on each of the two Icelandic ships, and these crews seem to have been Icelanders. Even before they left Iceland, there might have been some talk that they might ultimately go to Vínland; this would explain why none of them hesitated continuing their voyage after the decision to actually go was made in Greenland. Interpretations of either source on the matter must remain conjectural.

60. The Icelanders Hermund and Thorgils, like several other merchants from Norway, were found in the Western Settlement, closer than the Eastern Settlement to the important hunting area of Northrsetur: they must have been trying to get luxuries by hunting the walrus and other animals that were especially found there. It is also significant that the Icelandic brothers later went to Norway (*Grœnlendinga th.*, chs. 2, 6, ÍF 4:279, 292); the account does not say so, but they undoubtedly hoped to exchange their Greenlandic wares there, if they did not keep them for themselves.

61. *DI* 1:66.

62. This is the meaning accepted by Jón Jóhannesson, *Íslendinga saga* 1:138. Cf. Richard Cleasby, Gudbrand Vigfusson, and William A. Craigie, *An Icelandic-English Dictionary*, s.v. "ey": "Eyjar is often used on the Western Isles, Orkneys, Shetland, and Sudor [Hebrides], hence Eyja-jarl, earl of the Isles (i.e., Orkneys), Orkn[eys] (freq.)."

63. *Haralds s. hárfagra*, ch. 22, ÍF 26:120–22; *Óláfs s. helga*, chs. 96, 100, ÍF 27:158–60, 166–68; *Orkneyinga s.*, chs. 4, 17, ÍF 34:7–8, 36.

64. *Óláfs s. helga*, chs. 96, 100, pp. 158–60, 166–68; *Orkneyinga s.*, ch. 17, p. 36.

65. *Óláfs s. helga*, chs. 100–102, pp. 166–72; *Orkneyinga s.*, ch. 19, pp. 39–42.

66. From the time of Harald the Fairhaired's conquest of the Orkneys and Shetlands until 1195, the two island groups were administered as one political unit by the jarl of the Orkneys. In 1195 the Shetlands were placed under the direct control of King Sverrir of Norway (*Sverris s.*, ch. 125, p. 132; *Orkneyinga s.*, ch. 112, p. 297). In 1468 Christian I of Denmark-Norway pledged both groups as a dowry for his daughter upon her engagement to James III of Scotland, thus suggesting that they still were considered as essentially one political unit, despite Sverrir's administrative change.

67. Ch. 22, ÍF 26:122.

68. Ibid.

69. Óláfs s. helga, ch. 103, pp. 173–74; see, however, ibid., ch. 102, p. 170, where St. Óláf refers to the Orkney jarls giving him possession of the Orkneys and Shetlands: no mention is made of the Hebrides.

70. Ibid., ch. 127, pp. 218–19. St. Óláf never actually was able to receive any taxes due him from these islands (ibid., chs. 135, 142–43, pp. 236–40, 261–67); none were collected until 1035, during the reign of Magnús Óláfsson. But despite this difficulty, there is little question that after 1027 the Faeroes were as much a part of the Norwegian realm as the 1021 acquisitions were. This status is clearly acknowledged by a Faeroese, Thránd í Gata, who said in 1027 or 1028 to an unsuccessful royal tax collector, "I am happy that such a fine man has come here to our land with business from our king to whom we are all subject" (ibid., ch. 143, p. 263). On the Faeroe annexation and St. Óláf's problem with taxes there, see The Saga of the Faroe Islanders, chs. 39–43, pp. 79–92.

71. Land., Sturlubók, ch. 3, p. 34; Land., Hauksbók, ch. 3, p. 35.

72. Land., Sturlubók, ch. 5, p. 36.

73. Land., Hauksbók, ch. 5, p. 37.

74. Sailing direction from 1312: DI 3:17. Because of their position, these islands also were used as important directional guides for navigators on their way to Greenland (see Land., Hauksbók, ch. 2, p. 33).

75. Cf. Archibald Lewis, The Northern Seas, p. 218.

76. For archaeological indications of a Norwegian presence in the Shetlands during the first half of the 9th century, see Holger Arbman, The Vikings, p. 55. On the settlements, see also A. W. Brøgger, Ancient Emigrants; idem, "Den norske bosetningen på Færøyene," Norsk geografisk tidsskrift 5(1935):321–33; idem, Den norske bosetningen på Shetland-Orknøyene; and G. J. Marcus, "The Norse Emigration to the Faroe Islands," English Historical Review 71(1956):56–61.

77. See, for example, Land., Sturlubók, ch. 5, p. 36.

78. See KLNM, s.v. "Fåreavl, Färöarna" and "Hvalfangst, Færøerne"; Arbman, Vikings, p. 55. The Shetlands also seem to have produced some barley, for Orkneyinga s. (ch. 57, ÍF 34:126) mentions a Shetlander threshing some as late as December. Alan Small says that a little grain was grown in the Shetlands ("Shetland—Location the Key to Historical Geography," Scottish Geographical Magazine 85[1969]:158). Presumably he bases his statement on the fact that a plowshare and two querns were excavated in the Shetlands: see his "A Viking Longhouse on Unst, Shetland," in The Fifth Viking Congress, p. 66. Despite these signs, grain production on the

Shetlands must have been quite inadequate for its needs. There is not even a faint indication that the Faeroes produced any grain.

79. *Óláfs s. helga*, ch. 135, *ÍF* 25:237.

80. Thránd's ship went to Norway accompanied by another cargo vessel owned by another powerful Faeroese chieftain, Thorálf of Dímon (ibid., ch. 135, pp. 236–37). Faeroese merchants must have traveled abroad in limited numbers later, for they, with Shetland merchants, are mentioned by King Sverrir as being in Bergen about 1186 (*Sverris s.*, ch. 104, p. 110). Such traders must have been few because only about five years later *Historia profectione Danorum*, though it carefully enumerated others being in Bergen, failed to include in the list Faeroese and Shetlanders: see *Scriptores minores historicae Danicae medii aevi* 2:475–76. Though they were sometimes found in Bergen, no Faeroese merchant is known to have come to Iceland to trade. One Shetlander, who must have been a merchant because he owned a ship, is supposed to have come: he sold his ship while he was there (*Laxdœla s.*, ch. 11, *ÍF* 5:21), perhaps because, like Thránd in the Faeroes, he could not make enough use of it.

81. Alan Small ("Shetland—Location," p. 158) gives a population for the Shetlands of over 19,000 at the end of the 9th century, but he does not say how he arrives at this figure.

82. The Shetlands during the late 9th century would have had a reduction of population, apart from those going away on Viking expeditions or settling elsewhere, because King Harald the Fairhaired is supposed to have slain all the Vikings he found there (and on the Orkneys, Hebrides, and Man) because they had been in the habit of making raids on Norway (*Haralds s. hárfagra*, ch. 22, *ÍF* 26:120).

83. At least by the Reformation he owned 40% of the land (John F. West, *Faroe*, p. 6).

84. Lucien Musset, *Les Peuples scandinaves au moyen âge*, p. 211. Because the cathedral was started when a foreign market for fish began to develop, perhaps a new prosperity based on that product instead of those of sheep was anticipated, causing the cathedral's construction to be initiated. Because the structure was not completed, however, the Faeroes' poverty must have remained general even during the latter Middle Ages in spite of the new market for fish.

85. On the lack of commerce between Iceland and the Faeroes, see also Peter G. Foote, *On the Saga of the Faroe Islanders*, p. 10. An exceptional example of at least indirect trade between Iceland and the Shetlands is provided by *Fljótsdœla s.* (ch. 5, *ÍF* 11:227): it states that some Icelandic goods were found there.

86. In addition to early colonizers of Iceland, two Hebrideans can be mentioned who may have come only to trade. One was named Sæmund who brought his ship to harbor at Göguskarthsáróss (Land., ch. 188, p. 228). The other was more certainly a merchant, if we can believe a saga of uncertain date: coming at the end of the settlement period or shortly afterward, he is said to have been named Rauth ("Red") the Buyer; he was supposed to have made a practice of sailing to various lands, and he came to Iceland to sell what he had acquired on his travels (Hrana s. hrings, ch. 11, ÍS 9:433).

87. Orkneyinga s. says that when Jarl Rögnvald was building St. Magnús Cathedral at Kirkwall during the years around 1140, he began to run short of funds. His father suggested he sell farmers full ownership to their land. Rögnvald did so, "and there was to be paid to the jarl a mörk for every plowland in all the islands. And afterward there was no lack of money for church construction, and it was built very beautifully" (ch. 76, ÍF 34:174). "Plowlands," which must have been used mainly for raising barley, therefore probably were extensive, for otherwise ample revenue would not have been raised to finish the work of church construction. Finnbogi Guthmundsson, the editor of this edition of the saga, points out, though, that the word "plowland" ("plógsland") might well be a scribal error, for it does not occur elsewhere in the saga; if the scribe read in the manuscript he was copying, "pland," he could have mistakenly understood it as meaning plógsland rather than "pennigsland" ("penny-land"). This other interpretation would have made sense, because Orkney land was divided into such subdivisions. Therefore, too much weight cannot be placed on the word "plowland" mentioned here (ibid., n5). Elsewhere in this saga, however, there is another indication that barley was commonly grown in some abundance: a man fell off a stack of barley high enough apparently for him to break some ribs (ch. 57, p. 126). Still, the best testimony to a significant Orkney grain supply is that the islands occasionally had a surplus to sell to Icelanders, as shall be seen. Most of the evidence concerning barley is related to the Orkneys. But there is little reason to believe that the Hebrides did not grow rather plentiful amounts of it as well, for they would have enjoyed virtually the same conditions as the Orkneys that made it possible.

88. On the Shetlands, where terrain and climate were more similar than on the Faeroes to the Orkneys and Hebrides, and where grain seems to have been able to be grown, probably it was because the population was too dense that only a nominal number of acres could be devoted to grain cultivation. The Hebrides include 2,900 mi.^{2}; the Orkneys proper only 376 mi.^{2}, smaller than the Faeroes or Shetlands. During most of the medieval

period following the Orkney settlement by Scandinavians, however, the area of Caithness, which included much of northern Scotland virtually adjacent to the Orkneys, was included in the jarldom (see, for example, *Orkneyinga s.*, chs. 10, 11, 13, 19, *ÍF* 34:23, 24, 28, 42). Combined square miles for the Orkneys therefore would be comparable to the Hebrides.

89. No Hebridean merchants are known to have come to Norway. On the value of Icelandic woolens in England, see Chapter 6.

90. *Orkneyinga s.*, ch. 59, *ÍF* 34:130; Oscar Albert Johnsen, "Norges handel og skibsfart i middlelalderen," *NK* 16:131.

91. *Hrafns s. Sveinbjarnarsonar*, ch. 3, *Bisk.* 1:641.

92. An entry in the Pipe Roll for 1182 mentions cloth of various colors: "scarlat" was most expensive, less so were green and gray say (a soft cloth) (E. Lipson, *Economic History of England* 1:446).

93. Lipson, *Economic History* 1:196. Not very far from Grimsby, Norwich still traded in leather goods c. 1200, and only later did it specialize in weaving cloth (ibid., p. 444). *Íslendinga s.* mentions a sword in Iceland in the early 13th century that came from the Orkneys (ch. 108, *Stur.* 1:385). Like the fine cloth and saddles given to Hrafn, it may have come to the Orkneys earlier from England, to which it might have been imported even earlier from possibly Spain, renowned for its metalworking industry.

94. Ch. 50, *ÍF* 4:137–38.

95. Archibald Lewis says that textile artifacts on Eigg in the Hebrides give evidence of trade as far as Flanders and the Baltic (*Northern Seas*, p. 339), but it is not inconceivable that textiles also were sometimes stolen. The Old Icelandic word "ársal" ("bed-hangings") is foreign, introduced from Britain (Cleasby et al., *Dictionary*, s.v. "ársalr"). These too could have come from England.

96. *Thorláks s. helga hins yngri*, ch. 49, *Bisk.* 1:320–21; cf. *Thorláks s. biskups hins elzta*, ch. 24, *Bisk.* 1:120, where it is noted that merchants from the Orkneys sought the aid of St. Thorlák on their way to the Faeroes: they may have been on the same voyage.

97. *Íslendinga s.*, ch. 15, *Stur.* 1:240.

98. *Jóns s. helga hins elzta* (Vithbætir: *Jarteinir úr Jóns sögu hinni yngstu*, ch. 9), *Bisk.* 1:210.

99. *Vatndœla s.*, ch. 43, *ÍF* 8:115.

100. *Bandamanna s.*, ch. 11, *ÍF* 7:358.

101. *Orkneyinga s.*, ch. 81, *ÍF* 34:182.

102. Ibid., ch. 90, p. 238.

103. *Jóns s. helga hins elzta* (Vithbætir: *Jarteinir úr Jóns sögu hinni yngstu*, ch. 9), *Bisk.* 1:210.

104. *Grágás* provides for the disposal of property of Icelanders dying in the "Western Isles" (1a:239). Though these places could have included the Faeroes, Shetlands, and Hebrides, not just the Orkneys, it appears that the latter would have been the most likely of the "Western Isles" to which Icelanders would have gone.

105. *Brot úr mithsögu Guthmundar*, ch. 4, *Bisk.* 1:563–64; *Prests s. Guthmundar Arasonar*, ch. 29, *Stur.* 1:257. The latter says that Guthmund went to "Hirtir" (Hirta?), a Hebrides island, with Hrafn Sveinbjarnarson and thirteen other Icelanders. There they heard of the death of King Sverrir of Norway. Since that occurrence took place in 1202, the voyage must have been made that year or the next. Guthmund became bishop of Hólar in 1203.

106. See Lindsay Scott, "The Norse in the Hebrides," in *The [First] Viking Congress*, pp. 189–215; *Magnúss s. barfœtts*, chs. 8, 9, ÍF 28:219–22. Arne Odd Johnsen shows clearly, however, that by the late 12th century, though the Hebrides were independent of Norway in practice, they were not altogether so in theory ("The Payments from the Hebrides and the Isle of Man to the Crown of Norway, 1153–1263," *Scottish Historical Review* 48[1969]:18–34). In 1266 the Hebrides, with the Isle of Man, were formally ceded to Scotland.

107. In the absence of any data, these examples are intended only to indicate possible price disparities. Furthermore these examples are given to show only general tendencies; various circumstances could occur to change price relationships temporarily.

108. For many of the same reasons, Orkney merchants themselves would prefer going to a larger market area than Iceland. In England, for instance, they could sell their most important cargo—woolens—for a higher price, and they could obtain a more varied selection of articles in return. Icelanders, though, were willing to pay a good price for barley, and when the Orkneys had a surplus, its merchants could be expected to bring it to Iceland. They did, but only when the price was exceptionally high at the beginning of the 13th century. Before that time ordinarily Orkney merchants must have preferred the easier, but less profitable, practice of selling what barley they had available to Icelanders who came to their island for it, or even to Norwegians who might come for it when there was a severe shortage in Norway.

109. If the merchant went to Norway first, and intended to pick up some wares in the Orkneys on his return trip, he might have had to pay another landaurar on those islands because the exemption clause of the agreement does not seem to provide for a voyage in that direction.

110. The Faeroes would enjoy much the same distinction and would

tolerate much the same practical control when they were annexed in 1027.

CHAPTER SIX

1. *The Anglo-Saxon Chronicle*, p. 55. *The Annals of St. Neot's* states that the Norsemen landed at Portland; in the account of Ethelweard's *Chronicon*, the reeve was from the city of Dorchester (ibid., pp. 54–55n2).

2. According to a later law of King Alfred, traders were supposed to come before the king's sheriff to declare publicly "how many of them there are" (F. L. Attenborough, *The Laws of the Earliest English Kings* [Cambridge, Eng., 1922], pp. 78–79, cited in *Anglo-Saxon Chronicle*, pp. 54–55n2). Thus "evidently the reeve thought the pirates were merchants" (ibid.).

3. See F. M. Stenton, *Anglo-Saxon England*, p. 534. In spite of the agreement, only three years later Óláf, in alliance with King Sveinn of Denmark, again carried on forays against England (ibid., pp. 372–73).

4. See ibid., p. 534, citing *Historians of the Church of York*, ed. J. Raine [Rolls Series, 1879–94], 1:454.

5. More emphatic evidence for commercial relations, as Stenton also points out, is that Scandinavian monarchs copied English coinage, and, of the six men who acted as moneyers for Óláf skattkonung of Sweden (999–1022), at least four were Englishmen (ibid., pp. 534–35). During the pre-Norman period in England, Sweden maintained a more active trade there than afterward, as the large number of English coins found on Gotland from this period suggests (Peter A. Sawyer, *Age of the Vikings*, p. 92). Sweden was important to England and all of northwestern Europe as a main intermediary for Russian, Muslim, and Byzantine goods. The decline of this importance coincided with increasing anarchy in the Kievan state after the death of Yaroslav I in 1054. Thus after the mid-11th century, continental Scandinavian contact with England would be mainly limited to Denmark and Norway. England, during the years before the mid-11th century, also obtained several Muslim luxuries, among which could have been silk, from the caliphate of Cordova (*KLNM*, s.v. "Englandshandel, Norge").

6. For England, see M. M. Postan, "Mediaeval Agrarian Society in its Prime: England," in *The Cambridge Economic History of Europe* 1:560–65.

7. See A. Taranger, *Den angelsakiske kirkes indflydelse paa den norske;* Henry Goddard Leach, "The Relations of the Norwegian with the English Church," *Proceedings of the American Academy of Arts and Sciences* 44(1909):531–60; and Knut Helle, "Anglo-Norwegian Relations

in the Reign of Håkon Håkonsson (1217–63)," *Mediaeval Scandinavia* 1(1968):106–11.

8. Leach, "Relations," pp. 541, 543; Helle, "Relations," p. 107. The formal trade concessions to Lyse were preceded in 1212 when King John allowed a ship of the abbot of that monastery to export goods from England free of duty (Leach, "Relations," p. 541).

9. See *Magnússonar s.*, ch. 3, *ÍF* 28:239; see also Leach, "Relations," p. 534.

10. Helle, "Relations," pp. 104–6, where he mentions hawks and falcons sent to Henry III by Hákon Hákonarson. For instances of Kings Henry I, Henry II, and John being sent falcons from their Norwegian counterparts, see *Diplomatarium Norvegicum* 19:pt.1:66, 86, 89, 127, 137, 139, 141–43, 145, 158, 161. See also *DI* 10:1–4. Besides these birds, King Henry III also received a live elk from Hákon in 1222 and a polar bear in 1252 (Helle, "Relations," p. 106).

11. Helle, "Relations," pp. 101–2; *Patent Rolls of the Reign of Henry III . . . 1216–1225*, p. 384 (7 Henry III m. 1.).

12. *Egils s. Skallagrímssonar*, ch. 62, *ÍF* 2:196.

13. *Prestssaga Guthmundar gótha*, ch. 12, *Stur.* 1:136; see also *Guthmundar s. Arasonar, Hóla-biskups hins elzta*, ch. 16, *Bisk.* 1:433–34.

14. The high quality of some English fabrics is testified to by their export even to some continental centers renowned for their own fine cloth: see Austin Lane Poole, *From Domesday Book to Magna Carta*, p. 86.

15. Ch. 67, *ÍF* 2:213.

16. In 1163, Henry II had given a license for a weavers' guild in York, and he gave that city a monopoly in Yorkshire for manufacturing cloths, tunics, and "rays" (striped material, probably the saga's multi-colored cloth) (Poole, *Domesday*, p. 85).

17. *Prestssaga Guthmundar gótha*, ch. 12, *Stur.*, 1:136; see also *Guthmundar s. Arasonar, Hóla-biskups hins elzta*, ch. 16, *Bisk.* 1:433–34.

18. Hjalmar Falk points out that the "fustian" (OI "fustan") mentioned in *Egils s.* (ch. 78) was perhaps borrowed from the English word (*Altwestnordische Kleiderkunde*, p. 66). This English fustian would have been fairly well known in Iceland, but whether as a luxury or a common cloth cannot be determined. According to Falk, referring to *Egils s.*, chs. 67, 78, 79, the oldest foreign clothing fashions in Iceland came from England (ibid., p. 380).

19. Archibald Lewis, *The Northern Seas*, pp. 206–7.

20. *Hemings th. Áslákssonar*, ch. 14, *ÍF* 7:433; *Hrafns s. Sveinbjarnarsonar*, ch. 5, *Bisk.* 1:645. The evidence concerning Icelandic imports of metal objects in the late 13th century *Hemings th.* should not be al-

together discounted, for two English swords and English silver dating from the 11th century have been found in Iceland: see Kristján Eldjárn, *Kuml og haugfé*, p. 435.

21. Poole, *Domesday*, p. 86.

22. Ibid.; E. Lipson gives the date as 1197 (*Economic History of England* 1:446). Lipson erroneously gives 45" instead of c. 46 cm for the length of an ell (ibid., n5), two of which equalled a yard.

23. That it was linen, of all English cloth, that is mentioned in the "stika law" helps to confirm what we already know from the price lists of c. 1186 and afterward, that this particular type of cloth was common in Iceland at the time, as it probably was just after 1100 when the legal or "short" öln became standardized in Iceland, apparently also in response to typical English cloth measurement.

24. Even with continually more attention given to sheep raising, by the 13th century English wool production seems to have become inadequate for both the needs of the Low Countries and England itself, partly because cloth production probably greatly increased with the invention of the pedal-loom and spinning wheel during the years around 1200 (on the dates of these inventions, see Urban Tigner Holmes, Jr., *Daily Living in the Twelfth Century*, pp. 146–47; Lynn White, Jr., *Medieval Technology and Social Change*, p. 117; Eleanora Carus-Wilson. "The Woollen Industry," in *The Cambridge Economic History of Europe* 2:379, 412). The Oxford Parliament of 1258, in an apparent attempt to secure a more ample supply of wool for domestic weavers, ordered that "the wool of the country should be worked up in England and not be sold to foreigners . . ." (quoted in Lipson, *Economic History* 1:448); the need to retain more domestic wool in the country can be seen also in the various restrictions levied on wool exports, rules that were intended to stimulate a declining weaving industry during the 14th century and later (see ibid., pp. 453–55).

25. As mentioned, English linen in Iceland was three times the cost of ordinary vathmál. Similarly in England, Icelandic vathmál might have been about ⅓ the cost of linen, for, in each case, transportation costs and mercantile profits should have been comparable. Thus even as an import, the price for Icelandic vathmál in English towns probably was competitive with ordinary domestic woolens. The use of Icelandic vathmál by the urban poor in England is strongly suggested by analogy with practices in Germany: the Grimm brothers' *Dictionary* states that the word "watmal" was known since the 13th century in Low Germany as well as in Prussia, Pomerania, the Baltic area, and southern Germany; it meant a cloth used by the lower classes and paupers (Marta Hoffman, *The Warp-Weighted Loom*, p. 223). Because Hanseatic German merchants began coming to Norway in significant numbers during the 13th century, it seems likely

that this "watmal" was Icelandic vathmál obtained in Norway. If, beginning in the 13th century, Icelandic vathmál was used to clothe the poor in Germany, which did not export a large proportion of its domestic wool supplies and which almost certainly did not use as high a proportion of its wool as did England for weaving fine cloth, then it seems probable that England would have had a similar use for the Icelandic product from the 11th to the 13th centuries when its trade with Norway was also strong, its wool exports larger, and more of its own cloth of high quality.

26. For the specifically Icelandic falcons, see *DI* 10:1–2.

27. *Hrafns s. Sveinbjarnarsonar,* ch.4, *Bisk.* 1:641–42.

28. *DI* 1:482; *DI* 10:3.

29. For an example not otherwise mentioned here, see *Gísla s. Súrssonar,* ch. 5, *ÍF* 6:16, and *Gunnars th. Thithrandabana,* chs. 1-2, *ÍF* 11:195–200, where a man named Thórir the England-Farer is mentioned who lived around 1000: he must have earned his nickname because of frequent voyages to England. Provision for the property of Icelanders dying in England is made by *Grágás* 1a:239; it is not certain they were merchants, though surely in many cases they would have been.

30. Sweden, Denmark, Gautland, Gotland, Scotland, the Orkneys, Faeroes, Shetlands, Caithness, and Greenland are also mentioned: *Thorláks s. biskups hins elzta,* ch. 28, *Bisk.* 1:123–24.

31. *Thorláks s. biskups: Önnur jarteinabók Thorláks biskups,* ch. 1, *Bisk.* 1:357.

32. On the activity of commerce at Lynn, see Poole, *Domesday,* p. 96; for Norwegians at Lynn, see Helle, "Relations," pp. 103–4. A comment by Giraldus Cambrensis may also illustrate a general lack of knowledge about Iceland at the end of the 12th century. He says in his *Topographica Hibernica* that Icelanders are few in number, that they are truthful, and that priests are their kings (bk. 2: ch. 8: pp. 95–96). There is no reason to disagree with his first characterizations, but the last one is more questionable. Giraldus is notorious for his inventions, and this may be one of them, an effort to depict Iceland as a kind of ideal state from his point of view. Or it may reflect a proper characterization that was corrupted in the retelling over a long period. Since Giraldus says only that priests were kings, apparently he did not know that Iceland had bishops, for otherwise he might have credited them with royal power instead—as did Adam of Bremen who, c. 1075, wrote that Icelanders "hold their bishop as king" (*Gesta* bk. 4: ch. 36: p. 184; see also ibid., schol. 150). The origins of Giraldus's comment, if he did not make it up himself, thus might have been before 1056 when the first Icelandic bishopric was established. And perhaps the story originated before the Icelandic conversion in 1000, since Christian priests during the early 11th century did not act in an indepen-

dent manner and were hardly of the stature of kings, subservient as they were to the chieftains; pagan chieftains fulfilled the function of priest-kings far better. Icelanders probably were not frequent visitors to England or wherever else Giraldus might have picked up the idea, for, had they been, his information might have been more accurate.

33. Alexander Bugge states that William of Malmesbury, c. 1140, says that Bristol was " 'a harbor for vessels from Iceland, Norway, and other lands beyond the sea' " (*Vesterlandenes indflydelse*, pp. 182, 192; idem, *Den norske trælasthandels historie* 1:130). Jón Jóhannesson repeats this information (*Íslendinga saga* 1:386). William says only that Irish, Norwegian, and other ships visited Bristol (*De gestis pontificum Anglorum*, p. 292). For general contact of Scandinavians with Wales, however, see B. G. Charles, *Old Norse Relations with Wales*. The c. 1275 version of *Landnámabók, Sturlubók*, while mentioning a direct route to Ireland, does not do so for England (see *Land*, ch. 2, pp. 32, 34). This omission might suggest that it was not the habit of Icelanders, even if they still went to England, to sail there directly.

34. The royal order of 1224 mentioned above might be an instance of the enforcement of the treaty of 1223: if so, the ship(s) that brought the Icelandic goods must have been of Norwegian origin, not Icelandic.

35. Ia:229.

36. *Húngrvaka* mentions that an English bishop, Bjarnvarth the Book-Wise Vilráthsson, visited Iceland about 1070 (ch. 3, *Bisk*. 1:64–65); and *Landnámabók* says that Björn the Englishman was the father of an Abbott Arnis (*Land*., ch. 137, p. 178). Evidence of possible Icelandic-English trade relations are the English coins found on Iceland, brought there perhaps by Icelandic, English, or other merchants. But these coins do not incontestably prove that trade took place directly with England because they may have come to Iceland via Norway. And some coins may have nothing to do with trade but may have been part of booty or tribute collected at one time in England by Scandinavians (cf. Lewis, *Northern Seas*, p. 340).

37. *Book of Rights*, ed. [John?] O'Donovan (Dublin, 1847), p. 241, cited by Lewis, *Northern Seas*, p. 337; "National Characteristics," *Zeitschrift für keltische Philologie* 1(1897):112, cited by Lewis, *Northern Seas*, p. 337. Lewis mentions here, as evidence of continued Norse commerce after 1014, 365 tuns of wine, probably coming from abroad, which the Norse had to pay annually to the Irish.

38. *War of the Gaedhil with the Gaill*, p. 51. Surely at least the satins and silks must have been the result of Norse trade, perhaps with the Muslims via the Baltic and Russia (see Lewis, *Northern Seas*, p. 225).

39. Lewis, *Northern Seas*, p. 336.

40. *War of the Gaedhil*, p. 115.

41. Patrick Weston Joyce, *A Social History of Ancient Ireland* 2:433; Alice Stopford Green, *History of the Irish State to 1014*, p. 352.

42. There are only a limited number of Irish coins in Iceland, and even these may not have arrived directly or have been the result of trade. As an example of comparative scarcity, in the Gaulverjabær find there are only 2 Irish coins compared to 180 Anglo-Saxon (*KLNM*, s.v. "Arabiska mynt"). For pre-1000 Irish objects of various kinds found in Iceland, see Eldjárn, *Kuml og haugfé*, p. 435. *Kjalnesinga s.* gives some indication that either native Irish or Norse-Irish traded with Iceland. After Iceland was Christianized in 1000, a certain Örlyg is said to have been persuaded by a Bishop Patrick to travel from Ireland to Iceland and build a church there because "there is much sailing of rich men there now" (ch. 1, *ÍF* 14:4). By 1000 all of the best pieces of Icelandic land of any size had long been settled, therefore the "rich men" would have been more likely to be prosperous merchants than settlers.

43. Ch. 21, *ÍF* 5:52–54. For other instances of Icelanders in Ireland during the 10th century, all of whom went to Dublin, see *Eyrbyggja s.*, chs. 29, 64, *ÍF* 4:76, 176. Particular mention should be made of the skald Gunnlaug the Serpent-Tongued. In the 10th century he is supposed to have been given by King Sigtrygg Silkybeard, as a reward for a poem which he composed, two knerrir, skarlat cloth, a kirtel, and a cloak with valuable furs, as well as a gold ring that weighed a mörk. If this incident actually happened, perhaps he used his knerrir to bring back some Irish products to Iceland to trade (*Gunnlaugs s. ormstungu*, ch. 8, *ÍF* 3:76).

44. *Land.*, chs. 116, 122, pp. 158, 162.

45. Reference is made to Icelanders in Dublin by *Grágás* (1a:239), but it is impossible to know what their purpose was (though trade seems most likely), how frequent their voyages there were, or indeed during what period these trips were most likely to have been made.

46. *Land.*, ch. 2, pp. 32, 34.

47. *KLNM*, s.v. "Landnamabok."

48. When Hauk Erlendsson wrote his version of *Landnámabók* about 1307, he changed the five days' sailing to Ireland given by Sturla to only three (*Land.* [*Hauksbók*], ch. 2, p. 33). Because this discrepancy almost certainly cannot be attributed to an increased speed of vessels making the trip, either Hauk (or his copyist) made an error, or he was unsure of the length of time the voyage took. If the latter, it could be attributed to infrequent sailings, or none at all, to Ireland by his time.

49. Irish weaving must have been mainly intended for local use even in the earlier 13th century when a limited amount of Irish cloth apparently first began to be sent to England (Lipson, *Economic History* 1:489).

50. These same circumstances must have accounted for the lack of a strong Norwegian trade with Ireland after 1014. Snorri Sturluson, writing about 1230, says that at the end of the 10th century Jarl Hákon of Lade in Norway sent a man on a trading expedition to Dublin "which many did then . . ." (*Óláfs s. Tryggvasonar,* ch. 45, *ÍF* 26:291), thereby suggesting that the trade was not frequent in his own time. In addition to the lack of Irish luxuries, Norwegian trade with Ireland must have been curtailed more severely by Snorri's time because of increased competition there of English merchants due to Henry II's Irish conquest in the 1170s (see Oscar Albert Johnsen, "Norges handel og skibsfart i middelalderen," *NK* 16:133).

51. *Ann.,* pp. 110, 251, 471.

52. He also went to Lincoln: *Thorláks s. biskups hins elzta,* ch. 4, *Bisk.* 1:92. For the years abroad: Jóhannesson, *Íslendinga saga* 1:214. Two other bishops of Skálaholt are known to have been students abroad: Páll Jónsson (1195–1211) studied in England (*Páls s. byskups,* ch. 1, *Bisk.* 1:127); Jón Halldórsson, before taking office in 1322, studied at Bologna and Paris (*Ann.,* p. 267).

53. *Hrafns s. Sveinbjarnarsonar,* ch. 4, *Bisk.* 1:641–42.

54. Jóhannesson, *Íslendinga saga* 1:180–81; see also *Íslb.,* ch. 10, p. 22.

55. See Halldór Hermannsson, *Sæmund Sigfússon and the Oddaverjar,* pp. 5–9, 33–36.

56. For more than a century after the original grant, Scandinavians in Normandy, though at least superficially Christianized, retained ties with pagan Vikings who used the area as a base from which to launch attacks against England and as a refuge after attacking other parts of France itself (see David C. Douglas, *William the Conqueror,* pp. 16, 21–22; *Óláfs s. helga,* chs. 19, 20, 27, *ÍF* 27:25–27, 33). Cultural ambivalence among early Normans is revealed by an anecdote recorded by Dudo of Saint Quentin: the second duke, William Longsword, sent his son Richard to Bayeux to learn the language of his forefathers because it was no longer spoken in Rouen (*De moribus et actes primorum Normanniae ducum,* ed. J. Lair [Société des Antiquares de Normandie, 1865], p. 148, cited by Douglas, *William,* p. 22). The administrative center must have been subject to Frankish influences more than outlying areas like Bayeux, which thus retained older Scandinavian traditions longer; a mixture of Frankish and Scandinavian ties is quite obviously seen by William's desire that his son should learn the ancestral language even when it was being supplanted by Frankish.

57. *Sighvats th. skálds,* ch. 10, *ÍS* 12:150.

58. *Óláfs s. helga,* ch. 43, *ÍF* 27:54.

59. Ch. 18, *Riddarasögur* 1:30–31.

60. While the white fur and falcons could have been commonly brought to France from Norway well before the time *Tristrams s.* was written, importation of sulphur may have started only somewhat before because Greek-fire was not introduced to western Europe until c. 1200.

61. *DI* 1:718–19.

62. Division of opinion of this ship's origin is exemplified by Poul Enemark (*KLNM*, s.v. "Frankrigshandel") who believes it to be Norwegian, and Alexander Bugge (*Vesterlandenes indflydelse,* p. 198) who thinks it was Icelandic.

63. Maurice Powicke, *The Loss of Normandy,* p. 233.

64. *Calendar of Documents in France,* ed. J. H. Round (London, 1899), p. 34, cited by Lipson, *Economic History* 1:279.

65. Direct French trade with Iceland, it is safe to say, probably did not exist. There are only a few indications that any Frenchman reached Iceland. A bishop named Rúthólf, said to have received his name because he was from Rouen "in England" (i.e., Normandy), visited Iceland in the mid-11th century (*Húngrvaka,* ch. 3, *Bisk.* 1:65). There is no reason believe that he traded either in Iceland or any place else (see Jón Stefánsson, "Rútholf of Bæ and Rudolf of Rouen," *Saga Book of the Viking Society* 13[1950]:174–82). Another Frenchman in Iceland was a certain Rikinni, who taught poetry and music at the cathedral school of Hólar at the beginning of the 12th century (*Jóns s. helga hins elzta,* ch. 14, *Bisk.* 1:168; *Jóns s. hins helga eptir Gunnlaug múnk,* ch. 27, *Bisk.* 1:239). Again there is no indication that he ever traded or that he ever returned to France so that he might persuade his countrymen to travel to Iceland to trade. Finally, an Icelander of the earlier 13th century, Thormóth, had the nickname of "valsk" ("French") (*Íslendinga s.,* chs. 71, 72, 85, Stur. 1:377, 329, 356). Perhaps he gained this name because he, or an ancestor, had gone to France; or perhaps a Frenchman was an ancestor of his. Apart from these few cases, archaeological evidence shows some indication of contact with France, whether by Icelanders going there, Frenchmen coming to Iceland, or, more probably, Norwegians acting as intermediaries. For artifacts of French origin from before 1000 found in Iceland, see Eldjárn, *Kuml og haugfé,* p. 435.

66. Kristján Eldjárn, "Gaulverjabær-fundet og nogle mindre islandske møntfund fra vikingetiden," *Nordisk numismatisk årsskrift* 13(1948):53–62.

67. A Saxon bishop named Bjarnharth (Bernhard) also visited Iceland; he came about 1070 and stayed twenty years (*Húngrvaka,* ch. 3, *Bisk.* 1:65). See also *Íslendinga s.,* ch. 34, *Stur.* 1:267, where Herburt, a German, is mentioned.

68. *Brennu-Njáls s.*, ch. 100, *ÍF* 12:255; *Annales regii* and *Skálholts annáll* give 997 as the arrival date; *Oddaverja annáll* gives 998: *Ann.*, pp. 105, 178, 464.

69. "Leitharvísir," in *Alfræthi íslenzk* 1:13–15. Provision is made by *Grágás* (1a:239) for the disposal of property of Icelanders dying in Saxony or farther south: presumably most of them would have been pilgrims.

70. *DI* 171–72.

71. *Húngrvaka*, ch. 2, *Bisk.* 1:60–61; see also Roland Köhne, "Bischof Ísleifr Gizurarson," *Jahresbericht des historischen Vereins für die Grafschaft Ravensburg* 67(1970):1–38.

72. The only example, however, is a polar bear brought from Greenland given by Ísleif Gizurarson to the Holy Roman Emperor Henry III (*Húngrvaka*, ch. 2, Bisk. 1:61).

73. *Gesta* bk. 4: chs. 39–40: pp. 186–88.

74. Henry S. Lucas, "Medieval Economic Relations between Flanders and Greenland," *Speculum* 12(1937):174.

75. Müllenhoff and Scherer, eds., *Denkmäler deutscher Poesie und Prosa* (Augsburg, 1892), cited by Bugge, *Trælasthandels historie* 1:65. Konrad Maurer said that Iceland is mentioned in a 13th-century Leiden manuscript of Solinus; it also mentions burning ice (from Thorvald Thoroddsen, *Landfræthissaga Íslands* 1:58–59). See also Johannes A. Huisman, "Utrecht im Merigato," *Beiträge zur Geschichte der deutschen Sprache und Literatur* (Tübingen) 87(1966):379–89; and Hans Wilkins, "Zur Geschichte des niederländischen Handels im Mittelalter," *Hansische Geschichtsblätter* 15(1909):126–27.

76. Certain cloth came from Flanders originally, and the "broad linen," as distinct from the "English linen," mentioned in the Althing price list of c. 1200 may have been of Flemish origin; but these various cloths did not necessarily come to Iceland directly. The same is true of the German cloth known in Iceland.

77. Icelanders, however, sometimes may have gone to Frisia for Viking raids that may have involved trade; see *Egils s. Skallagrímssonar*, ch. 50, *ÍF* 2:128. And later Hall Teitsson, after having been chosen bishop in 1149 and having gone to Rome, died on his way back at Utrecht in 1150 (*Ann.*, p. 114). He was known for his travels to the Continent and for a book he wrote entitled *Flos peregrinationis* (*Haukdæla th.*, ch. 4, *Stur.* 1:60); but he was not known as a trader.

78. Lewis, *Northern Seas*, p. 433.

79. For Norwegian trade in general in this period, see Oscar Albert Johnsen, *Norwegische Wirtschaftsgeschichte*, pp. 91–128; for German active trade, see Lewis, *Northern Seas*, pp. 431–33, 479–80; for Frisian

active trade, see Wilkins, "Geschichte des niederländischen Handels," pp. 123–203; Lewis, *Northern Seas*, p. 480.

80. If Norway, usually served as intermediary in the Holy Roman Empire-Iceland trade, the inaccuracies of the Frisian literary evidence, purporting to state direct contact, might be explained thereby. The voyagers mentioned by Adam of Bremen and those mentioned by Reginbert may have in fact not gone to Iceland at all, but merely to Norway. Fearful that these traders might contact Iceland directly if they learned of Iceland's needs, Norwegian merchants may have sought to protect their profits gained as mediators in the trade by telling stories of the supernatural in the one case, or by deliberately lying in the other—by pointing out that there was no market for grain or wine in Iceland, the Norwegians would discourage Frisians from bringing these products to the island. Norwegian merchants might freely admit that timber was in short supply on Iceland, for Frisian merchants would not be able to compete with Norwegians in supplying this product.

81. Ch. 8, ÍF 6:159.

82. *Land. (Sturlubók)*, ch. 174, p. 212; *Land. (Melabók)*, ch. 174, p. 212 n2; *Thórthar s.*, ch. 2, ÍF 14:169.

83. *Thorsteins s. Geirnefjufóstra*, ch. 15, ÍS 8:432–33.

84. *Bjarnar s. Hítdœlakappa*, chs. 2–4, ÍF 3:113–20.

85. *Heitharvíga s.*, chs. 41, 43, ÍF 3:324, 328. According to A. Stender-Pedersen, the Old Norse word "varangi" ("varangian") originally had a commercial meaning which only later began to assume a military connotation ("Die Varägersage als Quelle der altrussischen Chronik," *Acta Jutlandica Aarsskrift for Aarhus Universitet* 6[1938]:11–12).

86. *Íslendinga s.*, ch. 32, Stur. 1:260–61. That Constantinople was known for its metalwork is supported by a story that King Harald the Harsh-Ruler Sigurtharson had had armor made while he was in that city. This armor was particularly strong, of two layers, and reached down to his feet when he stood upright (*Sneglu-Halla th.*, ch. 4, ÍF 9:269–70). Kiev was also known for its metalwork: see *Nordens historie i middelalderen efter arabiske kilder*, p. 52. For Scandinavian trade in eastern swords or possession of them, see G. Jacob, *Der nordisch-baltische Handel der Araber im Mittelalter*, pp. 148–49; see also *Nordens historie*, pp. 11, 58.

8. Thorvald Konráthsson, nicknamed "the Wide-farer," was an Icelandic pilgrim who was presumably on his way home through Russia when he died at a monastery, perhaps at Poloszk (*Thorvalds th. vithförla*, ch. 9, *Bisk*. 1:48–49). See also the example of Aron Hjörleifsson traveling to Russia early in the 13th century: *Íslendinga s.*, ch. 55, Stur. 1:308. A Norwegian, Andrés Skjalldarband, went on a pilgrimage to Jerusalem and

was never heard from again, despite persistent efforts to learn his fate (*Hákonar s. Hákonarsonar*, ch. 170, p. 476); because one of the Icelandic annals records that he perished in 1230 on a dromon in the "Sea of Greekland" (*Ann.*, 128), conceivably an Icelander went with him and eventually brought back the news.

88. Three bishops are described by Ári Thorgilsson as "ermskir," and they are said to have come to Iceland during the 11th century (*Íslb.*, ch. 8, p. 18); they may have been of the Paulician heresy from Armenia: see Frédéric Macler, "Armenie et Island," *Revue de l'histoire des religions* 87(1923):236–41; or instead they may have been orthodox from western Russia ("Ermland"): see Magnús Már Lárusson, "On the so-called 'Armenian' Bishops," *Studia Islandica* 18(1960):23–38.

89. See, for example, *Grettis s.*, chs. 85, 86, 90, 93, ÍF 7:271, 272, 285, 290. On the Varangian Guard, see Sigfús Blöndal and Benedikt S. Benedikz, *The Varangians of Byzantium*. That Icelanders were members of the Varangian Guard even under 13th-century Latin rulers of Byzantium is suggested by a story concerning St. Thorlák. *Önnur jarteinabók Thorláks biskups* states that some Norwegians, who had gone to Constantinople to join the guard soon after a certain Philip was chosen Byzantine ruler, told the other Varangians about Thorlák's recently declared sanctity; they received the news with great joy and a church was built in the city dedicated to him. When called upon, he was instrumental in a Varangian victory over certain pagans (ch. 14, *Bisk.* 1:363–64). Thorlák's sanctity of course would have been of particular interest to Icelandic Varangians. As Blöndal and Benedikz point out, after the death of Henry of Flanders in 1216 Philip of Namur was elected, but he refused the honor; the possibility that Icelanders or at least Scandinavians being in the guard at this time is enhanced by the Icelandic hagiographer's knowledge of at least Philip's election (*Varangians*, pp. 168–69). It may in fact have been Sigurth the Greek who, when he returned to Iceland in 1217 from Byzantium, brought news of Philip's election and matters concerning St. Thorlák; if this is the case, he could not have learned of Philip's refusal before he left.

90. Selma Jónsdóttir has argued convincingly (*An 11th Century Byzantine Last Judgment in Iceland*) that the carvings on the panels from Bjarnarstathahlíth are similar to representations of 11th- and 12th-century Byzantine Last Judgments. She mentions that models for carving these representations could have come to Iceland from the "Armenian" bishops who arrived during the mid-11th century. She further points out that according to *Thórthar s. hrethu*, the hero was a carpenter of great skill who was commissioned to build a hall at Flatatunga (ibid., pp. 50–51). Since the panels at Bjarnarstathahlíth may originally have come from

Flatatunga, it is not impossible that these are the very panels that Thórth carved. For a divergent opinion, see Kristján Eldjárn, "Carved Panels from Flatatunga," *Acta Archaeologica* 24(1953):81–101. *Thórthar s. hrethu* is the only saga that mentions that Fur-Björn traded in the east before coming to Iceland (ch. 2, *ÍF* 14:169). This comment alone shows an awareness on the part of the author with eastern Europe. Perhaps he had in mind, for this reason, the Byzantine-style panels when describing Thórth's work. See also Ellen Marie Magerøy, "Flatatunga Problems," *Acta Archaeologica* 32(1961):15$–72.

91. See T. J. Arne, *Det stora Svitjod*; S. H. Cross, "Medieval Russian Contact with the West," *Speculum* 10(1935):137–44; idem, "The Scandinavian Infiltration into Russia," *Speculum* 21(1946):505–14; and V. Thomsen, *The Relations between Ancient Russia and Scandinavia*.

92. See Alexander A. Vasiliev, *The Russian Attack on Constantinople in 860*.

93. See *Authunar th. vestfirzka*, ch. 3, *ÍF* 6:366; *Óláfs s. helga*, ch. 66, *ÍF* 27:83–85; *Magnúss s. gótha*, ch. 8, *ÍF* 28:18. Possibly general Scandinavian trade with Byzantium may be indicated by a carving of a ship found in a 10th-century church at Aghthamar. This carving depicts a ship that is an "emphatically northern, or even Scandinavian type. . . . Evidently the artist had a Northern ship in mind, not a Byzantine dromon" (R. E. Anderson, "Viking Ships of the Black Sea," *Mariner's Mirror* 51: [1965]:102).

94. As an example of mainland Scandinavian mediation, the Icelander Höskuld Dalla-Kolsson purchased, as we have already seen, an Irish slave from Gilli, nicknamed "the Russian," at the market at the Göta River, at the borders of Norway, Sweden, and Denmark: Gilli also sold products from Russia itself (*Laxdœla s.*, ch. 12, *ÍF* 5:22–23; see also *Brennu-Njáls s.*, ch. 28, *ÍF* 12:74–75).

CHAPTER SEVEN

1. Bogi Th. Melsteth, "Ferthir, siglingar og samgöngur milli Íslands og annara landa á dögum thjóthveldisins," *Safn til sögu Íslands* 4(1907–1915):727.

2. That the Viking Age in general can be divided into various periods, or at least into early and late ones, is usually accepted. Disagreement arises over how it changed, or more exactly how various motives were emphasized in one period and not in another. A stimulating debate bearing on this topic, insofar as it concerns Britain, Ireland, and Normandy, is P. H. Sawyer et al., "The Two Viking Ages of Britain: A Discussion," *Mediaeval Scandinavia* 2(1969):163–207.

3. The Icelandic sagas dealing with the period c. 1030–c. 1200 are much less numerous than those concerning the earlier and later periods, but in general they are more truthful than those of the earlier group. They mention 25 Icelandic and 30 Norwegian ships (Melsteth, "Ferthir," pp. 838–39). The total number of vessels engaged in the trade actually would have been, of course, much larger than 55 during this period, and furthermore it can be expected that in the sagas there would be more occasion to mention Icelandic than Norwegian ships. Even as the saga evidence for the period stands, however, it confirms a Norwegian dominance in the trade.

4. Georges Duby, *Rural Economy and Country Life in the Medieval West*, pp. 123, 127–28, 135, 418; see also Michael Postan, "The Trade of Mediaeval Europe: The North," in *The Cambridge Economic History of Europe* 2:166; D. L. Farmer, "Some Price Fluctuations in Angevin England," *Economic History Review*, 2nd ser., 9(1956):34–43; idem, "Some Grain Price Fluctuations in Thirteenth Century England," *Economic History Review*, 2nd. ser., 10(1957):207–20. By the second half of the 13th century, English grain supplies had become so insufficient even for domestic needs that England itself frequently had to import grain (Knut Helle, "Anglo-Norwegian Relations in the Reign of Håkon Håkonsson (1217–63)," *Mediaeval Scandinavia* 1[1968]:112).

5. *Diplomatarium Norvegicum* 5:1–2.

6. Eleanora Carus-Wilson, "The Woollen Industry," in *The Cambridge Economic History* 2:375–76.

7. The saga evidence for this period mentions only 25 Norwegian ships in Iceland compared to 30 for the previous period (Melsteth, "Ferthir," pp. 838–85). Even though this period is shorter than the previous, the amount of saga evidence is more abundant. There is thus some justification for treating the saga evidence for the two periods on a strictly comparative basis.

8. Melsteth, "Ferthir," pp. 844–47.

9. *Ann.*, pp. 125, 185, 326. *Oddaverja annáll* gives 1218: *Ann.*, p. 479.

10. *Ann.*, p. 189; see also Jón Jóhannesson, *Íslendinga saga* 1:305.

11. In 1201 a ship disappeared with 30 men aboard (*Ann.*, pp. 121, 181); in 1209 four ships were driven off course (ibid., pp. 123, 182) and perhaps five ships were lost at sea (ibid., p. 478); in 1210 one ship disappeared at sea (ibid., p. 123); in 1223 a certain Authbjörn's ships were lost (ibid., pp. 24, 63, 126, 186); in 1227 a certain Jón Petersson lost his ship and all men aboard were drowned (ibid., p. 186); the same year a ship from Nidaros went down near the Vestmannaeyjar and 6 men perished (ibid., p. 127); in 1232 there were four shipwrecks (ibid., pp. 25, 64, 129, 187, 327);

in 1234 there were many (ibid., p. 129); in 1248 there was one (ibid., pp. 132, 190, 329); in 1251 a búza went down near the Vestmannaeyjar (ibid., p. 482); in 1253 a certain Eysteinn the White's ship was lost (ibid., p. 66); in 1256 three ships were wrecked at Eyrar (ibid.); and in 1258 two ships were lost (ibid., pp. 27, 33).

12. See *DI* 1:619–25 for the full text of the agreement; this summary is based, in part, upon the interpretations of Jóhannesson, *Íslendinga saga* 1:332–38.

13. See Jóhannesson, *Íslendinga saga* 1:327–28, 330–31.

14. *DI* 1:635, 670. For the *Gamli Sáttmáli* (ibid., pp. 635–46, 669–716), see *KLNM*, s.v. "Gamli Sáttmáli."

15. *DI* 1:670.

16. Björn Thorsteinsson, "Þættir úr verzlunarsögu," *Saga* 4 (1964): 26.

EPILOGUE

1. Though prices for agricultural goods in England and elsewhere in western Europe had begun to increase sharply during the latter 12th century, the rise was less rapid after 1250. Though evidence for food supplies is somewhat contradictory for the 14th and 15th centuries, Georges Duby states that "we can subscribe to the opinion of those historians who consider that difficulties of victualling got worse in the last years of the thirteenth century, at least in the westernmost parts of Europe, and that after 1300 an age of catastrophic shortages commenced" (*Rural Economy and Country Life in the Medieval West*, p. 295). On prices and shortages, see also ibid., p. 135; Michael Postan, "The Trade of Mediaeval Europe: The North," in *The Cambridge Economic History of Europe* 2:166, 191–98, 201–2, 204–9, 211–16; D. L. Farmer, "Some Grain Price Fluctuations in Thirteenth Century England," *Economic History Review*, 2nd ser., 10(1957):212–15.

2. *Hansisches Urkundenbuch* 1:137–39. Earlier, in 1237, the Baltic merchants were granted exemption in England from tolls on all goods they imported or exported (ibid., p. 94); but they were not able to take effective advantage of this right because of opposition from Cologne merchants, who had been granted trading rights there as early as 1157 (ibid., p. 8), and who did not want to suffer additional competition. Reconciliation between Cologne and Baltic merchants in England did not come about until 1281. Nevertheless, Lübeckers were to remain less active in the trade with England than with Bruges and the Low Countries in general.

3. See *Hákonar s. Hákonarsonar*, ch. 280, pp. 542–43. The treaty was made 6 October 1250: *Diplomatarium Norvegicum* 5:4–5. It may have

been preceded by another about 1237 (Johan Schreiner, *Hanseatene og Norges nedgang,* p. 22), apparently agreed to by the Baltic Germans in response to the privileges they had gained that year in England; probably because the English privileges proved useless to them, they abrogated their early agreement with Norway soon after it was made despite King Hákon's complaints to the Lübeck city council (*Diplomatarium Norvegicum* 5:1–3).

4. *Detmar-Chronik,* in *Die Chroniker der niedersächsischen Städte* (Lübeck 1) 19:364. This statement is somewhat exaggerated because Detmar himself states that Bremen did not cooperate in the embargo.

5. The best treatment of Hanseatic activity in medieval Norway besides Schreiner's *Hanseatene* is John Allyne Gade, *The Hanseatic Control of Norwegian Commerce during the Late Middle Ages.*

6. First expressly stated in 1302: *DI* 2:333; *Norges gamle love* 3:134–35.

7. *DI* 2:287.

8. See *DI* 2:235, 370–71. *Laurentius s. biskups* (written before 1393) says that in 1322 a knörr from Iceland was wrecked on the Norwegian coast; the cargo was saved; it partly consisted of rolls and packs of vathmál, but "skreith was not taken then [from Iceland]" (ch. 40, *Bisk.* 1:842). This statement must be erroneous in view of the clear evidence that skreith was being exported in considerable amounts in 1294 as well as in 1320.

9. The origin of the tax is somewhat mysterious. The use of the word "sack" might well indicate that the tax was first levied when vathmál and perhaps raw wool were more important as exports than fish, because woolens and wool, not so feasibly fish, could be so carried. Woolens, however, are not referred to in documents as having been transported in such a manner, and so raw wool may have been the more popular export when the sekkjagjald was originally imposed. During Magnús Eiríksson's time, fish was already becoming more significant than wool or woolens as an Icelandic export, and thus a tax levied on sacks of wool products already or soon would be anachronistic. For this reason too the tax might have been first collected before 1319. In fact it could have been levied not very long after 1262 when the landaurar was first abolished by the *Gizurarsáttmáli.* The landaurar had become virtually a dead letter for Icelanders, but it still must have been paid until then by Norwegians engaged in the Iceland trade. In doing away with it, King Hákon Hákonarson may have tried to encourage Norwegian participation in the trade thereafter, just as St. Óláf had done for Norwegians long before. As Norwegian trade with the island increased, one of Hákon's near successors could have replaced

the lost revenue of the landaurar with that derived from the sekkjagjald. Whenever the sekkjagjald originated, and whether or not it first concerned woolen products, it was eventually generalized to include all Norwegian exports from Iceland, including fish. On the problem of the tax's origin, see Jón Jóhannesson, *Íslendinga saga* 2:71, 154–55.

10. *DI* 3:178–79.

11. If conditions at sea changed radically from one of these half-centuries to the next, the varying number of accidents might be explained largely or totally thereby instead of being attributed to a variance in the total volume of shipping activity. As seen in Chapter 1, climate seems to have steadily deteriorated after about 1200 until perhaps nearly the end of the 14th century. It could not have suddenly improved during the latter 14th century when the number of accidents sharply declined, even though some improvement may have come during the final years of that century. Gradually worsening weather conditions at sea during the period 1250 until almost 1399, though, must be considered when using accidents as an indication of total shipping during that time. Thus total trade would have increased somewhat less than the percentage indicated during 1300–49 compared to 1250–99 because part of the accident increase would have been due to a worsening climate; by the same token total trade would have declined somewhat less than the given percentage during 1350–99.

12. *Ann.*, pp. 225–27, 268, 276, 280, 284–85, 354–55, 356, 367.

13. *Ann.*, p. 399; see also *KLNM*, s.v. "Fiskehandel, Island."

14. Since the value of skreith is measured in relationship to that of vathmál, skreith's rise in value was probably not as great as it seems because that of vathmál was declining. Most of vathmál's decline in value, however, must have taken place during the century or so following the late 12th century when the impact of new technology abroad, which allowed strongly competitive production of low-cost cloth, would have been particularly strong. If vathmál continued to fall in value after c. 1300, the decline must have been much more gradual. Therefore, during the 14th and 15th centuries skreith's rising price must be attributed mostly to the increased market abroad for dried fish rather than to a diminished one for woolens.

15. Finnur Jónsson, "Islands mønt, mål og vægt," *NK* 30:158–59; *KLNM*, s.v. "Fiskehandel, Island."

16. *Jónsbók, DI* 2:168–70. This list is usually dated c. 1280, but Magnús Már Lárusson (*KLNM*, s.v. "Marked, Island"), citing Ólafur Lárusson, *Grágás og lögbækurnar* (Reykjavík, 1923), p. 71, and his own "Nokkrar athugasemdir um upphæth manngjalda," *Saga* 1(1960):76–91, suggests that it actually is from the beginning of the 14th century (1302).

17. *DI* 9:12.

18. *Ann.*, p. 290. For later visits of Englishmen to Iceland, see *Ann.*, especially *Lögmanns annáll*, for 1413, 1415, 1425, 1426, 1429, 1430.

19. G. J. Marcus, "The First English Voyages to Iceland," *Mariner's Mirror* 42(1956):315; Björn Thorsteinsson, *Enska öldin í sögu íslendinga*, pp. 28–31. Thorsteinsson's work is the most complete treatment of the Anglo-Icelandic trade during the 15th century; see also E. M. Carus-Wilson, "The Iceland Trade," in *Studies in English Trade in the Fifteenth Century*, pp. 155–82; E. Baasch, *Die Islandfahrt der Deutschen*.

20. *DI* 4:268.

21. *KLNM*, s.v. "Hansa, Island."

22. Ibid.

23. Ibid., citing *DI* 11: nos. 27, 32, 37, 38, 41, 47, 48.

24. Thorsteinsson, *Enska öldin*, pp. 251–52.

25. Raimondo de Raimondi di Soncino wrote to the duke of Milan from England in 1497 about the recent voyage of John Cabot; he said that the seas of Newfoundland contain a great deal of fish and "they say that so much fish will be taken from there that this kingdom [England] will not have much need for Iceland" (*DI* 7:374).

⚓ Bibliography of Cited Works

PRIMARY SOURCES
A. Sagas and Thættir

The approximate date of composition following each saga or tháttr in parentheses is usually that given by Halldór Hermannsson, *Bibliography of Icelandic Sagas and Minor Tales* or his *Bibliography of the Sagas of the Kings of Norway and Related Sagas and Tales.* If Hermannsson does not give the date, or if that provided by the editor of the edition cited is preferable, the editor's date is used, indicated by an asterisk.

Arna saga biskups (early 14th century). Edited by Jón Sigurthsson and Guthbrandur Vigfússon. *Biskupa sögur* 1:677–786. Copenhagen, 1856.

Authunar tháttr vestfirzka (end of 13th century). Edited by Björn K. Thórólfsson and Guthni Jónsson. *Íslenzk fornrit* 6:359–68. Reykjavík, 1943.

Bandamanna saga (end of 12th century). Edited by Guthni Jónsson. *Íslenzk fornrit* 7:291–363. Reykjavík, 1936.

Bjarnar saga Hítdœlakappa (c. 1200). Edited by Sigurthur Nordal and Guthni Jónsson. *Íslenzk fornrit* 3:109–211. Reykjavík, 1938.

Brennu-Njáls saga (latter 13th century). Edited by Einar Ól. Sveinsson. *Íslenzk fornrit* 12. Reykjavík, 1954.

Brot úr mithsögu Guthmundar (latter 13th century?). Edited by Jón Sigurthsson and Guthbrandur Vigfússon. *Biskupa sögur* 1:559–618. Copenhagen, 1856.

Draumr Thorsteins Síthu-Hallsonar (c. 1300). Edited by Jón Jóhannesson. *Íslenzk fornrit* 11:323–26. Reykjavík, 1950.

Egils saga Skallagrímssonar (c. 1200). Edited by Sigurthur Nordal. *Íslenzk fornrit* 2. Reykjavík, 1933.

Eiríks saga rautha (after 1264: Jóhannesson, "Date of the Composition of

268

the Saga of the Greenlanders"). Edited by Einar Ól. Sveinsson and Matthías Thórtharson. *Íslenzk fornrit* 4:193–237. Reykjavík, 1935. *The Vinland Sagas: The Norse Discovery of America.* Translated with an Introduction by Magnus Magnusson and Hermann Pálsson. Baltimore, 1965.

Eyrbyggja saga (c. 1200). Edited by Einar Ól. Sveinsson and Matthías Thórtharson. *Íslenzk fornrit* 4:1–186. Reykjavík, 1935.

[*Færeyinga saga*]: see *Saga of the Faroe Islanders.*

Fljótsdœla saga (12th century). Edited by Jón Jóhannesson. *Íslenzk fornrit* 11:213–96. Reykjavík, 1950.

Flóamanna saga (last quarter of 13th century). Edited by Finnur Jónsson. Copenhagen, 1932.

Fóstbrœthra saga (middle of the 13th century). Edited by Björn K. Thórólfsson and Guthni Jónsson. *Íslenzk fornrit* 6:119–276. Reykjavík, 1943.

Gísla saga Súrssonar (c. 1200). Edited by Björn K. Thórólfsson and Guthni Jónsson. *Íslenzk fornrit* 6:1–118. Reykjavík, 1943.

Grettis saga (end of the 13th century). Edited by Guthni Jónsson. *Íslenzk fornrit* 7:1–290. Reykjavík, 1936.

Grœnlendinga saga (c. 1200: Jóhannesson, "Date of the Composition of the Saga of the Greenlanders"). Edited by Einar Ól. Sveinsson and Matthías Thórtharson. *Íslenzk fornrit* 4:239–69. Reykjavík, 1935.

Grœnlendinga tháttr (latter 14th c.) Edited by Einar Ól. Sveinsson and Matthías Thórtharson. *Íslenzk fornrit* 4:271–92. Reykjavik, 1935.

Gunnars tháttr Thithrandabanda (13th century). Edited by Jón Jóhannesson. *Íslenzk fornrit* 11:193–211. Reykjavík, 1950.

Gunnlaugs saga ormstungu (second half of 12th century). Edited by Sigurthur Nordal and Guthni Jónsson. *Íslenzk fornrit* 3:49–107. Reykjavík, 1938.

Guthmundar saga Arasonar, Hóla-biskups, eptir Arngríms ábóta (mid-14th century). Edited by Jón Sigurthsson and Guthbrandur Vigfússon. *Biskupa sögur* 2:1–184. Copenhagen, 1878.

Guthmundar saga Arasonar, Hóla-biskups hins elzta (second half of 13th century). Edited by Jón Sigurthsson and Guthbrandur Vigfússon. *Biskupa sögur* 1:405–558. Copenhagen, 1856.

Guthmundar saga dýra (before 1300). Edited by Jón Jóhannesson, Magnús Finnbogason, and Kristján Eldjárn. *Sturlunga saga* 1:160–212. Reykjavík, 1946.

Hákonar saga gamla Hákonarsonar [by Sturla Thórtharson] (1264–1265). Edited by C. R. Unger. *Codex Frisianus: En samling af norske konge-sagaer,* pp. 385–583. Christiania, 1871.

Hálfdanar saga svarta [by Snorri Sturluson] (c. 1220–1230). Edited by Bjarni Athalbjarnarson. *Íslenzk fornrit* 26:84–93. Reykjavík, 1941.

Halldórs tháttr Snorrason hinn síthari (probably before c. 1230 *). Edited by Einar Ól. Sveinsson. *Íslenzk fornrit* 5:263–77. Reykjavík, 1934.

Hallfrethar saga (c. 1200). Edited by Einar Ól. Sveinsson. *Íslenzk fornrit* 8:133–200. Reykjavík, 1939.

Haralds saga gráfeldar [by Snorri Sturluson] (c. 1220–1230). Edited by Bjarni Athalbjarnarson. *Íslenzk fornrit* 26:198–224. Reykjavík, 1941.

Haralds saga hárfagra [by Snorri Sturluson] (c. 1220–1230). Edited by Bjarni Athalbjarnarson. *Íslenzk fornrit* 26:94–149.

Haralds saga Sigurtharsonar [by Snorri Sturluson] (c. 1220–1230). Edited by Bjarni Athalbjarnarson. *Íslenzk fornrit* 28:68–202. Reykjavík, 1951.

Haraldssona saga [by Snorri Sturluson] (c. 1220–1230). Edited by Bjarni Athalbjarnarson. *Íslenzk fornrit* 28:303–46. Reykjavík, 1951.

Haukdæla tháttr (before 1300). Edited by Jón Jóhannesson, Magnús Finnbogason, and Kristján Eldjárn. *Sturlunga saga* 1:57–62. Reykjavík, 1946.

Heitharvíga saga (second half of 12th century). Edited by Sigurthur Nordal and Guthni Jónsson. *Íslenzk fornrit* 3:213–328. Reykjavík, 1938.

[*Heimskringla*]: see individual kings' sagas.

Hemings tháttr Áslákssonar (second half of 13th century*). Edited by Guthni Jónsson. *Íslendinga sögur* 7:409–36. Reykjavík, 1953.

Hœnsa-Thóris saga (c. 1200 or second half of 13th century). Edited by Sigurthur Nordal and Guthni Jónsson. *Íslenzk fornrit* 3:1–47. Reykjavík, 1938.

Hrafns saga Sveinbjarnarsonar (c. 1230). Edited by Jón Sigurthsson and Guthbrandur Vigfússon. *Biskupa sögur* 1:639–76. Copenhagen, 1856.

Hrana saga hrings (date unknown). Edited by Guthni Jónsson. *Íslendinga sögur* 9:415–40. Reykjavík, 1953.

Húngrvaka (c. 1200). Edited by Jón Sigurthsson and Guthbrandur Vigfússon. *Biskupa sögur* 1:57–86. Copenhagen, 1856.

Íslendinga saga [by Sturla Thórtharson] (before 1284). Edited by Jón Jóhannesson, Magnús Finnbogason, and Kristján Eldjárn. *Sturlunga saga* 1:229–534. Reykjavík, 1946.

Jóns saga helga hins elzta (13th century). Edited by Jón Sigurthsson and Guthbrandur Vigfússon. *Biskupa sögur* 1:149–202. Copenhagen, 1856.

[*Jóns saga helga hins ýngsta*] *Jarteinir úr Jóns sögu hinni ýngstu* (14th century). Edited by Jón Sigurthsson and Guthbrandur Vigfússon. *Biskupa sögur* 1:203–12. Copenhagen, 1856.

Jóns saga hins helga eptir Gunnlaug múnk (shortly after 1200). Edited by

Jón Sigurthsson and Guthbrandur Vigfússon. *Biskupa sögur* 1:213–60. Copenhagen, 1856.

Kjalnesinga saga (first half of 14th century). Edited by Jóhannes Halldórsson. *Íslenzk fornrit* 14:1–44. Reykjavík, 1959.

Kristni saga (c. 1200). Edited by Jón Sigurthsson and Guthbrandur Vigfússon. *Biskupa sögur* 1:1–32. Copenhagen, 1856.

Laurentius saga [by Einar Haflithason] (before 1393). Edited by Jón Sigurthsson and Guthbrandur Vigfússon. *Biskupa sögur* 1:787–877. Copenhagen, 1856.

Laxdœla saga (first half of 13th century). Edited by Einar Ól. Sveinsson. *Íslenzk fornrit* 5:1–248. Reykjavík, 1934.

Ljósvetninga saga (c. 1200). Edited by Björn Sigfússon. *Íslenzk fornrit* 10:1–106. Reykjavík, 1940.

Magnúss saga bárfœtts [by Snorri Sturluson] (c. 1220–1230). Edited by Bjarni Athalbjarnarson. *Íslenzk fornrit* 28:210–37. Reykjavík, 1951.

Magnúss saga gótha [by Snorri Sturluson] (c. 1220–1230). Edited by Bjarni Athalbjarnarson. *Íslenzk fornrit* 28:1–67. Reykjavík, 1951.

Magnússona saga [by Snorri Sturluson] (c. 1220–1230). Edited by Bjarni Athalbjarnarson. *Íslenzk fornrit* 28:238–77. Reykjavík, 1951.

[*Njáls saga*]: see *Brennu-Njáls saga.*

Óláfs saga helga [by Snorri Sturluson] (c. 1220–1230). Edited by Bjarni Athalbjarnarson. *Íslenzk fornrit* 27. Reykjavík, 1945.

Óláfs saga kyrra [by Snorri Sturluson] (c. 1220–1230). Edited by Bjarni Athalbjarnarson. *Íslenzk fornrit* 28:203–9. Reykjavík, 1951.

Óláfs saga Tryggvasonar [by Snorri Sturluson] (c. 1220–1230). Edited by Bjarni Athalbjarnarson. *Íslenzk fornrit* 26:225–372. Reykjavík, 1941.

Orkneyinga saga (c. 1200). Edited by Finnbogi Guthmundsson. *Íslenzk fornrit* 34:1–300. Reykjavík, 1965.

Páls saga biskups (c. 1200). Edited by Jón Sigurthsson and Guthbrandur Vigfússon. *Biskupa sögur* 1:125–48. Copenhagen, 1856.

Prestssaga Guthmundar gótha (first or second decade 13th century). Edited by Jón Jóhannesson, Magnús Finnbogason, and Kristján Eldjárn. *Sturlunga saga* 1:116–59. Reykjavík, 1946.

Reykdœla saga ok Víga-Skutu (c. 1200). Edited by Björn Sigfússon. *Íslenzk fornrit* 10:149–243. Reykjavík, 1940.

The Saga of the Faroe Islanders (first half of 13th century). Translated by Muriel A. C. Press. London, 1934.

Sighvats tháttr skálds (early 13th century*). Edited by Guthni Jónsson. *Íslendinga sögur* 12:119–58. Reykjavík, 1953.

Sneglu-Halla tháttr (first half of 13th century). Edited by Jónas Kristjánsson. *Íslenzk fornrit* 9:261–95. Reykjavík, 1956.

272 / Bibliography

Sturlu saga (shortly after 1200). Edited by Jón Jóhannesson, Magnús Finnbogason, and Kristján Eldjárn. Sturlunga saga 1:63–114. Reykjavík, 1946.
[Sturlunga saga]: see individual sagas in the collection.
Svarfdœla saga (beginning of the 14th century). Edited by Jónas Kristjánsson. Íslenzk fornrit 9:127–211. Reykjavík, 1955.
Svatha tháttr ok Arnórs kerlingarnefs (probably much later than 1218*). Edited by Guthni Jónsson. Íslendinga sögur 8:335–44. Reykjavík, 1953.
Sverris saga [by Karl Jónsson] (before 1213). Edited by Gustav Indrebø. Christiania, 1920.
Svínfellinga saga (c. 1270–80). Edited by Jón Jóhannesson, Magnús Finnbogason, and Kristján Eldjárn. Sturlunga saga 2:87–103. Reykjavík, 1946.
Thorgils saga ok Haflitha (before or about 1200). Edited by Jón Jóhannesson, Magnús Finnbogason, and Kristján Eldjárn. Sturlunga saga 1:12–50. Reykjavík, 1946.
Thorgils saga skartha (shortly after 1258). Edited by Jón Jóhannesson, Magnús Finnbogason, and Kristján Eldjárn. Sturlunga saga 2:104–226. Reykjavík, 1946.
Thorláks saga biskups hins elzta (c. 1206). Edited by Jón Sigurthsson and Guthbrandur Vigfússon. Biskupa sögur 1:87–124. Copenhagen, 1856.
Thorláks saga biskups hins ýngri (c. 1225–1230). Edited by Jón Sigurthsson and Guthbrandur Vigfússon. Biskupa sögur 1:261–332. Copenhagen, 1856.
[Thorláks saga biskups] Önnur jarteinabók Thorláks biskups (first half of the 14th century?). Edited by Jón Sigurthsson and Guthbrandur Vigfússon. Biskupa sögur 1:357–74. Copenhagen, 1856.
Thorsteins saga Geirnefjúfóstra (date unknown). Edited by Guthni Jónsson. Íslendinga sögur 8:399–453. Reykjavík, 1953.
Thorsteins saga uxafóts (c. 1300). Edited by Guthni Jónsson. Íslendinga sögur 10:341–70. Reykjavík, 1953.
Thorsteins tháttr Síthu-Hallssonar (before the end of the 14th century). Edited by Guthni Jónsson. Íslendinga sögur 10:379–403. Reykjavík, 1953.
Thórthar saga hrethu (mid-14th century). Edited by Jóhannes Halldórsson. Íslenzk fornrit 14:61–226. Reykjavík, 1959.
Thorvalds tháttr vithförla (c. 1300). Edited by Jón Sigurthsson and Guthbrandur Vigfússon. Biskupa sögur 1:33–50. Copenhagen, 1856.
[Tristrams saga ok Ísöndar] Tristram og Ísönds saga [by Brother Róbert] (1226). Edited by Bjarni Vilhjálmsson. Riddarasögur 1:1–247. Reykjavík, 1954.

Vatnsdœla saga (c. 1200). Edited by Einar Ól. Sveinsson. *Íslenzk fornrit* 8:1–131. Reykjavík, 1939.

Ynglinga saga [by Snorri Sturluson] (c. 1220–1230). Edited by Bjarni Athalbjarnarson. *Íslenzk fornrit* 26:1–83. Reykjavík, 1941.

B. *Other Icelandic Sources*

Annales Islandici posteriorum saeculorum. Edited by Hannes Thorsteinsson. 2 vols. Reykjavík, 1932.

Diplomatarium Islandicum: Íslenzkt fornbréfasafn. Edited by Jón Sigurthsson et al. Copenhagen, 1857–.

Grágás: Elzta lögbók Íslendinga [*Konungsbók:* Royal Library of Copenhagen 1157 fol.]. Edited by Vilhjálmur Finsen. Copenhagen, 1852.

Hauksbók [by Hauk Erlendsson]. Edited by Jakob Benediktsson. *Íslenzk fornrit* 1:pts. 1–2. Reykjavík, 1968.

Islandske annaler indtil 1578. Edited by Gustav Storm. Christiania, 1888.

Íslendingabók. Edited by Jakob Benediktsson. *Íslenzk fornrit* 1:pt. 1:1–28. *The Book of the Icelanders (Íslendingabók) by Ari Thorgilsson.* Edited and translated by Halldór Hermannsson. Islandica 20. Ithaca, N.Y., 1930.

[*Landnámabók*]: see *Hauksbók, Melabók, Sturlubók.*

"Leitharvísir" [by Nikolás Bergthórsson]. Edited by Kr. Kålund. *Alfræthi íslenzk* 1:12–23. Copenhagen, 1908.

"Líknesjusmith." Edited by Kr. Kålund. *Alfræthi íslenzk* 1:89–91. Copenhagen, 1908.

Melabók [by Thórthur Jónsson]. Edited by Jakob Benediktsson. *Íslenzk fornrit* 1:pts. 1–2. Reykjavík, 1968.

Rím. Edited by N. Beckman and Kr. Kålund. *Alfræthi íslenzk* 2. Copenhagen, 1914–1916.

Sturlubók [by Sturla Thórtharson]. Edited by Jakob Benediktsson. *Íslenzk fornrit* 1:pts. 1–2. Reykjavík, 1968.

C. *Non-Icelandic Sources*

Adam of Bremen. *Gesta Hammaburgensis ecclesiae pontificum.* Edited by G. Waitz. *Monumenta Germaniae historica. Scriptores rerum Germanicarum in usum scholarum* 2. Hanover, 1876.

Alfred, king of England. *King Alfred's Orosius.* Edited by Henry Sweet. Early English Text Society 79. London, 1883.

The Anglo-Saxon Chronicle. Edited and translated by G. N. Garmonsway. London, 1955.

Detmar-Chronik. Die Chroniker der niedersächsischen Städte (Lübeck 1) 19. Edited by K. Koppmann. Leipzig, 1884.

Dicuil. *Liber de mensura orbis terra.* Edited by James F. Kenney. *Sources for the Early History of Ireland,* pp. 546–48. New York, 1929.

Diplomatarium Norvegicum. Edited by C. C. A. Lange, C. R. Unger, H. J. Huitfeldt-Kaas, G. Storm, A. Bugge, Christian Brinchmann, and O. Kolsrud. 19 vols. Christiania, 1847–1919.

Frederick II of Hohenstaufen, Holy Roman Emperor. *The Art of Falconry.* Edited and translated by Casey A. Wood and Majorie Fyfe. Boston, 1955.

Giraldus Cambrensis. *Topographica Hibernica.* Edited by James F. Dimonk. London, 1867.

Hansisches Urkundenbuch 1. Edited by Konstantin Höhlbaum. Halle, 1876.

Historia de profectione Danorum in Hiersolymam. Edited by M. CL. Gertz. *Scriptores minores historiae Danicae medii aevi* 2:443–92. Copenhagen, 1922.

Konungs skuggsiá. Edited by Ludvig Holm-Olsen. Oslo, 1945.

Latinske dokument til norsk historie fram til år 1204. Edited by Eirik Vandvik. Oslo, 1959.

Neckham, Alexander. *De nominibus utensilibus.* Edited by T. Wright. *A Volume of Vocabularies.* London, 1857.

Nordens historie i middelalderen efter arabiske kilder. Edited and translated by Harris Birkeland. Oslo, 1954.

Norges gamle love indtil 1387. Edited by R. Keyser, P. A. Munch, Gustav Storm, and Ebbe Hertzberg. 5 vols. Christiania, 1846–1890.

Ordericus Vitalis. *Historia ecclesiastica.* Edited by A. Le Prévost. 5 vols. Paris, 1838–1855.

Patent Rolls of the Reign of Henry III . . . 1216–1225. London, n.d.

Pavelige nuntiers regnskaps- og dagbøker førte under tiendeopkrævningen i norden, 1282–1334, med et anhang af diplomer. Edited by P. A. Munch. Oslo, 1864.

Saxo Grammaticus. Gesta Danorum. Edited by J. Olrik and H. Ræder. Copenhagen, 1931.

War of the Gaedhil with the Gaill or the Invasion of Ireland by the Danes and Other Norsemen. Edited and translated by James Henthorne Todd. London, 1867.

William of Malmsbury. *De gestis pontificum Anglorum.* Edited by N. E. S. A. Hamilton. London, 1870.

Secondary Works

Allen, Richard M. *Fire and Iron: Critical Approaches to Njáls saga.* Pittsburgh, 1971.

Andersen, Magnus. *Vikingefærden 1893.* Christiania, 1895.

Anderson, R. E. "Viking Ships on the Black Sea." *Mariner's Mirror* 51(1965):102.

Andersson, Theodore M. *The Problem of Icelandic Saga Origins: A Historical Survey.* New Haven, 1964.

Arbman, Holger, *The Vikings.* Translated by Alan Binns. New York, 1961.

Arne, T. J. *Det stora Svitjod.* Stockholm, 1917.

Athalsteinsson, Jón Hnefill. *Kristnitakan á Íslandi.* Reykjavík, 1971.

Baasch, E. *Die Islandsfahrt der Deutschen namentlich der Hamburger vom 15. bis 17. Jahrhundert.* Forschungen zur hamburgischen Handelsgeschichte 1. Hamburg, 1889.

Björnsson, Björn Th. *Íslenzk gullsmithi.* Reykjavík, 1959.

Blindheim, Charlotte. "The Market Place in Skiringssal: Early Opinion and Recent Studies." *Acta Archaeologica* 31(1960):83–100.

Blom, Grethe Authén, et al. *Trondheims bys historie.* 4 vols. Trondheim, 1956–1962.

Blöndal, Sigfús. *The Varangians of Byzantium: An Aspect of Military History.* Translated, revised, and rewritten by Benedikt S. Benedikz. Cambridge, Eng., 1978.

Bolin, Sture. "Medieval Agrarian Society in its Prime: Scandinavia." *The Cambridge Economic History of Europe.* Vol. 1, *The Agrarian Life of the Middle Ages,* 633–59. Edited by M. M. Postan and E. E. Rich. Cambridge, Eng., 1966.

Boyer, Regis. "L'Evêque Guthmundr Arason, témoin de son temps." *Etudes germaniques* 22(1967):427–44.

Brøgger, A. W. *Ancient Emigrants.* Oxford, 1929.

————. "Den norske bosetningen på Færøyene." *Norsk geografisk tidsskrift* 5 (1935):321–33.

————. *Den norske bosetningen på Shetland-Orknøyene.* Oslo, 1930.

————, and Haakon Shetelig. *Vikingeskipene.* Oslo, 1950; *The Viking Ships: Their Ancestry and Evolution.* Translated by Katherine John. London, 1971.

Bugge, Alexander. "Handelen mellem England og Norge indtil begyndelsen af det 15de aarhundrede." [*Norsk*] *Historisk tidsskrift,* 3rd ser., 4(1898):1–149.

————. *Nidaros's handel og skibsfart i middelalderen: Særaftryk af det Kongelige norske Videnskabers Selskabs festskrift ved Trondhjems 900 aars jubilæum 1897.* Trondheim, 1897.

————. *Den norske trælasthandels historie.* Vol. 1. Skien, 1925.

————. *Studier over de norske byers selvstyre og handel før hanseaternes tid.* Christiania, 1899.

————. *Vesterlandenes indflydelse paa nordboernes og særlig nordmændenes ydre kultur, levesaet og samfundsforhold.* Christiania, 1905.

Bull, Edvard. "Islands klima i oldtiden." *Geografisk tidsskrift* 23(1916):1–5.

Carus-Wilson, Eleanora. "The Iceland Trade." *Studies in English Trade in the Fifteenth Century,* pp. 155–82. Edited by Eileen Power and Michael M. Postan. London, 1933.

————. "The Woollen Industry." *The Cambridge Economic History of Europe.* Vol. 2, *Trade and Industry in the Middle Ages,* 355–428. Edited by M. M. Postan and E. E. Rich. Cambridge, Eng., 1952.

Chapman, Kenneth G. *Icelandic-Norwegian Linguistic Relationships.* Oslo, 1962.

Charles, B. G. *Old Norse Relations with Wales.* Cardiff, 1934.

Christensen, Aksel E. "Danmarks handel i middelalderen." *Nordisk kultur.* Vol. 16, *Handel och samfärdsel under medeltiden,* 108–27. Oslo, 1934.

————. "Scandinavia and the Advance of the Hanseatics." *Scandinavian Economic History Review* 5(1957):89–117.

Cleasby, Richard, Gudbrand Vigfusson, and W. Craigie. *An Icelandic-English Dictionary.* Oxford, 1962.

Cross, Samuel H. "Mediaeval Russian Contact with the West." *Speculum* 10(1935):137–44.

————. "The Scandinavian Infiltration into Russia." *Speculum* 21(1946):505–14.

Dasent, G. W. *The Story of Burnt Njal.* 2 vols. Edinburgh, 1861.

Degerbøl, Magnus. "Nogle bemærkninger om husdyrene paa Island i middelalderen." *Forntida gårdar i Island.* Edited by Mårten Stenberger. Copenhagen, 1943.

Douglas, David C. *William the Conqueror.* Berkeley and Los Angeles, 1965.

Duby, Georges. *Rural Economy and Country Life in the Medieval West.* Translated by Cynthia Postan. Columbia, S.C., 1968.

Einarsson, Bjarni. "On the Status of Free Men in Society and Saga." *Mediaeval Scandinavia* 7(1974):45–55.

Einarsson, Trausti. "Nokkur atrithi varthandi fund Íslands, siglingar og landnám." *Saga* 8(1970):43–63.

Eldjárn, Kristján. "Carved Panels from Flatatunga, Iceland." *Acta Archaeologica* 24(1953):81–101.

————. "Gaulverjabær-fundet og nogle mindre islandske møntfund fra vikingetiden." *Nordisk numismatisk årsskrift* 13(1948):39–62.

————. *Kuml og haugfé úr heithum sith á Íslandi.* Akureyri, 1956.

———. "Two Medieval Farm Sites in Iceland and Some Remarks on Tephrochronology." *The Fourth Viking Congress: York, August, 1961,* pp. 10–19. Edited by Alan Small. Edinburgh, 1965.

———. *Um Hólarkirkja: Leithsögn um kirku og kirkjugripi.* Reykjavík, 1950.

[Erichsen, Johannes] Johannes Erici. *Disqvisitiones de vetervm septentrionalivm inprimis Islandorvm peregrinationibvs et philippia sive amoris eqvorvm apvd eos cavsis.* Copenhagen, 1755.

———. "Udkast til en islandsk Handels Historie." Ludvig Holberg, *Dannemarks og Norges geistlige og verdslige staat.* Third edition. Sorø, 1762.

Eythórsson, Jón. "Um loftslagsbreytingar á Íslandi og Grænlandi síthan á landnámsöld." *Skírnir* 100(1926):113–33.

Falk, Hjalmar. "Altnordisches Seewesen." *Wörter und Sachen* 4(1912):1–122.

———. *Altwestnordische Kleiderkunde mit besonderer Berücksichtigung der Terminologie.* Christiania, 1919.

Farmer, D. L. "Some Grain Price Fluctuations in Thirteenth-Century England." *Economic History Review,* 2nd ser., 10(1957): 207–20.

———. "Some Price Fluctuations in Angevin England." *Economic History Review,* 2nd ser., 9(1956):34–43.

Finsen, Vilhjálmur. *Om den oprindelige ordning af nogle af den islandske fristats institutioner.* Copenhagen, 1888.

Foote, Peter G. *On the Saga of the Faroe Islanders.* London, 1965.

———. "Secular Attitudes in Early Iceland." *Mediaeval Scandinavia* 7(1974):31–44.

Forntida gårdar i Island. Edited by Mårten Stenberger. Copenhagen, 1943.

Frithriksson, Sturla. "Gras og grasnytjar á Íslandi." Unpublished MS. N.p. [Reykjavík ?], [1968?].

Gad, Finn. *The History of Greenland.* Vol. 1, *Earliest Times to 1700.* Translated by Ernst Dupont. London, 1970.

Gade, John Allyne. *The Hanseatic Control of Norwegian Commerce during the Late Middle Ages.* Leiden, 1951.

Gelsinger, Bruce E. "Lodestone and Sunstone in Medieval Iceland." *Mariner's Mirror* 56(1970):219–26.

———. "The Mediterranean Voyage of a Twelfth-Century Icelander." *Mariner's Mirror* 58(1972):155–65.

———. "The Norse 'Day's Sailing'." *Mariner's Mirror* 56(1970):107–9.

———. "Some Unusual Norwegian Thirteenth-Century Ships." *Mariner's Mirror,* forthcoming.

Green, Alice Stopford. *History of the Irish State to 1014.* London, 1925.

Gregersen, Aa. *L'Islande: Son Statut à travers les âges.* Paris, 1937.

Guthmundsson, Bardi. *The Origin of the Icelanders*. Translated by Lee M. Hollander. Lincoln, Neb., 1967.

Guthmundsson, Valtýr. *Privatboligen på Island i sagatiden*. Copenhagen, 1889.

Hallberg, Peter. *The Icelandic Saga*. Translated by Paul Schach. Lincoln, Neb., 1962.

―――. "The Syncretic Saga Mind." *Mediaeval Scandinavia* 7(1974):102–17.

Hamilton, J. R. C. *Jarlshof, Shetland*. Edinburgh, 1953.

Hannesson, Guthmundur. "Körpermasse und Körperproportionen der Isländer." *Fylgirit árbók háskóla Íslands*. Reykjavík, 1925.

Helgason, Jón. *Kristnisaga Íslands*. 2 vols. Reykjavík, 1925–1927.

Helle, Knut. "Anglo-Norwegian Relations in the Reign of Håkon Håkonsson (1217–63)." *Mediaeval Scandinavia* 1(1968):101–14.

―――. *Norge blir en stat: 1130–1319*. Second edition. Oslo, 1974.

Hermannsson, Halldór. *Bibliography of the Icelandic Sagas and Minor Tales*. Islandica 1. Ithaca, N.Y., 1908.

―――. *Bibliography of the Sagas of the Kings of Norway and Related Sagas and Tales*. Islandica 3. Ithaca, N.Y., 1910.

―――. "Introductory Essay." *The Book of the Icelanders (Íslendingabók)*. Islandica 20:1–46. Ithaca, N.Y., 1930.

―――. *Sæmundr Sigfússon and the Oddaverjar*. Islandica 22. Ithaca, N.Y., 1932.

Heusler, Andreas. *Die Anfänge der isländischen Saga*. Abhandlungen der Königliche Preussiche Akadamie der Wissenschaft, pp. 1–87. Berlin, 1913.

Hoffman, Marta. *The Warp-Weighted Loom. Studies in the History and Technology of an Ancient Implement*. Studia Norwegica 14. Oslo, 1964.

Hofmann, G. "Falkenjagd und Falkenhandel in den nordischen Ländern während des Mittelalters." *Zeitschrift für deutsches Altertum und deutsche Literatur* 80(1957):115–49.

Holmes, Urban Tigner, Jr. *Daily Living in the Twelfth Century, Based on Observations of Alexander Neckham in London and Paris*. Madison, Wis., 1952.

Huisman, Johannes A. "Utrecht im Merigato." *Beiträge zur Geschichte der deutschen Sprach und Literatur* (Tübigen) 87(1966):379–89.

Ingstad, Anne Stine, et al. *The Discovery of a Norse Settlement in America: Excavations at L'Anse aux Meadows, Newfoundland 1961–1968*. Oslo, 1977.

Ingstad, Helge. *Land under the Pole Star*. Translated by Naomi Walford. New York, 1967.

Jacob, Georg. *Der nordisch-baltische Handel der Araber im Mittelalter*. Leipzig, 1887.

Jóhannesson, Jón. "The Date of the Composition of the Saga of the Greenlanders." Translated by Tryggvi J. Oleson. *Saga Book of the Viking Society for Northern Research* 16(1962):54–66.

————. *Íslendinga saga*. 2 vols. Reykjavík, 1956–58; *A History of the Old Icelandic Commonwealth: Íslendinga Saga* [vol. 1]. Translated by Haraldur Bessason. Winnepeg, 1974.

Jóhannesson, Thorkell. "Plágan mikla 1402–1404." *Skírnir* 102(1928):73–95.

————. *Die Stellung der freien Arbeiter in Island*. Reykjavík, 1933.

Johnsen, Arne Odd. "The Payments from the Hebrides and Isle of Man to the Crown of Norway, 1153–1263." *Scottish Historical Review* 48(1969):18–34.

Johnsen, Oscar Albert. "Le Commerce et la navigation en Norvège au moyen âge." *Revue historique* 178(1936):385–410.

————. "Gildevæsenet i Norge i middelalderen: Oprindelse og utvikling." [*Norsk*] *Historisk tidsskrift*, 5th ser., 5(1924):73–101.

————. *Norges bønder: Utsyn over den norske bondestands historie*. Oslo, 1936.

————. "Norges folk i middelalderen." *Nordisk kultur*. Vol. 2, *Befolkning under medeltiden*, 58–105. Oslo, 1938.

————. "Norges handel og skibsfart i middelalderen." *Nordisk kultur*. Vol. 16, *Handel och samfärdsel under medeltiden*, 128–47. Stockholm, 1934.

————. *Norwegische Wirtschaftsgeschichte*. Jena, 1939.

Jónsdóttir, Selma. *An 11th Century Byzantine Last Judgment in Iceland*. Reykjavík, 1959.

Jónsson, Finnur. "Islands mønt, mål og vægt." *Nordisk kultur*. Vol. 30, *Maal og vægt*, 155–61. Copenhagen, 1936.

————, and Daniel Bruun. "Det gamle handelsstad Gásar (at Gásum), yngre Gæsir, ved Øfjord (Eyjafjörthur)." *Kongelige danske Videnskabernes Selskabs forhandlinger* (1908), pp. 95–111.

Joyce, Patrick Weston. *A Social History of Ancient Ireland*. 2 vols. London, 1903.

Kalifa, Simon. "L'Etat et l'organisation sociale dans l'Islande médiévale." *Etudes germaniques* 22(1967):404–26.

Kantorowicz, Ernst. *Frederick the Second*. London, 1931.

Köhne, Roland. "Bischof Ísleifr Gizurarson, ein berühmter Schüler des

Stifts Herford: Kirchliche Verbindungen zwischen Deutschland und Island in 11. Jahrhundert." *Jahresbericht des historischen Vereins für die Grafschaft Ravensburg* 67(1970):1–38.

Koht, Halfdan. "Gråfelden i nordisk historie." [*Norsk*] *Historisk tidsskrift*, 5th ser. 11(1930):19–36.

Kristjánsson, Lúthvík. "Grænlenzki landnemaflotinn og breithfirzki báturinn." *Árbók hins íslenzka fornleifafélags* (1964), pp. 20–68.

Kulturhistorisk leksikon for nordisk middelalder fra vikingetid til reformationstid. 22 vols. Copenhagen, 1956–78.

Lane, Frederick C. "The Economic Meaning of the Invention of the Compass." *American Historical Review* 68(1963):605–17.

Larson, Laurence Marcellus. *Canute the Great (c. 995–1035) and the Rise of Danish Imperialism during the Viking Age.* New York, 1912.

Lárusson, Magnús Már. "Íslenzkar mælieiningar." *Skírnir* 132(1958):240–45.

——. "Nokkrar athugasemdir um upphæth manngjalda." *Saga* 1(1960):76–91.

——. "On the so-called 'Armenian' Bishops." *Studia Islandica* 18(1960):23–38.

Lárusson, Ólafur. "Island." *Nordisk kultur.* Vol. 1, *Befolkning i oldtiden,* 121–37. Oslo, 1936.

Leach, Henry Goddard. "The Relations of the Norwegian with the English Church, 1066–1933 and their Importance for Comparative Literature." *Proceedings of the American Academy of Arts and Sciences* 44(1909):531–60.

Lethbridge, T. C. *Merlin's Island.* London, 1948.

——. *Hermits and Herdsmen: Celtic Seafarers in the Northern Seas.* Cambridge, Eng., 1950.

Lewis, Archibald. *The Northern Seas: Shipping and Commerce in Northern Europe: A.D 300–1100.* Princeton, 1958.

Lipson, E. *The Economic History of England.* Vol. 1, *The Middle Ages.* London, 1964.

Little, Lester K. "Pride Goes before Avarice: Social Changes and the Vices in Latin Christendom." *American Historical Review* 76(1971):16–49.

Lönnroth, Lars. *Njáls Saga: A Critical Introduction.* Berkeley and Los Angeles, 1976.

Lucas, Henry S. "Medieval Economic Relations between Flanders and Greenland." *Speculum* 12(1937):167–81.

Macler, Frédéric. "Arménie et Islande." *Revue de l'histoire des religions* 87(1923):236–41.

Mageröy, Ellen Marie. "Flatatunga Problems." *Acta Archaeologica*

32(1961):153–72.

Magerøy, Hallvard. *Norsk-islandske problem.* Omstridde spørsmål i Nordens historie 3. Oslo, 1964.

Magnússon, Finnur. "Om de Engelskes Handel og Færd paa Island i det 15de. Aarh." *Nordisk Tidskrift for Oldkyndighed* 2(1833):112–69.

Magnusson, Magnus, and Hermann Pálsson. "Introduction." *The Vinland Sagas: The Norse Discovery of America: Grœnlendinga Saga and Eirik's Saga.* Baltimore, 1965.

Marcus, G. J. "The First English Voyages to Iceland." *Mariner's Mirror* 42(1956):313–18.

————. "The Greenland Trade Route." *Economic History Review,* 2nd ser., 7(1954–1955):71–80.

————. "The Navigation of the Norsemen." *Mariner's Mirror* 39(1953):112–31.

————. "The Norse Emigration to the Faroe Islands." *English Historical Review* 71(1956):56–61.

————. "Norse Traffic with Iceland." *Economic History Review,* 2nd ser., 9(1957):408–19.

Maurer, Konrad. *Altisländische Strafrecht und Gerichtwesen.* Leipzig, 1910.

————. *Die Bekehrung des norwegischen Stammes zum Christentum.* 2 vols. Munich, 1855–1856.

————. *Die Entstehung des isländisches Staats und seiner Verfassung.* Munich, 1852.

————. *Island von seiner ersten Entdeckung bis zum Untergange des Freistaats.* Munich, 1874.

————. "Islands und Norwegens Verkehr mit dem Süden vom IX. bis XIII. Jahrhunderte." *Zeitschrift für deutsches Philologie* 2(1870):440–68.

————. "Kaflar úr verzlunarsögu Íslands." *Ný félagsrit* 21(1861): 100–35.

Melsteth, Bogi Th. "Ferthir, siglingar og samgöngur milli Íslands og annara landa á dögum thjóthveldisins." *Safn til sögu Íslands* 4(1907–1915):585–910.

————. "Hverjir ráku verzlun milli Íslands og annara landa á dögum hins íslenzkir thjóthveldis?" *Búnatharrit* 9(c. 1896):52–80.

————. "Utanstefnur og erindisrekar útlendra thjóthhjöfthingja á fyrri hluta Sturlungaaldar: 1200 til 1239." *Tímarit bókmentafélagsins* 21(1899):102–55.

Morcken, Roald. "The Norse 'Day's Sailing' (Doegr Sigling)." *Mariner's Mirror* 56(1970):347–49.

————. "Norse Nautical Units and Distance Measurements." *Mariner's Mirror* 54(1968): 393–401.

282 / Bibliography

———"Old Norse Nautical Distance Tables in the Mediterranean Sea." *Sjøfartshistorisk årbok 1971* (1972), pp. 165–238.

Musset, Lucien. *Les Peuples scandinaves au moyen âge.* Paris, 1951.

Nef, John U. "Mining and Metallurgy in Mediaeval Civilisation." *The Cambridge Economic History of Europe.* Vol. 2, *Trade and Industry in the Middle Ages,* 429–92. Edited by M. Postan and E. E. Rich. Cambridge, Eng., 1952.

Nicolaysen, N. *The Viking Ship Discovered at Gokstad.* Christiania, 1882.

Nilsson, Albert. "Den sentida bebyggelsen på Islands landsbygd." *Forntida gårdar i Island,* pp. 271–306. Edited by Mårten Stenberger. Copenhagen, 1943.

Nordal, Sigurdur. *The Historical Element in the Icelandic Family Sagas.* Glasgow, 1957.

Oleson, Tryggvi Julius. *Early Voyages and Northern Approaches: 1000–1632.* New York, 1964.

———. "Inventio Fortunata." *Annual of the Icelandic National League* 44 (1963):64–76.

———. "Polar Bears in the Middle Ages." *Canadian Historical Review* 31(1950):47–55.

Ólsen, Björn M. "Um íslendingasögur." *Safn til sögu Íslands* 6(1937–1939):1–427.

———. "Um skattbændatal 1311 og manntal á Íslandi fram ath theim tíma." *Safn til sögu Íslands* 4(1907–1915):359–84.

Olsen, Olaf, and Ole Crumlin-Pedersen. "The Skuldelev Ships. (II)." *Acta Archaeologica* 38(1967):73–174.

Pálsson, Árni. "Um lok thrældoms á Íslandi." *Skírnir* 106(1932): 191–203.

Petersen, Jan. "Handel i Norge i vikingetiden." *Nordisk kultur.* Vol. 16, *Handel og samfærdsel i oldtiden,* 39–48. Oslo, 1934.

Poole, A. L. *From Domesday Book to Magna Carta: 1087–1216.* Oxford, 1955.

Postan, Michael. "Mediaeval Agrarian Society in its Prime: England." *The Cambridge Economic History of Europe.* Vol. 1, *The Agrarian Life of the Middle Ages,* 548–632. Edited by M. M. Postan. Cambridge, Eng., 1966.

———. "The Trade of Mediaeval Europe: The North." *The Cambridge Economic History of Europe.* Vol. 2, *Trade and Industry in the Middle Ages,* 119–256. Edited by M. Postan and E. E. Rich. Cambridge, Eng., 1952.

Powicke, Maurice. *The Loss of Normandy: 1189–1204.* Manchester, 1961.

Proceedings of the Vnland Map Conference. Edited by Wilcomb E. Washburn. Chicago, 1971.

Ramskou, Th. *Solstenen: Primitiv navigation i Norden før kompasset.* Copenhagen, 1969.

Sawyer, Peter H. *The Age of the Vikings.* London, 1962.

———, et al. "The Two Viking Ages of Britain: A Discussion." *Mediaeval Scandinavia* 2(1969):163–207.

Schnall, Uwe. *Navigation der Wikinger: Nautische Probleme der Wikingerzeit im Spiegel der schriftlichen Quellen.* Schriften des Deutschen Schiffahrtsmuseums 6. Oldenburg, 1975.

Schreiner, Johan. *Hanseatene og Norges nedgang.* Oslo, 1935.

Scott, Lindsay. "The Norse in the Hebrides." *The [First]Viking Congress: Lerwick, July 1950,* pp. 189–215. Edited by W. Douglas Simpson, Edinburgh, 1954.

Shetelig, Haakon. "Íslenzkar dysjar og fornleifar frá víkingaöld." *Árbók hins íslenzka fornleifafélags,* (1937–1939), pp. 5–16.

———, and Hjalmar Falk. *Scandinavian Archaeology.* Oxford, 1937.

Sigurthsson, Jón. ["Introduction to number 23."] *Diplomatarium Islandicum* 1:162–64. Copenhagen, 1857.

———. ["Introduction to number 152."] *Diplomatarium Islandicum* 1:602–3. Copenhagen, 1857.

Sjøvold, Thorleif. *The Oseberg Find and the Other Viking Ship Finds.* Oslo, 1959.

Small, Alan. "Shetland—Location the Key to Historical Geography." *Scottish Geographical Magazine* 85(1969):155–61.

———. "A Viking Longhouse in Unst, Shetland." *The Fifth Viking Congress: Tórshavn, 1965,* pp. 62–70. Edited by Bjarni Niclasen. Tórshavn, 1968.

Sølver, Carl V. "Leitharsteinn: The Compass of the Vikings." *Old Lore Miscellany.* Viking Society for Northern Research 10(1946):293–321.

Steblin-Kamenskij, M. I. *The Saga Mind.* Translated by Kenneth H. Ober. Odense, 1973.

Stefánsson, Jón. "Rútholf of Bæ and Rudolf of Rouen." *Saga Book of the Viking Society for Northern Research* 13(1950):174–82.

Steinnes, Asgaut. "Mål, vekt og verderekning i Noreg i millomalderen og ei tid etter." *Nordisk kultur.* Vol. 30, *Maal og vægt,* 84–154. Copenhagen, 1936.

Stender-Pedersen, A. "Die Varägersaga als Quelle der altrussischen Chronik." *Acta Jutlandica: Aarsskrift for Aarhus Universitet* 6(1934):1–256.

Stenton, F. M. *Anglo-Saxon England*. Oxford, 1955.

Stephensen, Olav. *Kortfattet Underretning om den islandske Handels Førelse fra Aar 874 til 1788 med tilførede Tanker om hvorledes den nu værende frie Handel maate være at iværksætte til Fordeel for Island*. Copenhagen, 1798.

Sveinsson, Einar Ól. *The Age of the Sturlungs: Icelandic Civilization in the Thirteenth Century*. Islandica 36. Ithaca, N.Y., 1953.

———. *Dating the Icelandic Sagas: An Essay in Method*. London, 1958.

———. *Njáls Saga: A Literary Masterpiece*. Translated by Paul Schach. Lincoln, Neb., 1971.

———. "Papar." *Skírnir* 119(1945):170–203.

Taranger, A. *Den angelsakiske kirkes indflydelse paa den norske*. Christiania, 1890.

Taylor, E. G. R. *The Haven-Finding Art: A History of Navigation from Odysseus to Captain Cook*. London, 1956.

Thomsen, V. *The Relations between Ancient Russia and Scandinavia*. Oxford, 1877.

Thorarinsson, Sigurdur. *The Thousand Years Struggle Against Ice and Fire*. Reykjavík, 1956.

Thoroddsen, Thorvald. *Landfrœthissaga Íslands: Hugmyndir manna um Ísland, náttúruskothun thess og rannsóknir, fyrr og síthar*. 2 vols. Reykjavík, 1892–1896.

Thorsteinsson, Björn. *Enska öldin í sögu íslendinga*. Reykjavík, 1970.

———. *Íslenzka skattlandith*. Reykjavík, 1956.

———. "Some Observations on the Discoveries and the Cultural History of the Norsemen." *Saga Book of the Viking Society for Northern Research* 16(1963–1964):173–91.

———. "Thættir úr verzularsögu: Nokkur atrithi úr norskri verzulnarsögu fyrir 1350." *Saga* 4(1964):3–52.

Thórtharson, Björn. "Íslenzkir fálkar." *Safn til sögu Íslands*, 2nd ser., 1(1957).

Thórtharson, Matthías. "Island." *Nordisk kultur*. Vol. 23; *Kirkebygningerne og deres udstyr*, 288–316. Oslo, 1933.

———. "Manngerthir hellar í Árnessýslu og Rangárvallasýslu." *Árbók hins íslenzka fornleifafélags* (1930–1931), pp. 1–76.

Tønning, O. *Commerce and Trade on the North Atlantic: 850 A.D. to 1350 A.D.* Minneapolis, 1936.

Vandvik, Eirik. *Magnus Erlingssons privilegiebrev og kongevigsle*. Det norske Videnskaps-Akademie i Oslo, II, hist.-filos. klasse, ny serie. Oslo, 1962.

Vasiliev, A. A. *The Russian Attack on Constantinople in 860.* Cambridge, Mass., 1946.

The Vinland Map and the Tartar Relation. Edited by R. A. Skelton, Thomas E. Marston, George D. Painter with a forward by Alexander O. Vietor. New Haven, 1965.

Wahlgren, Erik. "Fact and Fancy in the Vinland Sagas." *Old Norse Literature and Mythology: A Symposium,* pp. 19–80. Edited by Edgar C. Polomé. Austin, Tex. 1969.

West, John F. *Faroe: The Emergence of a Nation.* London, 1972.

White, Lynn, Jr. *Medieval Technology and Social Change.* New York, 1966.

Wilkins, Hans. "Zur Geschichte des niederländischen Handels im Mittelalter." *Hanische Geschichtsblätter* 15(1909):123–203.

Wright, J. K. "Notes on the Knowledge of Latitudes and Longitudes in the Middle Ages." *Isis* 5(1923):75–98.

⚓ Index